WANGECHI MUTU

ADRIENNE EDWARDS
COURTNEY J. MARTIN
KELLIE JONES
CHIKA OKEKE-AGULU

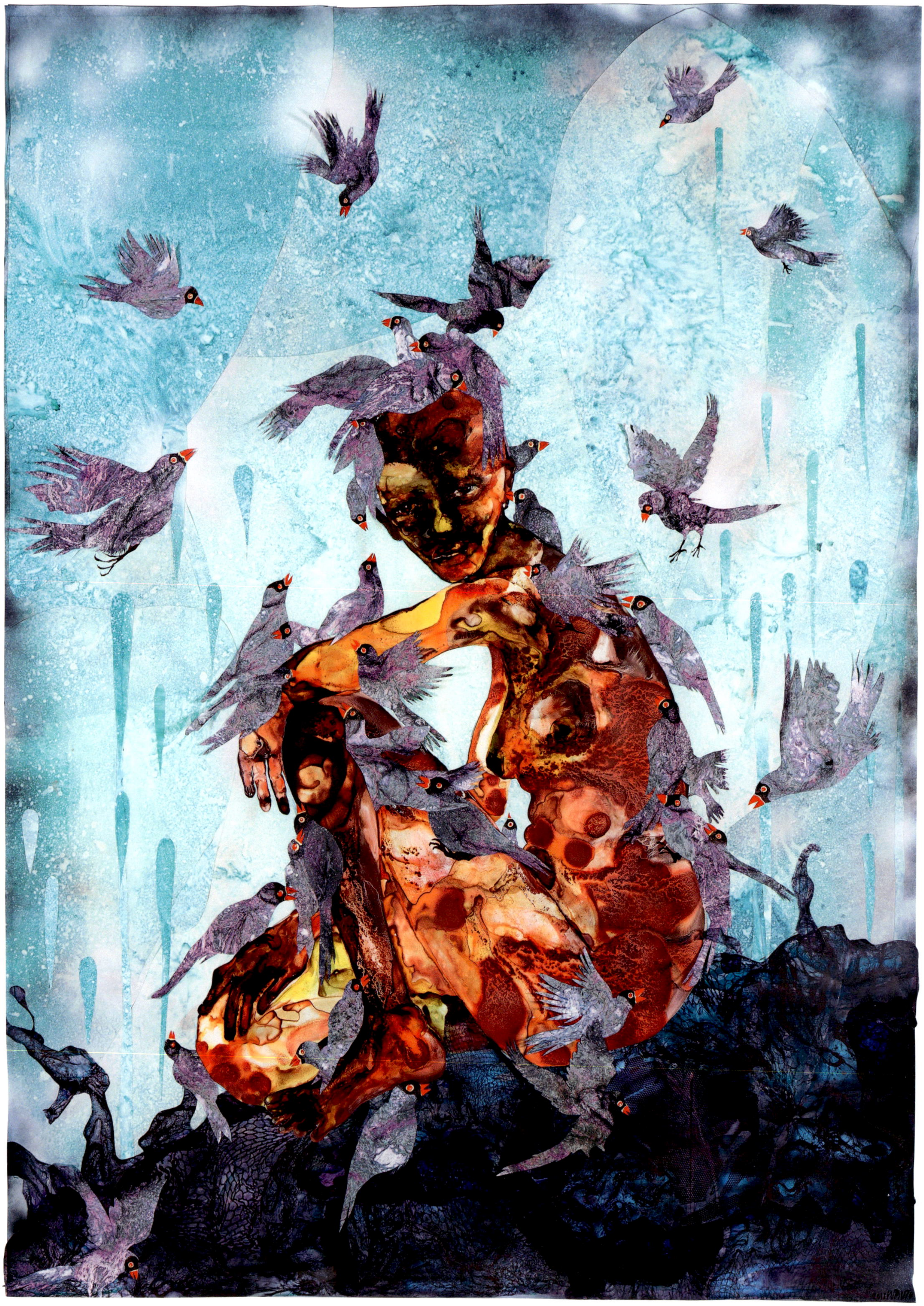

OX PECKED, 2018
INK, WATERCOLOUR AND
COLLAGE ON MYLAR
209 X 146 CM

CONTENTS

Understanding how and where we are situated in the world does not merely concern a taking account of the present moment but always necessitates a self-reflexivity that at its best is historical, which is to say, viewing oneself in juxtaposition to others and to events. Such a retro-perspective on the world meditates on the complexity of experience, and for Wangechi Mutu, is a contemplation of the sublime of existence that is the imagination materialized in her art.

I remember visiting Wangechi's Grand Street studio in Brooklyn in the Winter of 2014. This experience has stayed with me over the years because I have come to understand that it was a moment of witnessing what would become a radical turning point for the artist as much in her work as in her life, particularly because the fact of their profound entanglement would become clearer to me and perhaps to her over the ensuing years. There, in the studio, were bales of shredded papers – old newspapers, magazines, junk mail – the very materials she had used to make her fantastical collage paintings, rendered differently, even seemingly useless. Some of those bales of paper were soaking in a brew of tea, ink, soil and other liquids, fomenting into a viscous black pulp.

The body of *Sleeping Serpent* (2014), a sculpture that Wangechi showed at Victoria Miro Gallery that autumn, was stuffed with these lacerated sheets. *Sleeping Serpent* was Wangechi's first exhibited sculpture in a very long time – few people even knew that she had studied the form as a MFA student at the Yale School of Art, graduating in 2000. The work was located above the gallery's first floor, where her celebrated ornamental, two-dimensional variations on mythological water women she called *Nguva na Nyoka* were displayed. The large undulating floor sculpture was made of reptilian black vinyl with a cerulean blue ceramic head resting on a white embroidered pillow, surrounded by diminutive ritual objects. The head was actually a self-portrait, a cast of her own head made in 2001, just after finishing Yale, a time of great transition and therefore anxiety for her. The disembodied motif recurs in her collages, drawings and paintings. *Sleeping Serpent* was shown alongside the video *Nguva* (2013), in which the artist does not so much perform as embody the mythological presence in the work, something she has often done in her performances for the camera in pieces such as *She Seas Dance* and *Eat Cake* (both 2012), as well as *Mud Fountain* (2010). I imagine that making the serpent was profoundly cathartic for Wangechi, a kind of container for years of materials accumulated and preserved for some undefined purpose, and that the process of making this work – really the beginning of an end – initiated the necessary release, the letting go.

With hindsight, I realize that at this moment in Wangechi's career and life she was beginning to imagine otherwise and elsewhere. More specifically, she was contemplating her turn not only towards sculpture but to Nairobi, Kenya. She was reconciling her dream of living outside of New York and the reality of being an immigrant there for more than twenty years at that time. Possibilities were opening up, and New York had changed drastically since her arrival in 1992, as had she and her circumstances. From the mid-1990s up until 2012, Wangechi could not travel internationally, which included home to Nairobi, because of an immigration issue that took years to resolve. Pregnant with her second child, she made her first flight to Nairobi that October. It was a vastly different city from the one she had left – more technologically advanced, more cosmopolitan. After a second visit the following year with her husband Mario Lazzaroni and their two daughters, she realized she could make a life there without sacrificing her career while continuing to maintain a home and studio in New York. That realization was quite literally grounding. Within a couple of years, thanks to a long-standing mentor whom she had known since the age of fifteen, she serendipitously found a beautiful property completely immersed in nature in which to live and work, marking the transition to East Africa at the beginning of 2016.

Wangechi now owned a home in her country of birth. The same year, she participated in Okwui Enwezor's 2015 Venice Biennale 'All The World's Futures' with a video animation, *The End of carrying All,* of herself navigating landscapes, shown alongside the sculptural installation *She's got the whole world in her* (both 2015). The latter was enswathed in the alchemical black pulp, essentially debuting the transformed matter

007 INTRODUCTION

A thin place[1]

Adrienne Edwards

I'd seen stewing in buckets in her studio the previous year. When I invited Wangechi to participate in the show 'Blackness in Abstraction' in 2016, it was also with this feral matter that she made her wall work through a two-part private performance in the gallery. The material was again the animating force of *Banana Stroke* (2017), a three-part live performance and video installation presented in the Performa 17 biennial at the Metropolitan Museum of Art.

I had travelled to Nairobi to visit in August 2016 to work on our Performa project, and had seen the then nascent experiments instigated by Wangechi's return that would seismically change her work. I came to understand that everything that had preceded this moment had come out of a longing for it – was a projection of her natal rupture. But now, no longer lost, the Kenyan landscape provided the inspiration, the material and the space, a kind of expansionism that made the turn to sculpture inevitable and seamless. The land held material imbued with energy that was not accessible to her in the United States. Most resonant were the types of soil – black cotton, which is a clay, as well as red muurum earth. The former expands when it rains and bears a striking resemblance to the black pulp that Wangechi had been making in her Brooklyn studio, not only in colour but also because it, too, expands and contracts. Now she no longer needed to fabricate this material, for it was ready at hand. Black cotton soil was the foundation of the lush savannahs. Deeper in the terrain is the rocky red earth. These two types of earth balance one another and thus the landscape through a careful calibration that is metaphoric of the artist herself.

Wangechi agreed to do an exhibition of sculpture, drawing upon the craggy, crooked tree branches, trunks, and roots, as well as the deep red earth that surrounded her, at Gladstone Gallery in January 2017. These arborial materials were assembled alongside ambitious bronze sculptures – one of the mythological water women and the other of her head from *Sleeping Serpent,* although this time burnished gold. Taken together, they encompassed the two different worlds the artist occupied, as if to illuminate from whence she came, where she has arrived, and where she is heading. The origins of later work, such as her monumental caryatids for The Metropolitan Museum's façade *The NewOnes, will free Us* (2019) and her impressive 2021 solo exhibition 'I Am Speaking, Are you Listening?' at the Legion of Honour, are found here.

These entanglements that lead to wonder, with their resolved sense of metaphor, their means of resistance, their function of a self-expressivity that is no longer alienated, reminded me of the Derek Walcott poem that Wangechi recites in the video accompanying the *Banana Stroke* performance:

Between this Africa and the English tongue I love?
Betray them both, or give back what they give?
How can I face such slaughter and be cool?
How can I turn from Africa and live?

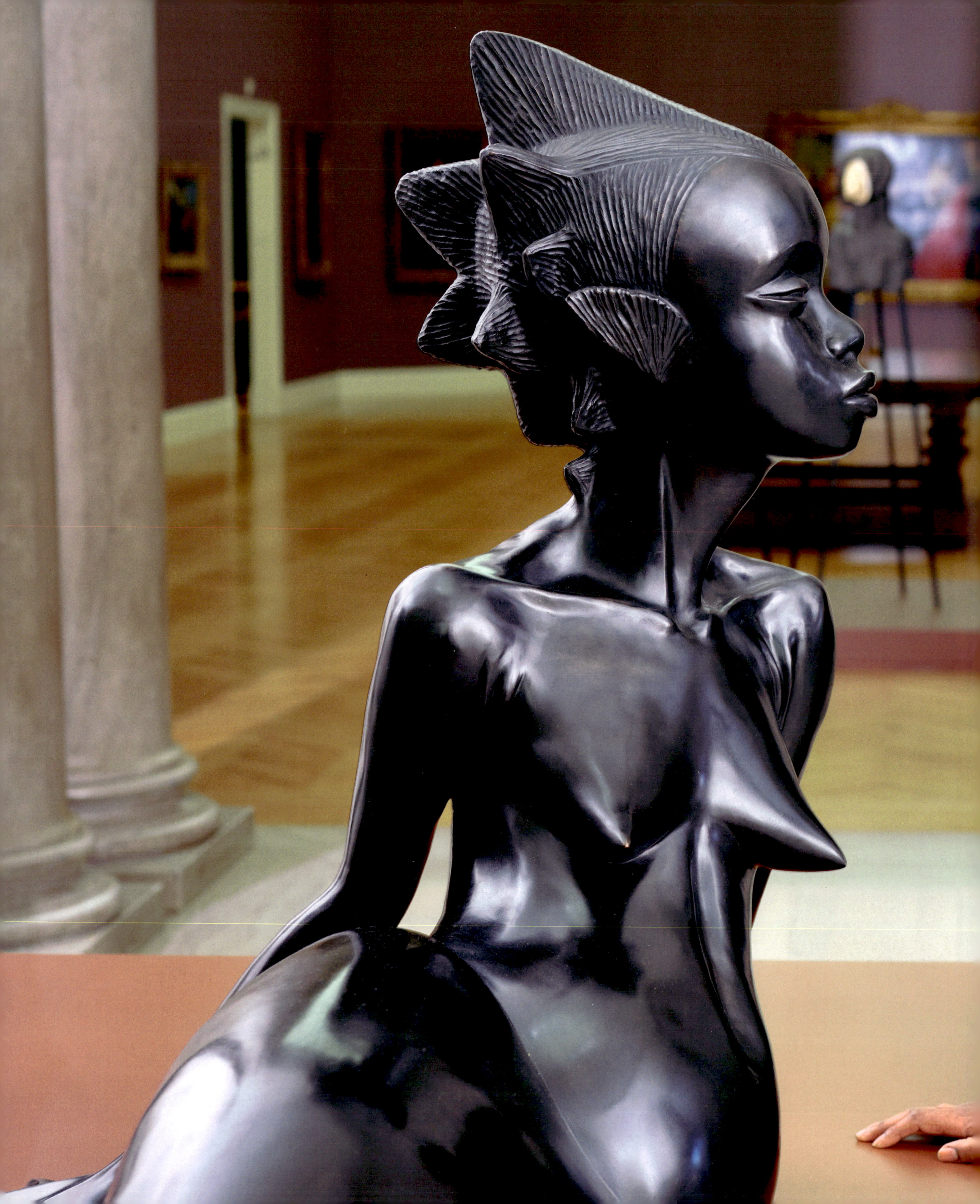

Courtney J. Martin in conversation with Wangechi Mutu

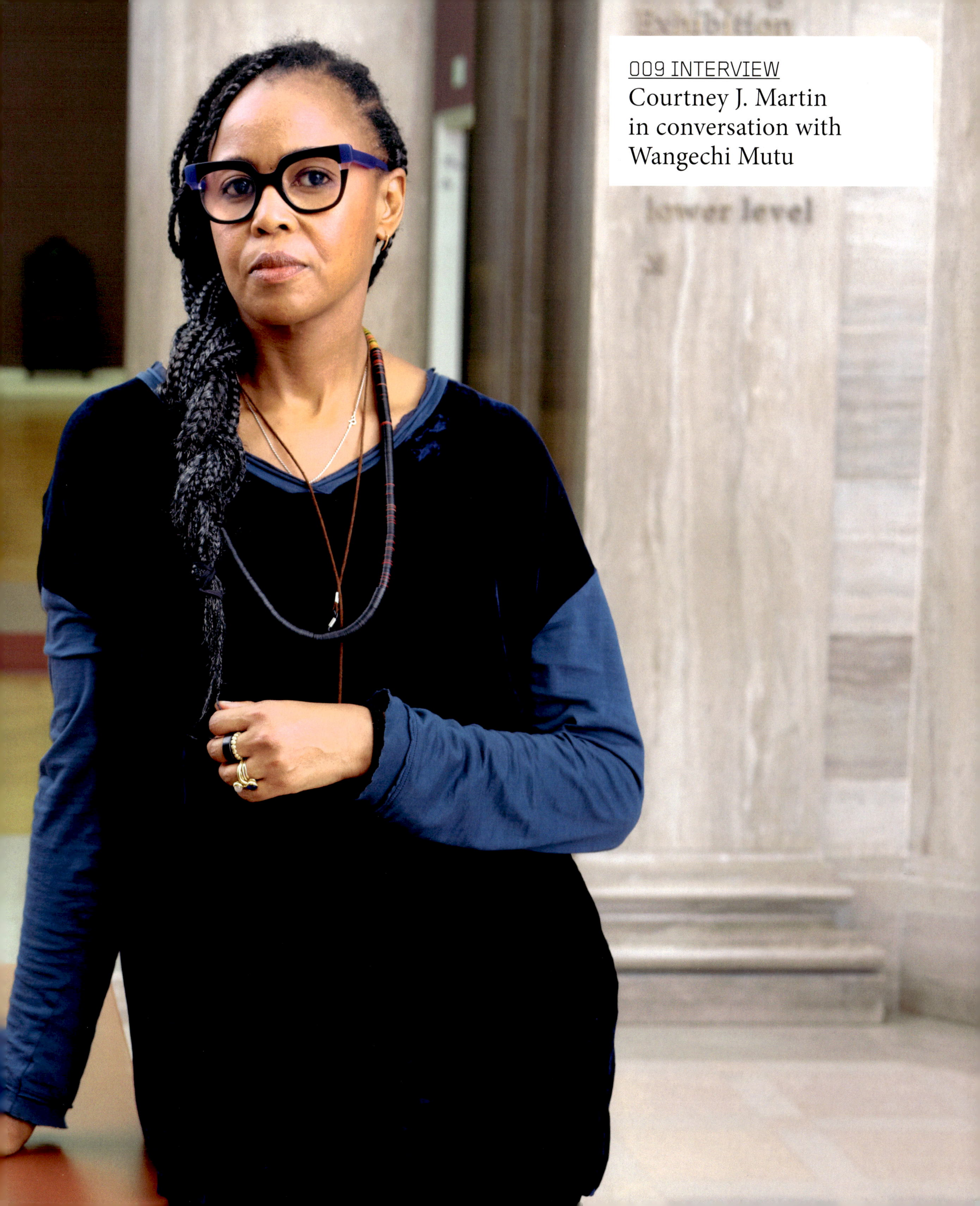

previous pages,
WANGECHI MUTU,
FINE ARTS MUSEUM OF
SAN FRANCISCO, 2021

opposite,
SHY SIDE-EYE, 2015
COLLAGE PAINTING
ON LINOLEUM
91 X 57 CM

COURTNEY J. MARTIN: *Where were you born?*

WANGECHI MUTU: I was born in Nairobi, at Nairobi Hospital, 22 June 1972, on the cusp of the evening and the night.

MARTIN: *Were you the first child in your family?*

MUTU: No, I was the second. I'm the first artist.

MARTIN: *What did your parents do?*

MUTU: My mum's a retired registered nurse and midwife. She worked in several hospitals in Nairobi, including the Aga Khan Hospital. This is where she finally landed, after enduring my crying every time she left, and the challenges of my sister's fragile health. She ran the CSSD department, which is in charge of sterilizing and sanitizing hospital instruments, so perfectly suited to her because she's a hygiene fanatic. But eventually she opened up her own pharmacy, which she did very well at.

MARTIN: *Is this why you know so much about bodies?*

MUTU: It's part of why I'm so intrigued by diseases and bodies and biology and scientific illustrations and anatomy and drawing the body. I think it comes from there, but then I also loved and did well in biology, which I studied until high school. In biology you have to draw all the time – even doctors have to draw – so I think that continued in my muscle memory. I loved drawing all those things that I saw in her nurse's books. She had a lot of books. They weren't very modern books. They were somewhat Victorian, with black and white photography and really precise hand-drawn illustrations. I loved looking at them. Yes, for sure, this played a role in forming my imagination.

MARTIN: *What about your father?*

MUTU: My dad did so many different things. He studied teaching. He was a geography teacher when my parents met.

MARTIN: *Is there nobody else in your family interested in art? Are they creative?*

MUTU: My brother is an actor. My dad is artsy.

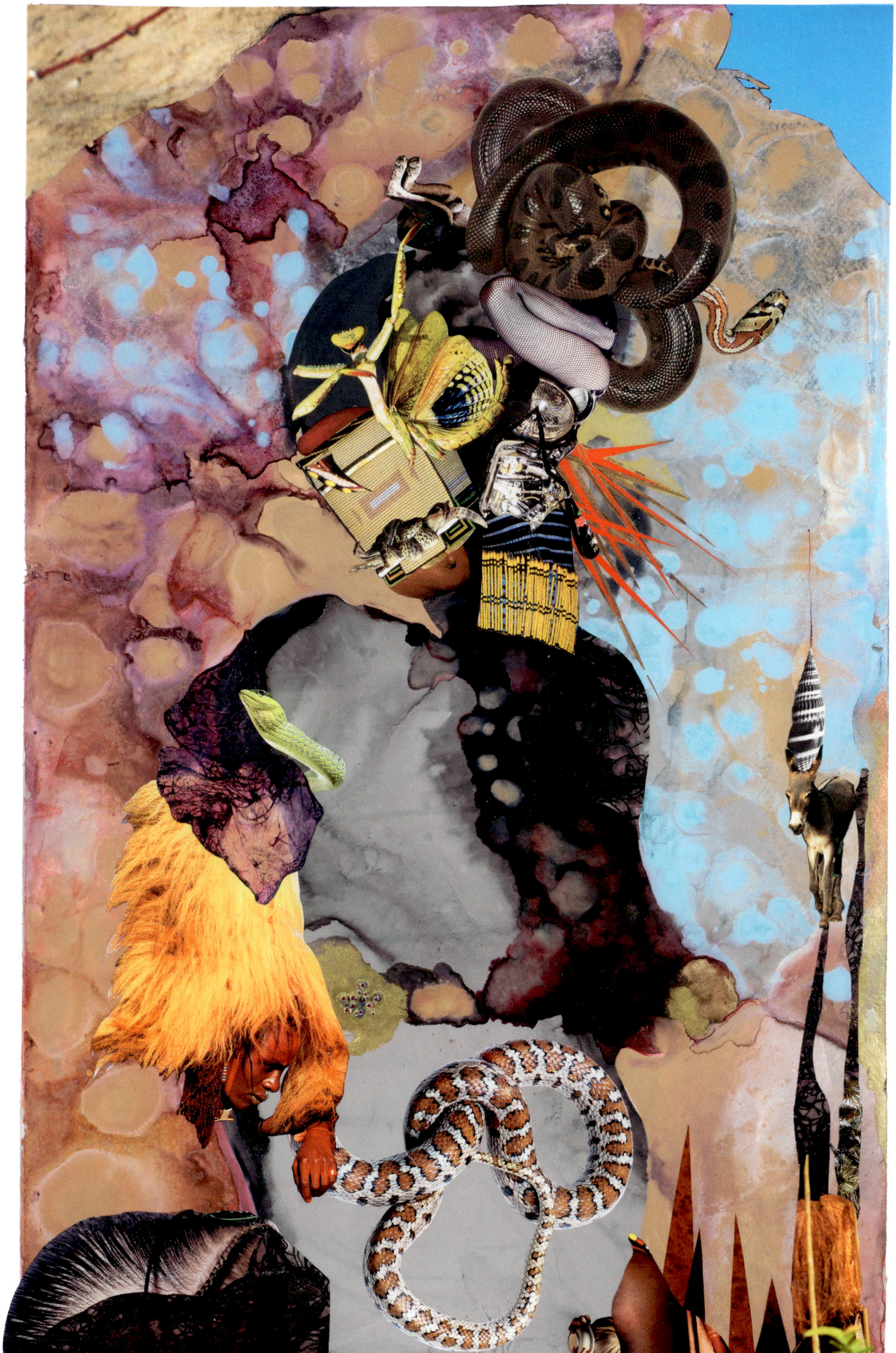

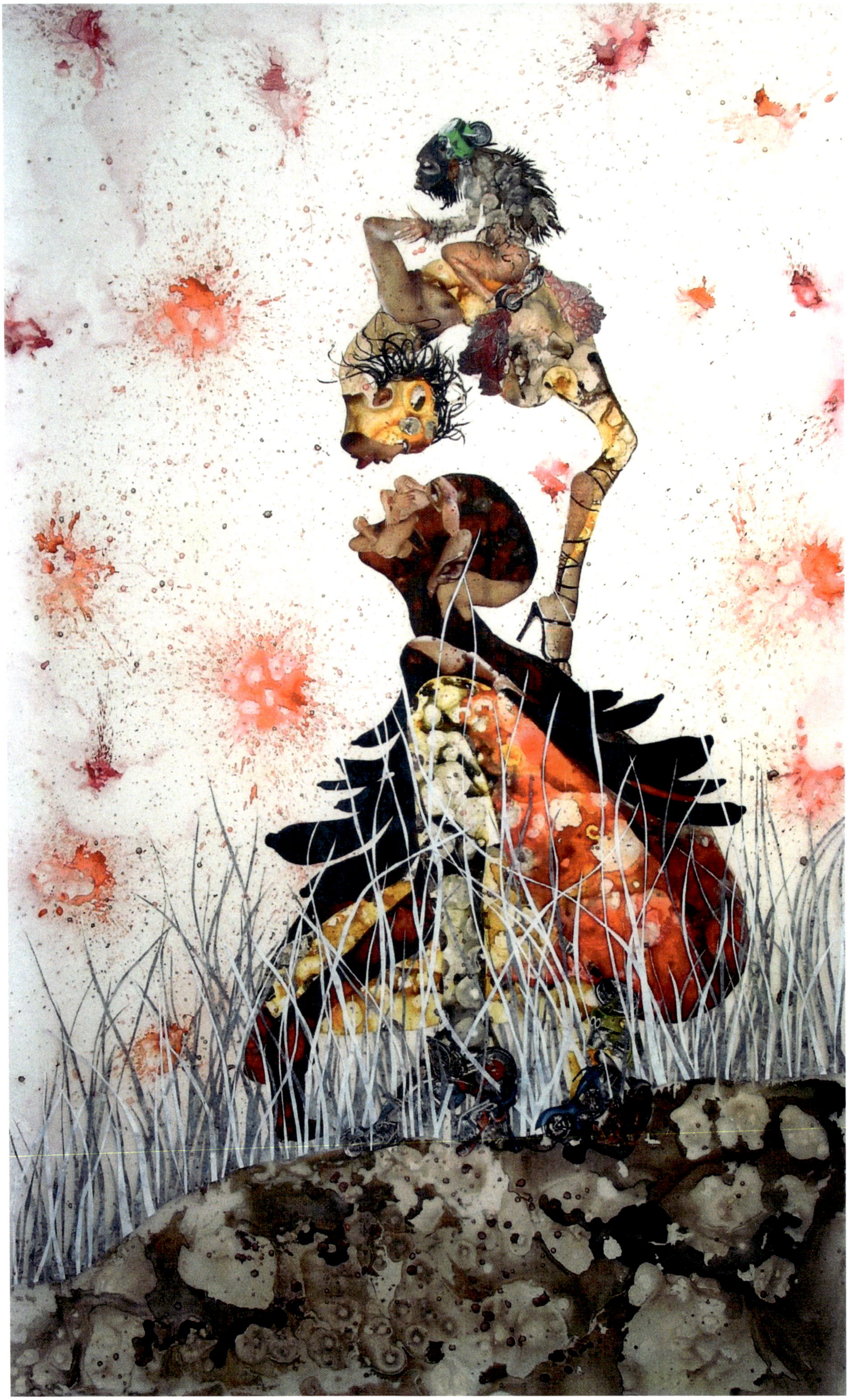

opposite,
MISGUIDED LITTLE UNFORGIVABLE HIERARCHIES, 2005
INK, ACRYLIC, COLLAGE AND CONTACT PAPER ON MYLAR
206 X 132 CM

MARTIN: *What does that mean?*

MUTU: If you ask anybody who's met him in the last twenty or thirty years, they'll say, 'He's a professor, he's a teacher, he's a writer, he's a poet.' But he was a businessman when we were kids. I think he had a bit of a midlife crisis. I remember looking at him thinking, 'If I get to be as old as him …', he was forty! [Laughter] I remember it so clearly: 'If I get to be as old as him and I'm not doing what I love doing, I'm going to take that steering wheel and do a U-turn and go and figure something else out.' By the time he turned forty he'd started writing poetry. He'd make us read and do odd things like stop by the road when we were driving somewhere, and get out of the car and learn the names of indigenous trees. He was admired as a teacher and his students seemed to like listening to him. He trained as a teacher in Kenya, but studied political science in Northern Michigan University. His first degree was in Kenya, then his Master's was in the States. He was in the States right before Kenya's independence. It was a really critical time because of the civil rights movement and the relationship between the two freedom-fighting independence movements. He has a strange relationship with communism. He's very paranoid about communism.

MARTIN: *Does that come from having been in the States during the Cold War?*

MUTU: It was that time in the States when there was a witch hunt for radicals and political dissenters. He was probably one of the only Black students around. I'm sure there was a lot going on and being said that made him very afraid and made him associate communism with chaos. There was also a big effort to divide the African countries that went socialist and the ones that went capitalist. Forces were placed upon countries that chose communism, which distanced them and punished them for choosing what seemed un-American.

MARTIN: *I imagine Nairobi as a massive and cosmopolitan city. What was it like to grow up there? Is there a rural/urban divide between Nairobi and other parts of the country?*

MUTU: Nairobi was an idyllic city that was easy to drive through from one end to another. It was called 'the green city in the sun', because it was sunny and lush, lots of trees and the perfect climate. The country was still very young when I was growing up; we got our independence in 1972. There were still a lot of people whose families had recently moved to Nairobi or whose parents had moved and met in the city. There was a real mix of rural and urban, lots of farm animals, herds of cows, donkeys and chickens, and even today you'll spot an occasional camel. People grow and sell food crops everywhere, in little tiny spaces behind their houses and by the road. There's still a lot of agricultural life within the city because there are many poor people who, essentially, move to the city and then they realize the food is expensive and unhealthy. People take buses and smaller Matatus everywhere, but for many, transportation is expensive, so when I was growing up, people used to walk, and still do trek all the way from home and back to work many hours away. People make do and kind of continue their rural self-sufficiency, and frugality.

MARTIN: *What's changed in Nairobi since your childhood?*

MUTU: It's a little hard to tell who's rural and urban these days. There's this massive population of young people, many born in the city, but many who've been forced to come to town for work. There's also this peculiarity of a massive market of second-hand clothing. People look like they're wearing hip Western-American clothes. Wealthy country populations discard a lot of clothes before they're worn out. Most wealthy people, most middle-class people, don't wear their clothes to the bone. A lot of that clothing gets recycled and has another life in markets far away. There's a huge industry of second-hand clothing in most urban centres in Africa, which is a big problem because it doesn't encourage manufacturing. We have hardly any manufacturing of clothing. We used to have factories that made everything. I recently took a close look at childhood uniforms and there were all these beautifully made clothes and they were manufactured in Kenya. The quality was exceptional.

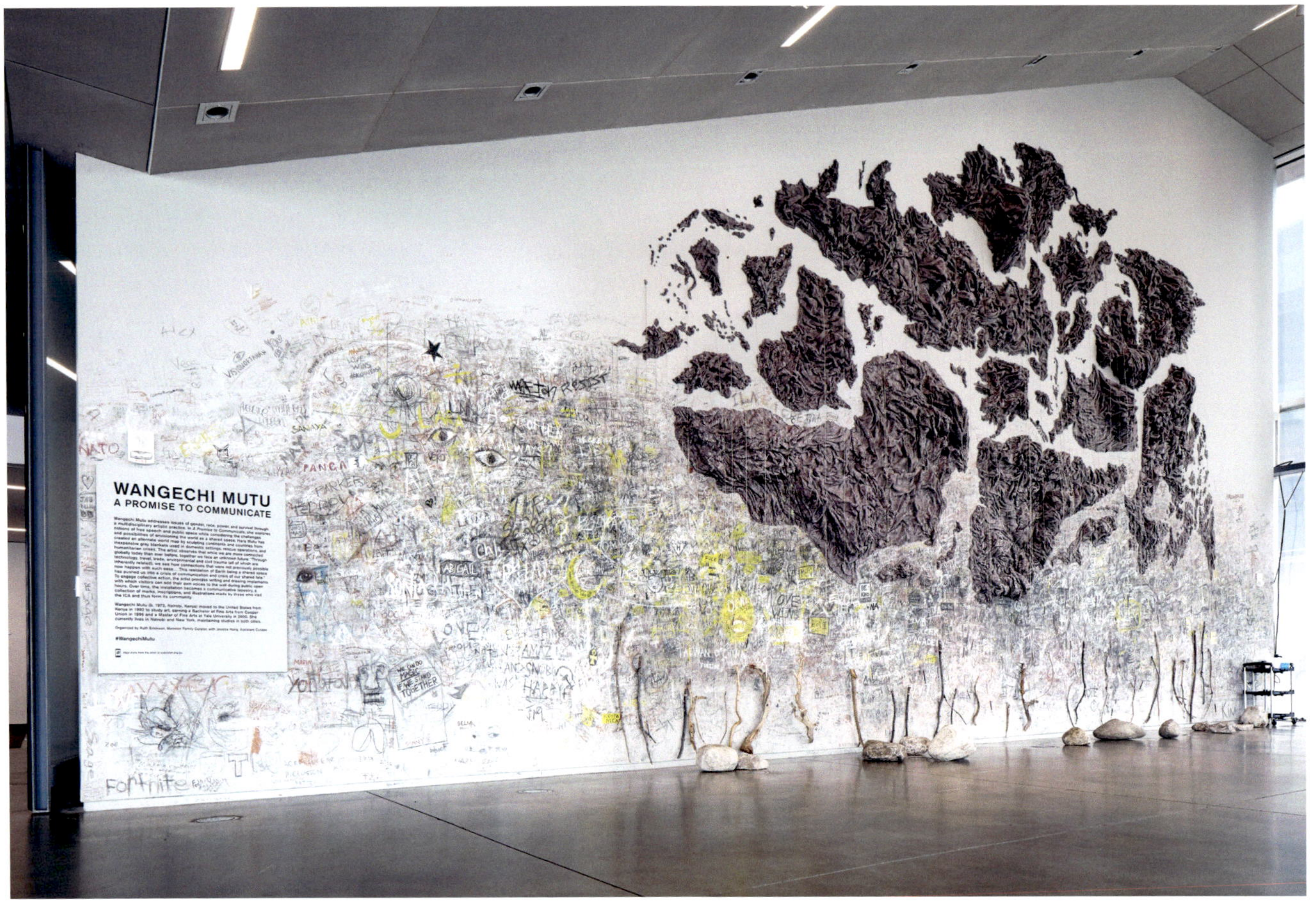

A PROMISE TO COMMUNICATE, 2018
BLANKETS, PACKING TAPE, PAINTED WALL, STICKS, STONES, CHALK, STRING

INSTALLATION VIEW AT THE INSTITUTE OF CONTEMPORARY ART, BOSTON, 2018

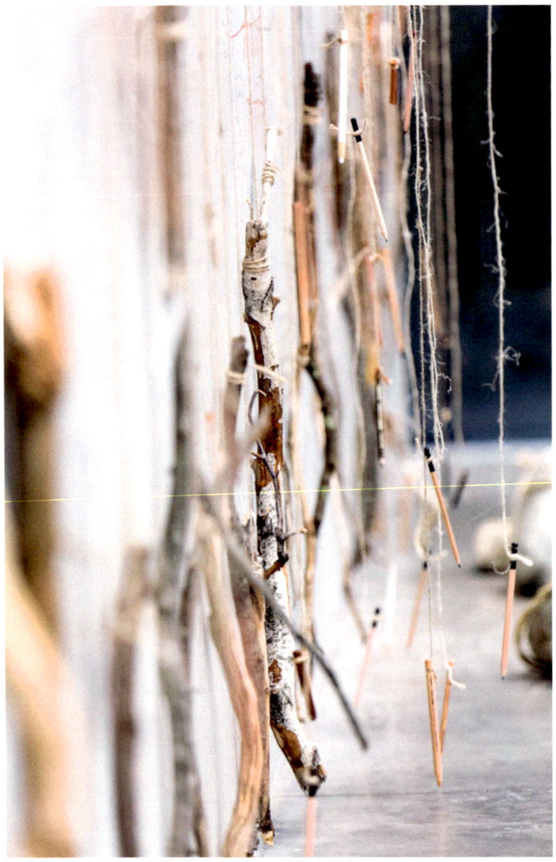

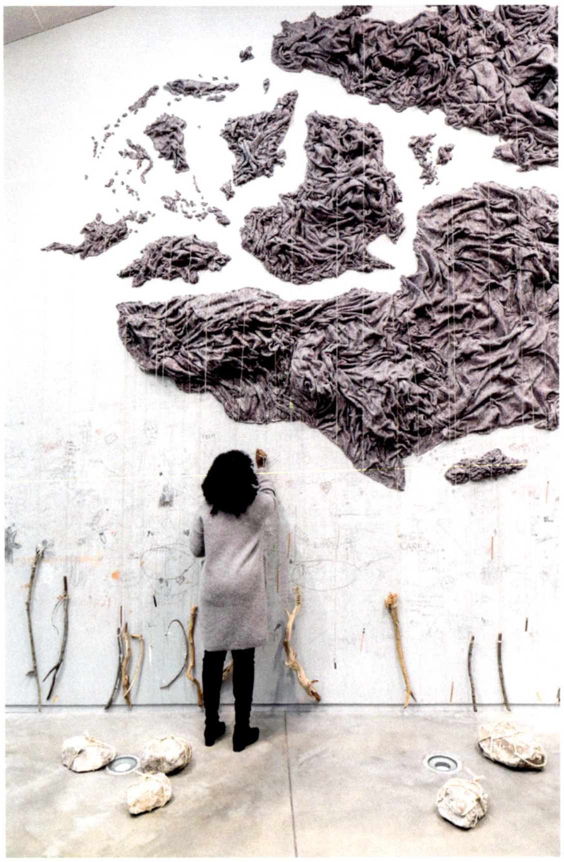

A PROMISE TO COMMUNICATE
(DETAIL), 2018
BLANKETS, PACKING TAPE,
PAINTED WALL, STICKS,
STONES, CHALK, STRING

There are tons of vehicles, and the skyline has grown ferociously. The big Marabou storks are still sitting on thorn trees on the highway, though, and the Nairobi national park still spoons the edge of the city.

MARTIN: *Did your parents know that you were an artist early on in your childhood?*

MUTU: They knew I loved drawing and colouring and making things. But I also loved singing, playing my flute and swimming. I loved reading and being theatrical. I did water ballet or synchronized swimming for several years. I was very creative. I think they just thought I was this kid who had a hyperactive imagination, and it would wear off as I grew up.

MARTIN: *Were you encouraged in school?*

MUTU: Yes, by two teachers in my Catholic school and one in my high school in Wales. My English teacher named Ms Joel, with an incredibly long last Madagascan name, she constantly encouraged me and smoked tons of cigarettes. There was also Mr Yiga, a wonderful Ugandan music teacher, who could speak about classical European music. My mentor, father figure, was Richard Leakey. He recognized something in me, and I listened to that.

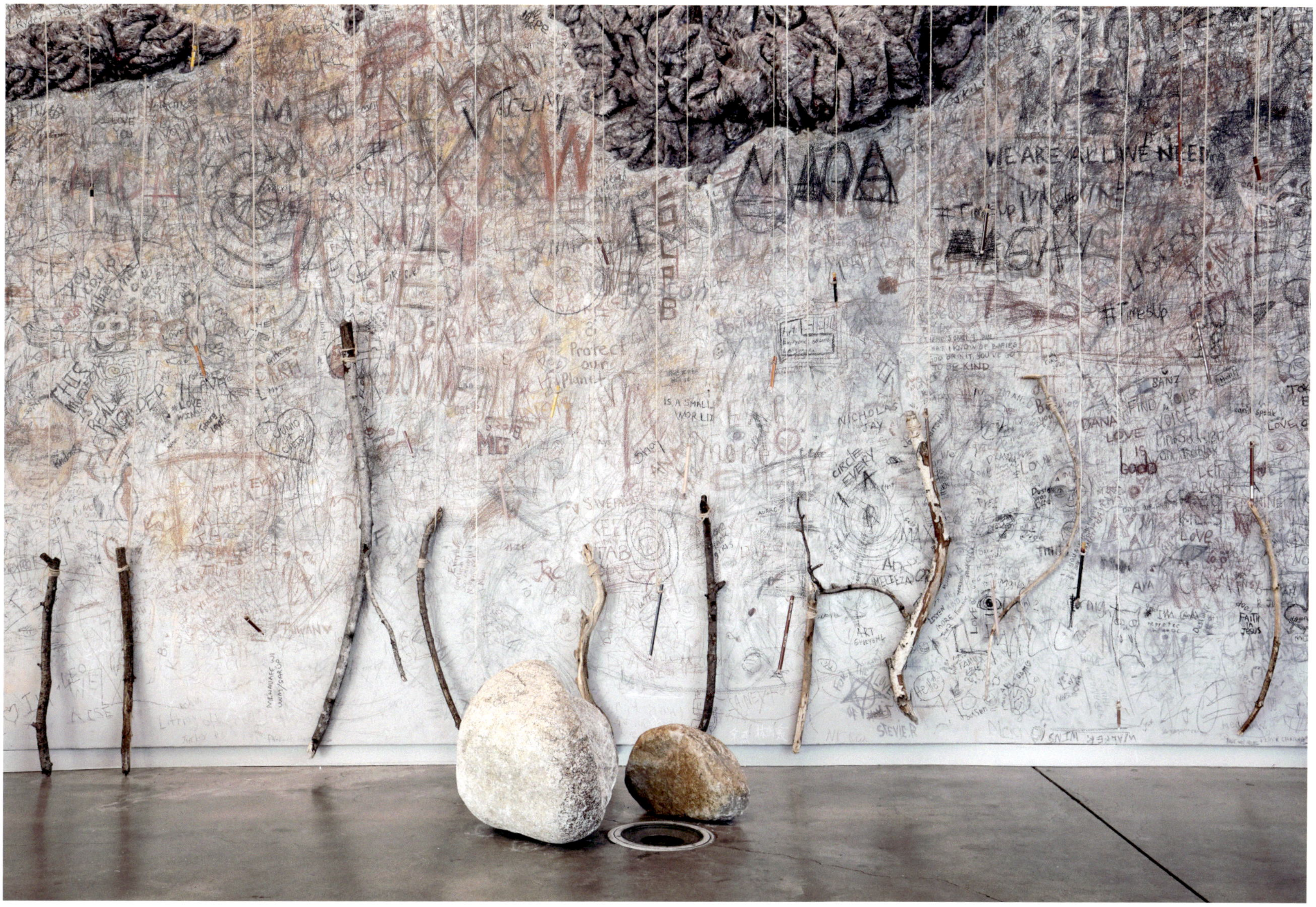

opposite,
TREE WOMAN, 2016
RED SOIL, PAPER PULP, SOIL, WOOD GLUE, WOOD
198 X 86 X 76 CM

MARTIN: *You left Kenya for Wales?*

MUTU: I wasn't intending to leave Nairobi, because that's where I'd been my whole life, that's what and who I knew. I was going to stay and enroll in university here. I was a total artsy-shmartsy girl in a school that didn't have a real plan for its artists. Anyway, I auditioned for a play called *The Desert Song* and I was the principle role, the Red Shadow, who was actually a young Frenchman disguised as a Moroccan rebel. Our school was a girls-only school, so I was the male lead. This was a play about the Moroccan rebellion against French colonization, in a Catholic school, run by English and Irish nuns, set in the northern part of Africa, where the desert nomads were rebels fighting for their freedom. Our school, my brother's school too, produced really good plays so everyone would come from all over the city to see us perform for about two weeks of performances. The reason I'm telling you this story isn't to make you laugh, but to say that it was Richard Leakey who came to the play and ignited this insane idea in me that I should go to school abroad. Soon after he'd come to see this play, he said to me 'You need to go to this international school in Wales where kids come from all over the world.'

MARTIN: *What school did you attend?*

MUTU: The Atlantic College, which sits on the southern coast of Wales, on the Bristol Channel. It's one of dozens of United World College IB schools, which are now scattered all over the world. They're really incredible schools, because they pioneered the idea that if you educate kids from different places, you create a population of people who can get along with each other and solve problems diplomatically through dialogue as opposed to conflict. At that age, we were able to see both sides of the coin. Every time there was a world crisis, the entire school would congregate and discuss the issues from the perspective of different worldviews. Whatever arguments and agreements came up in those discussions were often very accurate assessments and readings of the situation. We often had spot-on analysis and sometimes even solutions to global problems, because we were genuinely trying to get along, without political motivations and very little to lose. I mean, sometimes you'd hear what sounded like patriotism, but it was often sentimental attachment to our countries and families. For the most part, if we talked about a war we always got down to the fundamental underlying problem: 'Oh, this is about oil.' We were all teenagers, so we didn't have any responsibilities but to our authenticities, and we could always work through a complex problem and come to the end of it and then go to the social-centre and dance off the tensions.

MARTIN: *Was it difficult to go from the city of Nairobi to rural Wales?*

MUTU: The school was in a village. It was next to this little town called Llantwit Major, so we were basically on the water, on these beautiful brutal cliffs. It's a very romantic, very rural, sheep-farming Anglo-welsh area. Being in the hills and the cliffs was good because it was essentially a bit of a liability to have all these teenagers miles away from home in a foreign place. Culturally, we were so different from one another, but in our heart of hearts we were young and idealistic and hopeful and smart and talented and open to change. It was safer to have us in a village, where the school could monitor our social life.

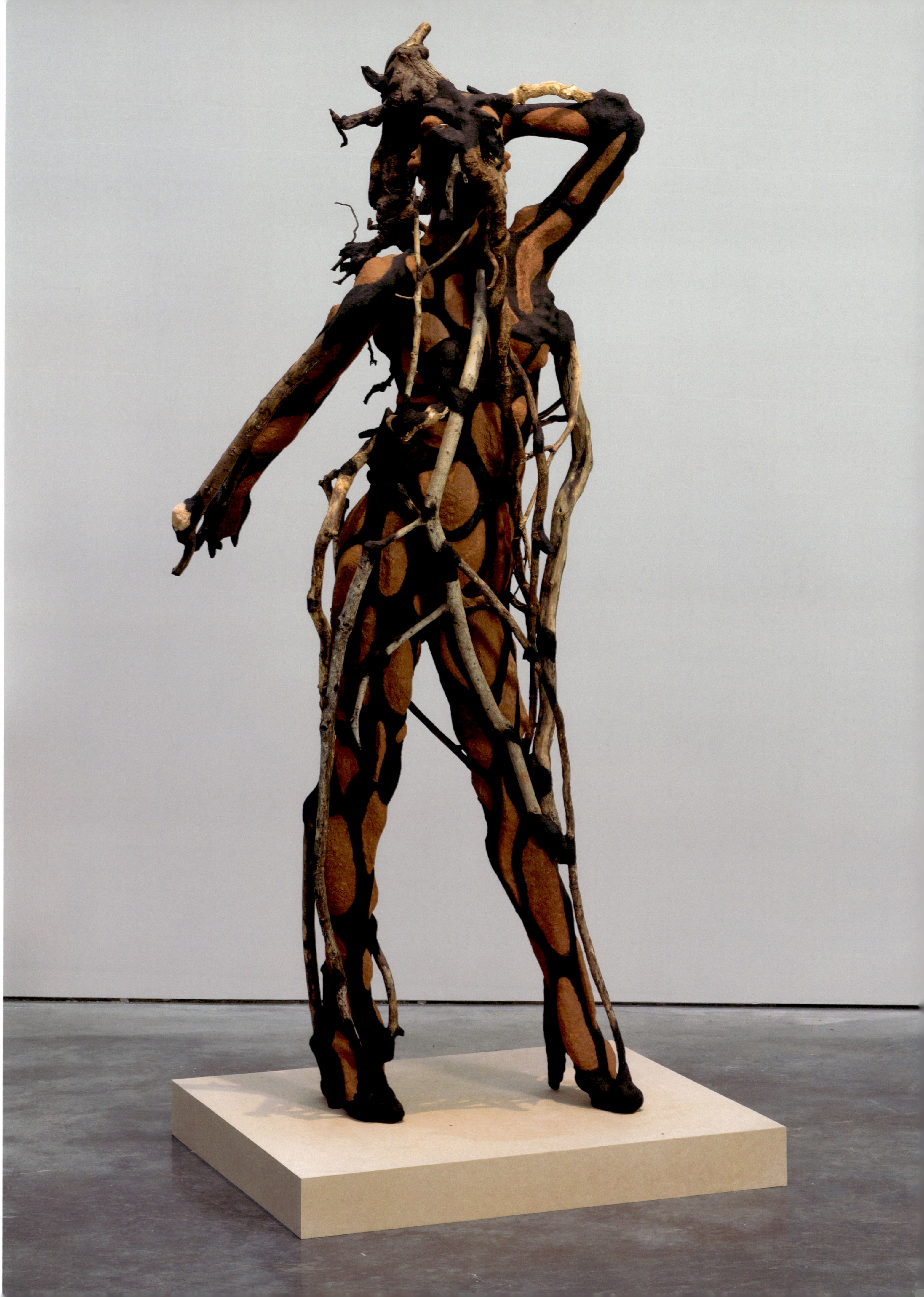

CREATURA V, 2018
RED SOIL, PAPER PULP, WOOD GLUE, EMULSION PAINT, SPRAY PAINT, COW BONES, COW HORN ORNAMENTS, GLASS, BRASS, WOOD BEADS, WOOD
55 X 17 X 58 CM

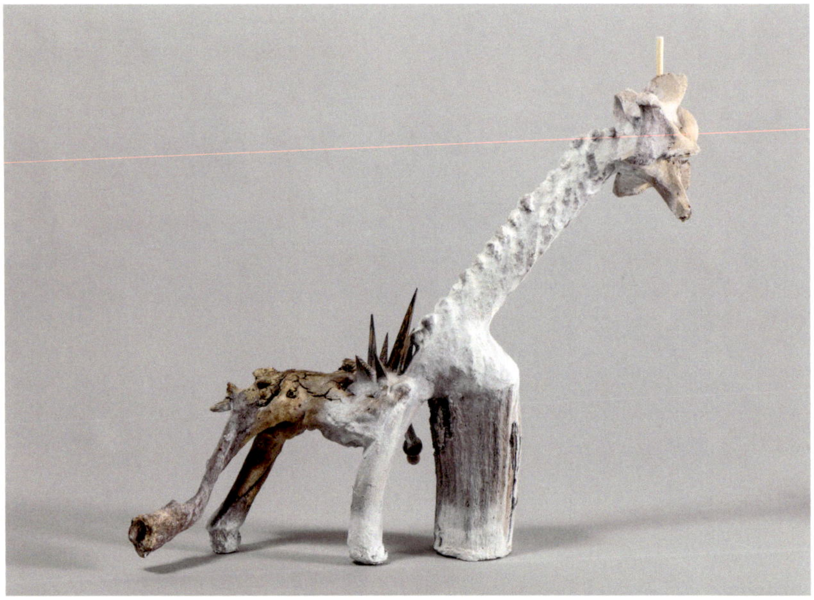

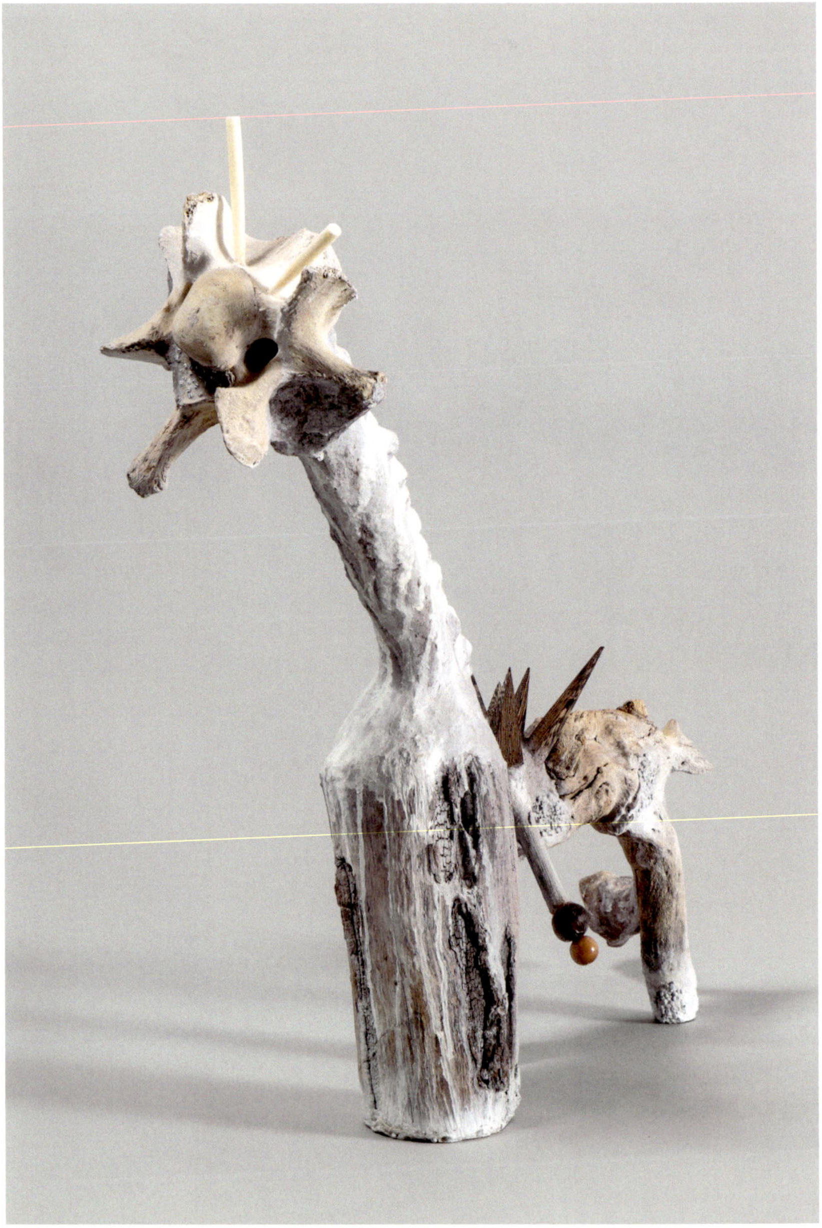

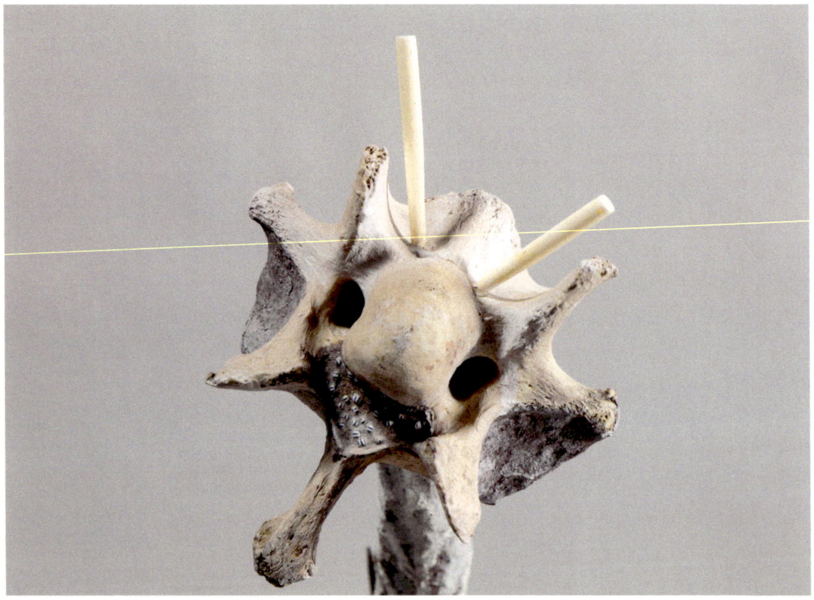

CREATURA IX, 2019
RED SOIL, PAPER PULP,
WOOD GLUE, ORNAMENTS,
GLASS BEADS, SNAIL SHELLS,
WOOD, EMULSION PAINT,
SPRAY PAINT
44 X 21 X 52 CM

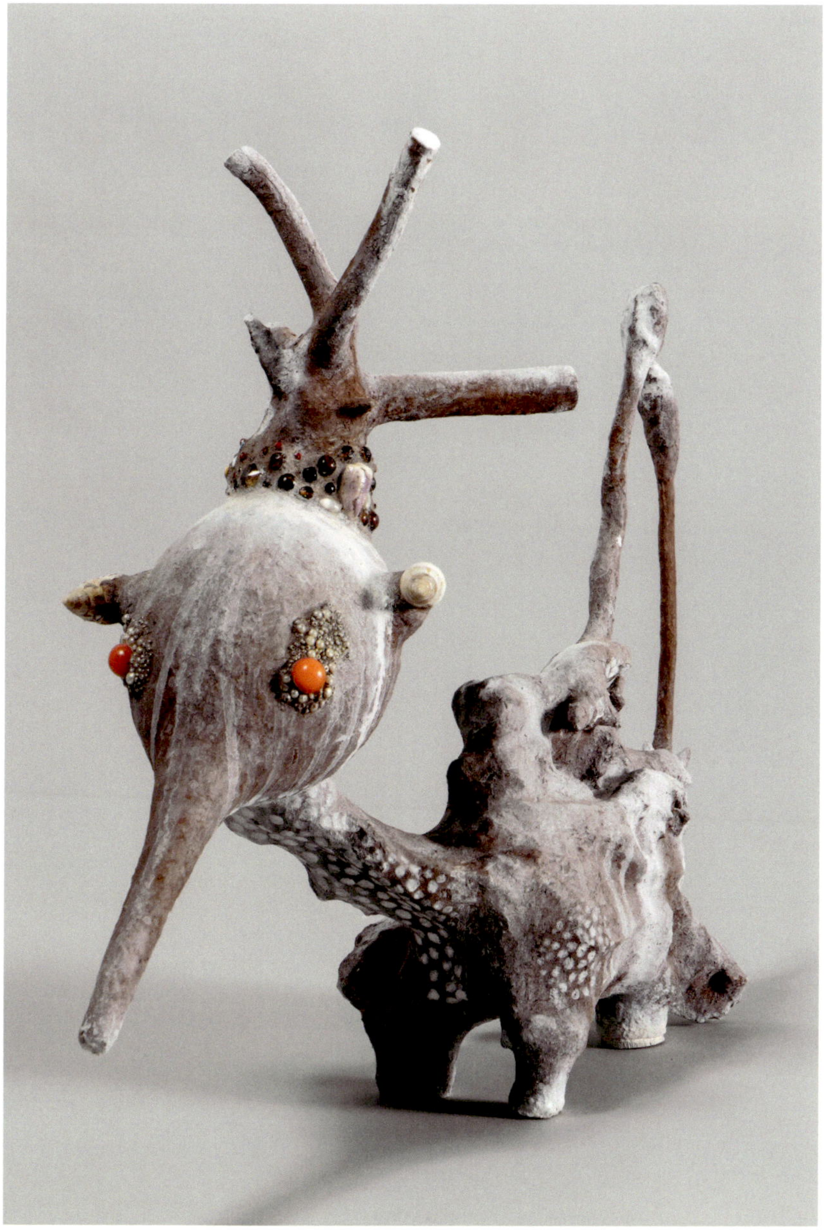

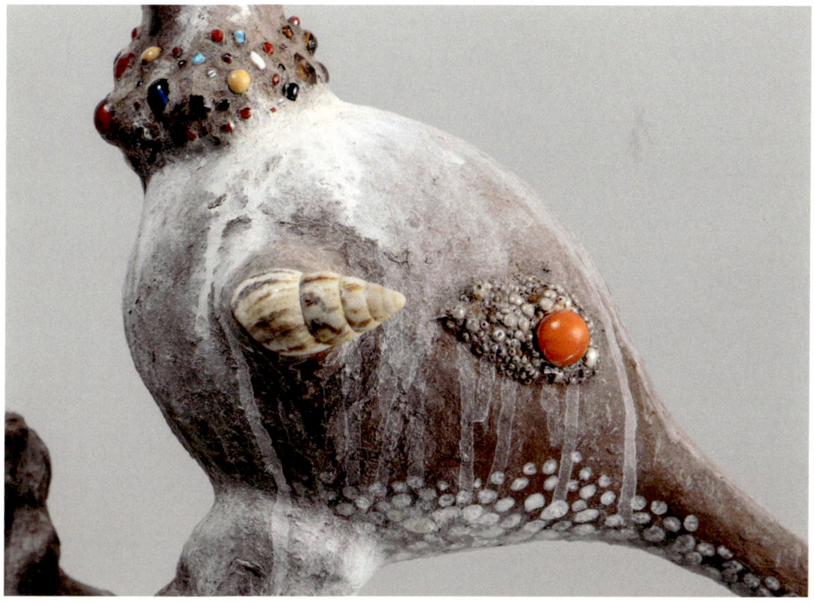

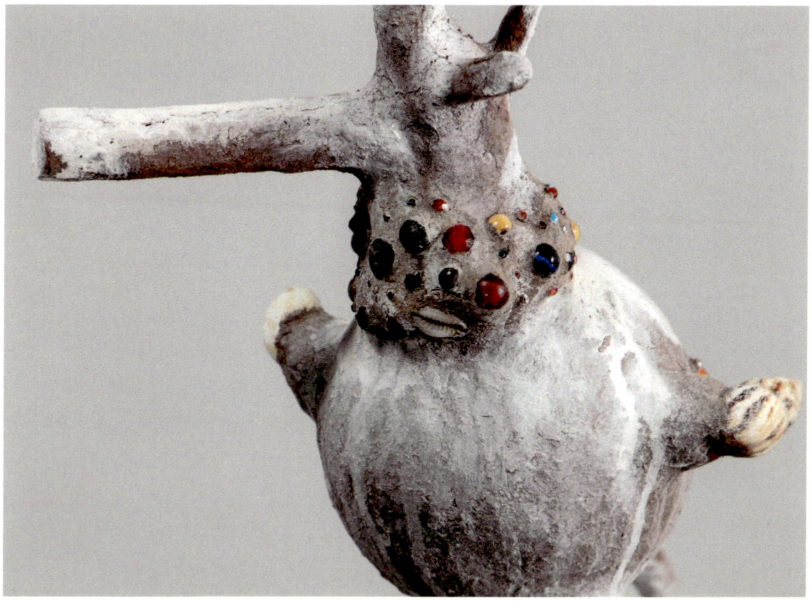

MARTIN: *Were there art classes?*

MUTU: There was an incredible art department. Kids made art because it was a cool subject, because of the teacher, because of the department, even though they had no desire to pursue it professionally. A lot of people just showed up in the art classes. I didn't know much about art or art histories at the time. But even while I was applying, I just knew I loved making art. Once we enrolled in the classes, we were given studios and our superbly dedicated teacher took us to museums and local galleries, often with very traditional ideas. Then, sometimes, we'd go to London, to the Tate. We also went to studios and did studio visits – that was the beautiful thing about this teacher: he taught us by showing us what professional artists do. It was the first time I realized, 'Oh God, the studios are in these filthy ends of the city, places where artists germinate their work and art and paint and make.' It was very interesting to look at these rooms and the people who were so inspired, and the work in their studios, and on the walls. For me, it was an indication of how much enthusiasm and how many ideas they had to offer.

At the time, I took a couple of trips around the Mediterranean. I remember going to the Reina Sofia. I was obsessed with Giacometti, so wherever I could, I'd go look at Giacometti. I remember seeing art in Istanbul, in Cyprus, in Thessaloniki in Greece, and being both in awe and perplexity.

MARTIN: *Was your interest in Giacometti because it was 3D or because it was figural?*

MUTU: I think it was because it was figurative. I feel like I got it, I understood. There was something very melancholic and existential: just the bare minimum to insinuate a human figure. I also didn't know what scale they were. I remember when I finally saw one, I was in shock. I don't know why I thought they were tiny. Yes, there are some tiny ones, but a lot of them are these gargantuan things, but they just look like they've been made with a movement of the fingertips.

I also saw my first Gauguins and fell in love with the colours and the fleshy softness of the figures. I don't know when I first saw Frida Kahlo, but I remember liking her natural worlds and her tortured-soul painstaking painting method.

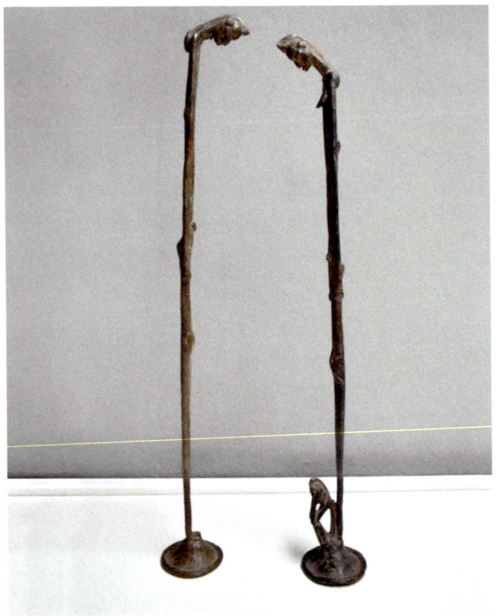

UNKNOWN ARTIST
DOGÓN SCULPTURES FROM MALI, 1890–1919
BRONZE
46 X 5 CM

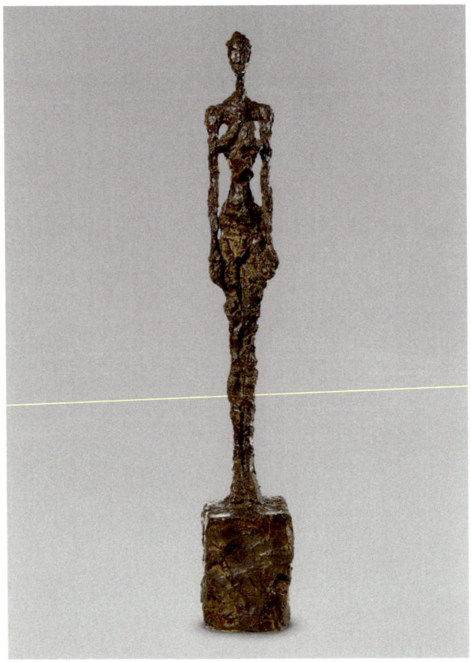

ALBERTO GIACOMETTI
STANDING WOMAN, 1958–59
BRONZE
131 X W. 20 X 35 CM

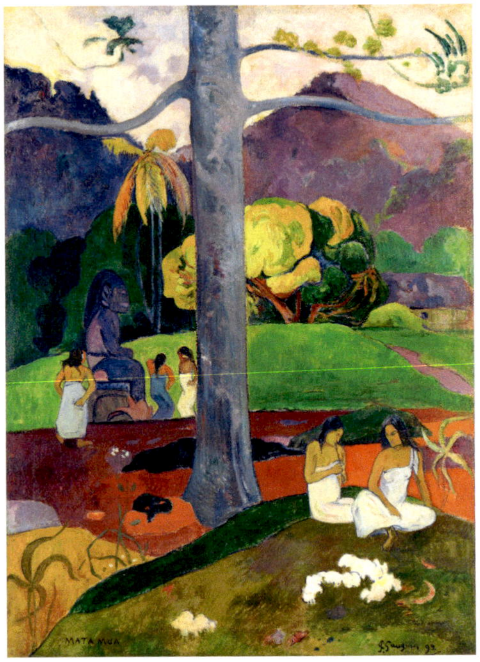

PAUL GAUGUIN,
MATA MUA (IN OLDEN TIMES), 1892
OIL ON CANVAS
91 X 69 CM

MARY & MAGDA, 2018
VARIEGATED LEATHER (PIGSKIN), DYED AND PAINTED BY HAND, HAND STITCH-ASSEMBLED WITH COTTON THREAD, SYNTHETIC FIBER FILL AND SAND WEIGHTS, IN TWO PARTS, ON WELDED STEEL BED WITH BLACKENED WAX FINISH
EACH: 114 CM
LENGTH: 46–91 CM
CIRCUMFERENCE: 152 X 97 X 46 CM

MARTIN: *Did you decide to go to art school after graduating?*

MUTU: After graduation, I said, 'Let me go back to Kenya and think about this because I'm clearly feeling so strongly about this art bug I've caught, but I don't know how I'm going to justify, explain, this huge leap I need to take in order to study and get a degree in art.' So I went back home, and I got a job. My dad helped me make a connection to this advertising company called McCann Erickson. I was hired as an illustrator. This was the age of cut-and-paste graphic design. It wasn't like some collage, edgy thing, it was the real-deal old-school but international, pre-digital, big company. These were people who were doing ads for Johnson & Johnson and Coca-Cola. I learned a lot about these big companies and big products as a minion. I was that little person who did the drawings and figured out how to make them attractive to the public. But really, I played a very minor role in what the finished product was going to be. I think that working this way inspired a lot of my collages. My love of cut and pasting wasn't born here, but it was reinforced. I got really good at and really interested in that way of working, like grafting images together and distorting them and changing them by adding something new, as opposed to painting over them or obscuring parts of them.

I did that for a few months. I didn't like it. It wasn't in any way what I was suited for, nor was it what I wanted to do, even with a salary. I had to do a lot of soul-searching and I went back to my mentor, and said, 'You got me to go to this high school and now I'm sort of trapped in between my Kenyan life, my desire to study art, my IB diploma, my lack of funds for art school. I want to study art, but I need to work and according to my father, I should return to my job.' He was involved with the Kenyan National Museums and told me there was a project in Lamu at the Lamu Fort.

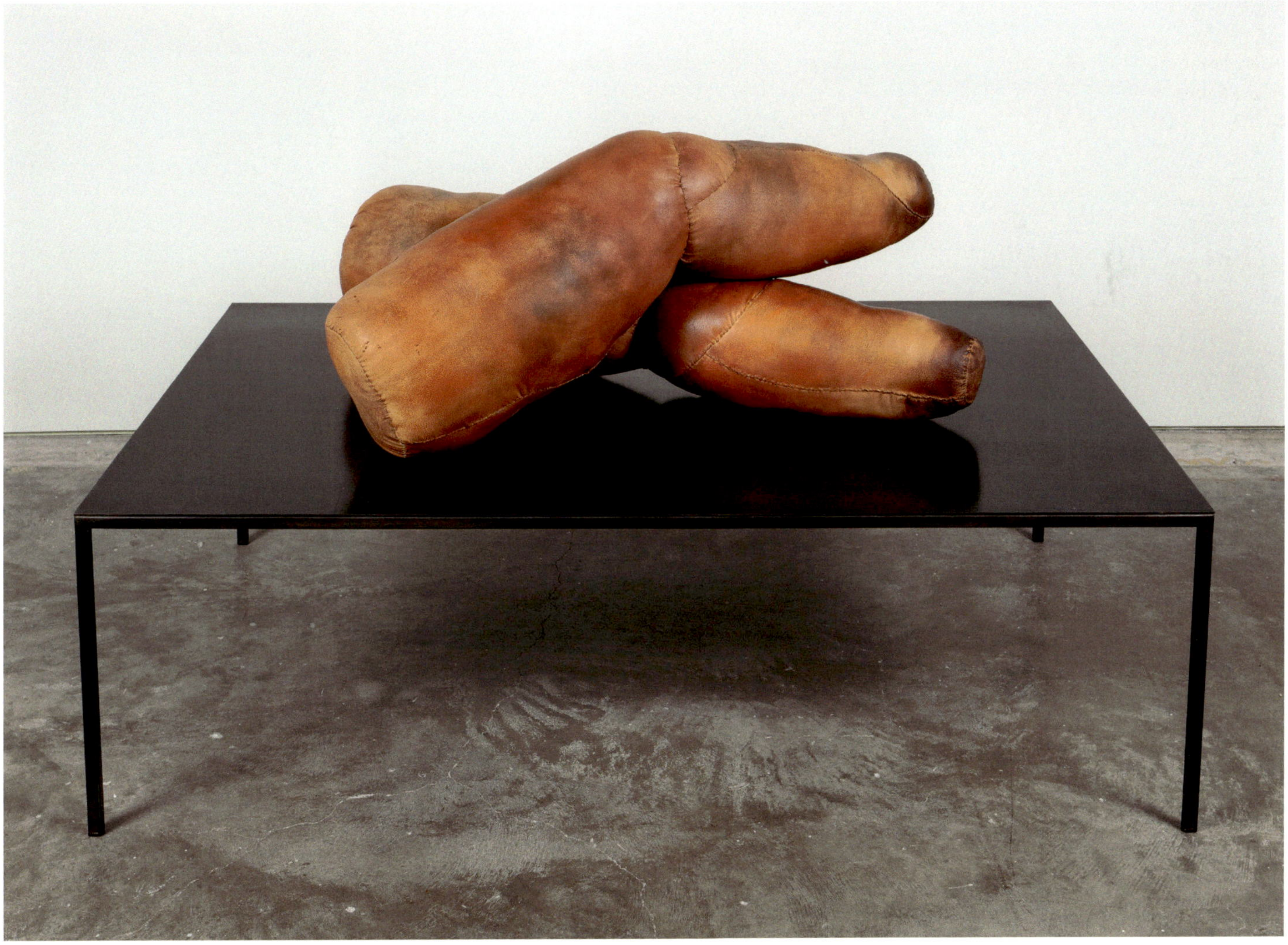

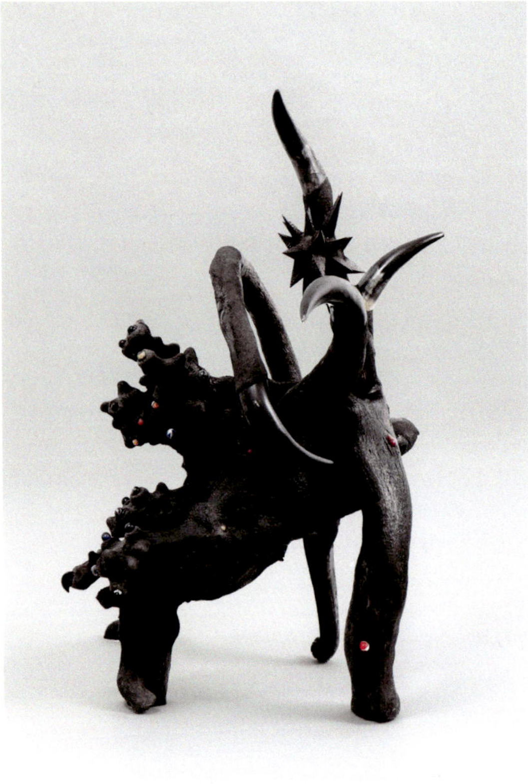

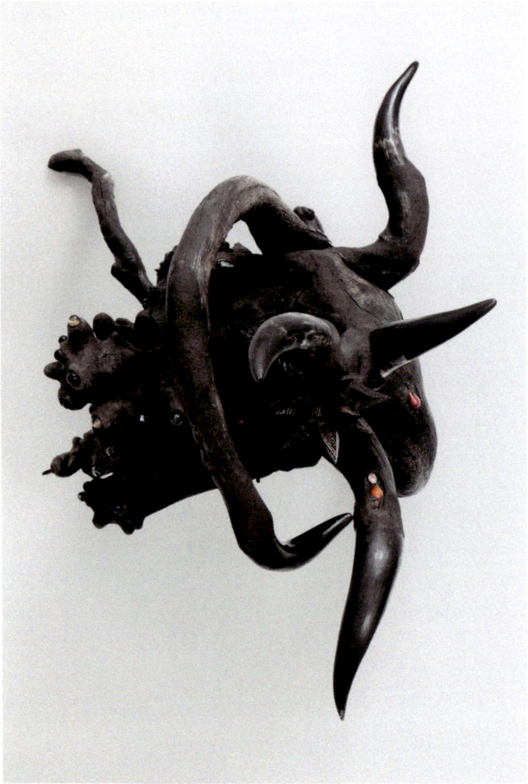

THE CLAW, 2018
SOIL, WOOD, COW HORNS, PAPER PULP, WOOD GLUE, CHARCOAL, ACRYLIC AND GLASS BEADS
94 X 61 X 84 CM

opposite,
SHAVASANA I, 2019
BRONZE
211 X 135 X 24 CM

MARTIN: *Lamu. The island in the Indian Ocean?*

MUTU: Yes, the small island on the northern coast of Kenya. I went to work on this island, in this historical fort that was used by the British military, but also served as a prison. It's an enormous structure in the middle of this boat-village, called Lamu. The National Museums of Kenya decided to turn the fort into an environmental museum with funding from the Swedish government, as far as I remember. For some reason, the Swedes decided, 'We're going to give you all this money to turn this historical monument into an environmental museum that begins thematically with the Big Bang. We want the entire museum to be turned into a kind of diary of the Earth's history, from the beginning of time. Literally from the birth of our solar system to how the earth was created, to explaining plate tectonics and different climates and continents, and eventually with a focus on Lamu.' It was laid out like a google view of Lamu, from the sky all the way to planet Earth. I was tasked with the early part. I remember drawing the various planets in a dark sky surrounded by stars and meteorites.

MARTIN: *So you made the museum's didactics?*

MUTU: Yes, I was one of several students producing the museum exhibits, one mural at a time. There were also other young artists and designers and architects who were part of the project and were responsible for other rooms and sections. It was a seriously daunting chaotic and impossible project. But it turned out to be very magical time for me, living out in the less polluted part of this little island in Kenya. It allowed all these thoughts to keep swirling around my young head, and gave me time to experience and see things I never had, either in my city life in Nairobi or in my country life in Wales, or anywhere I'd travelled to. Lamu made time slow down and gave me permission to dance around in my headspace and with the vast seascape in front, it fuelled and encouraged my meandering imagination. My eight months there influenced my work and my sense of confidence so tremendously. It was the place that gave wings to my imagination and to my intellect and it allowed me to feed something ridiculously courageous and gave me the right to feel I could be unpredictable.

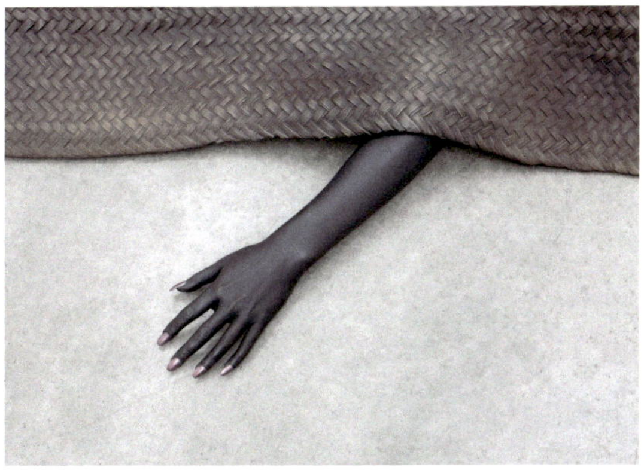

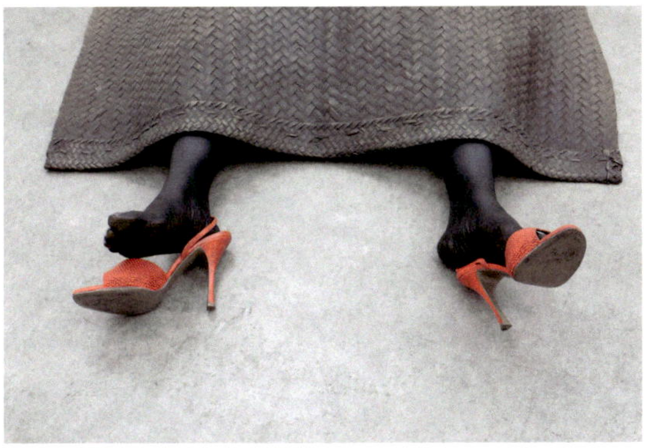

I think it was swimming in the morning, watching the small boats full of early morning commuters, the daily wading on the shore, finding little gems in the Indian ocean and coming back out and drawing, walking, napping, brooding, reading and going out to start again on the next day, that gave me a feeling of daily renewal and infinite playfulness in my creativity.

The house I lived in had a shortage of water. There was a generator that pulled water out of rocks deep beneath the house and often it wouldn't work for days. I remember having to fetch water for cooking and filtering, so I could have a drink, and how that little gesture changed my sense of survival. Cooking for myself, picking mangos off the trees on my way to and back from work, making friends with and hanging out with my Muslim lady friends who were all married and observant and hilarious and smart and worried for me: all of that stuff just filled my imagination with big questions and joy and independence and it just made me want to go further than I'd already gone and do more than I'd already done. I knew at that point, 'I can't stay here in a small place in my mind. I can't stay in Nairobi, I can't stay in Kenya. I have to do everything I can to pursue this thing that has absolutely no guarantees of any type of success or completion or income or whatever.'

MARTIN: *How long were you there?*

MUTU: I was there for maybe seven months, eight months. I had so much free time and aside from being able to read, draw and cook by myself, I was able to apply to five or six art schools in the States.

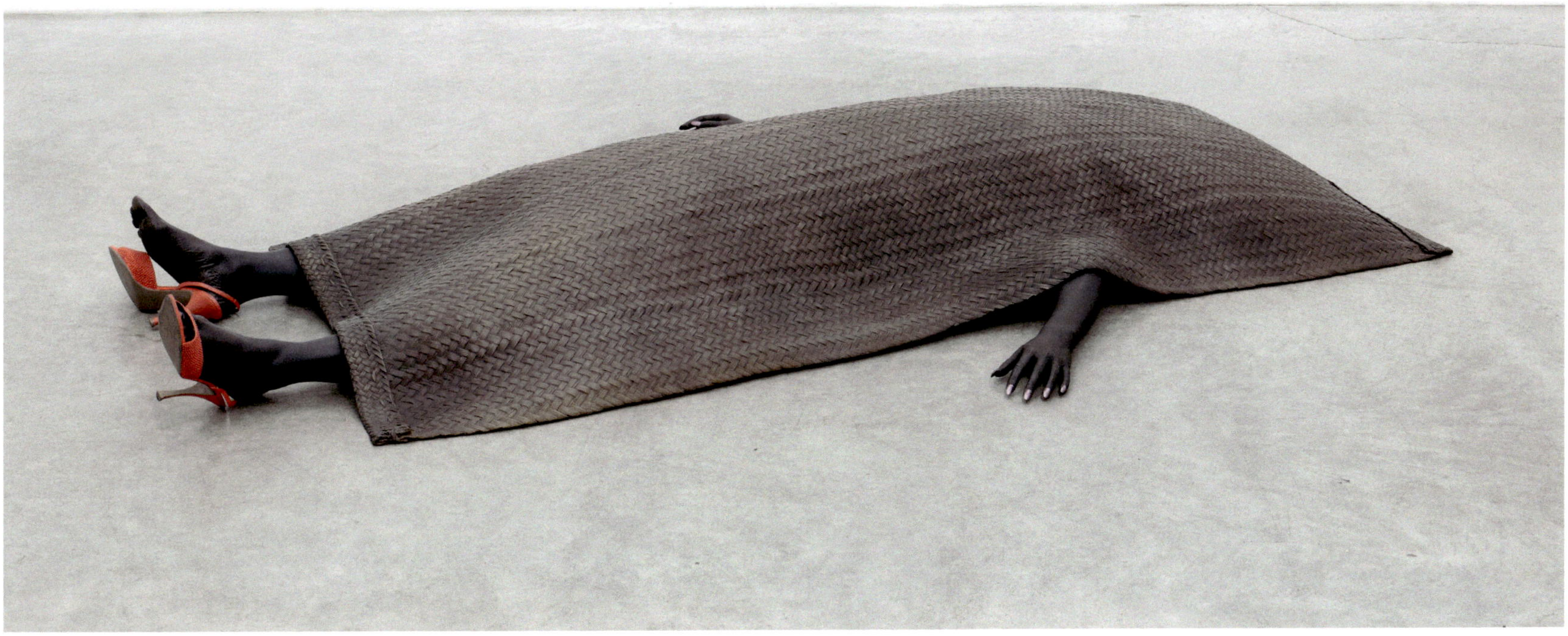

MARTIN: *You put together a portfolio and applied to art school from Lamu?*

MUTU: Oh yes, absolutely, I picked up my applications when I was visiting my parents in Nairobi. I'd written and received all the applications from Cal Arts, RISD, Pratt, Parsons, Philadelphia School of Art. I decided on Parsons School of Design. The art department was good, but it wasn't amazing. I hated feeling like I was in the wrong school, and I wasn't getting repaid for what the tuition cost. I just felt, 'I'm being charged for all of these design students to be able to do all of the expensive stuff that they have to do to be on Fifth Avenue. But really, I'm a nerdy art kid who just wants to explore everything even if all I have is only ink and paper and basic stuff.' I knew that I wasn't in the right school. So with one conversation after another, I discovered that there was a school a few blocks away, Cooper Union, that was tuition-free. Right there in New York City, literally ten to fifteen minutes away from my Parsons dormitory, and that I could try to get in as a transfer student if I applied. So I started to tell my teachers at Parsons I was going to apply to this small tuition-free school, and except for one teacher, all of them said, 'You're not going to get in.' Or, 'Cooper? You don't have what it takes. There are hardly any transfer positions.' All I could think was, 'What is this place, this magical school, that I can never be allowed get in to? [Laughter] I have to go find it.'

It was another big step. Probably one of the most important, because it was like another portal had opened in this space of New York, that I'd jump over into. I should add that to my list of accomplishments, because I got in and I got in as a transfer student, which means they have a slot or two every year when people drop out or have to leave, or move from art to architecture. I got offered one of those rare art slots.

MARTIN: *Cooper is about methodology, not technique. How did you learn to paint? How did you learn to sculpt? How did you learn about materials?*

MUTU: I was at Parsons for my foundation year, so that's actually where you do all of the basics of art-making, including drawing, printmaking, sculpture, colour theory. You learn how to weld. You learn how to cast in plaster and sculpt marble. You learn how to use the table saw, the circular saw. You learn what's going to cut your fingers off, and what's going to poison you in oil paints. You do loads of life drawing until you go crazy with an understanding that drawing is that singular melody of your imagination's voice. I drew all these naked people until I no longer saw nudity. I saw shape and colour and negative space. The politics of life drawing in art school is also very interesting, both in Nairobi and the UK. It was jarring because I was like, 'Wow, okay, this is a human being's body and we're going to learn how to render it, but that exactitude and representation is the least important aspect of this long-term project.' I took painting classes at Parsons, which is when I realized I wasn't going to enjoy being only in painting school.

That's when I started taking anthropology classes. I wanted a bit more. I took on a second Bachelor's, which is how I got to do all the Eugene Lang New School graduate school classes, which was important.

MARTIN: *What felt different about Cooper?*

MUTU: What felt different was that we were discouraged, at Cooper Union, from focusing too much on one medium. It was about exploration and growth and keeping open to new ideas. If your advisor saw that you'd signed up for yet more painting classes, they'd advise you to take calligraphy or join an architectural drawing class. You could make interdepartmental selections – you could even do engineering classes, but that took the maths that many art students didn't have.

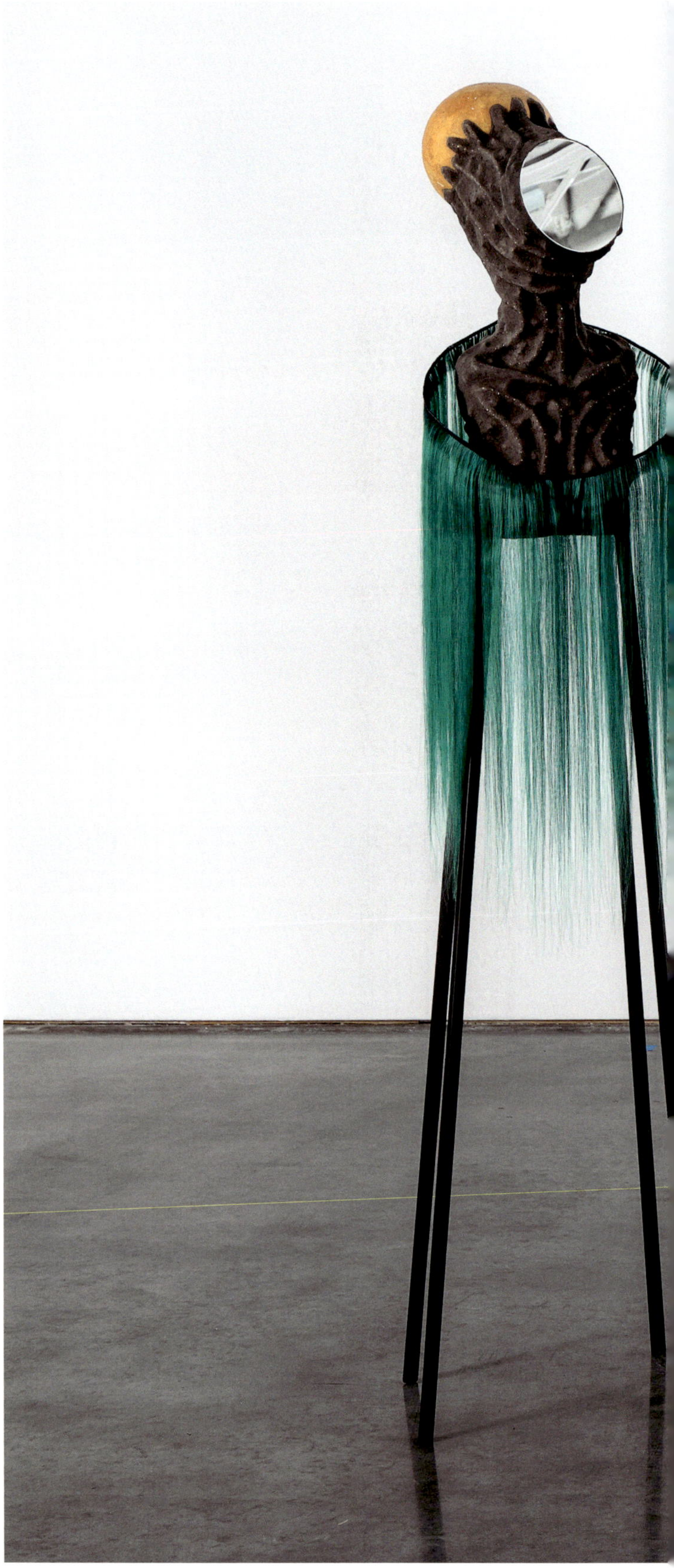

from left,
MIRROR FACED I, 2020
SOIL, CHARCOAL, PAPER PULP, WOOD GLUE, EMULSION PAINT, GOURD, BRASS BEADS, MIRROR, TEAK BASE, HAIR, WROUGHT IRON STAND
174 X 37 X 34 CM
BUST: 58 X 28 X 31 CM

MIRROR FACED II, 2020
SOIL, CHARCOAL, PAPER PULP, WOOD GLUE, EMULSION PAINT, DESICCATED BAOBAB FRUIT, BRASS BEADS, MIRROR, TEAK BASE, HAIR, WROUGHT IRON STAND
168 X 31 X 36 CM
BUST: 50 X 25 X 28 CM

MIRROR FACED III, 2020
SOIL, CHARCOAL, PAPER PULP, WOOD GLUE, EMULSION PAINT, BRASS BEADS, ROSE QUARTZ, MIRROR, TEAK BASE, HAIR, WROUGHT IRON STAND
176 X 43 X 37 CM
BUST: 60 X 27 X 33 CM

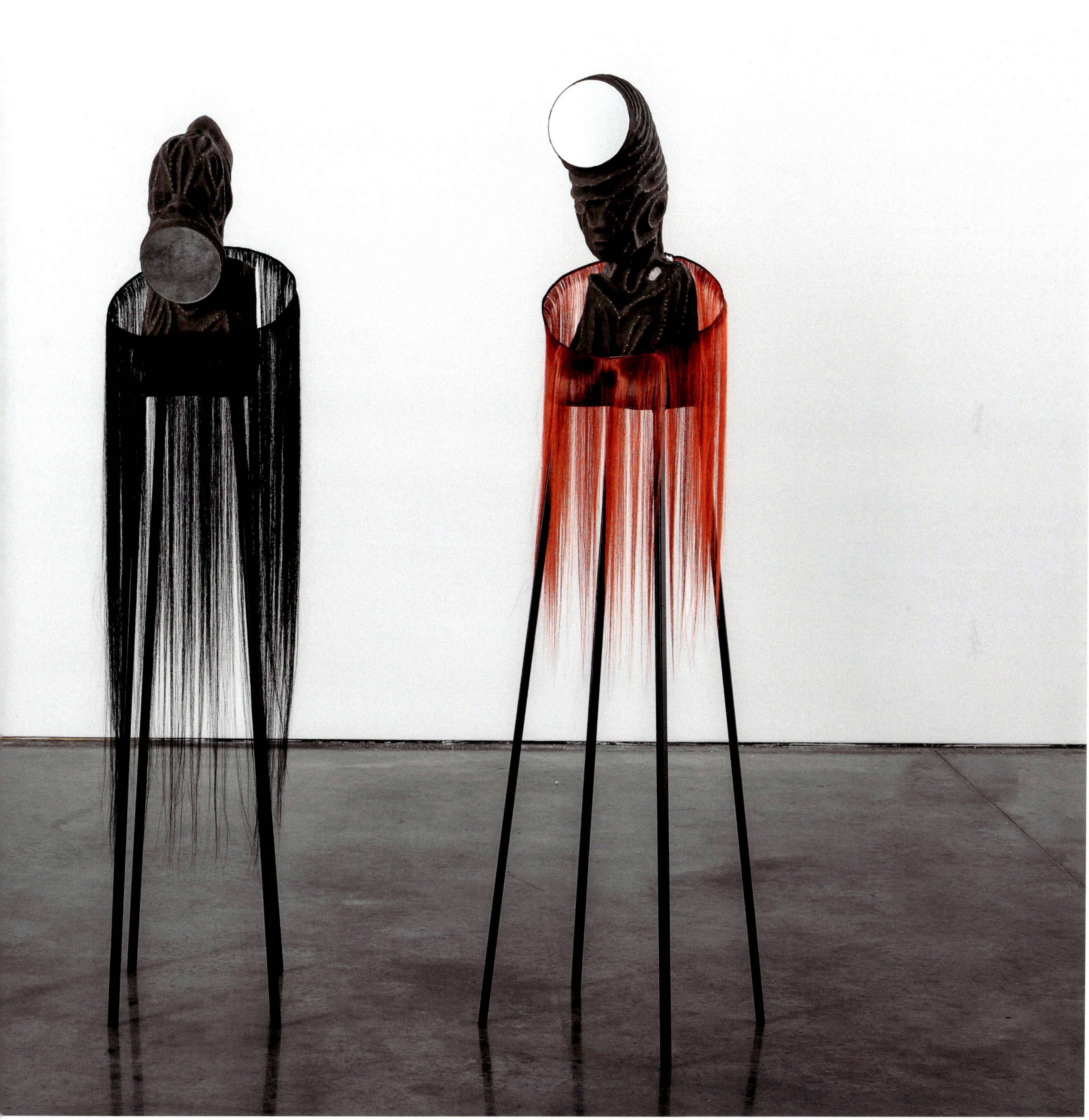

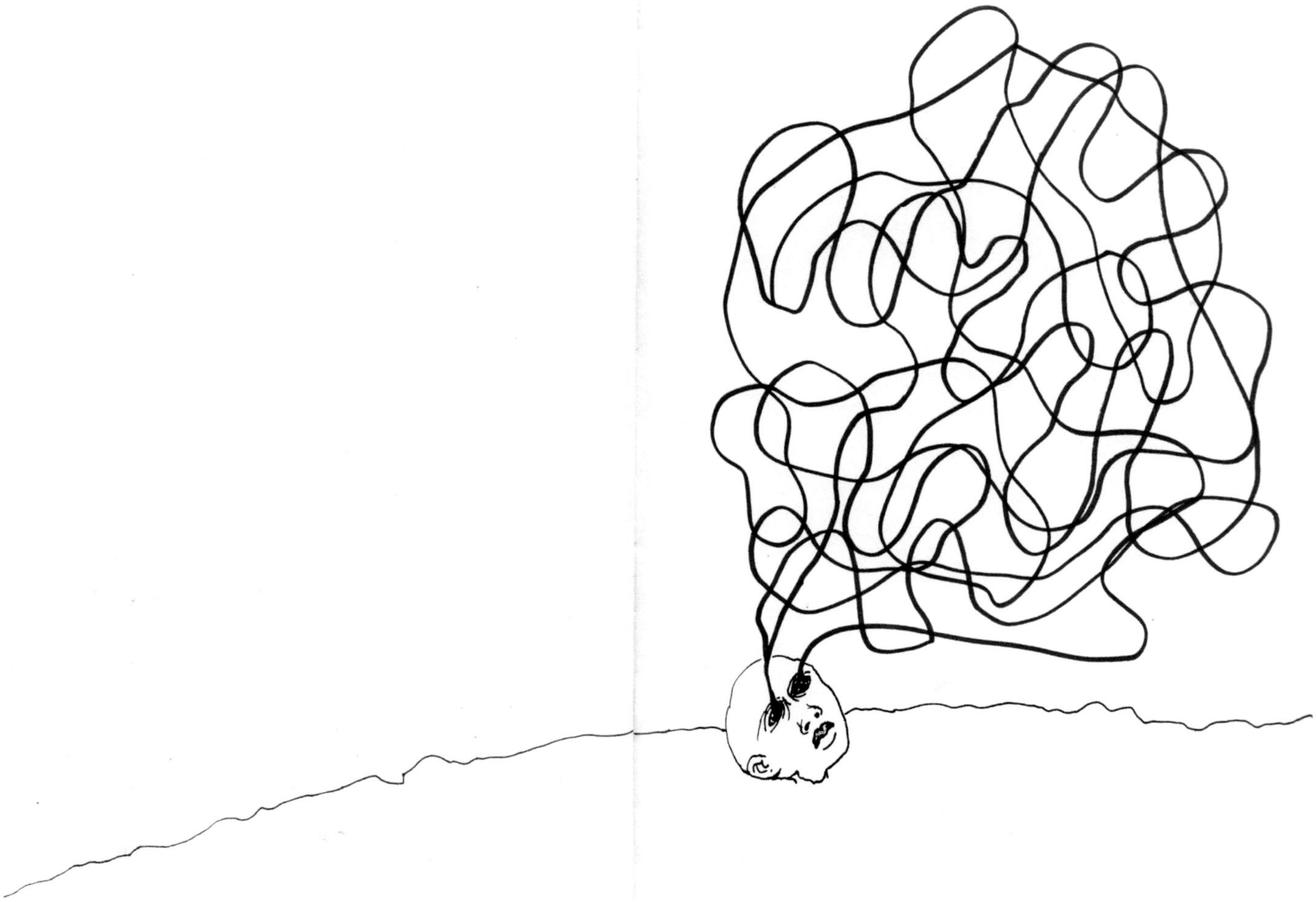

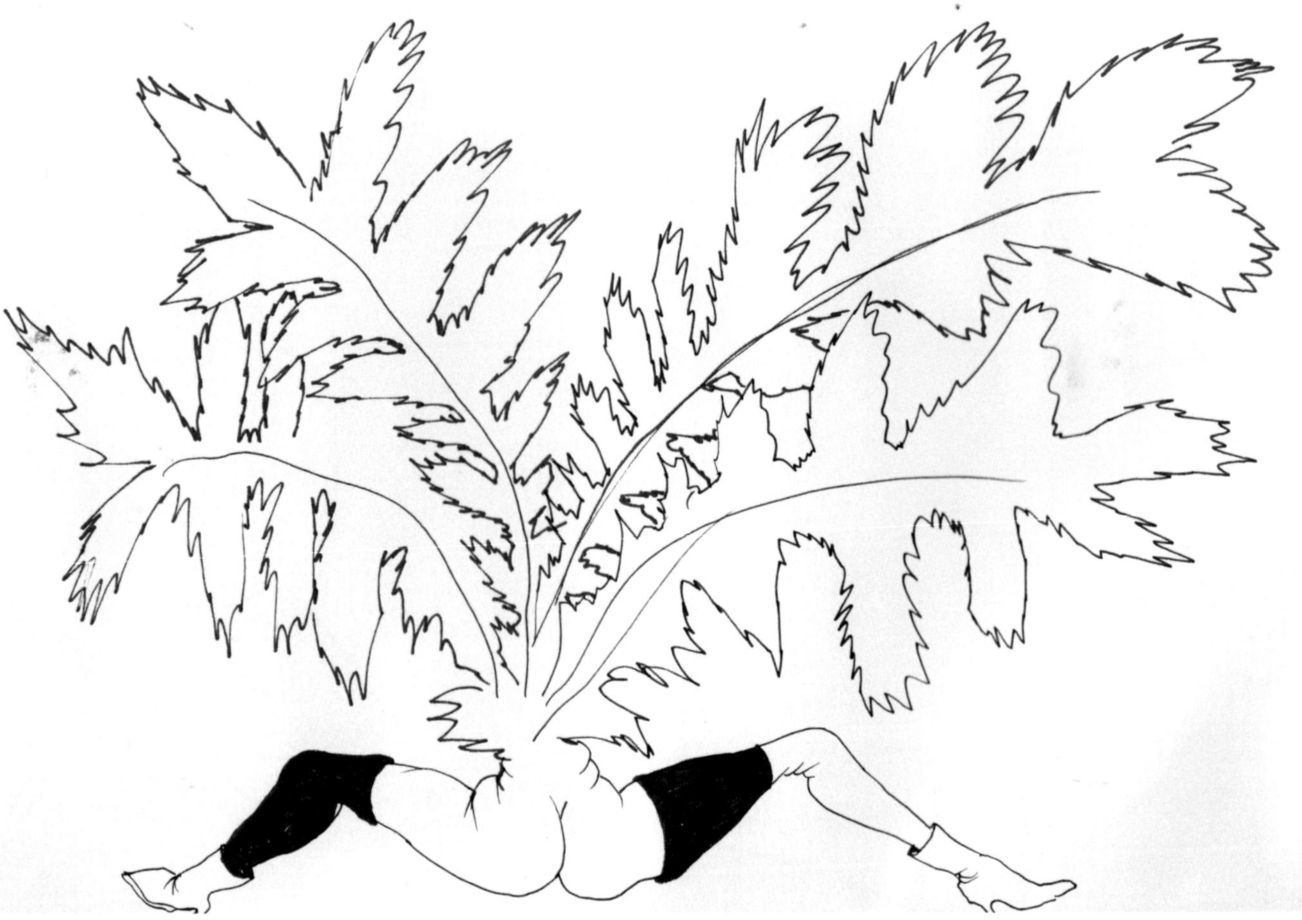

opposite,
SKETCHBOOK DRAWINGS
2011–12

SKETCHBOOK DRAWINGS
2009–10

Cooper was different, yes. The school was very loud about its political underpinnings as a type of platform for dialogues around change and democracy and representing the oppressed. There were many reverberations of the Marxist, socialist, non-consumer, non-capitalist fundaments that Peter Cooper espoused. But there were, ironically, a lot of very privileged, white, upper-middle-class kids who came from schools with good art programmes and art teachers; a lot of students who loved to only make abstract beautiful things that weren't particularly conceptual or soulful, and nor did they challenge or ask questions like 'Why make art in the first place?'. The Black and Latino kids painted more than anyone else. I remember my friends there all painted, a lot of them in a street-art, irreverent and anti-establishment fashion. (Whatever anti-establishment means when it comes to painting.) Let's say, very Basquiat-like. There was a ton of that kind of street calligraphy, urban grime marks, together with street signage. It was that moment, left over from the 1980s and the East Village location and the persistent city problems. When you think about New York in the early 1980s and 1990s, Basquiat is such a powerful icon for the struggling young Black man and the artist as a metaphor for cracking the code and beating the system. He's the messiah figure who completely invents his own language, in spite of the aggressive terrain he was living in. He then catapults to the top and then dies from the intensity.

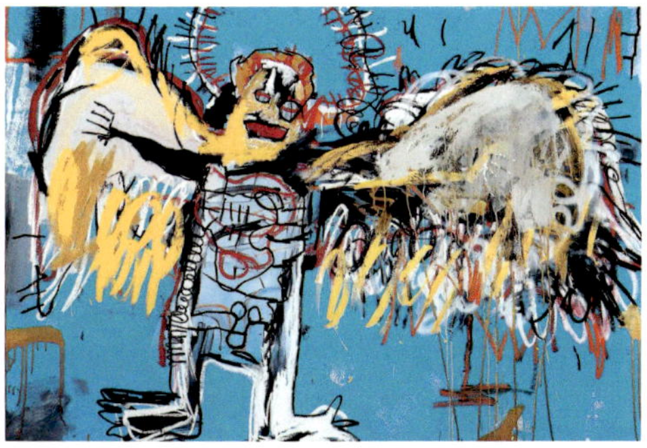

JEAN-MICHEL BASQUIAT
UNTITLED (FALLEN ANGEL), 1981
ACRYLIC AND OILSTICK ON CANVAS
168 X 198 CM

MARTIN: *In the 1990s, nobody else was as close to our age and close to the experience as Basquiat was at that moment. If you moved to New York in the early 1990s, you're there: the same club scene that he was a part of was still very much alive. The skaters and graffiti artists that he knew were still very active on the lower east side.*

MUTU: Absolutely, exactly.

MARTIN: *He's emblematic of that moment. It felt as if he'd just left the room.*

MUTU: He had, he literally had, and you felt it. You felt that breaking all the rules of classical painting in a street, nerdy way could actually create a formula for something really powerful and radical and redemptive. So we all looked at him a lot. We talked about him a lot.

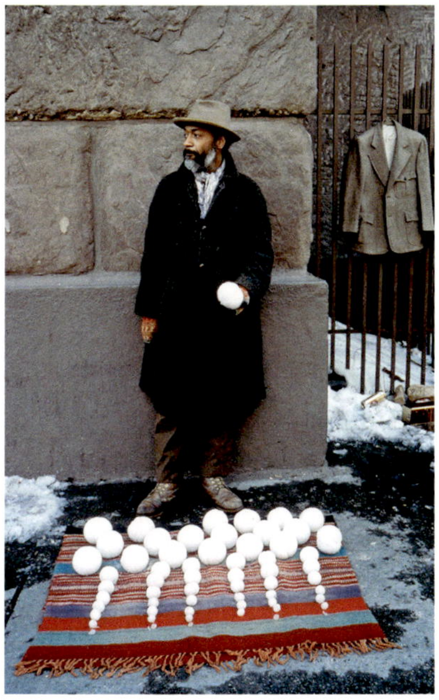

DAVID HAMMONS
BLIZ-AARD BALL SALE, 1983
PERFORMANCE
COOPER SQUARE, NEW YORK

David Hammons was also very influential, because he sold his blizzard snowballs in front of Cooper, but also produced these powerful street pieces and left spells on the corners of streets. A lot of kids were using detritus because they emulated him. I was definitely into using detritus and junk for my sculpture, which I kind of still am, except now I have soil and branches and sticks and stones and butterfly wings amongst the man-made things.

MARTIN: *If you were to make a list of the things that you took away from Cooper, what would they be?*

MUTU: Cooper gave me so much. I honestly feel, from an education and from a critical thinking perspective, that it was way more than graduate school. I felt, at Cooper, this enormous confidence that was given to us through the kinds of discussions we had about art. We talked about art to talk about everything.

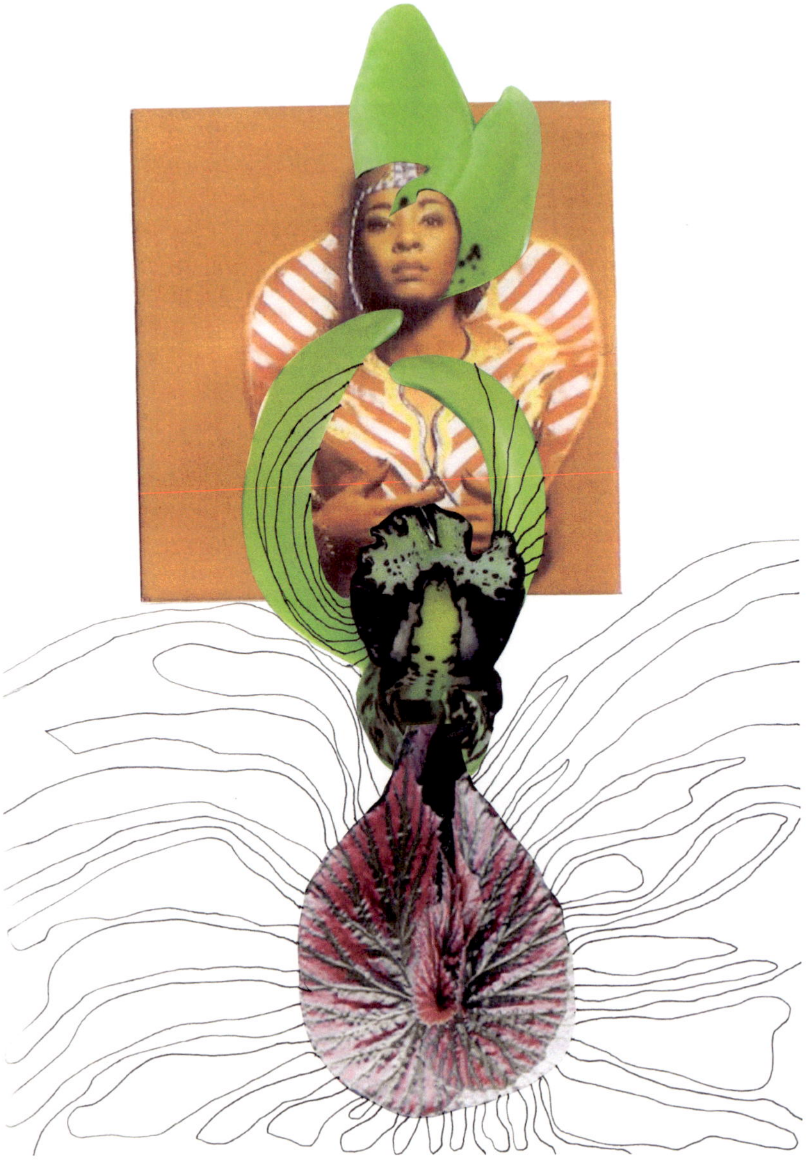

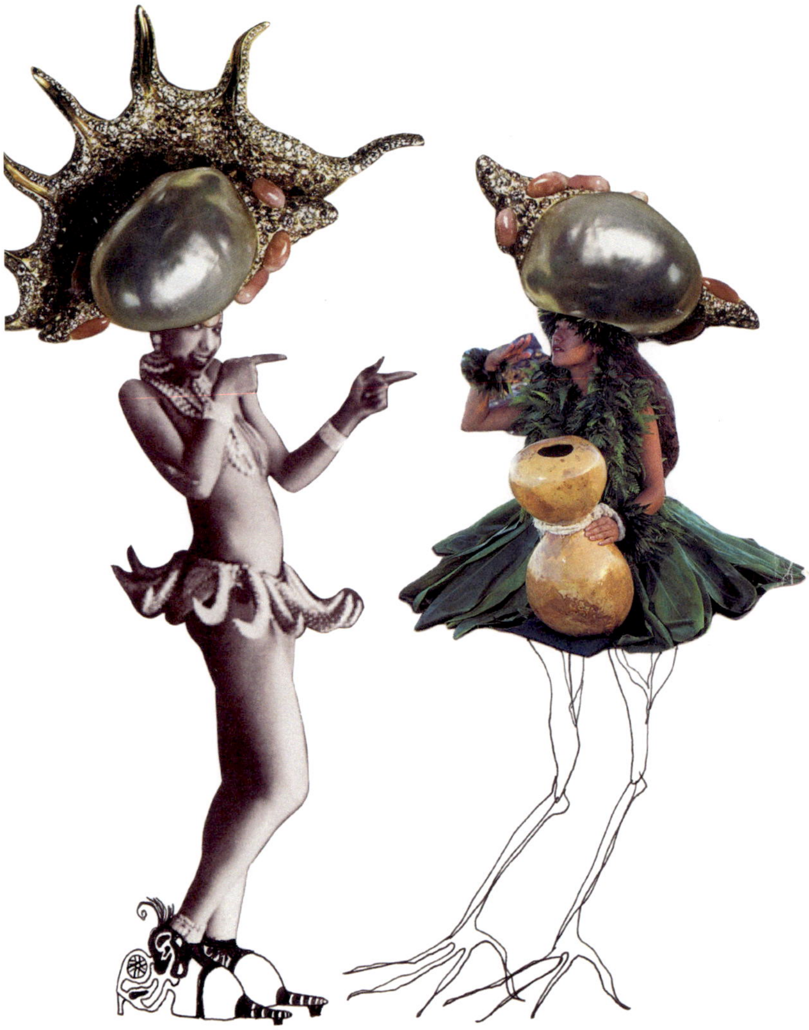

next pages,
FLORAL INSIDEOUT VII & VIII,
2018
WATERCOLOUR AND COLLAGE
ON PAPER
EACH 41 X 31 CM

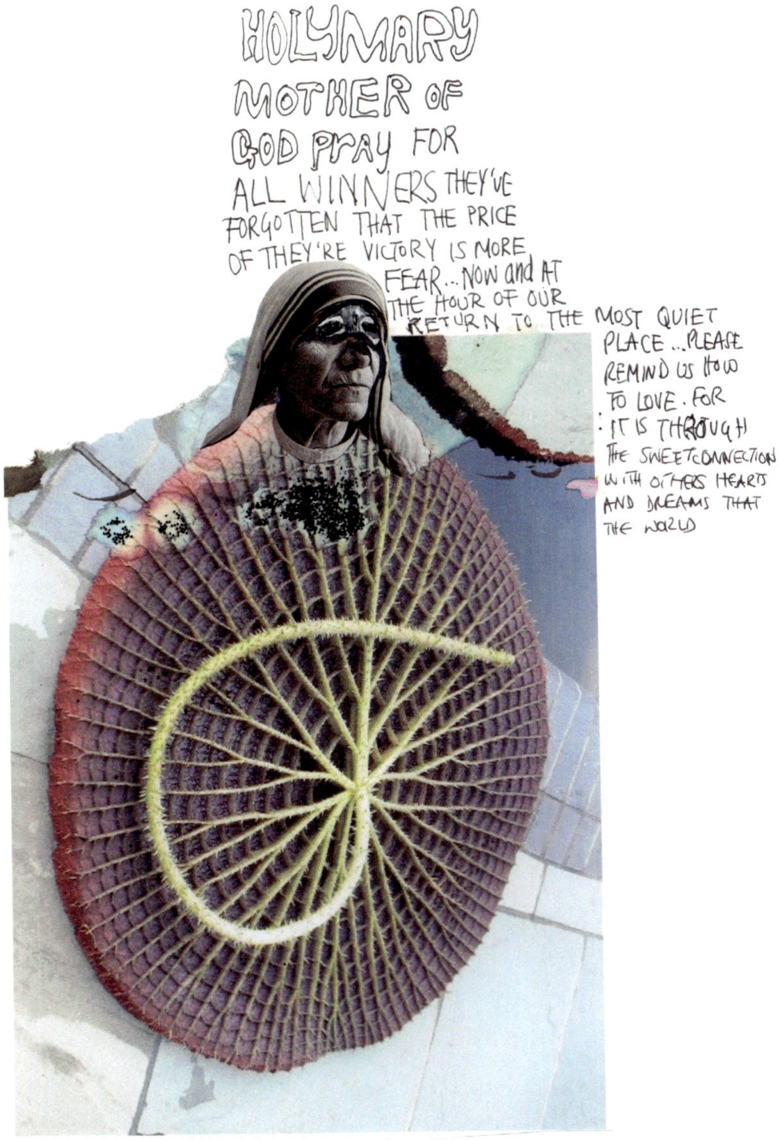

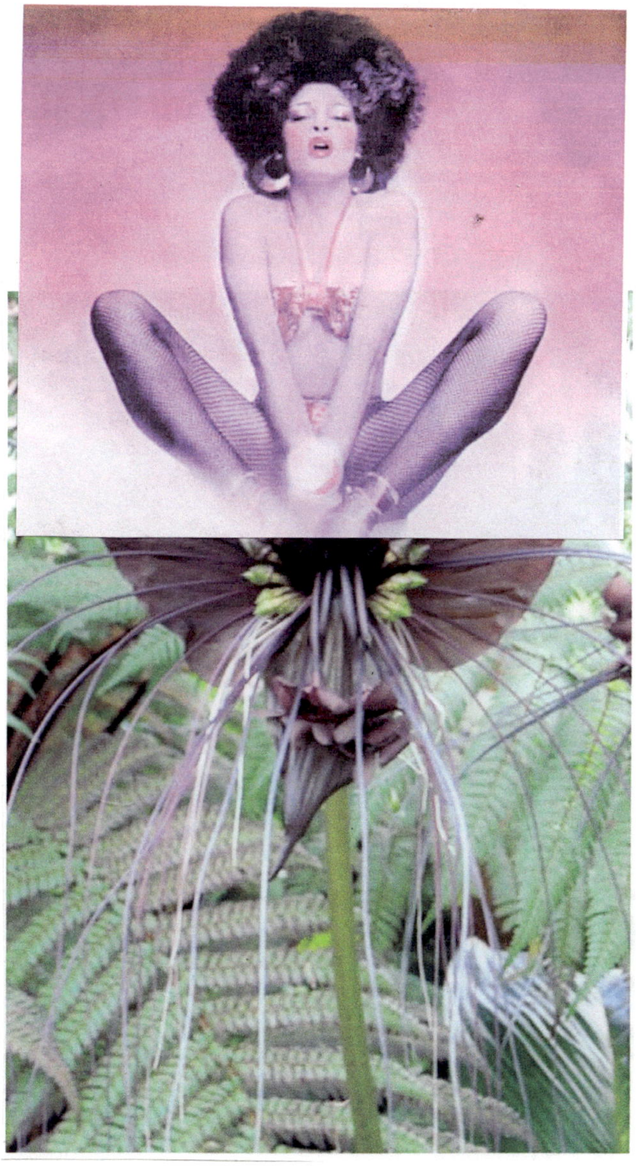

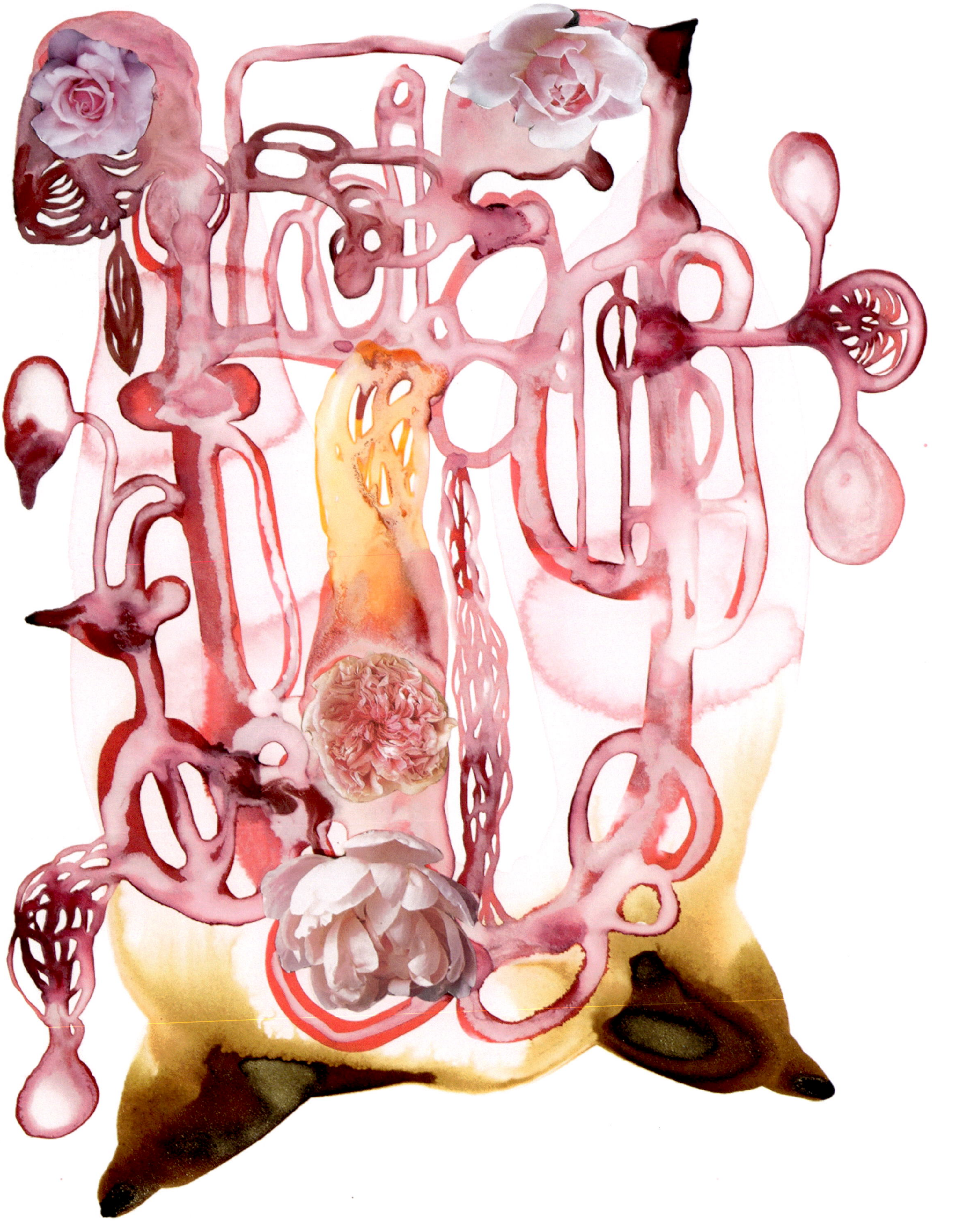

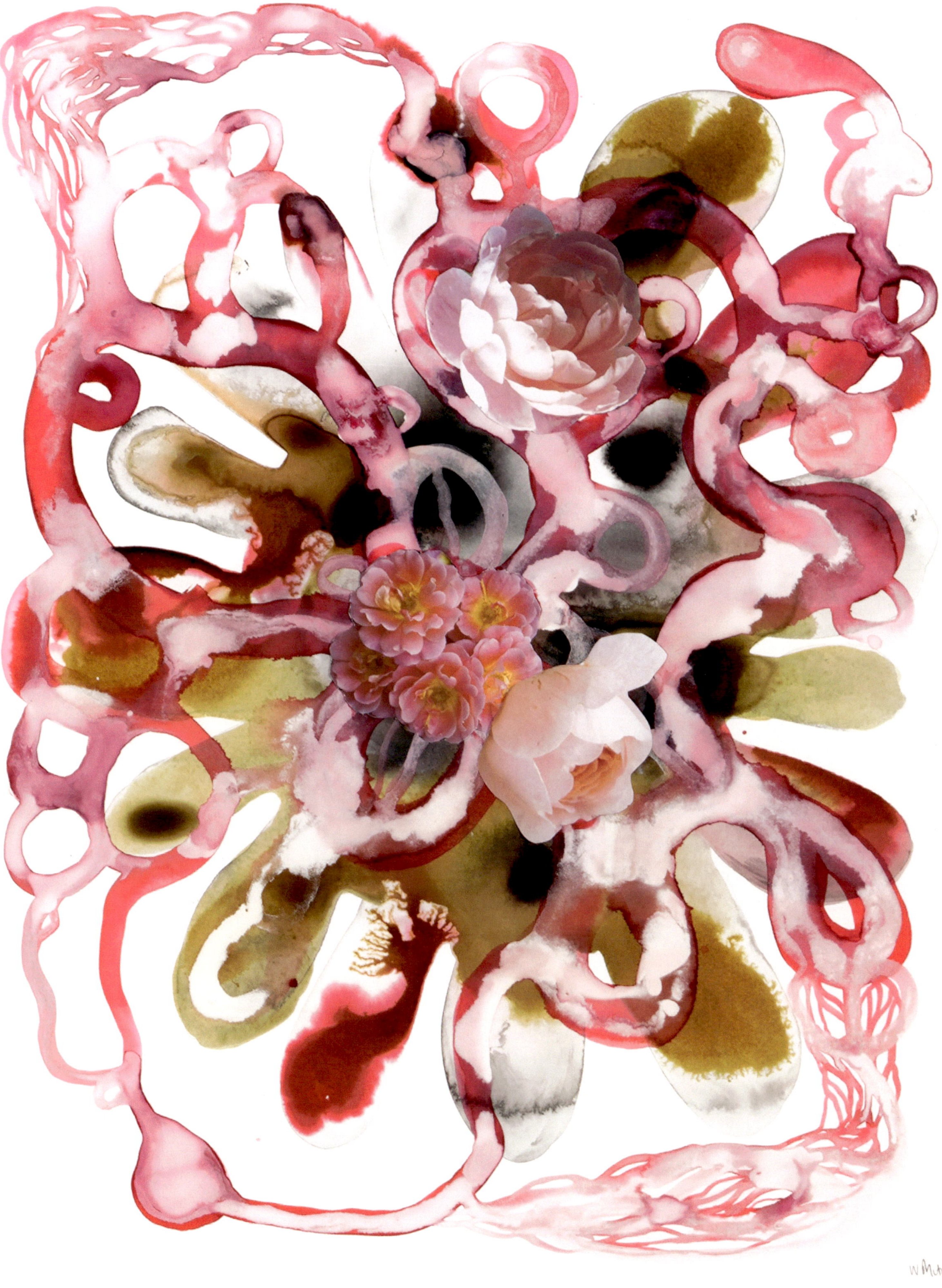

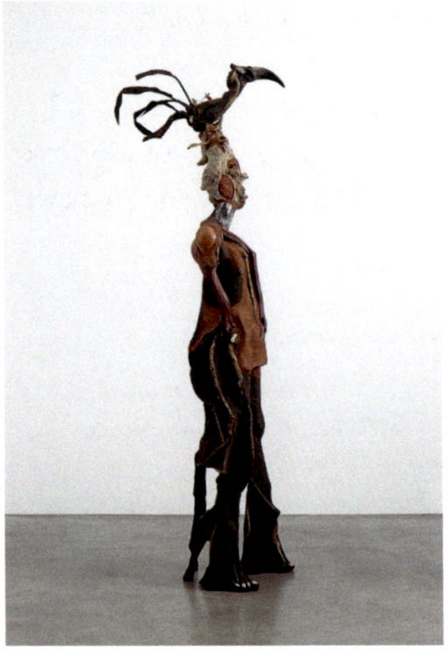

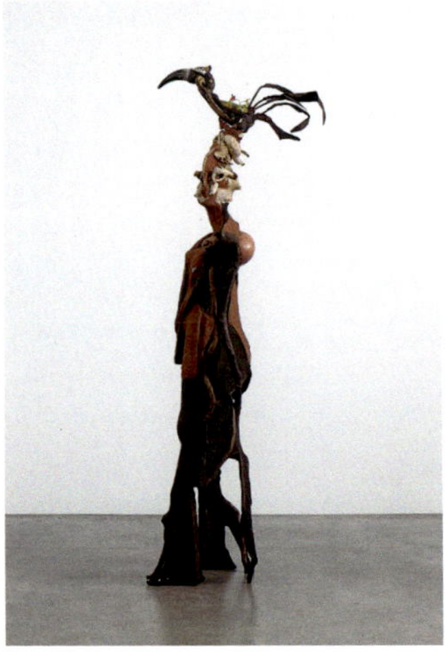

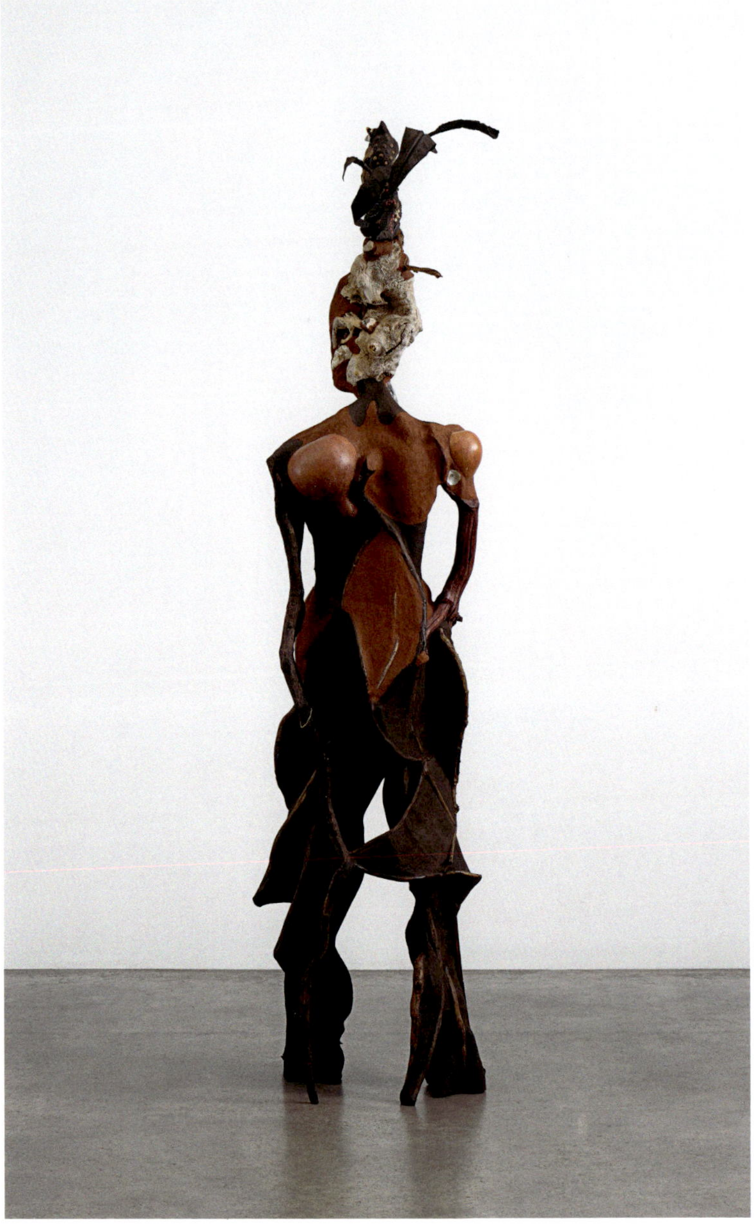

A lot of schools are defined by the teachers who are most dominant. We had people like Laura Cottingham. She had a reputation for making boys cry, because she was such a strict and sharp-tongued feminist. Even though she's kind of small, she was relentless and pushed us. She refused our arguments until we were kind of sweating blood and crying and then she'd say, 'That makes sense, I can see how it's a good point.' Then there were people like Hans Haacke, a gentler but very firm type of teacher, very disciplined and didactic in his work. A lot of what he did was visible in real-time: the stuff that was going on in New York at the time; the way the mayor was dealing with arrests of Black men, and the 'clean up' of the city, the way public transportation and real estate was divvied and gentrified. All that stuff was in his work. We saw it and we felt it and we understood it. We saw how it affected our lives and we also saw how, in his work, it was art. Then Fred Wilson was extremely influential in how we discussed and thought about museums. Here we are, a museum-heavy city with not nearly enough Black artists and not enough recognition of the things that they were saying. A lot of the stuff that Fred Wilson was critiquing is only just being addressed within institutions. Museums and schools are still so big and slow. We had people like Dennis Adams, Julie Ault, Doug Ashford … I didn't take Lorna Simpson's class, but she was there too. Alfredo Jaar, Coco Fusco and Andres Serrano came to speak. Jimmie Durham was in New York and came to do a visiting artist talk. So, you know, really important, interesting people.

MARTIN: *Every single person that you've named has, at some point, been identified as a conceptual artist.*

MUTU: That was Cooper. Cooper is a conceptual school. Cooper wasn't saying it was a conceptual school, but it was. Even aesthetics weren't necessarily applauded in that way. 'Beauty' was a big problem word, which I thought was fascinating. I thought, 'That's powerful, to say that you don't want to use that word. The status quo is in charge of what counts as beautiful.' Anyway, it was very different from Yale in that way. Yale painters applaud the canon of Western art through their paintings.

opposite,
SENTINEL V, 2021
RED SOIL, PAPER PULP, WOOD GLUE, EMULSION PAINT, CHARCOAL, INK, GOURD, WOOD, HORN, PUMICE STONE
208 X 61 X 56 CM

below,
SENTINEL IV, 2020
RED SOIL, PAPER PULP, WOOD GLUE, EMULSION PAINT, CHARCOAL, INK, COCONUT, SYNTHETIC HAIR, WOOD
216 X 85 X 59 CM

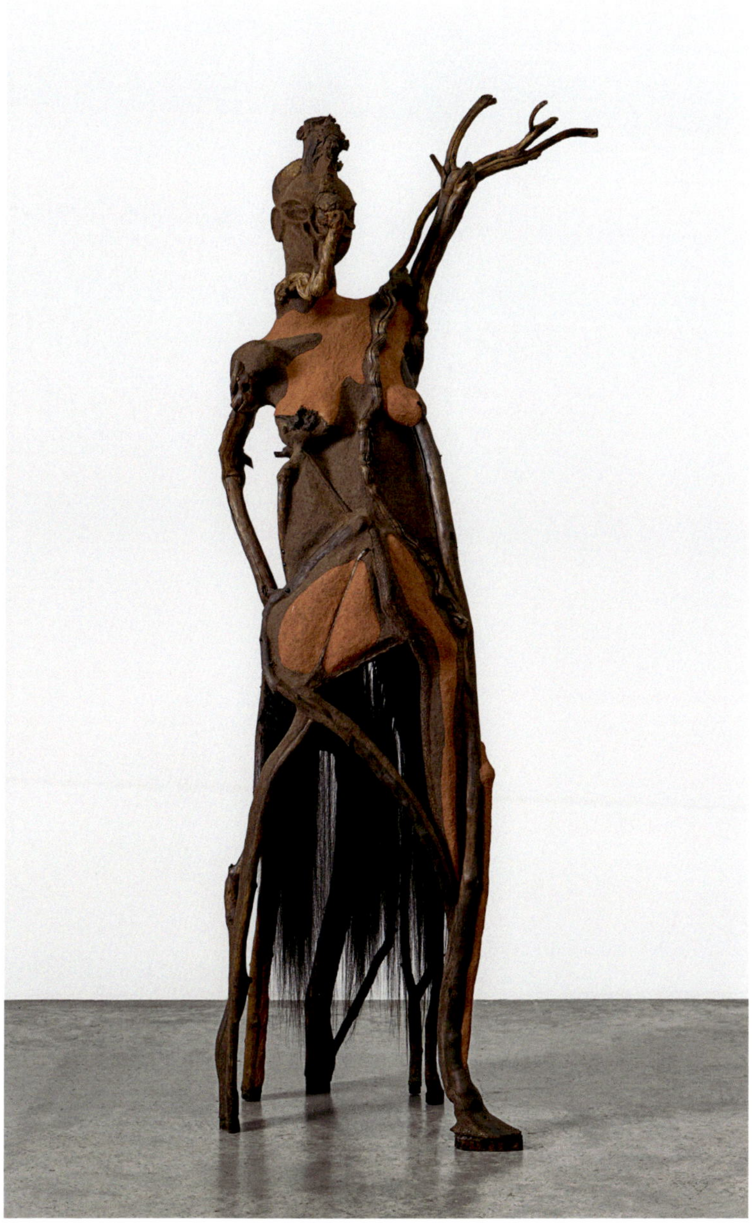

MARTIN: *Did you think of yourself as a conceptual artist when you left Cooper?*

MUTU: I did, but I didn't want that label per se. I didn't want any label. I knew that I didn't want to limit myself to one specific way of working. I'm not a conceptualist or a sculptress, sculptor, paintress. No, I didn't want any of that. I knew I was going to have to figure out my own path and direction.

MARTIN: *Did you believe in the collective thinking that came out of Cooper?*

MUTU: I did, and I do. I'm from many generations of farmer people, agrarians who till the earth, raise animals and work until food is plentiful. So the idea that you can make anything happen on your own isn't how I was raised, or believable for me. But to be perfectly honest, I was so poor when I first lived in the city of New York. I was always on the edge, not sure how I'd be able to make it, constantly running from one part-time job to another. The idea that any collective could have alleviated my very particular immigrant art-student hardship and stress and protect me seemed unthinkable, because I really didn't have the time to check who was looking out for me. I didn't fully buy into our school's collective thinking because of the reality of my life then. I found being poor in America particularly difficult because I come from a middle-class background in Nairobi. I was in the city trying (mostly failing) to pay basic rent and bills. I said 'No, I need to make some money. I can't be twenty-four, leaving university and still be calling on my parents to help me get a room in an apartment or buy a set of books. I have to try to make a living.'

There were certain types of discussions in art school amongst students from very privileged positions. I thought to myself, 'You know, what we're discussing right now has nothing to do with real life struggles, right? It has to do with art struggles, intellectual and conceptual struggles, which are important but…' That always brought it back home for me, because I said, 'Well, I must figure this impoverished-art-school-life thing out. Many of my fellow students are quite well-off, but this art-life I'm embarking on needs me to be strong enough to hold me, because because I'm living in harsh reality.' In the end I think we were rather courageous young people for taking on New York and for deciding to step into the arts.

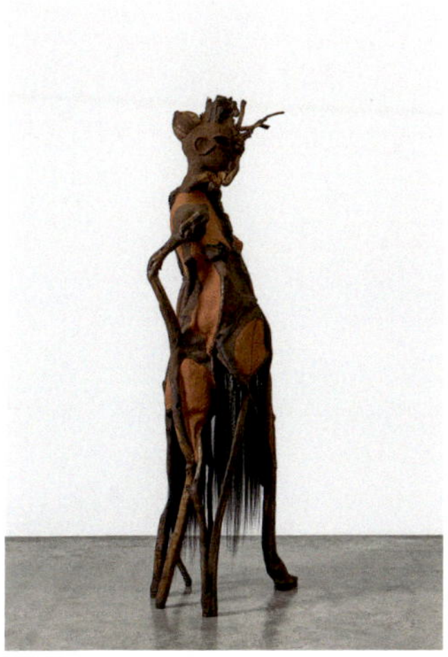

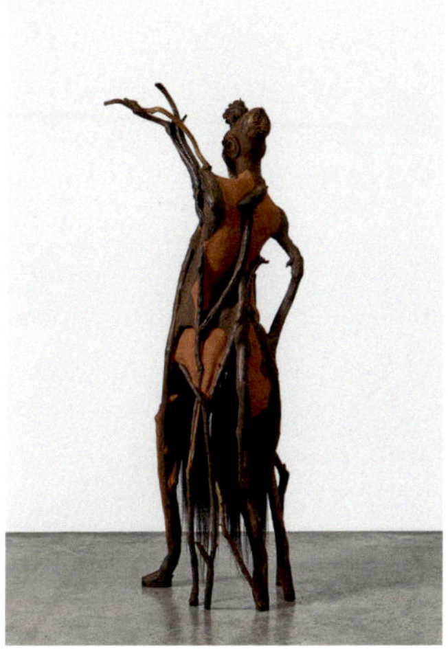

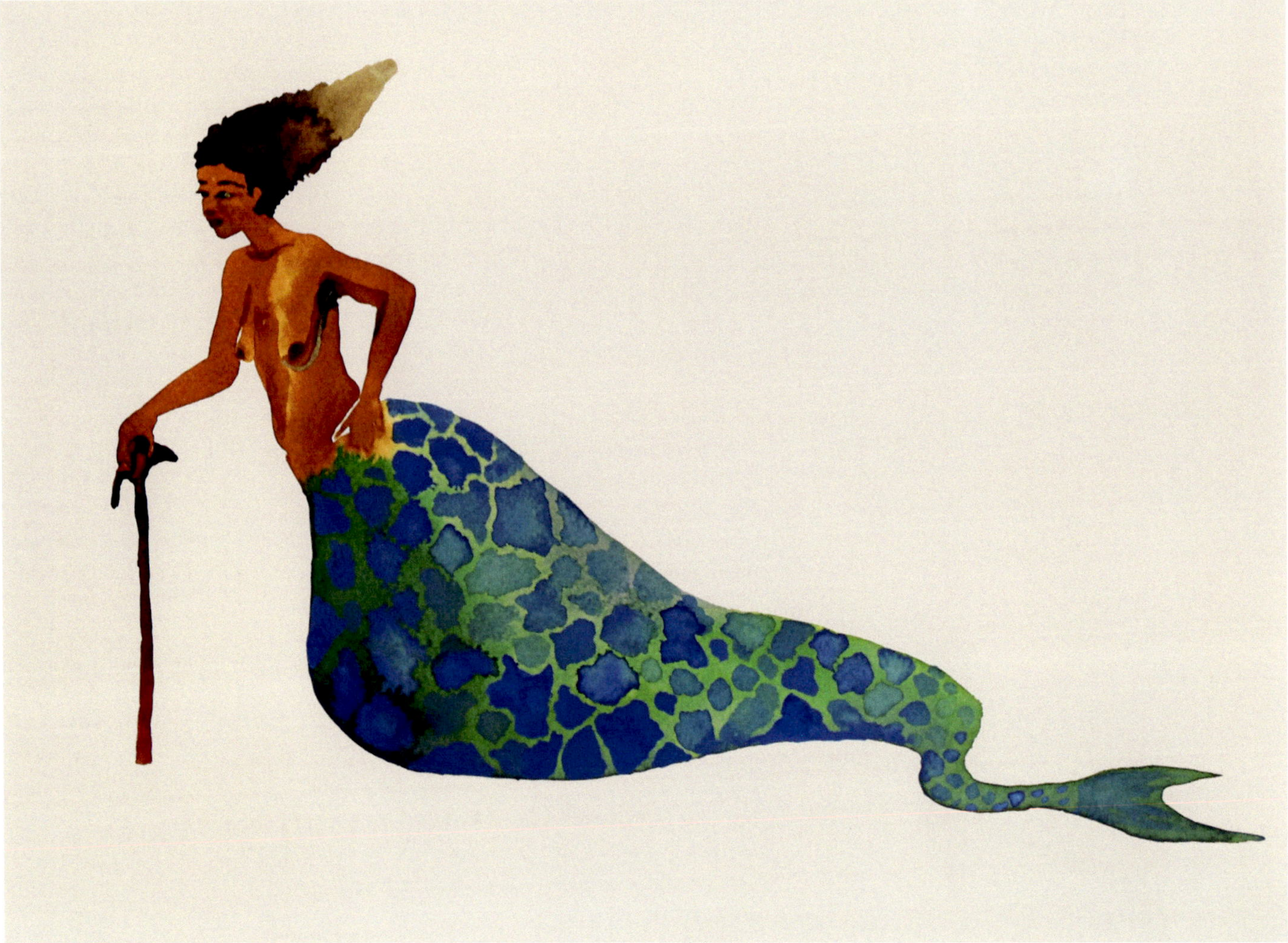

MARTIN: *Was the transition to Yale difficult?*

MUTU: I was there 1998 to 2000. I was interviewed for the sculpture course by John Newham and by Gary Simmons. There was no leadership/professor in charge when I got into the Sculpture department in 1998. They were putting out a call for the head of the department. Jessica Stockholder came in the second year. We're second years, she's brand new, which isn't the best combination, but she was one of the people who was in charge of our critiques.

MARTIN: *Did it feel disjointed?*

MUTU: Yes, that was the main issue for us: it felt like we'd inherited a broken department. There was so much that had happened three or four years before that, which had caused other people to leave the department. So they were still in upheaval about what this department ought to be and how to structure it.

You know, they have this amazing application process for tutors, where they apply and then come in and do the interview in front of a group of first-year students, who are potentially going to be their second years. The students in Sculpture actually play a huge role as first years in picking the people who they want to learn with. But we were sort of outweighed by professors we weren't familiar with. If we had professors who we didn't like, we really had to work hard to convince them. It's a strange kind of fraternity, performance artwork, or something. It's like people are sort of hazing each other in these really undetectable ways that I think racist white-America tends to do. You could cut the tension and the resentment with a knife. But we survived it. I survived it.

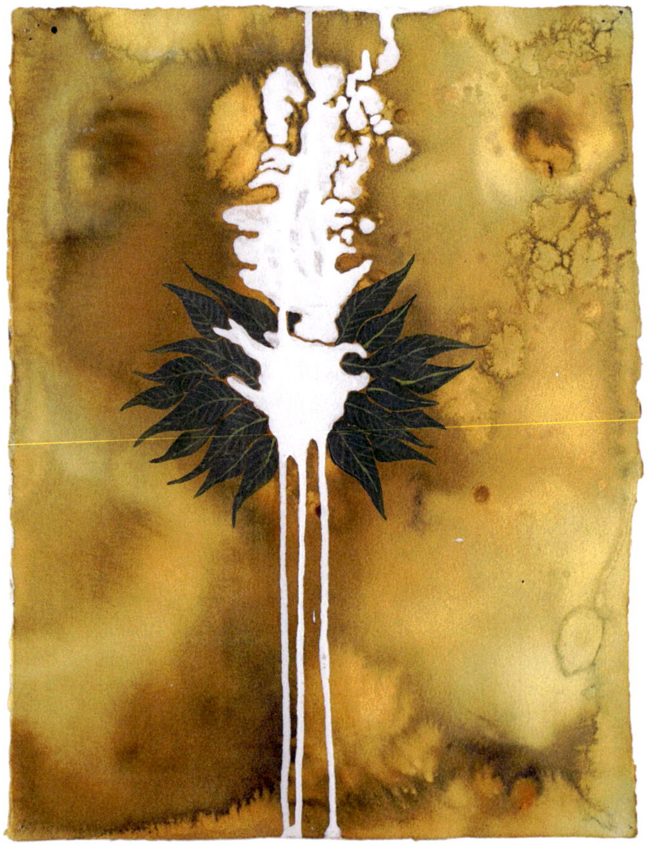

opposite, from top,
SKETCH, 2000

SKETCH, 2000

MARTIN: *Did you survive it because you came from a place like Cooper?*

MUTU: I survived it because I came from Cooper, as well as from Nairobi, and because I was an African immigrant and a dreamer and an extremely stubborn young woman with a determination that was greater than my fears and obstacles. I was also very vocal, because I'd learnt that as the first tool to express my opinion. I was very critical and questioned everything. I was probably also very argumentative. I was able to navigate these aggressive terrains with my bark before I even knew how to bite. Essentially, we're talking about ideas and art as it was being made in our little studios by ourselves and our peers. All these dynamics in the heart of downtown Manhattan were unfolding in front of our eyes. David Hammons was making his wizardly street art, Greg Tate sat in front of Barnes and Noble holding court like the village griot. There were books sold on the street everywhere, graffiti, Curtis the street sculptor made art in front of Cooper Union. We had to make sense of all these things in real time. And that's not always easy and it's not always something that you get trained to do in an institution. But Cooper made sense of these living-ideas and gave me a socio-politically, Marxist, anti-consumerist understanding that helped me with the language of art-seeing. So I felt I could always critique what I saw, not just in a western art-historical fashion, but based on ethical motivations and considering human rights, and women's rights and all these kinds of things that are important for my practice and my art-making.

I didn't notice it initially, but at some point I realised I was the only one talking about the global south and about non-western histories. 'There are other women here who could say something, there are other people of colour here', I kept thinking. But I told myself, 'No, you have a certain kind of confidence, you speak up, you say what you're going to say', but at some point, I realized that it was exhausting to be so responsible for everyone else and for so many perspectives. I realized I was operating from insecurity and overcompensation, not trust and self-confidence. I wasn't educating anyone. In many racing competitions, there's that horse that's placed there to run next to the actual racing horses, to make them faster. I thought, 'I'm not that horse. [Laughter] I'm in the race to be part of it. I'm not the horse that makes you run faster.'

MARTIN: *You were the pacesetter. This is such a fascinating trajectory. You started at Parsons, which brought you to the New School, then you moved to Cooper, which is much more aligned with the populist ethos and social critique.*

MUTU: Yes.

MARTIN: *That totally makes sense, but then you go to Yale?*

MUTU: [Laughter] Because I'm an African student [Laughter]

MARTIN: *What does that mean? As a Black American, what does that mean, Wangechi, that you're an African?*

MUTU: You want me to spell it out?

MARTIN: *I want you to 'unpack it', as Okwui Enwezor would instruct us to do.*

MUTU: What it means is that I was coming from a family and a background and a country and a time when pursuing art – going to America to study art – was already ridiculous and not seen as a path towards success: 'You're going to spend all this money to go abroad to do, essentially, what's going to put you in a position where you're going to be broke, or unemployed.' I chose Yale because I felt it was a school where art was just one of many different fields of knowledge, and where pedagogy was respected. Well, so I thought. So, I have to say, I was in it to practice and learn at the most prestigious place. I didn't want to go halfway or back off. There was no, 'Oh, let me see what happens, let me feel this out.' Every obstacle I ran into had to be overcome because, to come back with my tail between my legs would've been, number one, exactly what I was expected to do. Number two, I would've had absolutely no ability to argue for myself, no power, no voice. But my one problem was that this was never an obstacle race, and it took me a while to understand that.

MARTIN: *Did it work?*

MUTU: You know what's interesting? I thought of Yale recently and one of the times I went back there to visit after Robert Storr had been appointed. I went back there because I'd been invited to speak about having been a Yale art student and about my trials and tribulations. It gave me an opportunity to check it out, and I was stunned. I thought, 'This is amazing, there are plenty of Black students up here. They're having a challenging time, but they're surviving.' They were all doing rigorous work. All of them were operating with all engines blasting. There was no one who was doing anything simple or monosyllabic. They were all massively thoughtful.

So my answer is yes, of course it worked, even though that wasn't why I should have applied, it was part of the workingness of it. It's a lesson I learnt to understand, by applying, by enduring, by fighting and by getting out of the boxing ring. I think it took being a Yale art student to realize how inconsequential and yet how important Yale is/was simultaneously for my development.

MARTIN: *What did you do after you left Yale?*

MUTU: I started teaching at public school art programmes in New York. I taught at Studio in a School, Agnes Gund's organisation. I worked at the Children's Art Carnival, in Harlem. And then I started getting into shows. I did a show called 'The Magic City', at Sikkema Jenkins. I did a solo show at the Jamaica Centre for Arts and Learning. That helped to solidify and crystalize my ideas of hybrid, fantastical people and creatures and portraiture in the form of questions about, what is a face? What is a person's identity? Why do we decide that someone who doesn't look like us is unrecognizable or is unfavourable?

I then applied to the Artists-in-Residence programme at the Studio Museum in Harlem. It was a huge opportunity. I needed to be in a clean, beautiful studio. I also got into Artpace in San Antonio during my Studio Museum residency.

In between Studio Museum and Artpace, I moved to a bigger loft space, where I had a lot more room and I got a separate studio from that, because Taaffe Place in Brooklyn had all these empty loft studios in the space. Things picked up with regards to critical and public recognition of my work. There was an acknowledgement and discussion that was going on, especially post-September 11. New York, which was really heartbroken after September 11, understood that immigrant voices had wisdom and insight about the American condition. It was also a traumatized city, embracing the people who made it distinct.

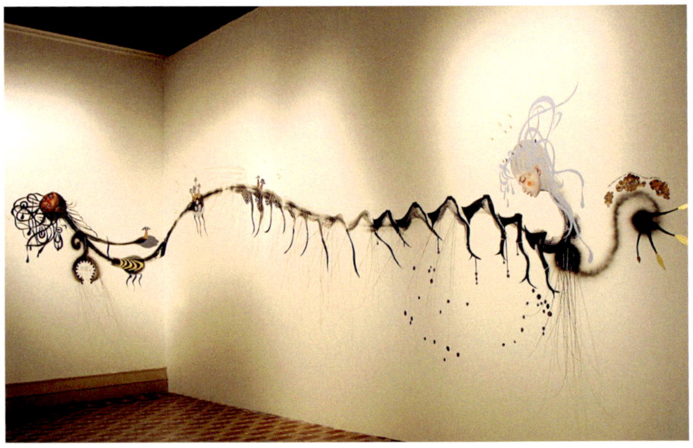

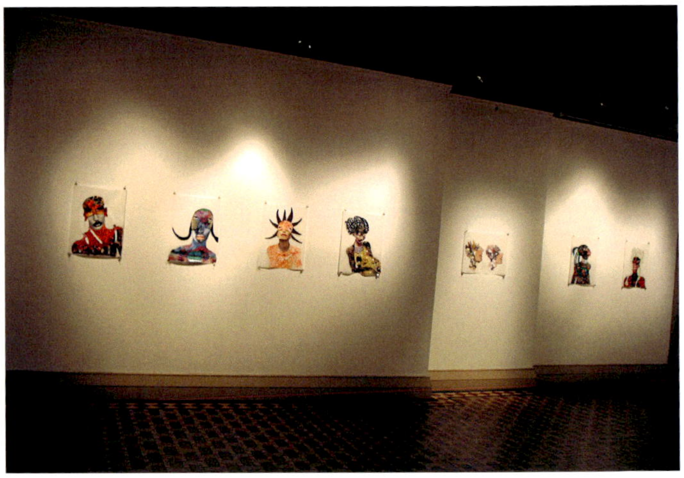

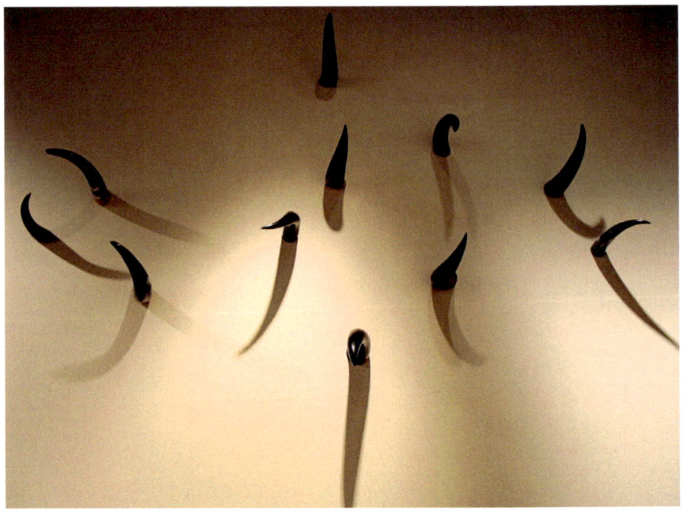

opposite,
EXHIBITION VIEWS OF
CREATURAS AT JAMAICA
CENTER FOR ART AND
LEARNING, NEW YORK, 2003

EXHUMING GLUTTONY
(ANOTHER REQUIEM), 2006–11
MIXED MEDIA INSTALLATION,
ANIMAL PELTS, WOOD,
BOTTLES, WINE, PACKING TAPE,
AND BLANKETS
983 X 465 CM

MARTIN: *Was there ever a moment when you felt trapped in New York?*

MUTU: Oh, yes. At some point, I thought about moving to New Orleans.

MARTIN: *Was that post-Katrina?*

MUTU: Yes, after Katrina, after Prospect I. Artists had an incredible time creating for a city that was begging to be heard and healed. I felt that New Orleans was culturally vibrant enough that I'd have fun there and, at the same time, was affordable and, at the same time, I could make my art.

MARTIN: *The first time that we officially worked together was on the installation,* Exhuming Gluttony: A Lover's Requiem in 2006.

MUTU: With the architect David Adjaye. It was a very dystopic kind of theatrical installation, something very different from what he does.

MARTIN: *Why had you chosen to work together?*

MUTU: I went to see him speak and it was one of the most impressive discussions I've ever heard. Two people discussing art, art history, architecture, blackness, and it was just astoundingly beautiful; it was a wonderful thing to witness. And he asked me, 'Would you like to collaborate?' And I said, 'Oh, how would that work?' He said, 'Well, you do whatever you want, and we could work together, and I could help you build it.' And I thought, 'Oh wow, that would be crazy and amazing and intense.' But I didn't really know much about what a collaboration would be like with an architect. Neither did I know what a collaboration would be like with somebody who has a very deep sense of what their work should look like and should feel like. I eventually agreed. We started

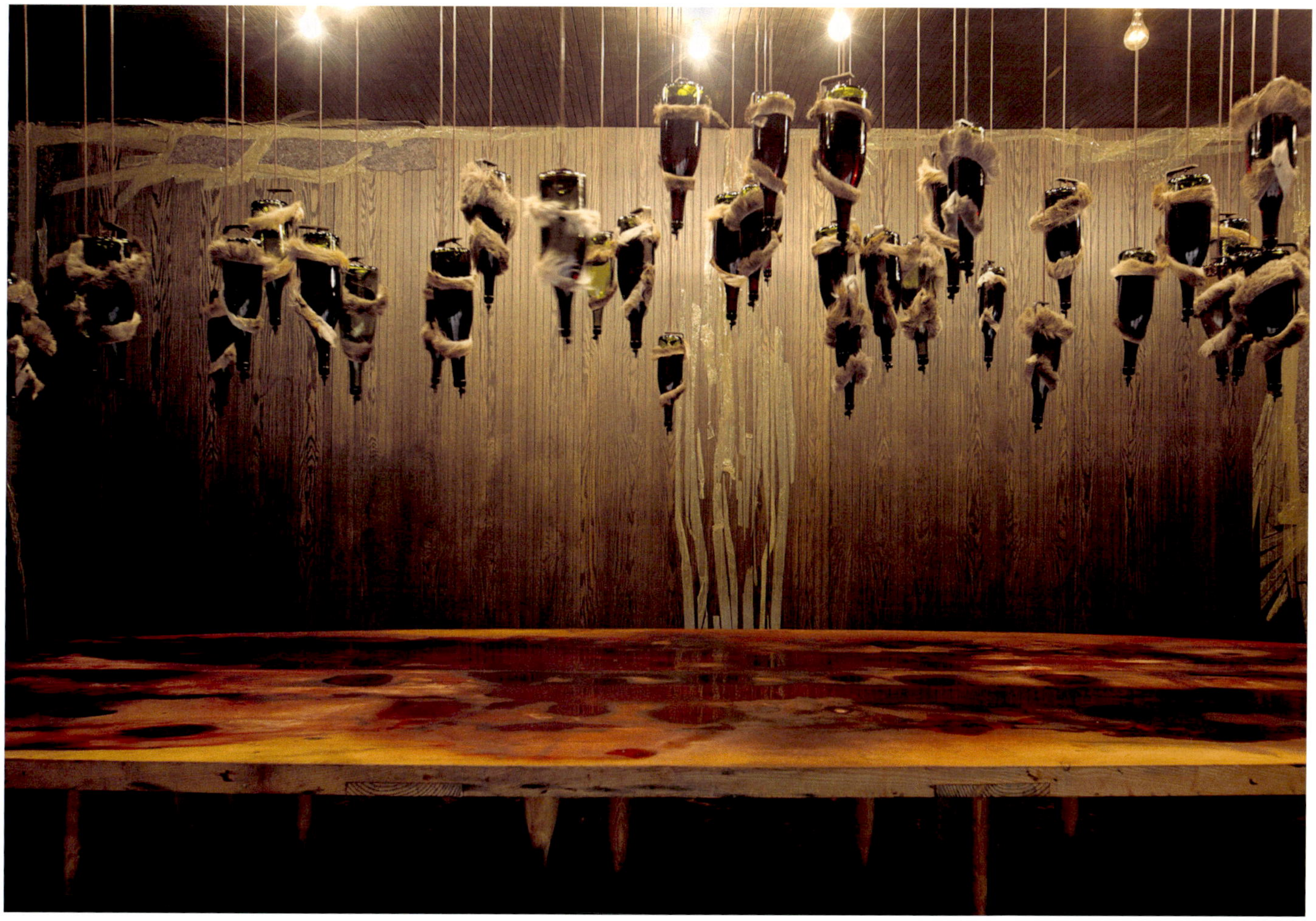

thinking about what that meant and what ideas I'd like to work out. I immediately had this idea of a communing of people, gathering around a table, in anticipation of a big meal, in anticipation of devouring and eating and consuming things together, but in a way that was very problematic and dark, and essentially led to destruction. I was very clear about that idea from the time I came up with it to the time we produced this piece. There was dripping wine and there was a gargantuan table that was this sort of butcher block. Very carnal. It was very fecund. There was hair on the ground and on the walls. There was also fur. There was a big altar, a kind of trophy piece made of these decadent furs. It was so opulent and sensual and disturbing and dark. It was so different from this very masculine, clean aesthetic that David is genius at.

MARTIN: *It's the first time that I experienced your 3D work. Up until that moment, I thought that you had been in sculpture at Yale because the sculptors at Yale could do everything, whereas the painters were only allowed to paint.*

MUTU: That's true, yes. I felt like painting restricted you to only painting and only learning about paint, whereas sculpture, for me, was learning about art. You could paint in sculpture if you could pull it off. At that point, you couldn't talk about installation in painting.

MARTIN: Exhuming Gluttony *was fully immersive, multi-layered, sensorial. As a visitor, I was overwhelmed by the experience because one risked interacting with some disturbing aspect of it, if you walked around that installation. Did you make sculpture because it allowed you the freedom to do everything and anything?*

MUTU: Yes, I did. I always loved making these environments, because it was a way of creating the artwork that said what I wanted to say, which I couldn't do in painting and I couldn't do in collage, I couldn't do in performance: to place the viewer in a position where they're the protagonists of this scenario, this vignette, this space. I hoped they'd react by sniffing and viewing and recoiling as they looked at the work, and this was part of the reason for doing this piece and what motivated me to make it so intensely interactive.

MARTIN: *How had your studio practice changed?*

MUTU: In 2006, I bought an old Brownstone in Brooklyn and there I painted many of my works that are considered seminal. By around 2010, I'd added a new space on Grand Street in the Clinton Hill area. I'm straddling the painting, collage work, as well as these new sculptural ideas that are coming out of *Exhuming Gluttony*. I'm still hanging up a lot of wine bottles – suspended bottles dripping like live fruit emitting their essence. These, together with multiple other elements, are crammed into these environments. The cacophony was representative of these galaxies or systems or organizations. I created installations with collections of objects like the 'Moth' works, the 'Moth Girls', the 'Sleeping Heads'. All of these were made around 2010 at Grand Street, when I was trying to redefine what an exhibit was. It was a precursor to some of the large works that I eventually did within the 'Nguva na Nyoka', the 'Water Woman' series, that eventually led me into the objects that I'm making now. There was a swelling or a cacophony of different kinds of materials, styles and ideas. It was an extremely fertile, rich moment in the studio, but it did prompt me to make certain decisions about how I wanted to work with 3D.

WATER WOMAN, 2017
BRONZE
91 X 165 X 178 CM

INSTALLATION VIEW AT
THE CONTEMPORARY AUSTIN
– LAGUNA GLORIA, 2017

MARTIN: *In what way?*

MUTU: I really wanted to make discrete objects, the way I was making paintings. I was definitely interested in installation, because of what I was able to do with it, but from a perspective of economizing my own energy intellectually – and even physically because I was now a mum. I wanted to make objects that I could focus on and think about step by step, one particular object at a time. I also wasn't sure I wanted to force them to exist in one theatre together. I wanted to be able to have them in a group show in discussion with other works by other thinkers. The 'Thrones' idea had been in my work since graduate school, but it was around this time that I truly individualized them into a unique series of 'Blackthrones'. That was a real attempt to grapple with this idea of individual objects, and what that means, and how they can exist and live in spaces and galleries, with other works and other discussion, with other works in discussion next to them.

I was also thinking about my palette. I was trying to pare down or simplify my palette. I was really obsessed with colour, but I think in sculpture I was trying to simplify the palette, to bring the idea forth without necessarily worrying about hue and tone. I was fighting with the reality of how much work I was making, or how much work I wanted to make while raising a little human.

MARTIN: *Does your sense of the figure change once you have a child?*

MUTU: Yes, absolutely. I think there's something about having babies that makes you feel quite heroic, and quite distended [Laughter], but another part of it makes you feel, unfortunately, somewhat repulsed by your body. There are just so many things that you're not in control of, that are not inherently your choice or your desire, or in your interest to have as part of your body. So there's a bit of a resentment towards the inevitable changes that come with the sacrifice of your time and your body in carrying a child. I think some of that unease comes through in the work, that ambivalence

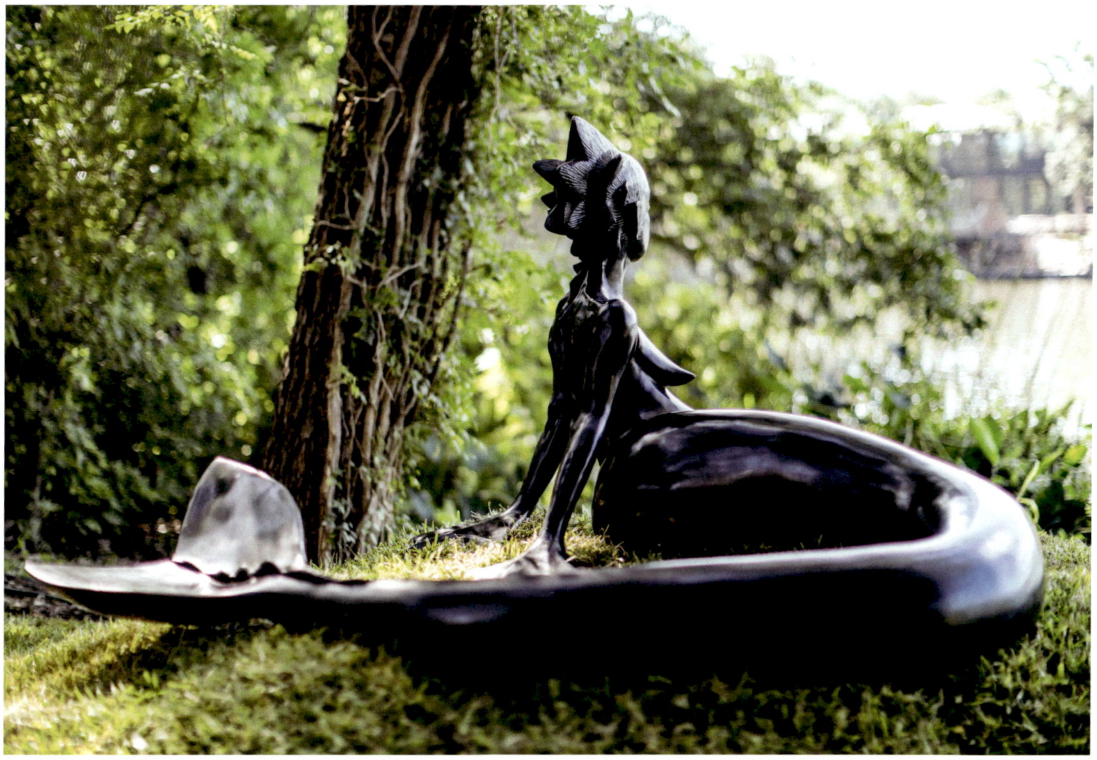

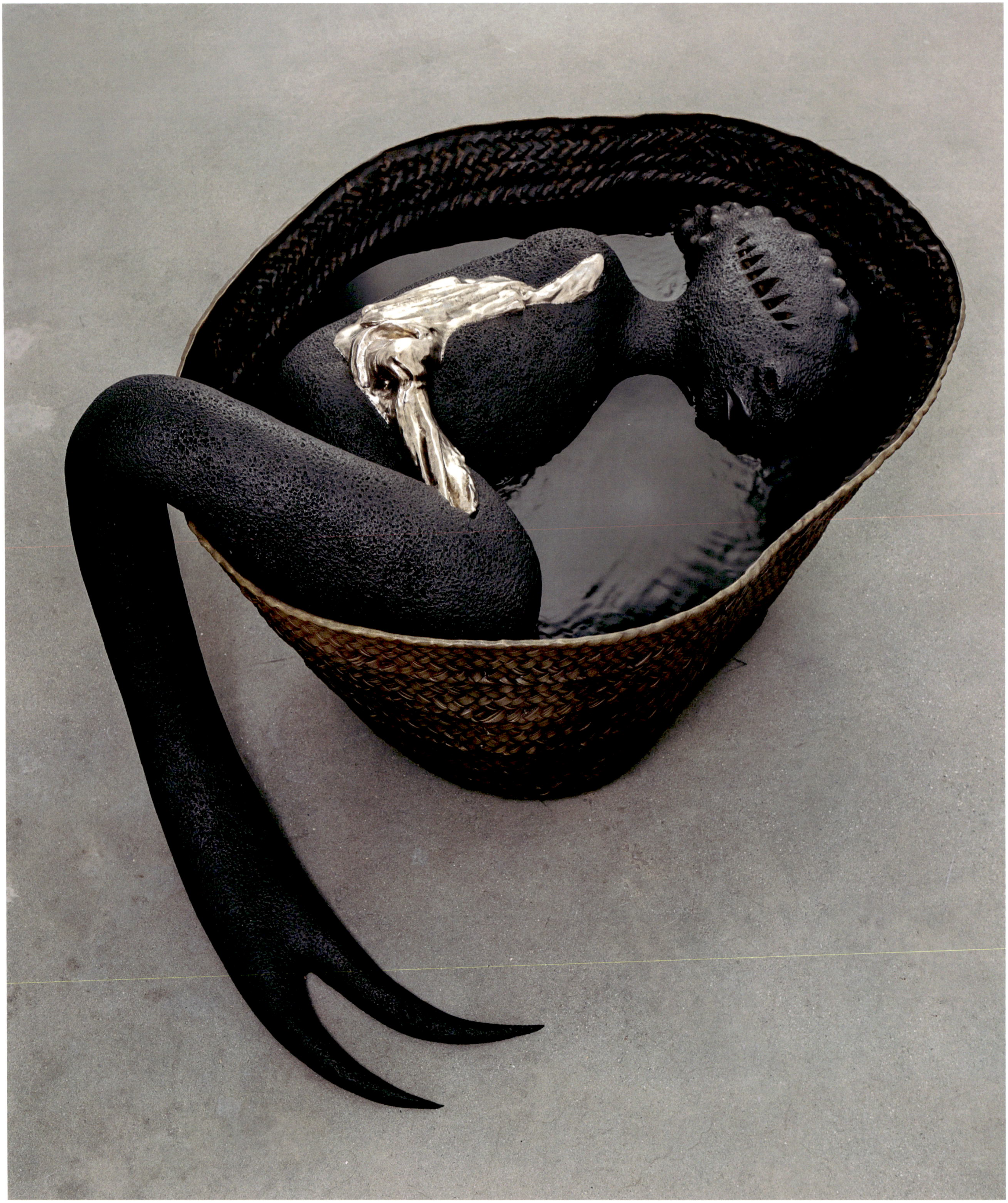

MUSA, 2021
BRONZE
138 X 98 X 73 CM

and the complicatedness. The feelings that I was harbouring at the time were, 'This is the best thing that could happen to me, but it's also unfortunate how much it takes me from my work, how different I look and how much of my mind is shaped by the enormity of the task.' Mothering a child was one of the rites of passage that I was so longing for, and which I still underestimated even when I was finally ready. I also felt quite restless. These places, these regions, these spaces, these cities that had the capacity to nurture an artist and a studio without such insurmountable hardship were in my thoughts a lot. I was yearning to get out of New York, but I didn't want to let go or lose what I'd built there: my friendships and my networks, my studio and my house. I wanted to figure out another site. That migratory restlessness, that feeling, I think, has a lot to do with how I came up with the 'Water Woman'. I feel it has a lot to do with the migration across the screen of *The End of carrying All.* There are certain things that I know I was trying to gather together and take somewhere new.

MARTIN: *At about the same time the moving blankets became a central element in your work.*

MUTU: The blankets were a strange kind of familiar comfort material that just happened to come to the studio as artwork packaging. I remember it struck a note in me because I was so aware of what these blankets meant in my memory. I was so clear that they were used in rural and village Kenyan life.

MARTIN: I *assume you mean that they came to you as utilitarian moving materials?*

MUTU: Exactly, totally utilitarian, almost industrial materials for wrapping objects – in my case artworks – for keeping the work from bumping against the surface of the box. I remembered from my childhood, from being raised in Kenya, in a developing nation, that these blankets were used by older village people: old, poor village or city people who, essentially, used them as shawls. You see them being used as shawls still in remote areas. As I said, there's a huge second-hand clothing industry. You still see them on little sculptures and tchotchkes that are emulating old people, old village people sitting on their little wooden stools, with a club in their hand. I guess I got a little sentimental and I got attached, and then the minute I got my hands on them, I loved the materiality and how sculptable they were. They're made of this repurposed fabric and plastic. It's felt. They were almost like an extremely layered collage, all of these fabrics, and materials, and textiles that had been ground together and reworked into one material, one colour. They look like they're one colour, but actually they're multi-coloured. The reason why they look grey is because all the colours are boiled or washed together and blend to become greyish. I love that idea of the aggregate nature of the man-made world. These blankets said all of those things for me that collage had been saying. I was able to shape them. I could rearrange and repurpose them, and in every given place I could reuse bits and pieces from the last installation. I like that ability to be resourceful with materials, and not just discard them or buy something brand new. So there was something about the blanket that also felt like it matched my sense of frugality and recycling, my repurposing obsession.

MARTIN: *That attraction to felt evokes the kind of modernism that Joseph Beuys signalled with his use of felt in installations and in static objects. It's the cloak for his modernity. In its base sense, which is what you're talking about, it is this aggregate material that provides warmth to the neediest. In its best and most refined sense, it is the thing that allows someone to have a fully impenetrable corporate suit. Either way, felt is a barrier.*

MUTU: That's right, yes. I'd seen Beuys' suits and felt sculptures and the photography of his performances, and these piles and columns of blankets that he folded and positioned in his installations. I'd seen these works physically and understood his material. There is something about Beuys's wizard-style, shamanistic performance that may have been imitating our long-gone elders, sitting on small stools, under big trees, with the protective hide around their shoulders, protecting them from a new time, protecting them from the weather, protecting them from the scrutiny of the Western eye, because now you should be clothed.

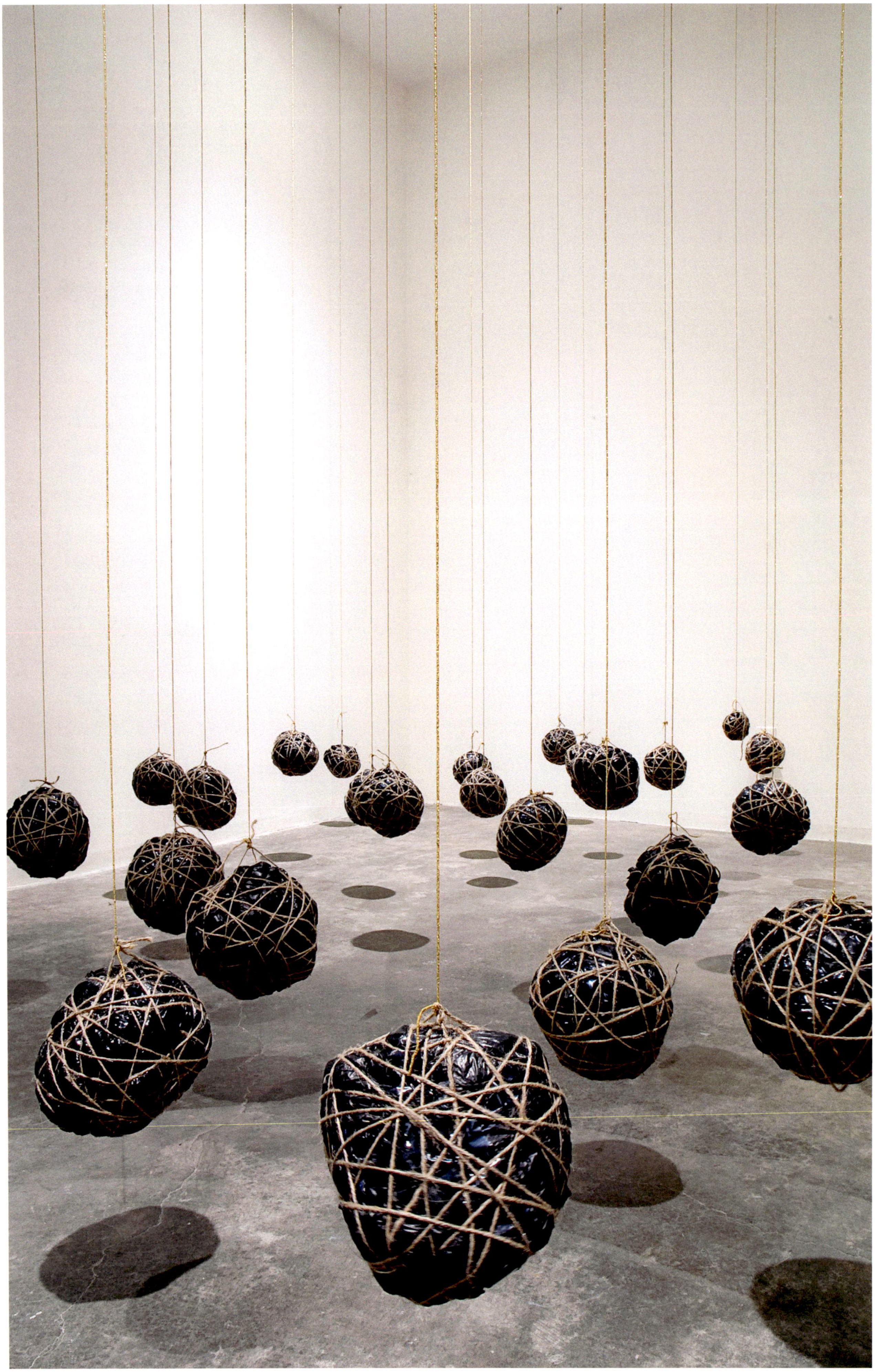

SUSPENDED PLAYTIME, 2008
GARBAGE BAGS, TWINE 44 PARTS
SIZE VARIES FROM 8 TO 20 CM

For me, the use of the grey blanket was coming from a place of nostalgia and remembering home. Yes, I was interested in how industrial it is, how very modern it is – it's a material that marks this kind of transition between an agrarian life or agricultural time, and this urban moment where factories are churning out clothing and textiles, enough material, enough stuff that they can repurpose it into something that can yet again be used: the grey felt blanket. But, of course, there's no way that every inch of a community, a place, or a nation, or a region is modernized at the same time. So there are some people who are using the materials in ways that are unexpected and unusual. In big cities in developing nations, people are picking up empty cans or jars and turning them into little cooking stoves or moving toys or a whole other set of things that they were never meant for. Once items are used and emptied, they're supposed to be thrown in the garbage and discarded, and you go buy something new. But if you can't afford to buy new things, you're resourceful and cunning with materials and you find that there's a new life for all this stuff.

There was something about the blanket that very much spoke to an understanding of that liminal space between two moments in history: the idyllic life before the colonial European takeover, the wisdom of material that made sense to your specific world, and your culture, and your people, your taste buds, and your climate. Then this new thing appears, that's brought from far away, that's foreign, factory manufactured, slightly bland, yet extremely useful. Once you get forced into producing it, into manufacturing it, into having it in your society, you begin to use it for what it was intended for and in these really odd ways.

When I use the grey blanket, it operates as a shield. I use it to conceal the detail of an object or architecture, I use it for nuance, for the metaphoric and poetic representation of a unifying membrane. I'm asking where all this clothing that is felted into the blankets was from, before it was churned into one grey patch of blanket.

MARTIN: *Does the felt connect materially to the round sculptural balls in* Suspended Playtime?

MUTU: That installation was another one of those riddles. It was a play on making a modern toy, using very basic materials in order to create the same effect, which is a bouncing football or soccer ball. Of course, this isn't something that you see anymore, because now a football is very cheap, relative to people's income. I don't know how better to describe it. It's definitely a bit of a poem, a soliloquy, a hymn about longing. Something that has been caught and frozen in time; another example of how something could be made out of things it was never supposed to be made from. Playing and games and a child's life, it carries on, despite all of the societal upheavals, and all of the weight of class differences and all of that kind of heart-wrenching reality. Games are, in some ways, the opium of children's harsh reality. Kids can survive pretty much anything if they're able to play and be with one another. Kids grow up, forget about family trauma, war, migration and poverty because they can disappear into their huge imaginations and play.

But I also like that they were these very minimal works, these very gentle, kinetic works. They move a lot, these pieces. You can touch one of them and it makes all the others vibrate a little bit, but they're also light enough that a little breeze can move them. They sway and swing. I love that piece in a wide-open space. I can't wait to install it one day again, especially after all of this new work has emerged. It would be an interesting thing to see that installation next to the figure and the figurative. Especially in this case, I was working with the idea that the protagonist, the player, the central role, was being enacted by the viewers. They were the characters in the painting, or the characters in the performance.

MARTIN: *You have made eight films. When did you make the first one?*

MUTU: Cutting was made in 2004. Then I did *Cleaning Earth* in 2006.

MARTIN: *Why the move to filmmaking?*

MUTU: I made films in graduate school. There's a film called, *The Promise*. It was a film that I put in 'The Magic City', Trevor Schoonmaker's gallery exhibition. One day, if someone does a deep dive into my shorts, they'll find some other films that explain why I made films: my feelings of alienation and my attempt to appear like I'd disappeared. They were ideas that I wanted to continue investigating in motion art pieces by enacting and reacting.

Either way, I love creating these small stories, short stories with film. I loved using the time-based aspect of film. I loved creating places that had never been visited or were from a different time and history and presenting them in a very open-ended, non-linear narrative, not particularly accurate to that time and place.

The Promise, I think, was my graduate school schism. I made that in Yale. It was basically about this European man who encounters this woman who's a black shaman, who he's attracted to but has no clue about. She's like a medicine woman. She's making a spell with the use of the entrails of a chicken. I was working out how to express the awe of what art could mean, but also how I felt at this big fancy art school with colleagues who hadn't travelled much physically or mentally and so were completely small-minded about meeting an African woman. It also brought to the forefront my respect for ancient knowledge and herbal medicine, magical spells, oral poetry and dance as the original and most fundamental way in which we first made art.

I was, and I am still, very much a believer that the limitations that we've placed upon what art represents – like, 'Art is a painting' or 'Art belongs in a museum' – have a lot to do with colonization and the attempt to own things that are sacred and un-ownable. This false narrative about the art histories that are out there has driven my art-making. The most dominant idea of acceptable art is the art of the European canons. Everything else is Voodoo, [Laughter] is lesser than, is craft, is folklore, is anthropology. Who knows who made these terms up?

All of those questions had come to me through making and studying, all the way back to *The Desert Song* play, to my high school, to the New School and Parsons, where I did cultural studies and anthropology. These issues are still haunting our knowledge platforms and have persisted. As I worked to debunk this very male-centred, Eurocentric view of what makes serious art, I was taught to be confrontational. But with time and through making, I've understood that I have nothing to prove, because by making my work, the joy and the authenticity, the complexity of being human is transmitted and explains everything. So the films have allowed me to play out this variety of art forms and the variety of roles that I and other artists have played where they're both healers and creators of new languages.

And the films are at the centre of a life performance that's essentially art in motion: wearable art, ephemeral art, art that has olfactory qualities. Nothing lasts forever because it transforms or rots or it evaporates or dies. Those ways of thinking about art were really important and fundamental, and still are to me the secret code of why we speak through art. Historically, most of the world's art isn't on a canvas, or in a frame.

MARTIN: *Are the films a way for you to preserve a performance?*

MUTU: Some are a performance and a film at the same time. All of them are related to my performances, the way I enact and how I perform them in real-time live. You'll see a lot of parallels and similarities in my films to that kind of movement: a rhythmic motion or a dance-like repetitive movement. But they're films in the sense of there's often a narrative arc in them, even if it's not a very literal narrative. it's some kind of a narrative that begins, and has a middle and has something of an end. Then it loops around intentionally as part of a post-apocalyptic cycle. I think about the loop as very much a part of how the works exist as stories: they die and are re-born again. Some of my performances are filmed as nonlinear narrative works, time-based and chance-driven works.

below,
SHE'S GOT THE WHOLE WORLD IN HER, 2015
MIXED MEDIA
274 X 152 X 107 CM

opposite,
SHE'S GOT THE WHOLE WORLD IN HER, 2015
MIXED MEDIA
274 X 152 X 107 CM

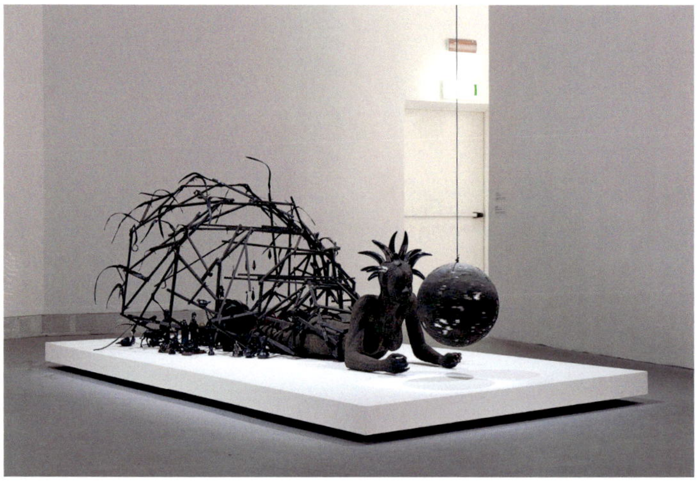

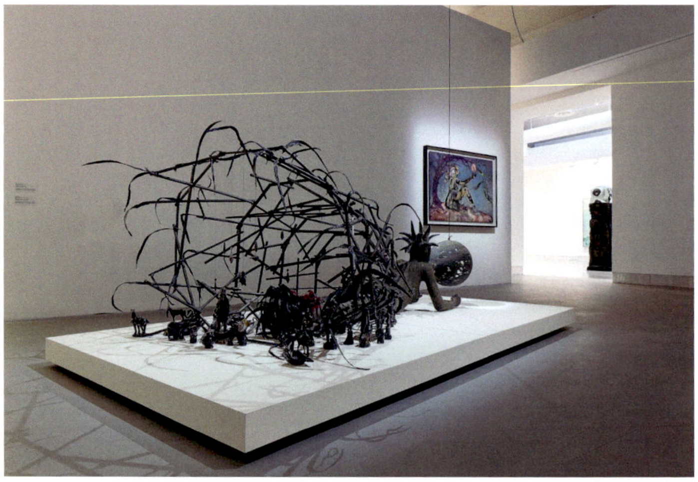

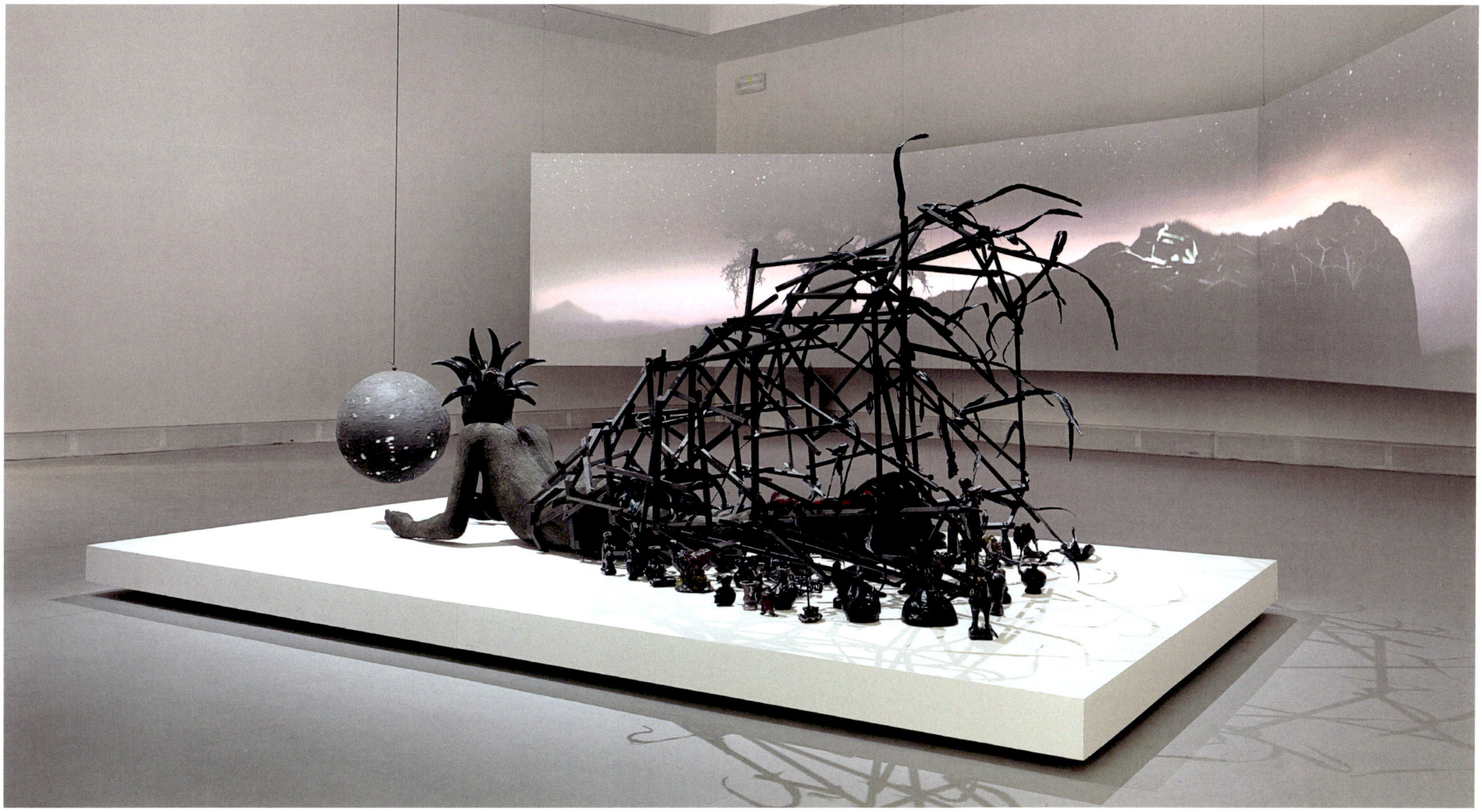

MARTIN: *The cinematic quality of your installation and sculpture became apparent in the sculptures that you made for the Venice Biennale in 2015. When I saw* She's got the whole world in her (2015) *in your studio, I was shocked because I recognized her. It dawned on me that you'd been making this figure for all of these years. Is she a pastiche of those bodies in your older work?*

MUTU: I don't know if I could encapsulate it in a better way than you just said it. I was trying for years to create new humans or a new way to make an 'us', to speak about us through our avatars. I'd been trying to conjure them, not just as two-dimensional representations but as actual objects that occupied and moved in a space – and the same space as the viewer, not only imaginary space like the picture-scape. I'd never been able to put it all together. I didn't want to simply replicate my paintings in 3D. I wanted this object to have its own reason for existing. It wasn't just to cobble together this kind of physical thing that had been happening in a photographic and paint-based collage space. For me, the collage had a different motivation and rationale in how it was made. The object needs to have its own significance, its own atmosphere, its own seat at the table of my ideas.

I finally figured it out without quite understanding how I got there. I didn't stop trying until I finally saw her. I saw what I wanted as a landscape-like figure that confronts us with her all-encompassing arms and garment and organisms and knick-knacks and people. She's not paying too much attention to us or why we're there, or looking at us in the eye (like a lot of my collages tend to do), or attending to how we're looking at her. She's completely self-involved and yet not self-conscious. She has her own business to take care of, her own challenges, her own conversation and gravity and art history and what her imagination had made. She's looking at this object rotating in front of her and swirling around like our planet Earth. She's hypnotized and transfixed by something that has been created by her and her selfhood. I wanted it to be an entire little world within which the sculpture belonged, that gave her a real sense of self-possession. I also wanted the material that I'd been using all these years to somehow still be usable and apparent.

from top,
THE SEATED IV (DETAIL), 2019
BRONZE
205 X 93 X 85 CM

THE SEATED IV, 2019
BRONZE
205 X 93 X 85 CM

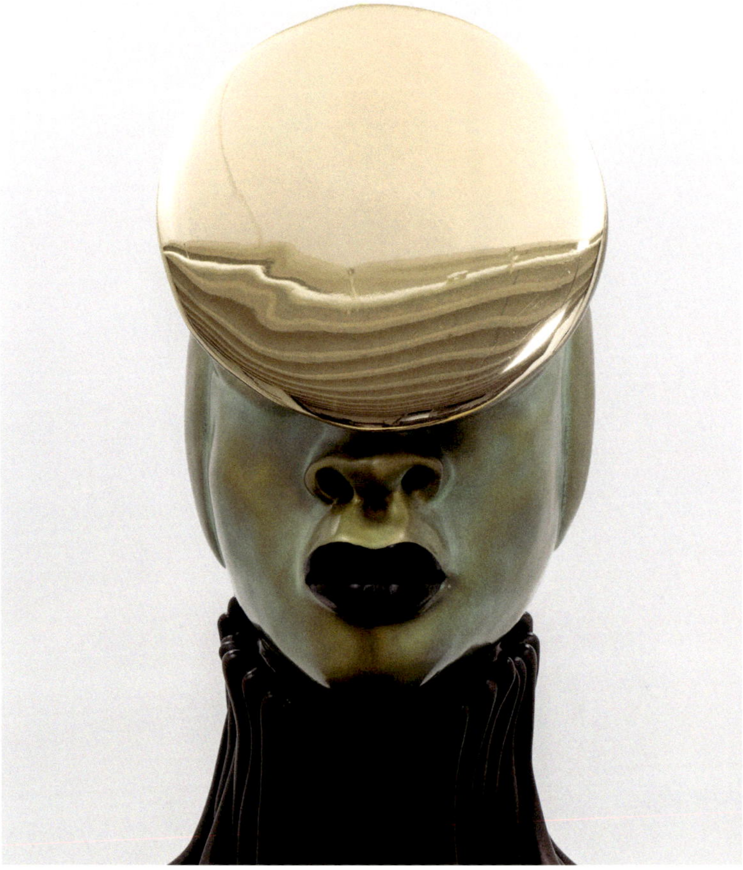

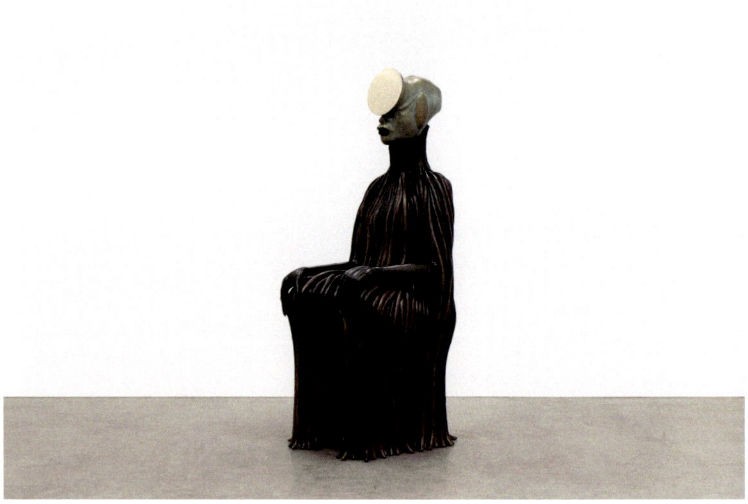

I pulverized and pulped all of these collage papers. I started shredding them. In shredding them, I was able to create these flakes, the particle equivalent of my collages. This shredded paper was what I put into water, and then put teas into, and poured inks, pigments and all of these powders and substances into. I created this muddy porridge, this viscous matter that was clay, my first clay, which is what the sculptural works are created and covered with. That's how I unify the whole figure. I recreate the image by grinding it into the particles of images that will eventually recreate it. I'd tried for years to do this. It was never, ever possible, or doable, in my mind, my imagination, or my capacity. I have to cut and mix and stir and blend and boil this material in order to become a sculptor. Until then, I wasn't able to get to a place where the material was the matter of the idea, a shape made from sculpting cells or particles or my 'atoms'.

When I finally made my mud, and I was able to mould it with my fingers and keep my mind active in thought and imagination, I was so triumphant. I was really happy about it, this epiphany. It was almost biblical. We really do have the whole world and the universe inside of us.

MARTIN: *How did you let go of all of the ephemeral materials and the more handmade processes to keep the aesthetic for the exterior bronzes shown at the Met,* The Seated I, II, III, and IV?

MUTU: I had to rise to the occasion. The material had to rise to the occasion. I had no choice but to literally lift myself up into those niches. I was very conscious of the fact that this piece was going to be seen by people who never bothered or thought about looking at my work, or who had looked at my work but weren't necessarily in agreement that I should be the one in those niches. Or who weren't accustomed to looking at art. It's almost like I had to find exactly the right woman who could sit in that position and, with such dignity and confidence, position herself as the one who ought to be there at that time.

That material felt, feels that way. It feels like it can withstand. It feels like it has the strength and the weight and the resilience and the beauty. It's also a wonderful material because of the solution I came up with. The way I protected her was using sculpture as armour. The garments I put on her are themselves a sculpting technique that's as ancient as the human imagination. I feel like I was able to enhance her, to lift her up, to clothe her, to protect her, to heal her from within and in front of the viewer, and at the same time to present her to the world with the essence of the material that she was sculpted from. I worked with my assistant sculptor, Maisie, to roll out all this clay and it became her embellishments and her identity. It's her cloak, her throne, her pedestal that holds her up and aloft.

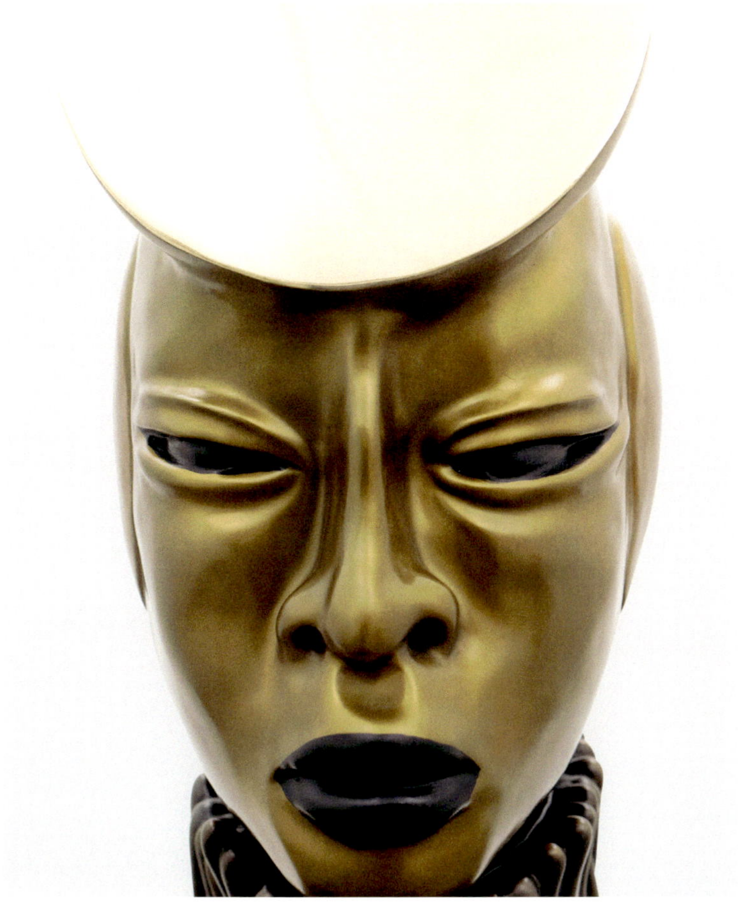

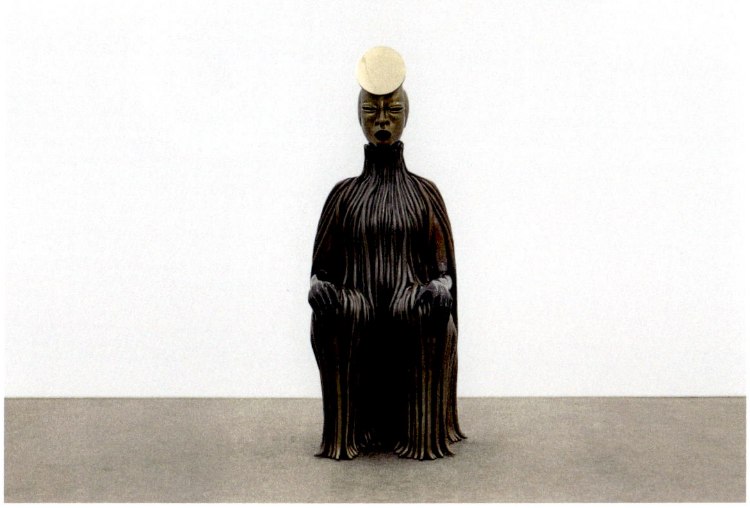

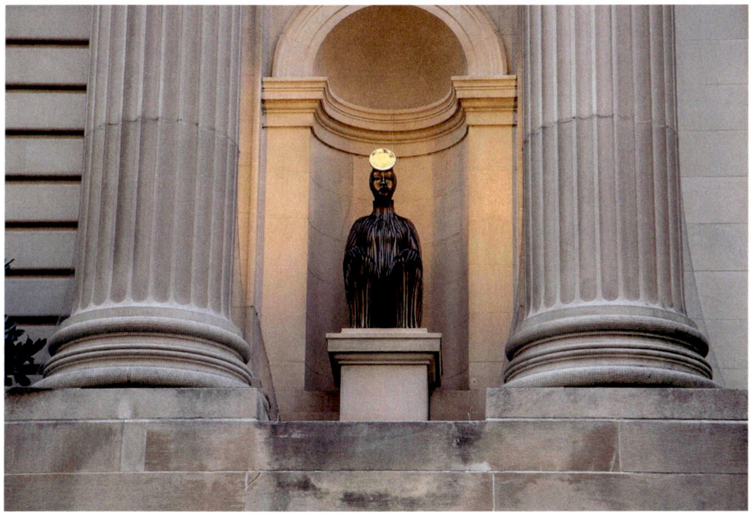

from top,
THE SEATED II (DETAIL), 2019
BRONZE
205 X 95 X 81 CM

THE SEATED II, 2019
BRONZE
205 X 95 X 81 CM

THE SEATED II, 2019
BRONZE
205 X 95 X 81 CM

INSTALLATION VIEW AT THE METROPOLITAN MUSEUM OF ART, NEW YORK, 2020

That was another moment when imagination, and serendipity, and a lot of previous trial and error came together and allowed me to make almost the perfect space to see ourselves as hopeful and dignified and connected and magical. For me, it felt like I made the perfect hymn, for the perfect ceremony, [Laughter] in the perfect pitch. The four of them, I thought, did really well together as a chorus.

MARTIN: *Yes, absolutely. They're amazing. It's funny as well, though, because, if you live in New York and you're used to seeing public sculpture, you take it for granted. I remember coming to the Met and thinking, 'There's going to be a point at which people look at these and don't even see them, which will actually be the test of their success.'*

MUTU: Yes! It's strange because I was very aware that they weren't going to be there for very long. The commission was only for five months. Then, of course, as luck would have it, the pandemic comes along and they were there for over a year, which is still not that long, but it was much longer than The Met had planned. The figures seem to have decided how long they wanted to be there and when they were done being seated at The Met. They had carried the power that this pre-pandemic/post-pandemic moment has exuded: the power of the reiteration of human rights, social justice, environmental awareness, as well as the kismet that came with the severity of the conditions that they were made in. This of course also reflects the strict deadline I was given, and the magnitude of the Museum's 'ask'. I feel like they came exactly at the right time, exactly when they were supposed to. They came in and enveloped that façade during a time of deep crisis and change and fear and transition, and reset awareness and creation.

I use the child metaphor a lot, but they are a little bit like children who come at exactly the time, giving you that bridge between the thing that you're not able to get through and the thing that you must go through. They just force you, the viewer, to cross the street and come closer. That's what they did for me, and I think that was the role that they played in those niches in that museum.

clockwise, from top left,
THE SEATED I, 2019
BRONZE
201 X 107 X 81 CM

THE SEATED I (DETAIL), 2019
BRONZE
201 X 107 X 81 CM

THE SEATED III, 2019
BRONZE
210 X 108 X 91 CM

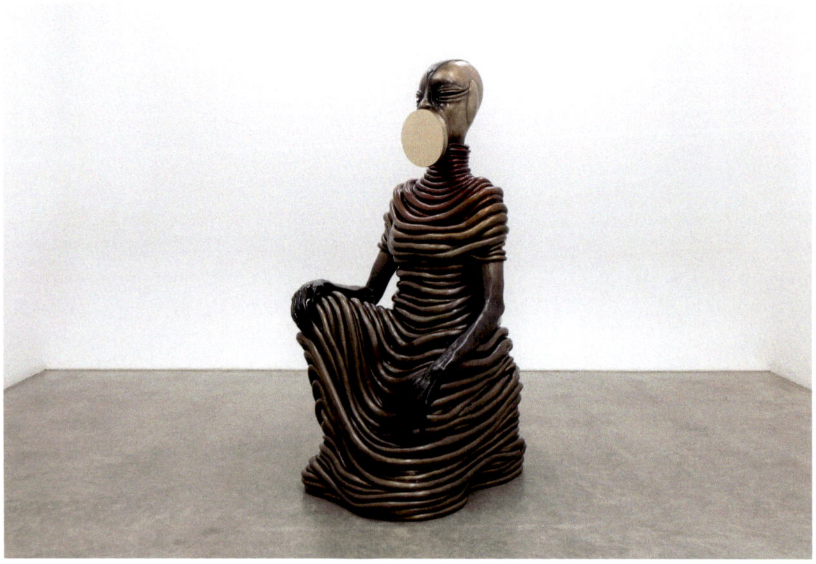

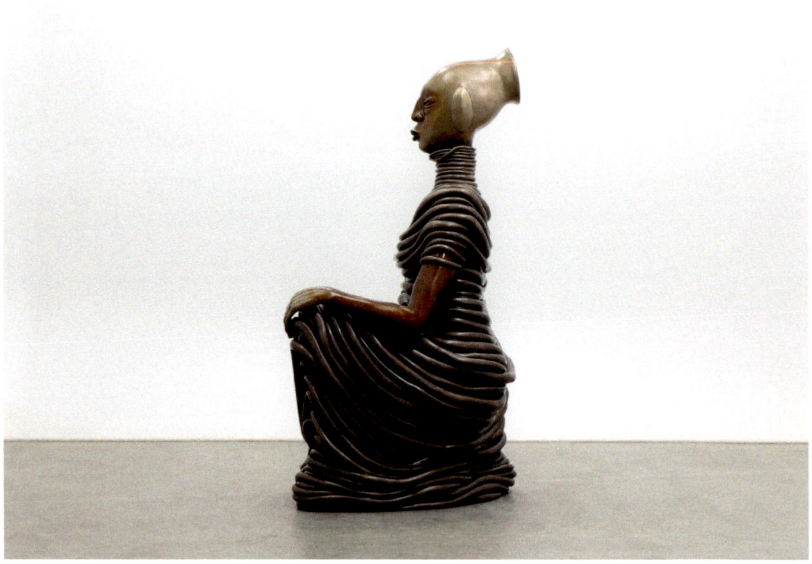

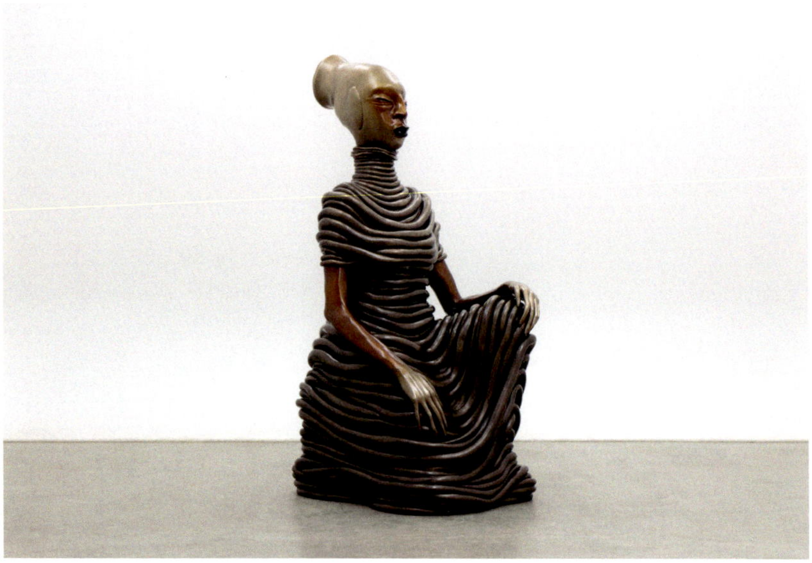

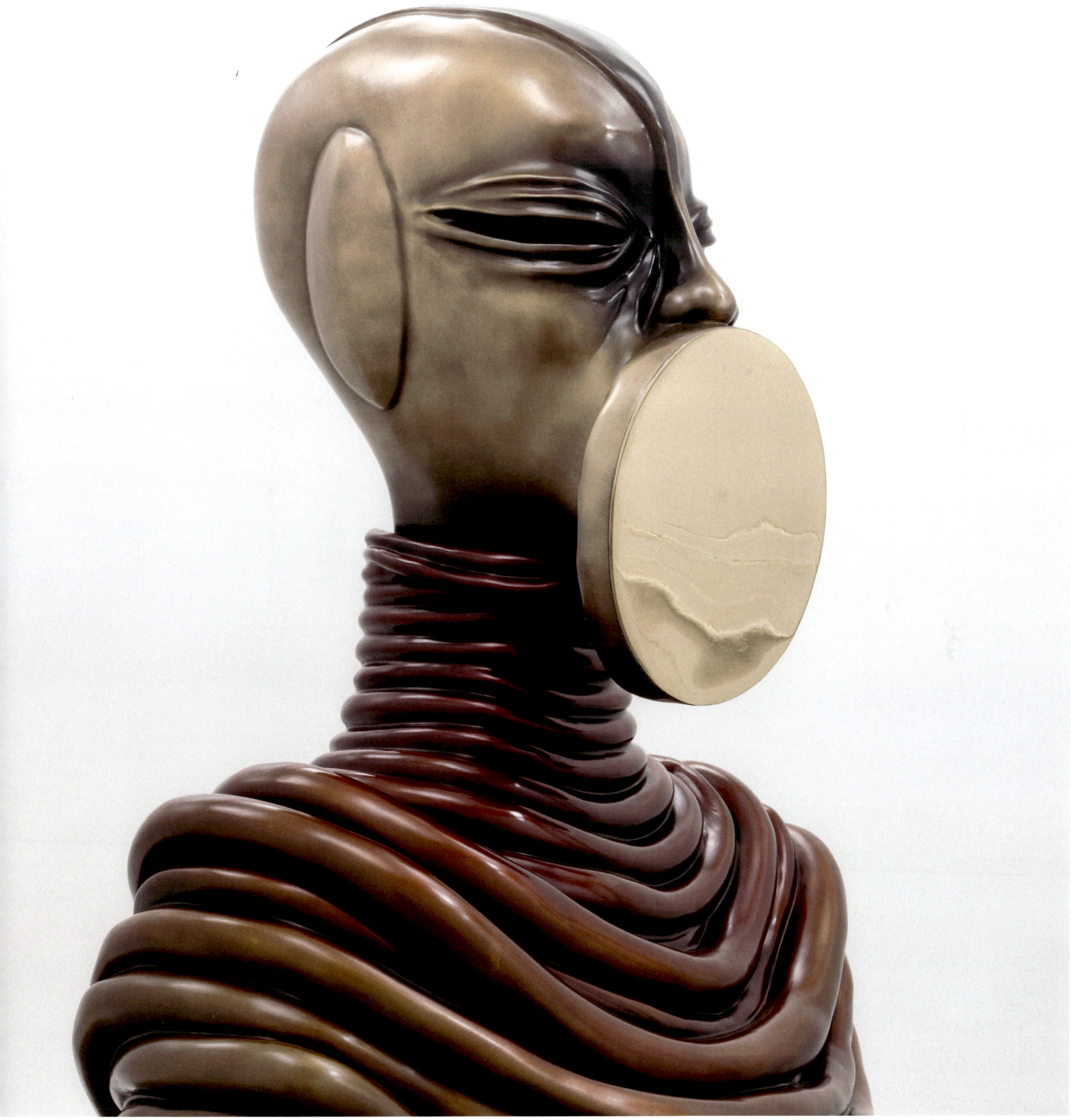

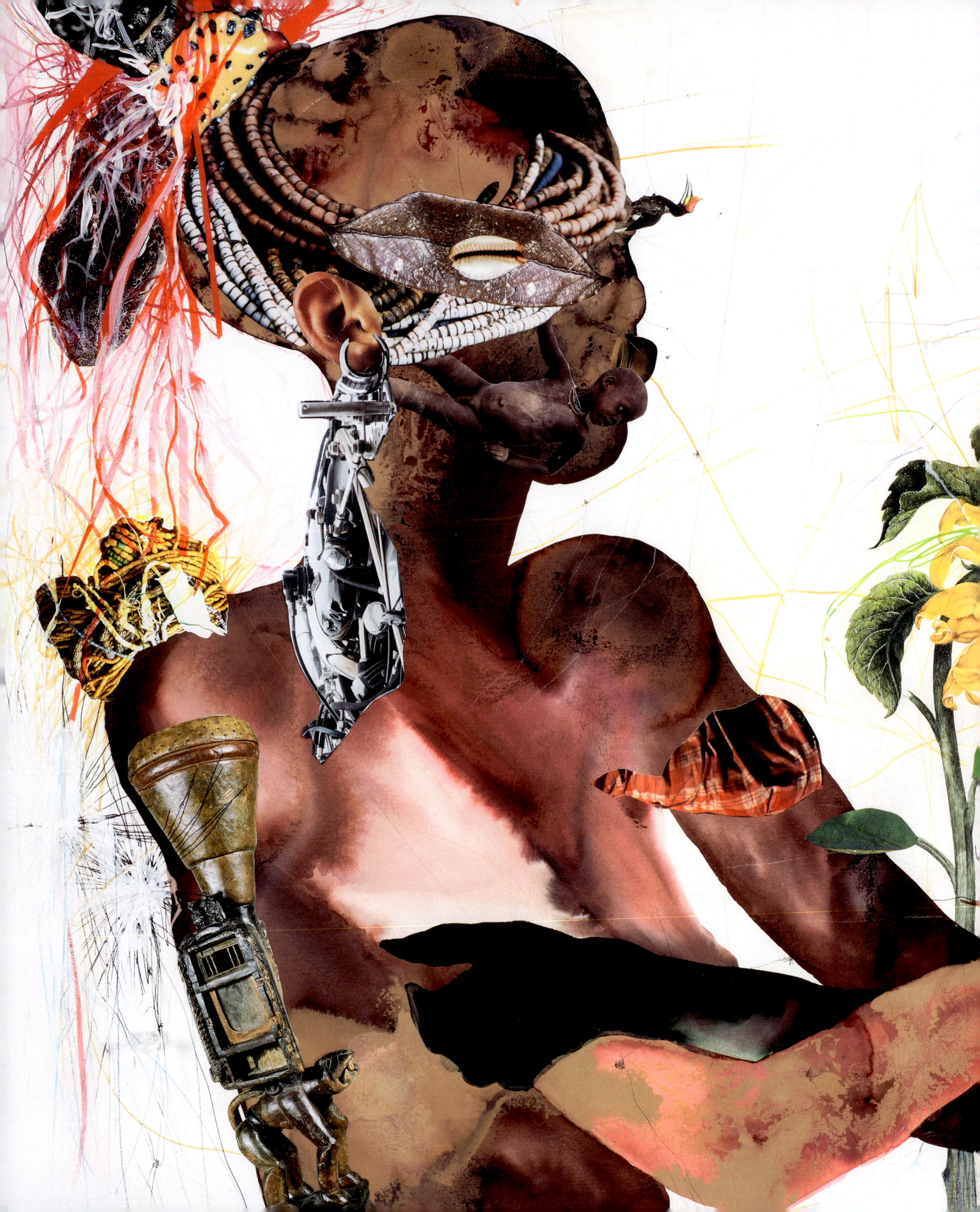

051 SURVEY

Sirens: Wangechi Mutu Pounds the Alarm

Kellie Jones

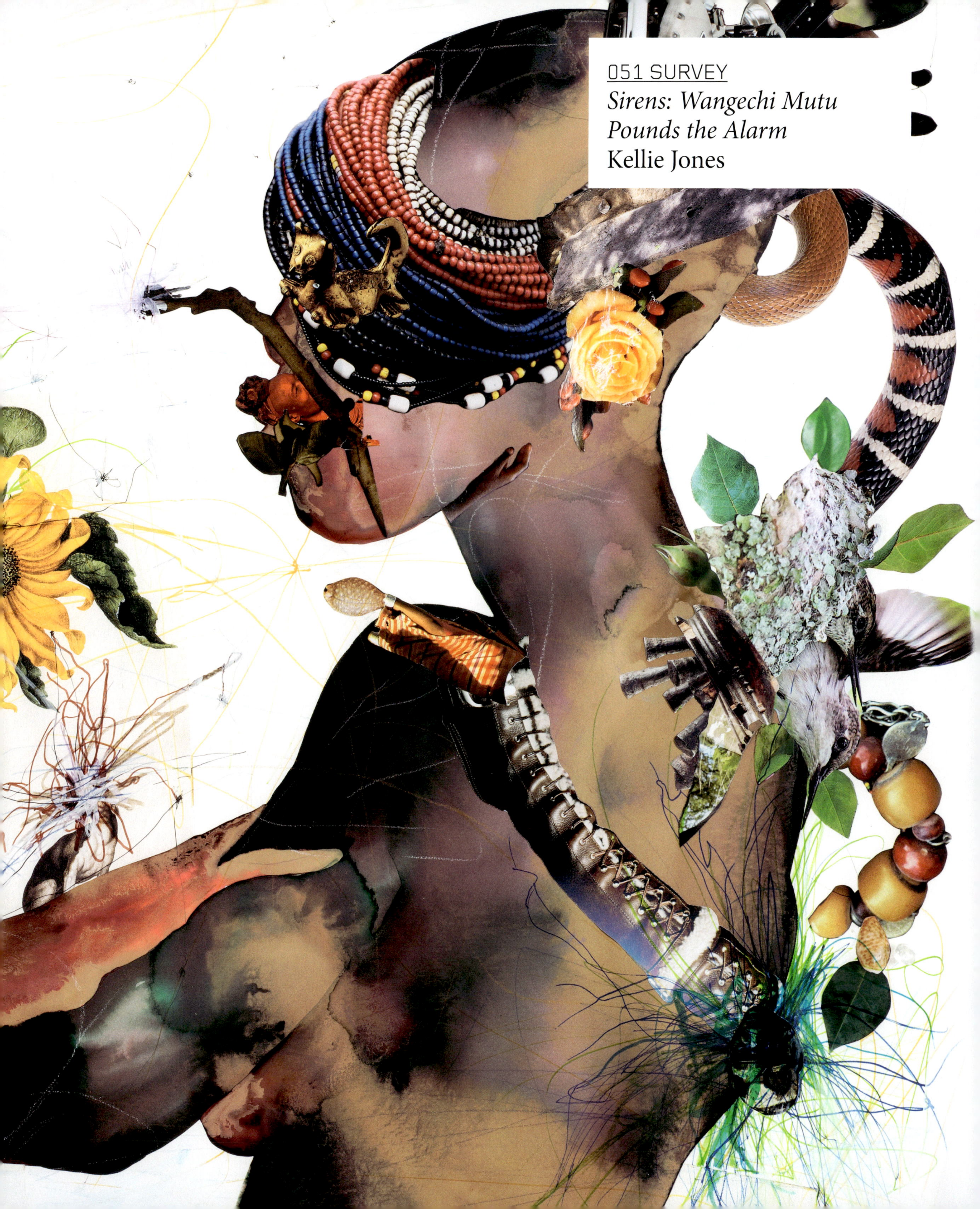

I – Gourd

It seems appropriate that I first met Wangechi Mutu when I was looking into 'the places [where] women's voices erupted in the critique of globalization', prompted by the invitation from Okwui Enwezor to organize an exhibition for South Africa's 2nd Johannesburg Biennale in 1997.[1] My show responded to Enwezor's overall project, 'Trade Routes, History and Geography', to examine the ways in which 'immense aggregates of human communities circulate in the complex vectors of class, race, gender, religious beliefs, ideology, commodity, and labor'.[2] The significance of issues of diaspora as part of the 'crosslayering of discourse that describe issues of globalization' also motivated me.[3] Through my exhibition 'Life's Little Necessities: Installations by Women in the 1990s', I wanted to think about women as global actors, commanding discursive universes that launch the world into its futures.

Mutu was among the thirteen women from across the globe included in that exhibition, working in all manner of installation, as mixed media sculptural site, as room-scale video and lightboxes. I reminded the artists to bring their own tools (cordless please) and get to work, be a part of and witness to the great transformation of South Africa into a multiethnic democracy, and the jettisoning of the racist apartheid state. While texts written since then have assumed (based on the catalogue image) that Mutu's 'Bottle People' series of 1997 formed her contribution to 'Life's Little Necessities', that wasn't the case. Her project was *Four Square Pillahs* (1997, also known as the 'Body Parts' series), consisting of sand, light and sixteen soft sculptures. The allusion to measurement in the title mimics an architectural plan outlined by the sixteen odd objects. The pillow-like elements embedded with horns, gourds and other materials demonstrate the artist's earliest interest in the sculptural, amalgamation and the alchemical.[4]

Her fascination with biology and zoology, and her condemnation of a staid anthropological framing that has trailed African art, is evident in the project, as is the rebuke of archaic notions of authenticity and gender politics, themes she has continued to address to varying degrees and in different ways over time. *Four Square Pillahs* is also evidence of Mutu's ongoing conversation with the nation of her birth through its exhibitionary complex. One strand of that dialogue could be seen at the Nairobi National Museum when it installed a monumental centrepiece based on the gourd as a unifying icon of Kenyan culture.[5]

The sixteen objects in *Four Square Pillahs* are domestic but uneasy. They are emblematic of the discomforts of home for those who feel estranged from its common routines, and visualize the difficulties of sustaining its stability for those set flowing into the tailspin of diaspora. The work also sketches out the violence in this existence, to which Mutu would continue to call our attention. As I wrote at the time:

While visiting her parents in Kenya, it is revealed that Mutu's mother refuses to serve lake fish, since they have been feeding on massacred villagers escaping the turmoil in Rwanda and Burundi. Writes the artist: 'The population of fish, even the size of them, had increased relative to the enormity of the tragedy … The people who have "disappeared" (and are still disappearing) because of the Central African Holocaust have re-emerged and are being redistributed amongst the living.'[6]

As with the myriad artists who participated in the 2nd Johannesburg Biennale, Mutu's project traced Enwezor's broad notion of modernity, one that was inclusive of colonial and postcolonial actors, and 'a more fascinating modernity than has been properly allowed in broader cultural discussions. Far from being aberrations, [art] instead suggest[s] partial ways of living, working, and travelling in a restless world of social, political, economic, and cultural transformation.'[7]

The other framing device for my exhibition was decidedly feminist and embodied in the rise of the female hip hop artist as a powerful image of self-making. Whether through a dynamic sexual and sensual femme body, or one presenting as more masculine, these musical artists' own sense of themselves and gendered identities offered paradigms of women as global actors. Their voices were strident, 'throwin' tantrums', focused on their own self-determination, or as journalist Karen R. Good put it in the *Village Voice*, 'both femme and butch, bitch and requisite n___'.[8] The commitment of 1990s figures such as Lil Kim and Da Brat continues today with women like Nikki Minaj, Cardi B and Megan Thee Stallion, whose vexing presence champions 'sexualized meanings of [the] black diasporic body as an apparatus to trouble discourses of respectability, taste, and femininity.'[9] Interestingly, Megan Thee Stallion's sounds pay homage to the nineties rap that she listened to growing up. Like numerous creators in this genre, her work celebrates sexual pleasure but 'is a provocative invitation to consider what it means when a woman wields sexual, economic, and artistic power in a world designed and defined by men.'[10]

About a year apart, Wangechi Mutu and Megan Thee Stallion penned op-ed articles for the *New York Times* decrying violence against women, those on the margins or at the intersections, transgender and gender-nonconforming people, who bear the brunt of sexual violence. In this context, the beings that populate Mutu's work are sirens, at once embodied women in control of their sexuality and pleasure, and audible warnings who do not just sound, but in the words of Minaj, 'pound the alarm'. They stand as a full liberatory force that turns on sexual freedoms but heralds and champions a social emancipation enfolding *all* humanity and life.[11]

opposite,
BOTTLE PEOPLE SERIES, 1997
GLASS, STRING, PAINT, VARNISH, SHELL, BOTTLE CAP, LEATHER, WIRE AND FOUND OBJECTS
DIMENSIONS VARIABLE

previous pages,
YOU ARE MY SUNSHINE, 2015
COLLAGE PAINTING ON PAPER
61 X 91 CM

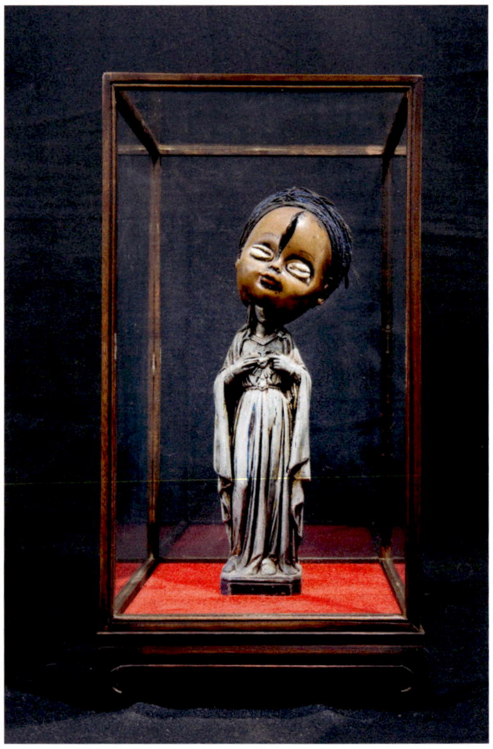

MARIA, 1997
PLASTIC, STRING, PAINT, SHELLS, FOUND OBJECT
53 X 11 X 10 CM

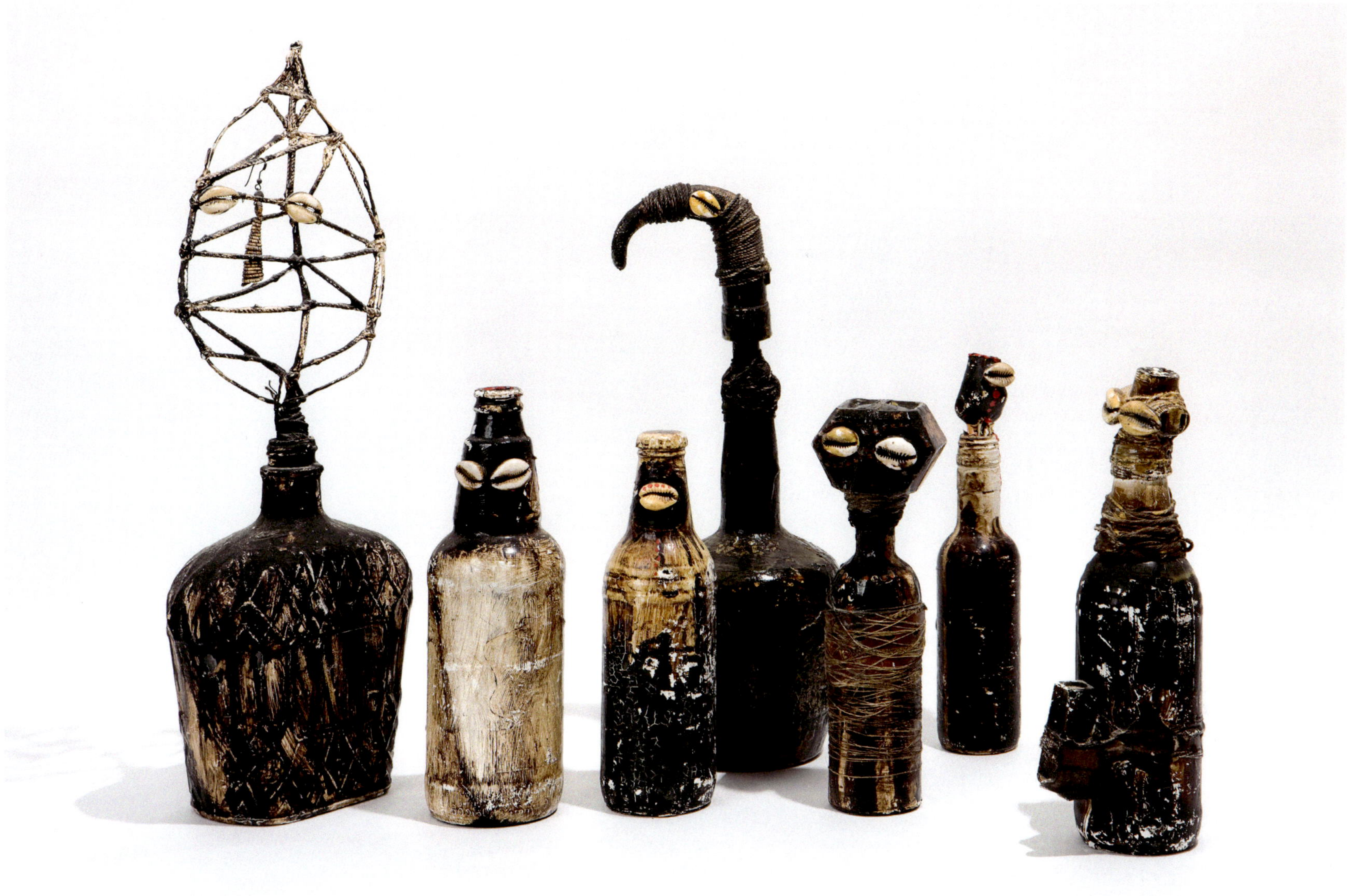

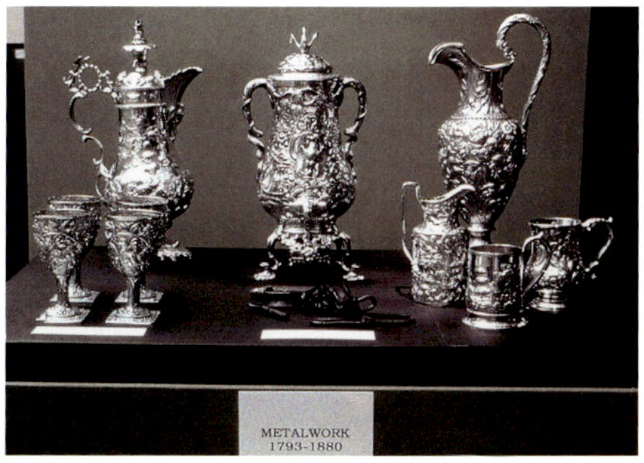

FRED WILSON
MINING THE MUSEUM (METALWORK 1793–1880), 1992
SLAVE SHAKES, COLONIAL SILVER
DIMENSIONS VARIABLE

Mutu arrived in the US to a 1990s New York and an art world that was flexing its multicultural muscle (again). As she recounts to photographer and historian Deborah Willis, she was excited and energized by a milieu that centred a discourse around race, agency and Black bodies. The Whitney Museum buzzed with exhibitions organized by Thelma Golden: there was the game-changing 'Black Male' (1994) but also Golden's continual showcasing of work by contemporary Black artists such as Lorna Simpson, Glenn Ligon and Gary Simmons that spanned the decade. Mutu's training at Cooper Union, where she received a BA in 1996, mirrored what she found in the city, with teachers like Hans Haacke and his politicized conceptualism, and Fred Wilson, whose installational practice like the 1992 site-specific *Mining the Museum*, critiqued colonial and racial structures within art-historical and museological contexts. Such sculptural and contextual vectors would continue to undergird Mutu's practice.[12]

Certain women artists exerted other influences. Mutu repeatedly cites photographer Claude Cahun, painter Frida Kahlo and conceptualist Ana Mendieta, all known for self-imaging that presents ambiguous, composite identities, beyond traditional gendered images. Their poses with the natural world were also significant, as reflected in Mutu's sumptuous 2008 portrait photograph.[13]

II – Paper

Paper was Mutu's first muse. During her childhood, her father had a paper import business in which figured a warehouse with stacks of papers of all types. It became Mutu's playground. During her studies at Cooper Union, she didn't have much use for the weighted histories and techniques of traditional western painting. She would find herself more comfortable thinking with paper and drawing implements at hand, enjoying the immediacy of sketching, the freshness of watercolour and quickness of collage.[14]

Mutu's line drawings open a path for an increasingly more ambitious and confident practice. They demonstrate to the artist herself what is possible on art's shifting horizon. They also early on reveal for the discerning viewer the enormity of the artist's talent.

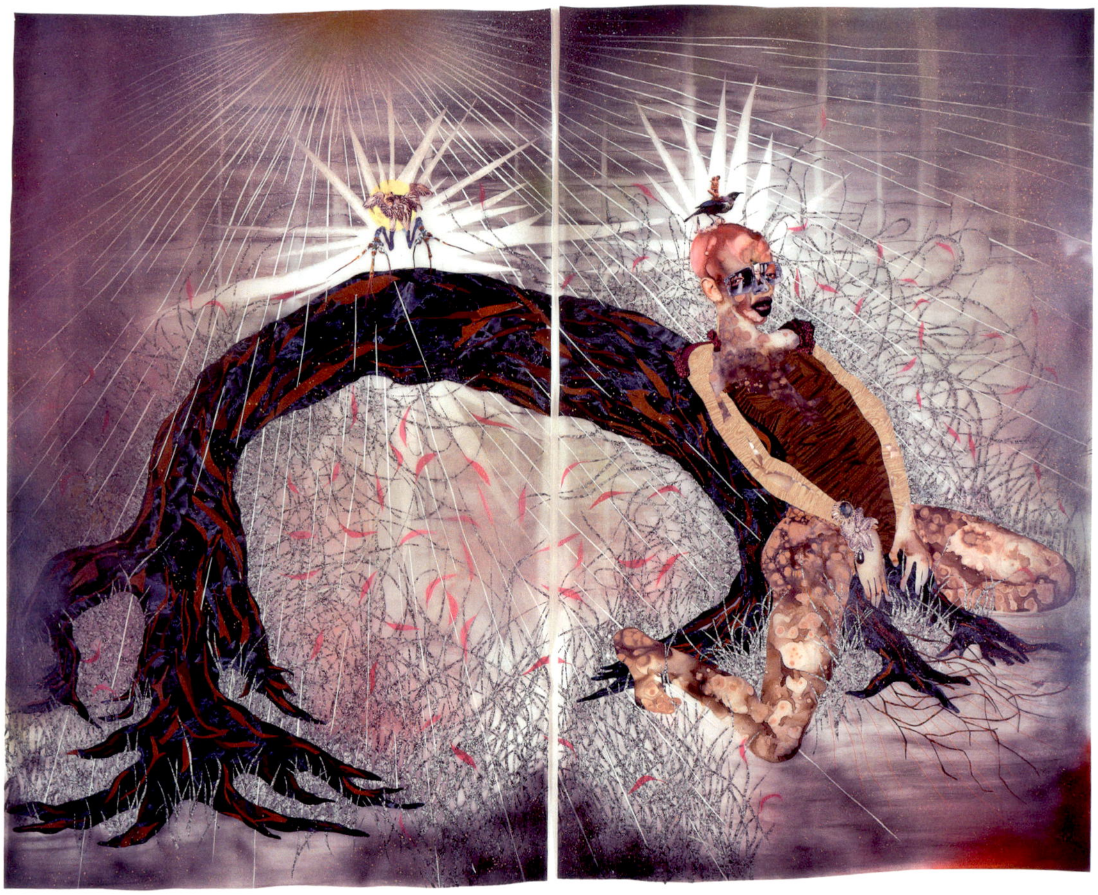

A SHADY PROMISE, 2006
MIXED MEDIA ON MYLAR
222 X 276 CM

opposite, clockwise from top,
PIN-UP, 2001
INK AND COLLAGE ON PAPER
33 X 25 CM

PIN-UP, 2001
INK AND COLLAGE ON PAPER
33 X 25 CM

PIN-UP, 2001
INK AND COLLAGE ON PAPER
33 X 25 CM

PIN-UP, 2001
WATERCOLOUR, COLLAGE AND
CONTACT PAPER ON PAPER
31 X 24 CM

Meandering and explosive ideas in line populate her first major book, *Wangechi Mutu, A Shady Promise* (2008). The initial section is comprised of sketchbook drawings from 1996 to 2001, the years between finishing at Cooper Union and completing her MFA at Yale. Her line is pervasive and infectious, spilling into areas of the text, reminding us of the ever-flowing marks and thoughts of any sketchbook.

The images in *A Shady Promise* demonstrate the precision of Mutu's line. The imagery is robust and fecund, yet executed with a knowing economy, with ink and collage making guest appearances. Page after page comes with the caption 'Actual Size', pulling us into the sketchbook world to focus on the artist's fastidiousness and balance. Mutu is motivated by the figure, always female presenting, driven by its own lean, youthful and sexual being that often morphs into other species and displays marks of cruelty. Sitting on a masklike head, one character holds her stitched and stuffed legs wide open; a nun supports her own amputated arms, her trunk a crucifix seemingly explained by the legend 'their job today'. These pictures are reminiscent of Adrian Piper's *The Barbie Doll Drawings* (1967), whose feminist critiques of the ideal body revolve around an equally surreal model, but it is more (or mere) puppet rather than animal hybrid. The aura of brutality that Mutu's figures emit is closer to that of Kara Walker, who works with a black outline and silhouette to depict equally fearless female protagonists.

Other aspects of Mutu's drawings take us to a starting point beyond contemporary art histories, particularly those in which the animal figures, with teats and udders, are unknowable except as female (as one of Mutu's sketches states, 'Mary was a little lamb'). An improbable being floats in purgatory in one drawing, high above the earth but watched (protected?) by an all-seeing eye that beams from heaven. Its drifting presence is little more than a head with an exquisite coiffure topping a ball of sexual organs; the figure sucks its own breast while simultaneously defecating. Here Mutu's precise grotesqueries reflect illustrations seen in European texts from the seventeenth century forward of African women who could 'suckle over their shoulder'. In her marvellous article of same title, Jennifer L. Morgan traces the development of the monstrous African woman as sign in such early European missives. The African woman was articulated as an incredible labourer, an embodied machine that felt no pain (unlike her European counterparts). Not marked by beauty but fertility, the trope of pendulous, hanging 'dugs' or teats (not necessarily 'breasts', which could suggest their humanity), drag the ground and are sometimes confused with legs. These monstrous mothers were beasts who were only civilized by the colonial encounter. That Mutu's visual musing and Morgan's article appeared within a year of each other is perhaps indicative of the rising influence of the discourse around blackness, the body and the importance of gender and sexuality in both the art and academic worlds of the 1990s.[15]

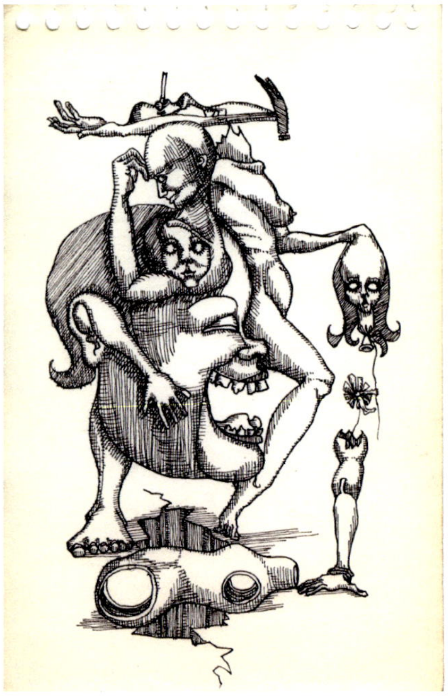

ADRIAN PIPER
THE BARBIE DOLL DRAWINGS, 1967
INK AND PENCIL ON THIRTY-FIVE SHEETS
OF NOTEBOOK PAPER
EACH 22 X 14 CM

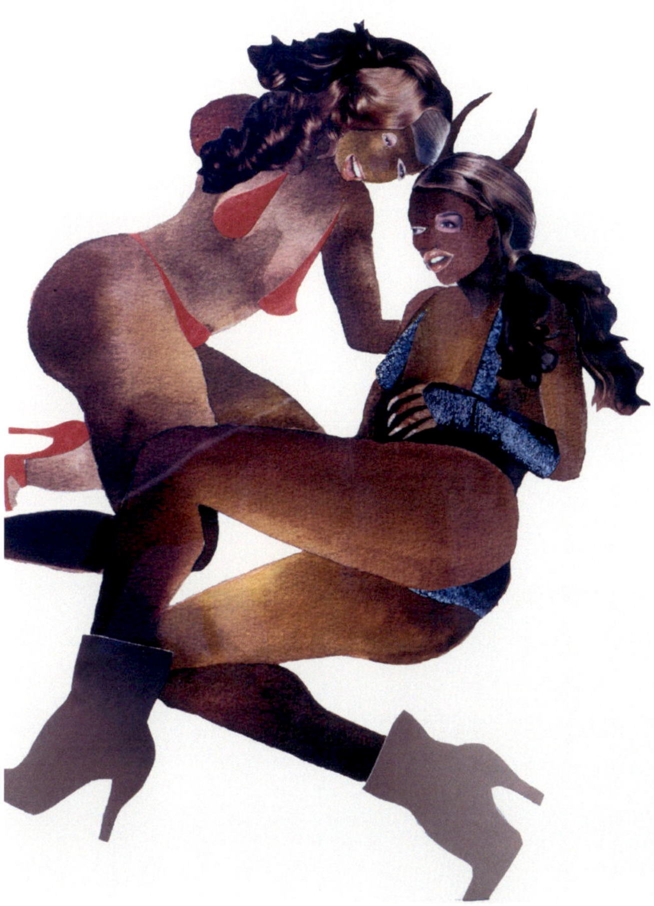
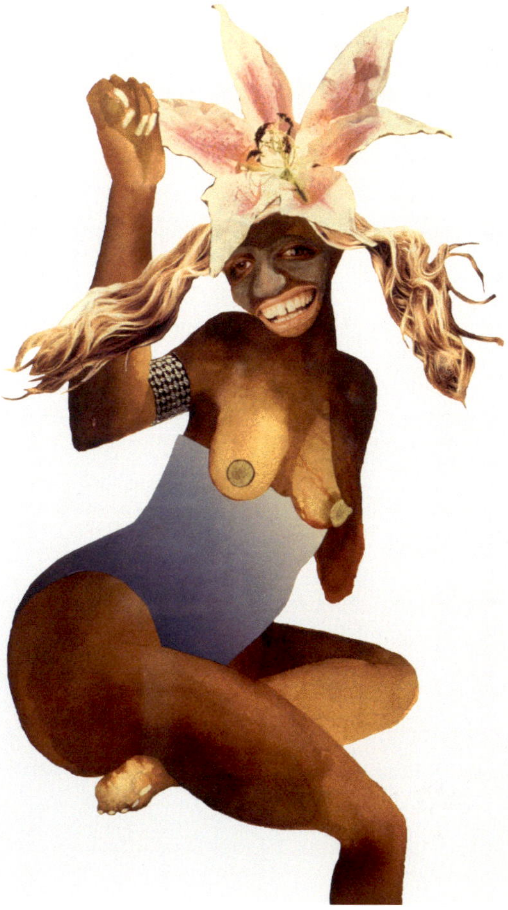
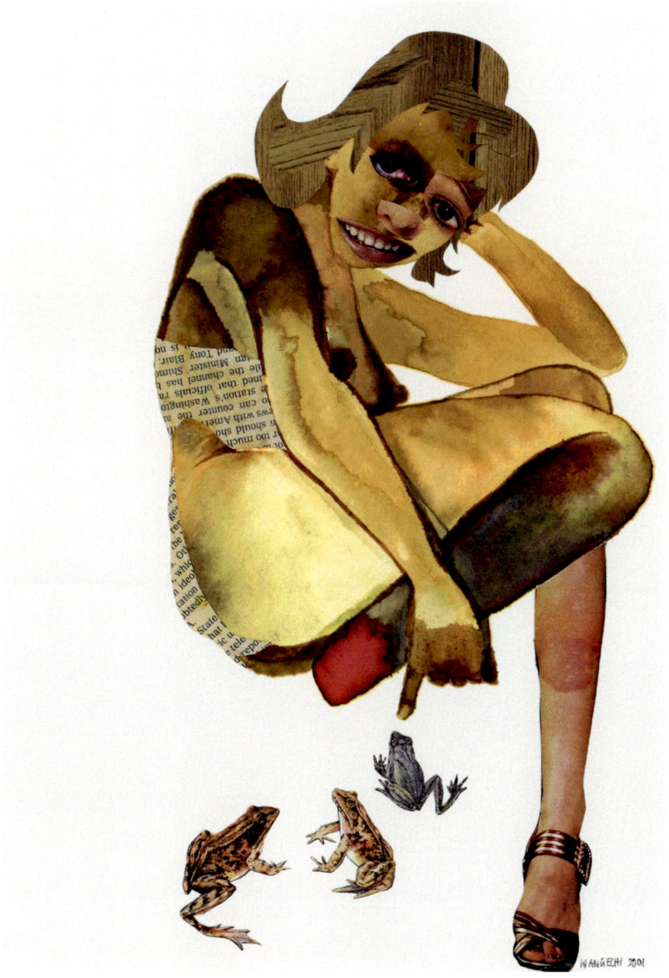
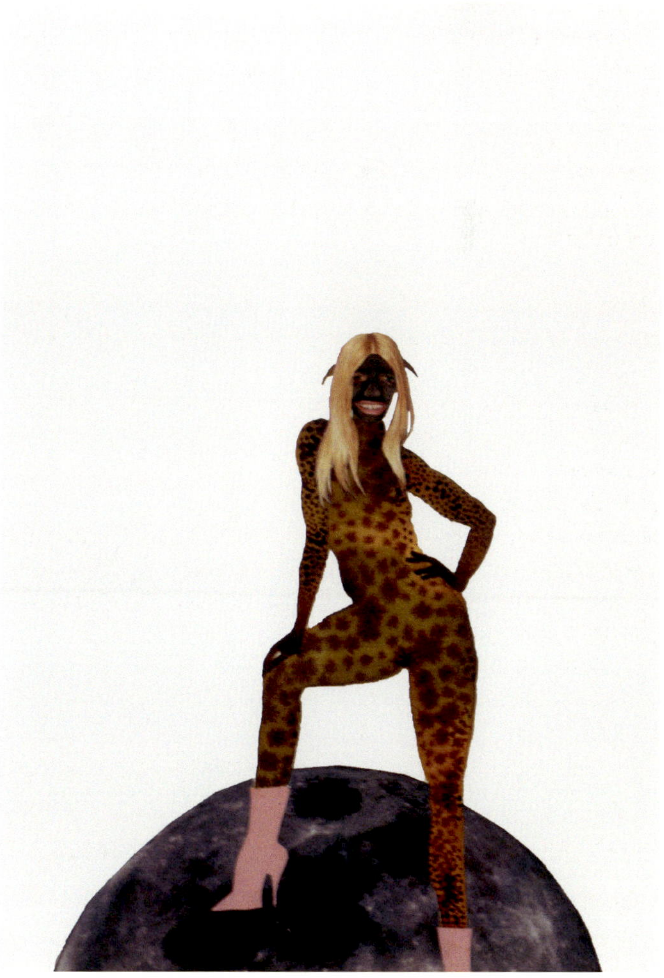

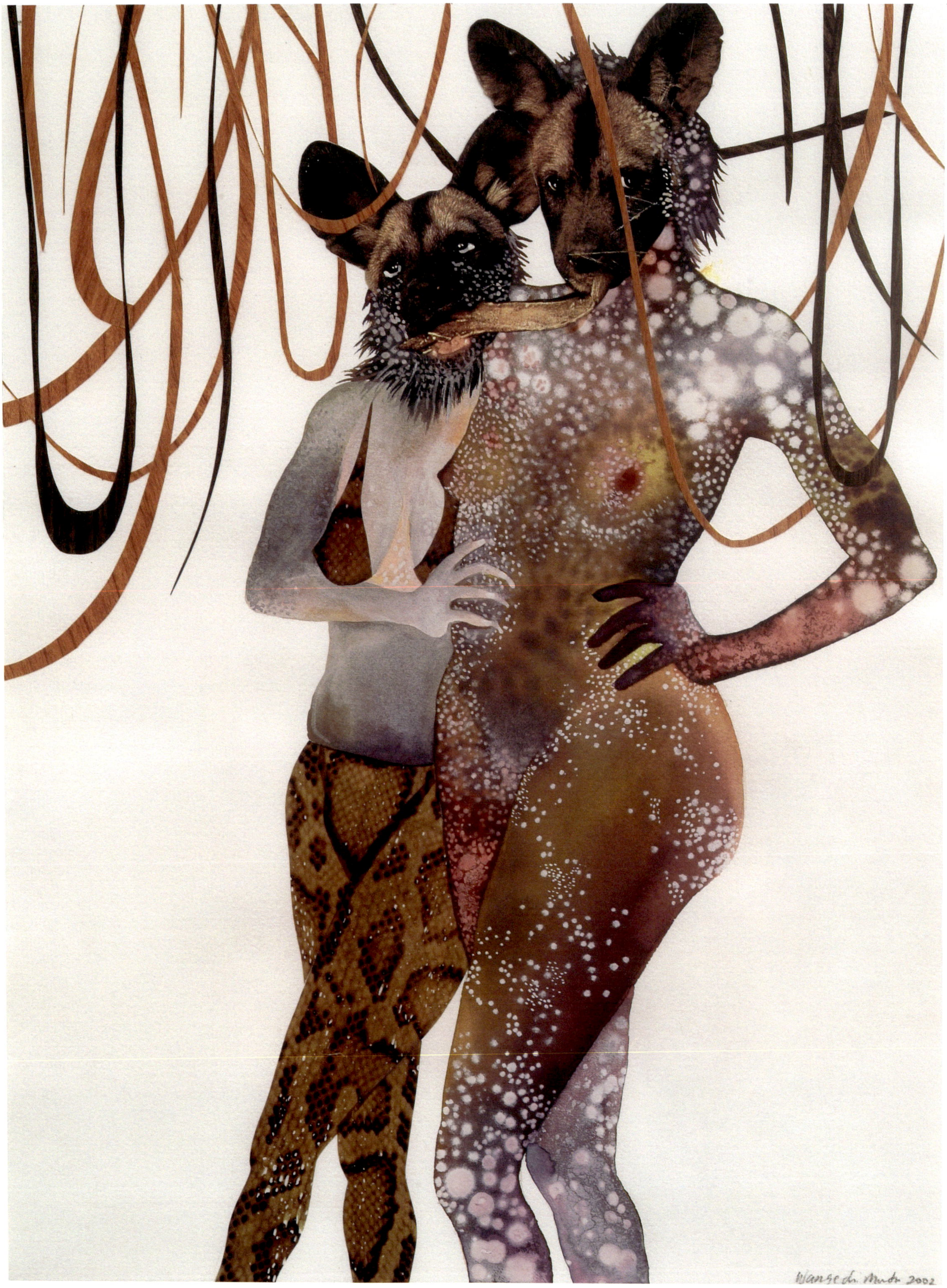
Wangechi Mutu 2002

opposite,
INTERTWINED, 2003
COLLAGE AND WATERCOLOUR
ON PAPER
51 X 41 CM

This was the moment when the artist began to circle in on 'the human figure as an exploratory site'.[16] In the her hands, the body was a pliable form that could speak to her position as a Black female artist but also as an African immigrant who only found herself Black outside the context of a homeland where blackness was dominant. In New York, French-speaking Africans from Senegal and Guinea were the prevalent groups when Mutu arrived in the early 1990s, evidence of growing waves of migration impacted by a globalized neo-liberalism. By the decade's end there was an increasing presence of those from Liberia, Sierra Leone and Rwanda, who had fled civil strife.[17] The mature voice to which the artist came in the new century would make a place for all this, while also hailing past histories of carnage and colonialism.

It was Mutu's meditations on the body conflicted by racial ideology, inequity, war and desire that first made an impact on the traditional Western art world in her Pin-Up series, which emerged at the beginning of the twenty-first century. We witness the artist conflating, refashioning and literally hacking skin magazines and fashion glossies to create a form both mutilated and mutant (like any superhero worth her salt). Some of the first pieces feel like an expansion of her sketchbook drawings. Somewhat larger, they rely on the expert handling of watercolour, with collaged accessories, coiffure and facial features. In many instances the joining of the latter two approximate masks, a semblance of those traditionally thought of as African, and of those associated with the conceits and poses of femininity. Mutu's skill with watercolour is exquisite, modulations of shadow and light adroitly handled. Alluring brown-toned limbs trail off into bloodied stumps and are supported by pasted-on prosthetics. When Mutu cites Romare Bearden as an inspiration, it is felt first here, in the adept melding of cut paper and watery medium.

Musicologist Michael Veal, whose writing on African soundscapes impressed Mutu while she was in graduate school at Yale, has written most stirringly about both the context of these breakout works and their impact, seeing in the artist's protagonists African female figures as the most vulnerable and yet 'most potent agent[s] of regeneration'. Embedded here is a critique of outmoded national formations and world-making; indeed, Mutu handily discards the 'big-men' narratives of postcolonial Africa in favour of frightfully powerful animal-spirit women. Veal's commentary on the monstrous and the visceral in what the artist calls her watercolour collage is worth quoting at length. The beings Mutu imagines are:

survivors of all the violence and material/psychic toxins dumped upon their bodies and environs. Striking the alluring poses of skin magazine models, their animalistic, exaggerated features coyly invite the viewer to mount stumps, calluses, and bloodied scabs […] In what future, present or past world will these hairy pin-up babies – in their stained plantation finery and jungle garb – find their places in locker rooms, bathrooms, boardrooms, powder rooms, dormitories and prison cells? And in which genre will the film adaptation be categorized? Adult? Horror? Sci-fi? Fantasy? Or, as the elegantly serpentine arm in the final image suggests, in what religious iconography will they serve as devotional images?[18]

By 2019, African women were being touted as powerful contemporary artistic voices of the continent.[19] Clearly, though, this had been the case at least since the beginning of the century. One gage might be 'Africaine', the exhibition organized by Christine Y. Kim at New York's Studio Museum in Harlem in 2002. Here, photo- and media-based practices were platforms for the interrogation of gender and its norms in the works of Fatimah Tuggar (Nigeria), Tracey Rose and Candace Breitz (South Africa) and Wangechi Mutu (Kenya). Each took on embattled media images, ideas of artifice and representation, through seemingly awkward and disjunctive articulations of the feminine. They scrutinized ideas of coloniality and white supremacy along with its eruption in modern tourist imagery and its circulation in photography, collage and digital mediums. Their use of media self-aware technologies joined with the nostalgic; a reconstructed and reimagined African female body was their battlefield. In the place of a fixed authenticity, Mutu and others instead trafficked in unruly images, a sexually abject ethnographic re-engineered for its own pleasure, a celebratory grotesque, embracing negation and repulsion as power.[20]

What is important to note about Mutu and the artists gathered in the 'Africaine' show is the significance of collage in their hands as what Courtney J. Martin calls 'the aesthetics of fractured assembly'.[21] Martin outlines the mechanics and disjunctions of collage and photomontage, but also reminds us of its basis in falling apart, of *décollage,* a tearing away made famous by Parisian affichists in the 1950s and 1960s. It is also felt in Brent Hayes Edwards's conception of *décalage*, the discrepancies and mistranslations of diaspora that are perpetually undone, unresolved, unmade. Here, collage is mobile, on the knife's edge between solidarity and incoherence, emblematic of 'radical, democratic, and decolonial publics as they combust, regenerate, or undergo erasure'.[22]

THE ARK COLLECTION
(DETAIL), 2006
COLLAGE ON POSTCARD
18 X 12 CM

The Ark Collection (2006) was a project in which Mutu drew on these same ideas of misrecognition and transformation. It also traded on its diminutiveness. Part of the logic of *The Ark Collection*, like the Pin-Ups before it, was that the size of these small collages approximated the dimension of the skin magazine. The traffic in intimacy was part of its power and control; you needed to come close. Instead of living on the wall, these pieces resided in a quadrangle of black vitrines housed in its own black room, the specter of ethnographic display ordered against the modern's blinding white cube. Grouped in pairs like their biblical predecessors, they are on a journey into the future.

As with the Pin-Ups, Mutu skims her imagery from fashion and skin magazines. But *The Ark Collection* also more directly engages the ethnographic imagination by striping images from sources like postcards, calendars, books and magazines such as *National Geographic*, in which the nude bodies of African women are circulated and exchanged in the name of science and knowledge.[23] These are joined by *Black Tail* and *Player's Girl Pictorial,* the other end of the literary spectrum, which, in their fashion, rely equally on performances of racial primitivism and rawness. As curator David Moos writes, 'the expectations encoded in these pornographic poses give way to ethnographic clichés'.[24] Sexual organs, native fabrics and jewellery along with accessories that gesture to porn (like lace or animal prints) are remixed, misplaced, unsettled. Even, or perhaps especially, in these recombinant forms, we are shown 'how black women's bodies make race a pornographic subject', as Jennifer C. Nash argues.[25]

Jillian Hernandez probes the ambivalence vested in *The Ark Collection* as a project that redeems Black sensuality and sexuality while destabilizing 'the exoticizing colonialist gaze'.[26] Hernandez raises the spectre of class invested in the artist's imagery – its press-on nails, Lucite shoes and spandex. In its troubling of boundaries, collage brings forth pleasure and enjoyment but in the same motion cuts it off, thwarting any anticipated gratification. These are performances of 'the colonized woman' where the fantasies of colonization are obliterated and no longer quite legible. In *The Ark Collection* Hernandez instead imagines Mutu 'embracing a lack of wholeness' and enfleshment as a sign of life.[27]

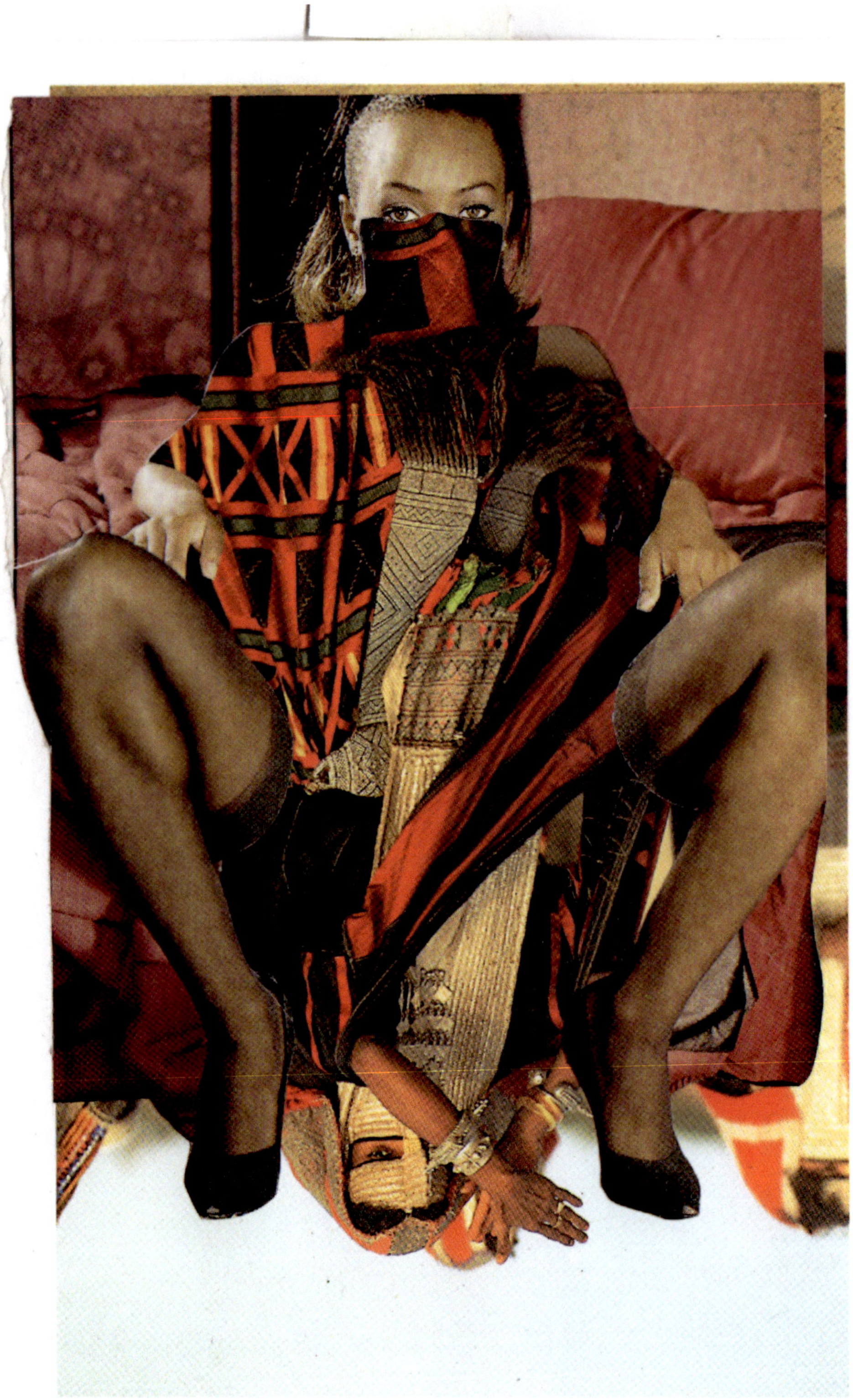

from top,
THE ARK COLLECTION
(DETAIL), 2006
COLLAGE ON POSTCARD
18 X 12 CM

THE ARK COLLECTION
(DETAIL), 2006
COLLAGE ON POSTCARD
18 X 12 CM

THE ARK COLLECTION
(DETAIL), 2006
COLLAGE ON POSTCARD
18 X 12 CM

THE ARK COLLECTION
(DETAIL), 2006
COLLAGE ON POSTCARD
18 X 12 CM

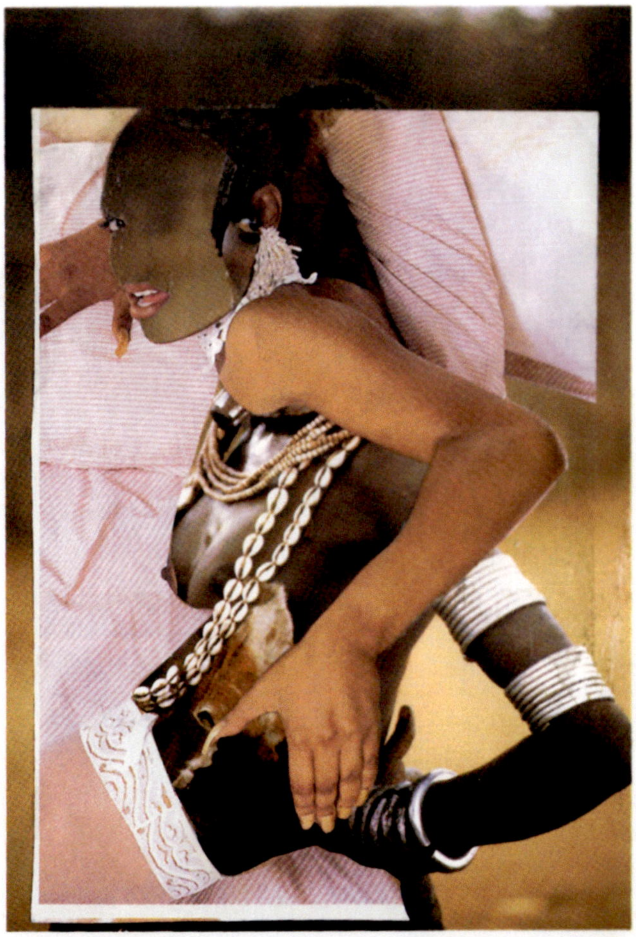

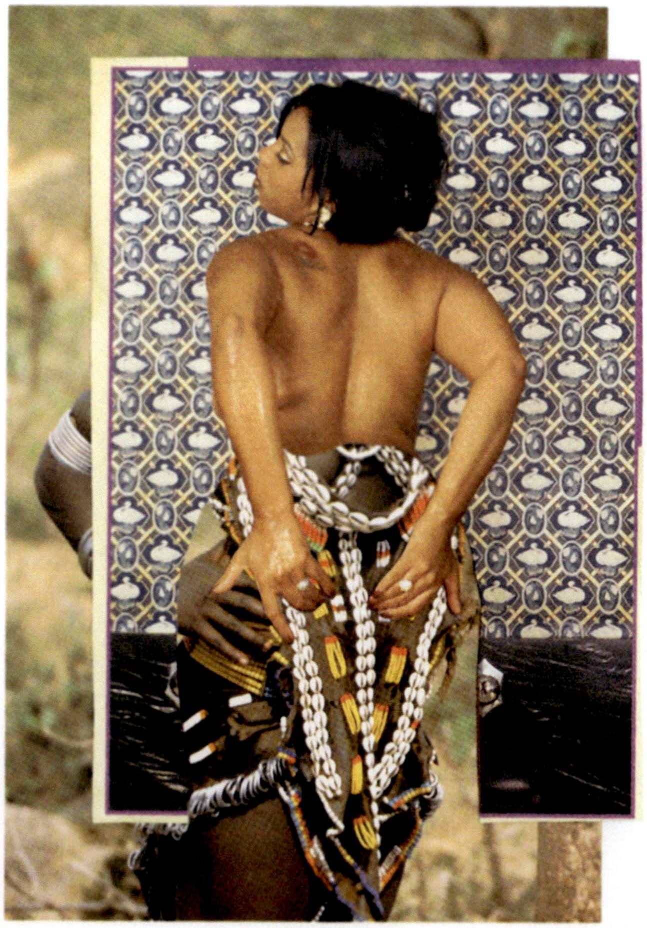

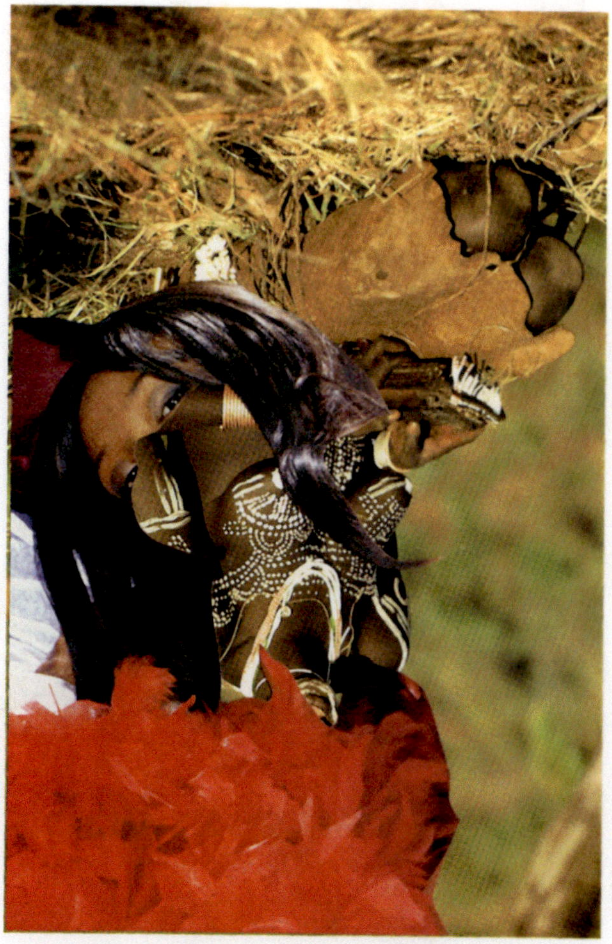

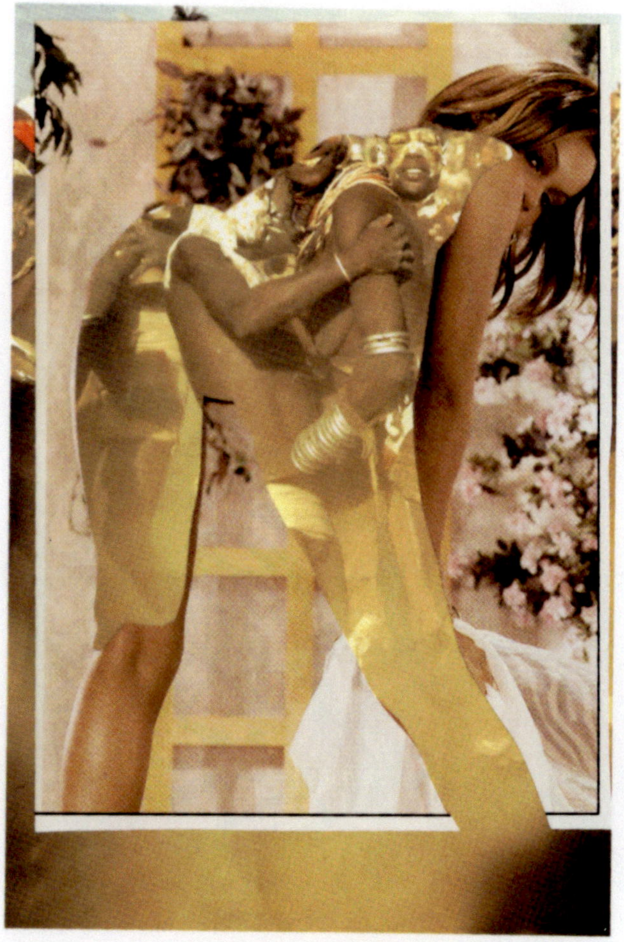

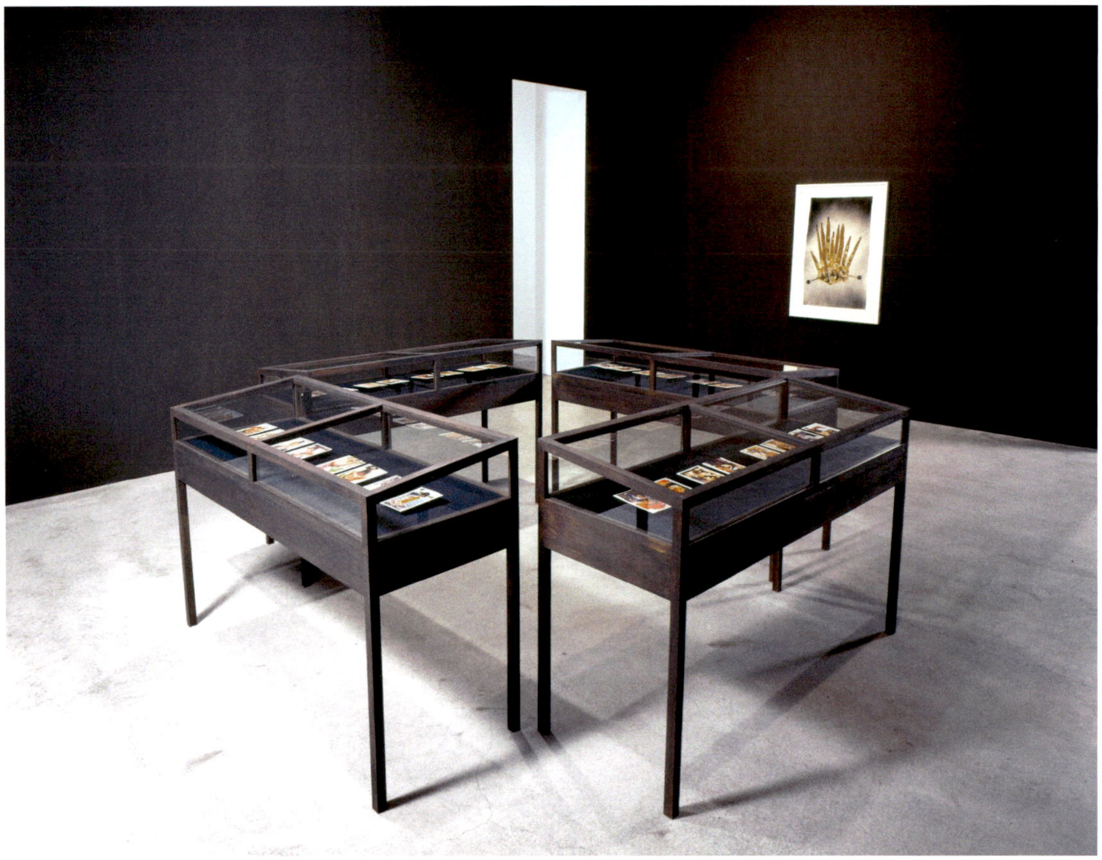

THE ARK COLLECTION, 2006
INSTALLATION VIEW

It is particularly with The Ark Collection project that Mutu's work has been compared to that of Hannah Höch, the German photomontage artist working in the early twentieth century, espeically her series *From an Ethnographic Museum*. At first finding the comparison specious due to art history's ever-easy habit of making comparisons with the European tradition, along with the dyadic structure she perceived in Höch's production, Mutu has more recently embraced the practice of this predecessor, seeing that she also worked in a time of upheaval and that her work was arrayed against ethnic hatred.[28] Indeed, Höch's appraisal in *From an Ethnographic Museum* was aimed at colonial engagement and fantasy in the wake of Germany's waning imperial might following WWI.[29] Her series challenged normative cultural histories, institutions and creative practices.

In *From an Ethnographic Museum,* Höch critiques ethnographically embedded institutions such as Berlin's Museum für Völkerkunde (Museum of Ethnology) and museological method that privileged the sublimation of Africans and others as a method of subjection in the wake of European colonial loss. In the exhibitionary complex Höch saw only slight shades of difference between de jure rule and the manipulation of cultural narratives. In a number of works in Höch's series, such as *Monument II: Vanity* (1926), the artist centralizes the action of the photomontage on a pedestal, critiquing modes of display and value, and like Mutu foregrounding those ideas through the feminine form. Höch also focused on a mediatized culture, occasioned by the explosion of print media in her time, and the depiction of women in it. As Enwezor has indicated, Höch's 'analysis of mass-media images hinged on exploiting the dialectic between primitivism and modernism, ethnography and surrealism, African art and photography.'[30] After Courtney J. Martin, we might see Höch as remaking narrative within collage's concept of disassembly.

As Z.S. Strother has indicated, some early histories of African art in the languages of Europe depended not on trying to understand and contextualize art of that place and people, but were more simply based on obtaining and sequencing photographic images drawn from public and private colonial collections. Such was the case with the book *Negerplastik (Negro Sculpture)* (1915) by the German Carl Einstein. The ninety-four objects of study were photographed in a uniform manner, most often stripped of materials (organic or human in facture) that extended their wooden structure. Circulated as an 'atlas of images' that presented 'stylistic unity', the text in Einstein's *Negerplastik* was more criticism than history.[31] Höch's own piece titled *Negerplastik* (1929) can be seen as taking to task both print and museological spectatorship. But her imagery is similarly a free-hand mix, hardly acknowledging the true sources of Africa's cultures and peoples; it is based in the perception, psychology, and experience of the spectators and not the makers. As Strother remarks, 'There are not many traces of Africa', but instead, as Enwezor intones, a view from the 'ethnographic fetish cabinet.'[32]

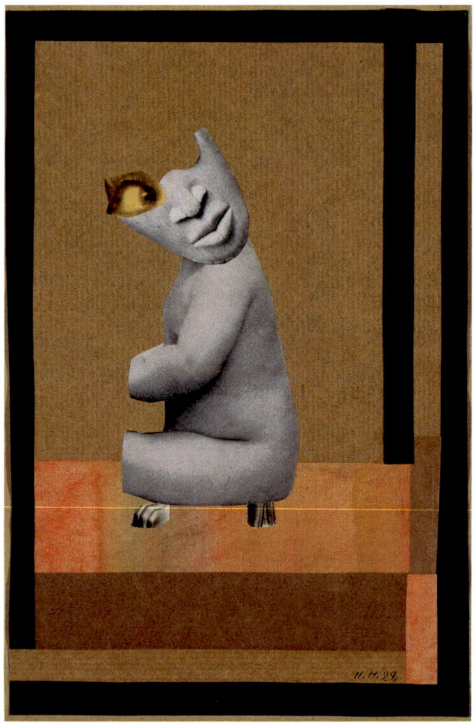

HANNAH HÖCH
AUS DER SAMMLUNG: AUS EINEM ETHNOGRAPHISCHEN MUSEUM, 1929
COLLAGE AND GOUACHE ON PAPER
26 X 18 CM

from top,
THE ARK COLLECTION
(DETAIL), 2006
COLLAGE ON POSTCARD
18 X 12 CM

THE ARK COLLECTION
(DETAIL), 2006
COLLAGE ON POSTCARD
18 X 12 CM

THE ARK COLLECTION
(DETAIL), 2006
COLLAGE ON POSTCARD
18 X 12 CM

THE ARK COLLECTION
(DETAIL), 2006
COLLAGE ON POSTCARD
18 X 12 CM

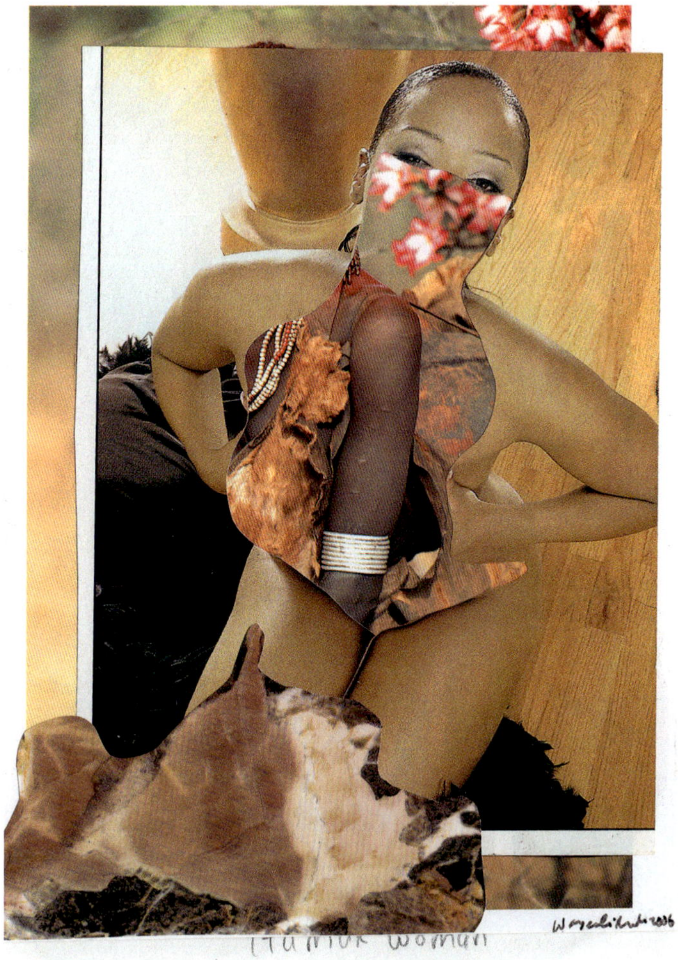

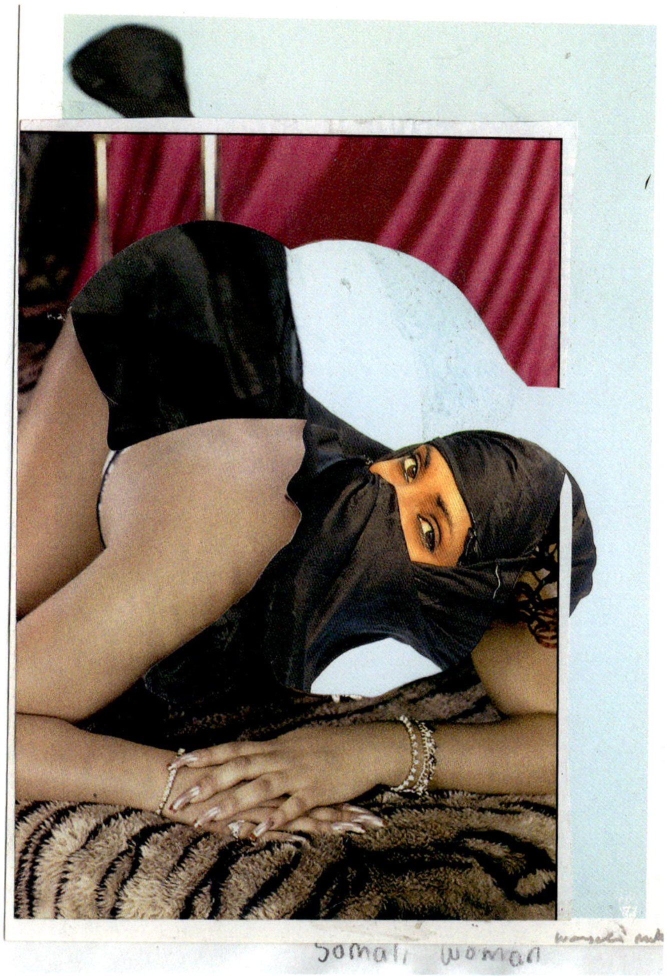

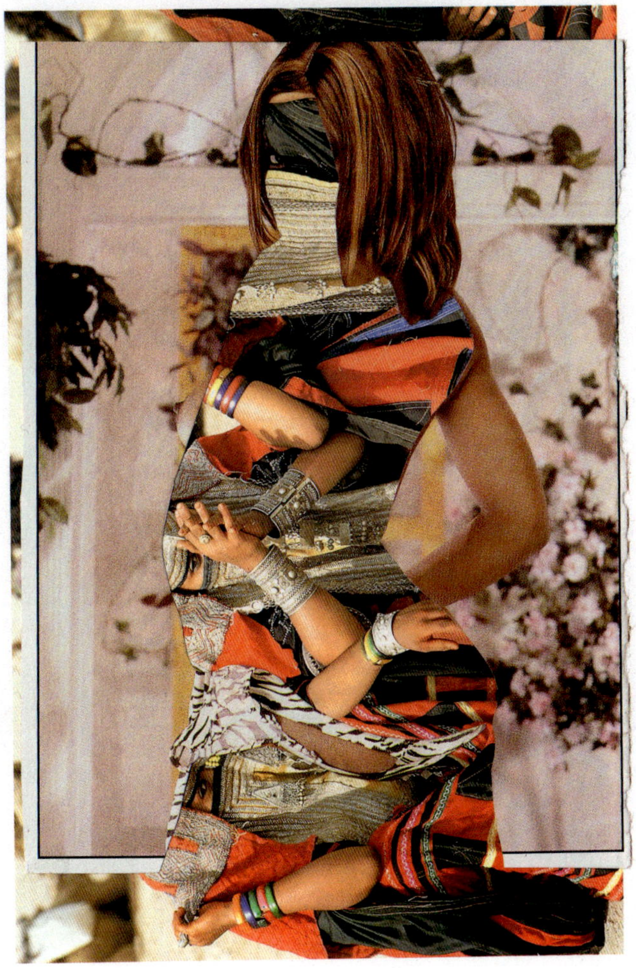

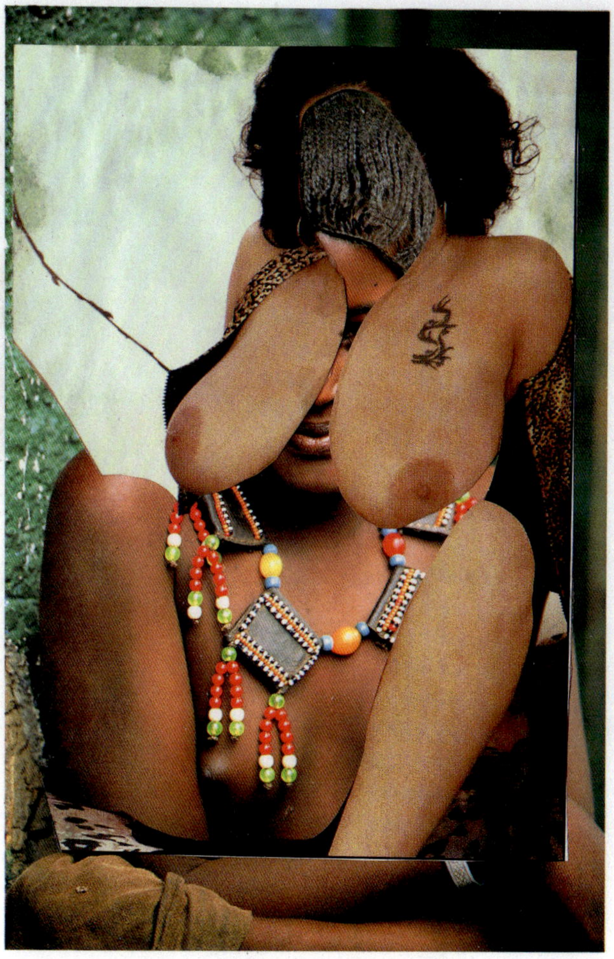

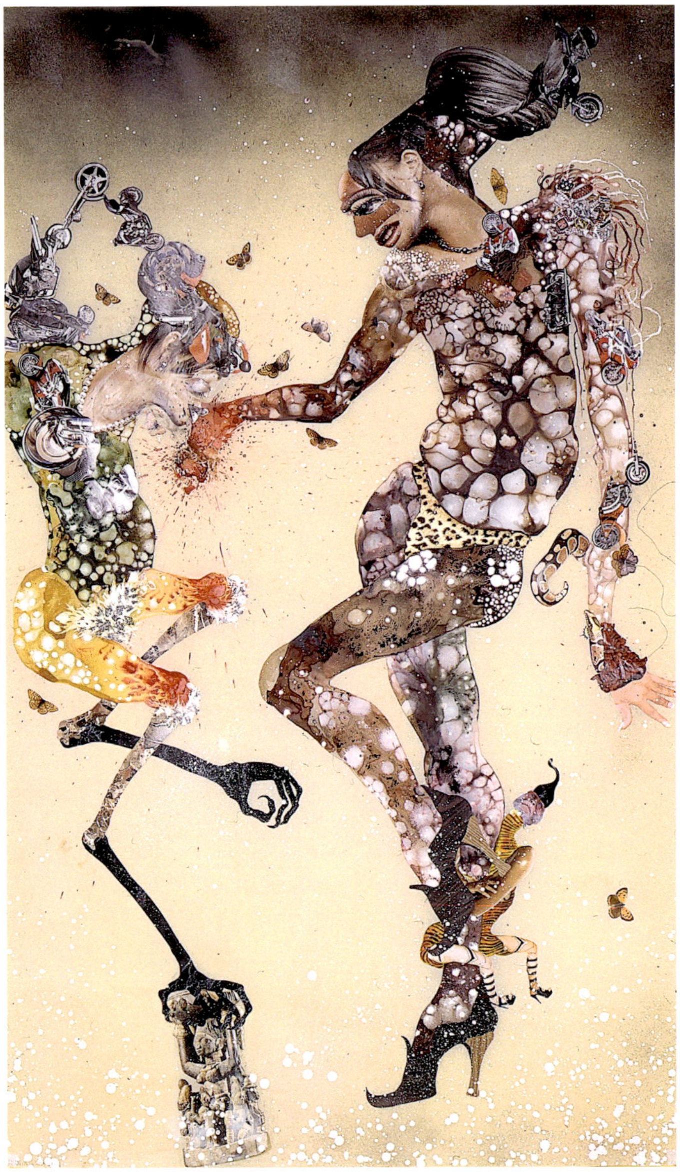

PATRICIAN'S CURSE, 2004
INK, ACRYLIC, COLLAGE AND CONTACT PAPER ON MYLAR
169 X 102 CM

III – Stiletto

The stilettos appear often in my work, especially the collages. I have contradictory reasons for using them – they're weapons, prosthetics, embellishments, armor, and obviously, titillating power symbols. High heels are the quintessential heightening apparatus that constrains and deforms the body whilst functioning as an indicator of modernity, urbanization and 'foreign' ideals of beauty.[33]

If paper was Mutu's first muse, the second was shoes. They begin showing up in the sketchbooks and become painted details in the Pin Up series. In *The Ark Collection* they appear as pleasurable features, fetishes ripped from porn magazines. While versions of stilettos abound in pieces like *The Patrician's New Curse* (2004), or *Lockness* (2006), limbs are equally likely to end in bird-like claws, or the mechanical wheels, gears and frames clipped from publications like *Motorbike*.[34] Those two works are exemplary of how Mutu's images explode, carving out ever-larger spaces for themselves as she moves from collage on paper to those on Mylar or contact paper – high-tensile plastic sheeting that was durable and allowed her to control water-based pigment and expand from the intimacy of magazine scale to more than six feet.[35]

In Mutu's large, mural-like collages, watercolor is substituted with ink, and the artist is able to achieve a mottled definition primarily applied to the skin or bodily surfaces, adding more dimension and depth. While Mutu herself acknowledges Romare Bearden as important to her own sense of development, this is not just defined by the cut-and-pasted assembly of collage. It is also in the painterliness onto which Bearden held throughout his career, from 1940s ink and watercolours on paper whose strong composed sections of black lines herald his coming collage practice, to experiments with abstract piecing, to later landscapes and monotypes, so much so that he understood the work that would become his mature practice as 'collage paintings'.[36] Mutu's facility with the play of surface and atmospheric

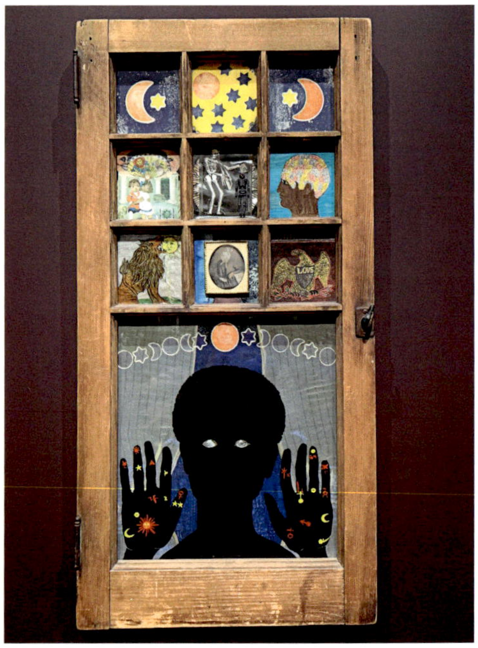

BETYE SAAR
BLACK GIRL'S WINDOW, 1969
WOODEN WINDOW FRAME WITH PAINT, CUT-AND-PASTED PRINTED AND PAINTED PAPERS, DAGUERREOTYPE, LENTICULAR PRINT, AND PLASTIC FIGURINE
91 X 46 X 4 CM

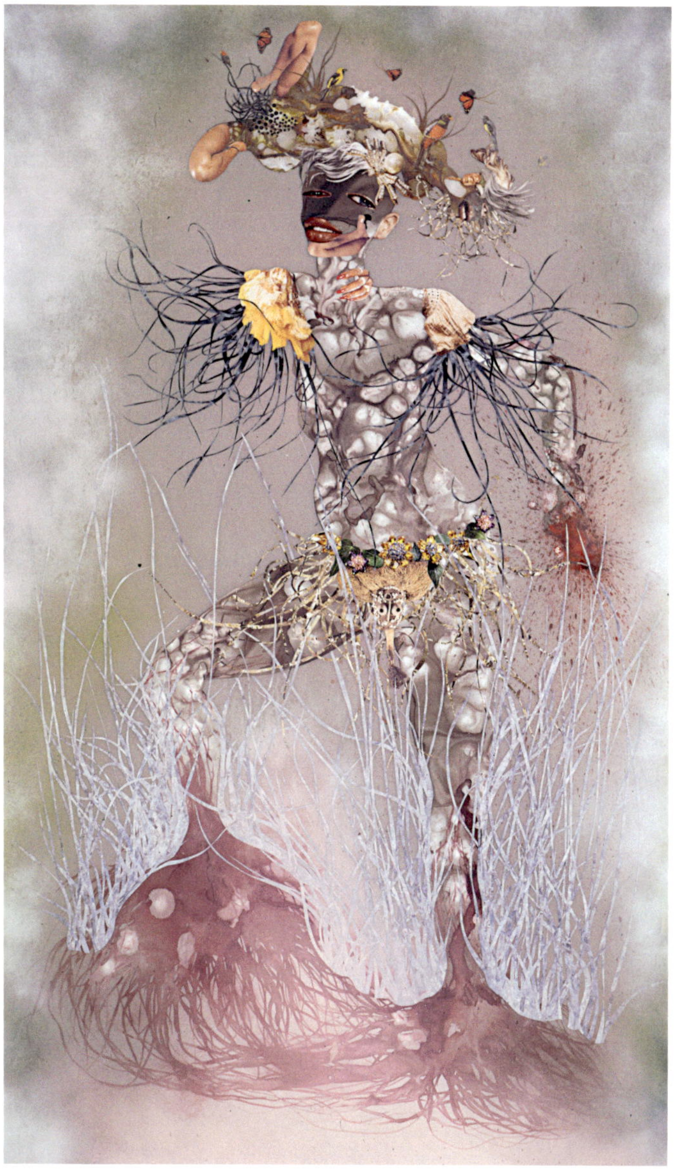

ME CARRY MY HEAD ON MY HOME ON MY HEAD, 2005
INK, ACRYLIC, GLITTER, CONTACT PAPER AND COLLAGE ON MYLAR
224 X 131 CM

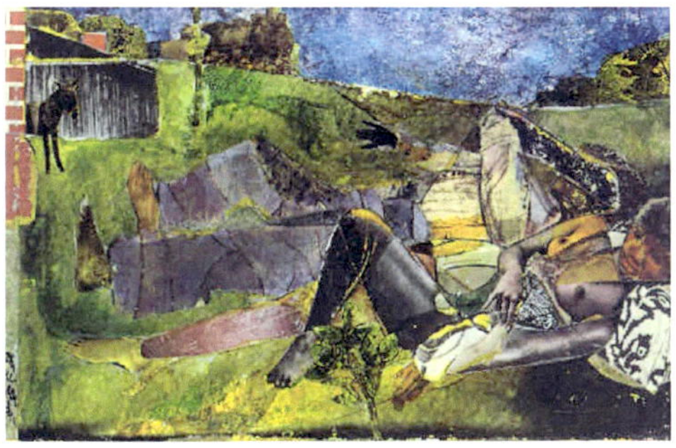

ROMARE H. BEARDEN
DOWN HOME, ALSO, 1971
PHOTOCOLLAGE
24 X 38 CM

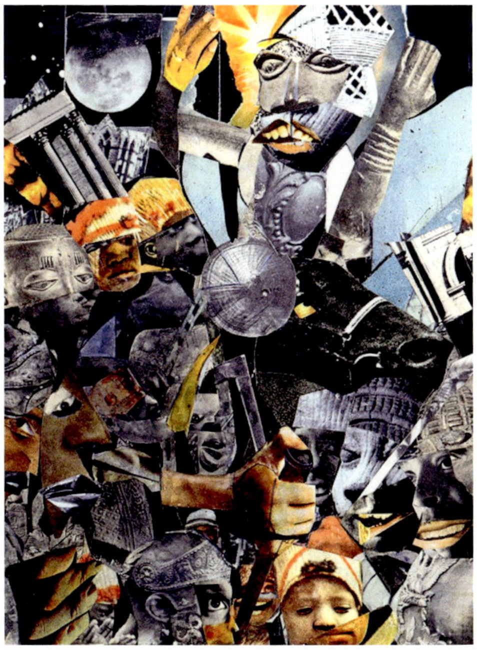

ROMARE H. BEARDEN
SERMONS: THE WALLS OF JERICHO, 1964
COLLAGE OF PRINTED PAPERS, PAINT, INK AND GRAPHITE PENCIL ON BOARD
30 X 24 CM

ground is seen in large pieces such as *She's Egungun Again* (2005) and *Me Carry My Head on My Home on My Head* (2004), where painting merges seamlessly with collage, held fast and even amplified by its synthetic paper base. The dialogue between collage and painting is subtle, obscured, worked through; we glean the excitement of mixing media, the gracefulness of the join. We can compare Mutu's touch in such pieces to Betye Saar's assemblages, in which her painterly hand, often unremarked, contributes much to creating a sense of the work's wholeness.

Bearden's celebration of the Black female nude in classic Western art poses of bath and brothel also famously used pornography (see *Down Home, Also* or *The Apprenticeship of Jelly Roll Morton*, both 1971, for example). The problematizing of this aspect of his practice after his death would have been part of Mutu's New York art education in the 1990s.[37] But there was also Bearden's decades-long engagement with African art. He remarked on the show 'African Negro Art' at New York's Museum of Modern Art in the spring of 1935 and on his desire 'to try and understand the African vision of the world' in structure and design.[38] Pieces that do just that, *Village of Yo* and *Sermons: Walls of Jericho,* date from 1964, when his turn to collage set him on the road to art stardom. The confluence of African subject matter in the midst of the US Civil Rights and African independence movements only added to the power of Bearden's new course. For him, Africa was also embedded in African America and Black diasporic life, and the secular and spiritual rituals around which much of his oeuvre revolved. Iconographies of women roam throughout his work, from sensual muses to formidable healers or Conjur women. However, *Sermons: Walls of Jericho* also holds lessons for our understanding of Mutu's practice here, summoning an African American spiritual (and Bible passage) in which the sounding of righteous trumpets brings down the walls of oppression, vanquishing tyrants. In the midst of late twentieth-century decolonial movements, Bearden pounds the alarm.[39]

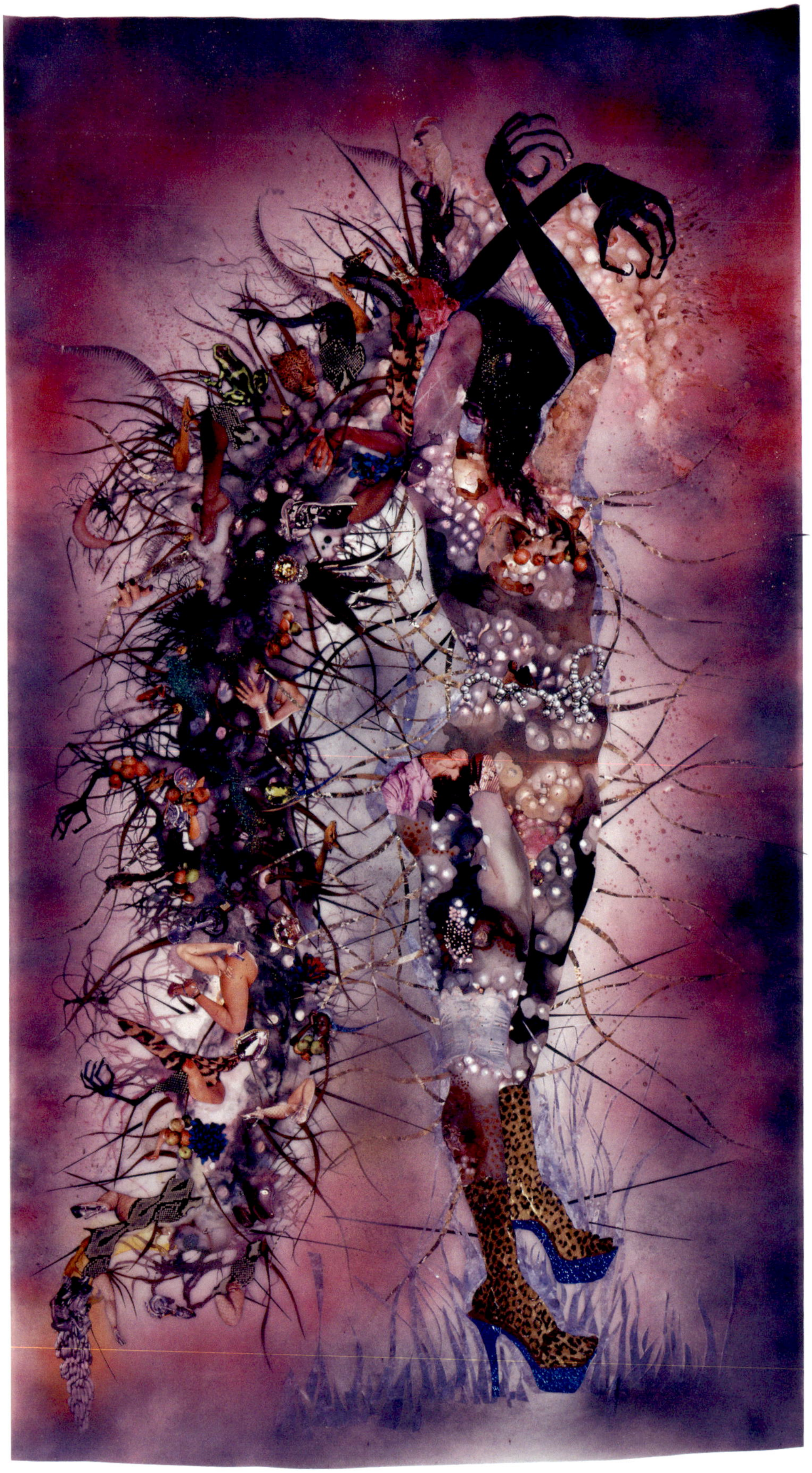

LOCKNESS, 2006
MIXED MEDIA ON MYLAR
242 X 137 CM

SHE'S EGUNGUN AGAIN, 2005
INK, ACRYLIC, COLLAGE AND
CONTACT PAPER ON MYLAR
221 X 133 CM

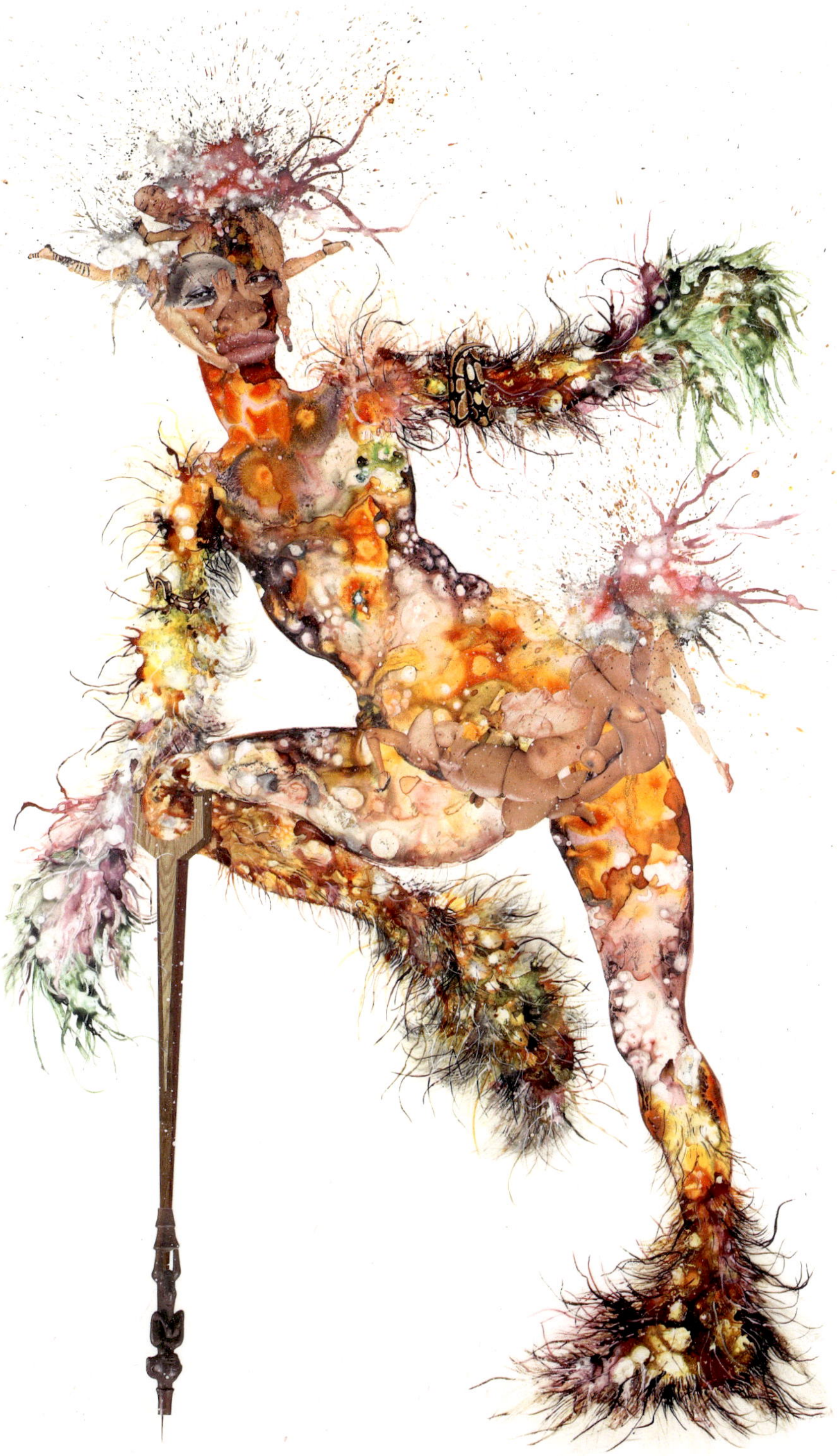

While African mask forms seem to have been preferred by Bearden, Mutu is partial to the sculptural. In *Sleeping Sickness Saved Me* (2005) the bottom-most of three cavorting figures arches her back and throws her legs in the air, one ending in a Fang head, the other in a seated wooden figure. She balances on other sculptural tiers, one a traditional neck or head rest. In the diptych *People in Glass Towers Should Not Imagine Us* (2003) neck/headrests become the stiletto heels of one siren who crouches in leopard-skin boots and a bodysuit, her coiffure a mix of more sculpture. A prosthesis in *She's Egungun Again* models a West African staff. In these works, traditional sculpture from West and Central Africa literally provides physical but also divine support.[40]

In other more intimate collages from the same time period – *Mask (Yoruba)* (2006) and *Pin-Up* (2005) – masks overlay and fill up the bodies of women drawn from skin magazines. In *Pin-Up* a deep ebony head with exquisitely patterned hair pairs with black fishnets; however, the stand-out is the red patent-leather platform stilettos, connecting a sexual obsession with footwear and feet to Western beliefs that African objects belonged only to the 'ethnographic fetish cabinet'.

In their unification of 'human, animal, plant, and mechanical parts' the protagonists in Mutu's large collages have been characterized as cyborgs.[41] They access the parahuman or posthuman, living beyond binaries. They are also vehicles to upend social hierarchies, fusions that transgress boundaries, their speculative forms unlocking possibilities. These figures wander, opening new pathways, proclaiming the right to reassemble, reconfigure, regenerate; their mischievous body parts rebel against norms both social and material. In doing so, Mutu's configurations speak to 'experiences of alienation and dislocation'.[42] As Zakiyyah Iman Jackson reminds us, 'antiblackness produces differential biocultural effects of gender and sex', with the colonized nonwhite body that is female always already not a woman but some kind of machine of production and reproduction.[43] Or as Tiffany E. Barber asks, 'is Black womanhood always already cyborgian?'[44]

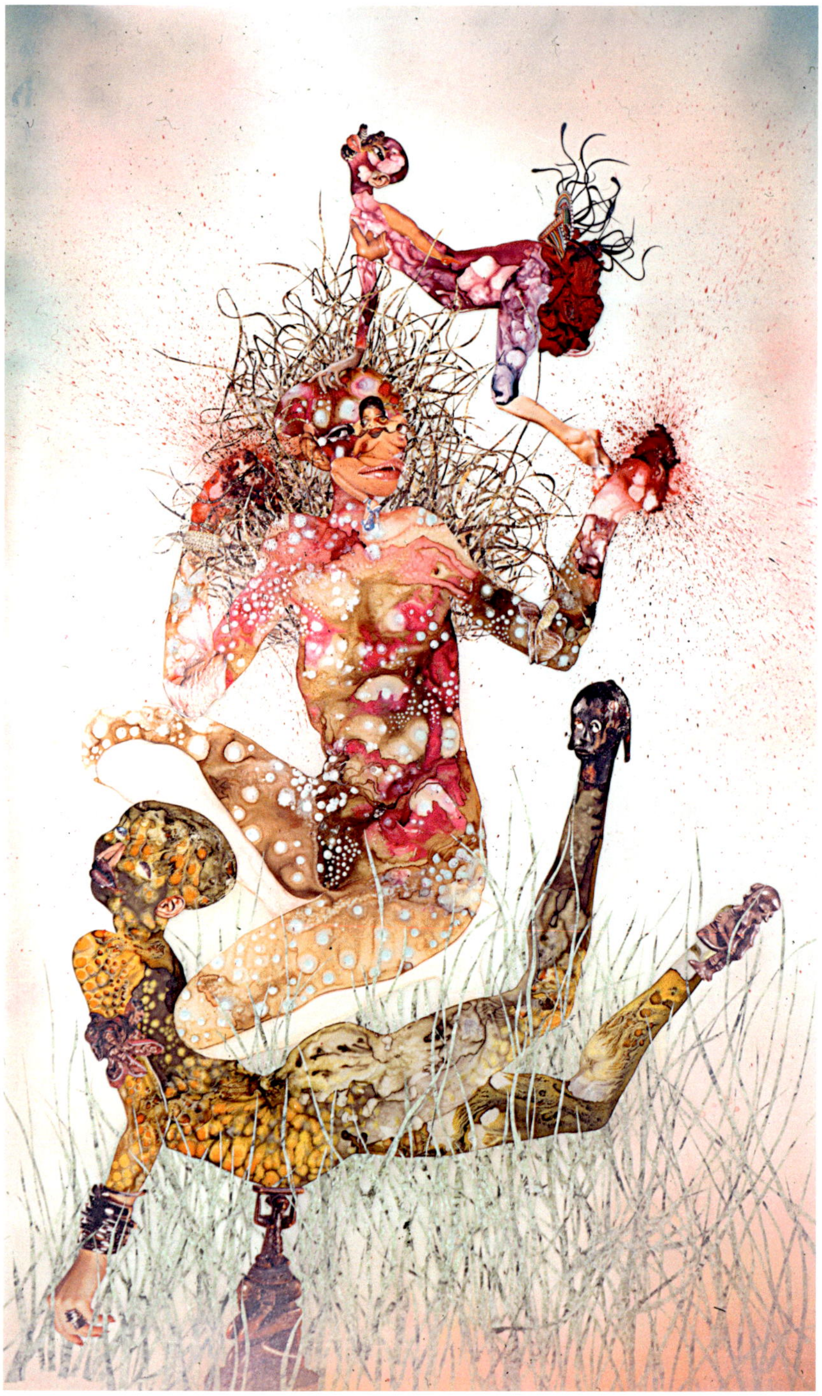

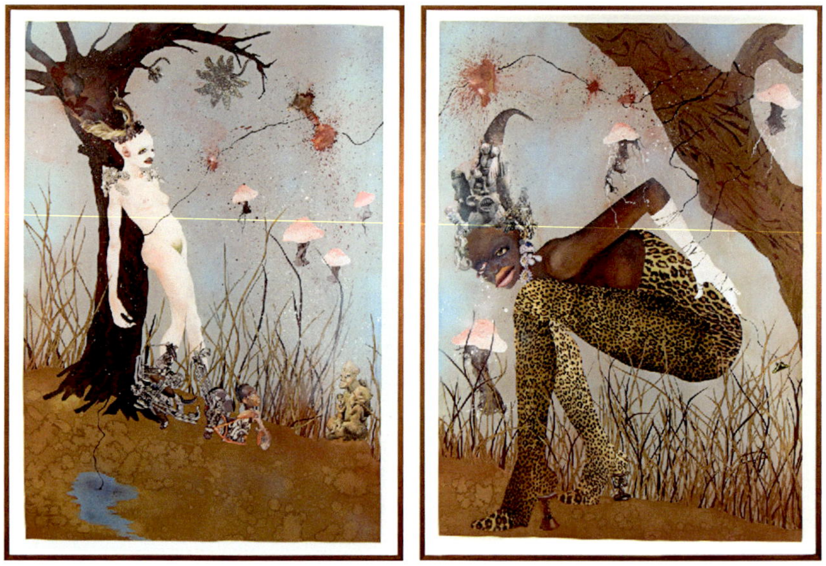

opposite, from top,
SLEEPING SICKNESS SAVED ME, 2005
INK, ACRYLIC, GLITTER, FUR, CONTACT PAPER AND COLLAGE ON MYLAR
219 X 130 CM

PEOPLE IN GLASS TOWERS SHOULD NOT IMAGINE US, 2003
MIXED MEDIA COLLAGE ON PAPER
356 X 259 CM

from top,
BEDROOM MASK, 2006
CONTACT PAPER AND PHOTO COLLAGE
166 X 12 CM

BEDROOM MASK, 2005
INK AND MAGAZINE COLLAGE
20 X 10 CM

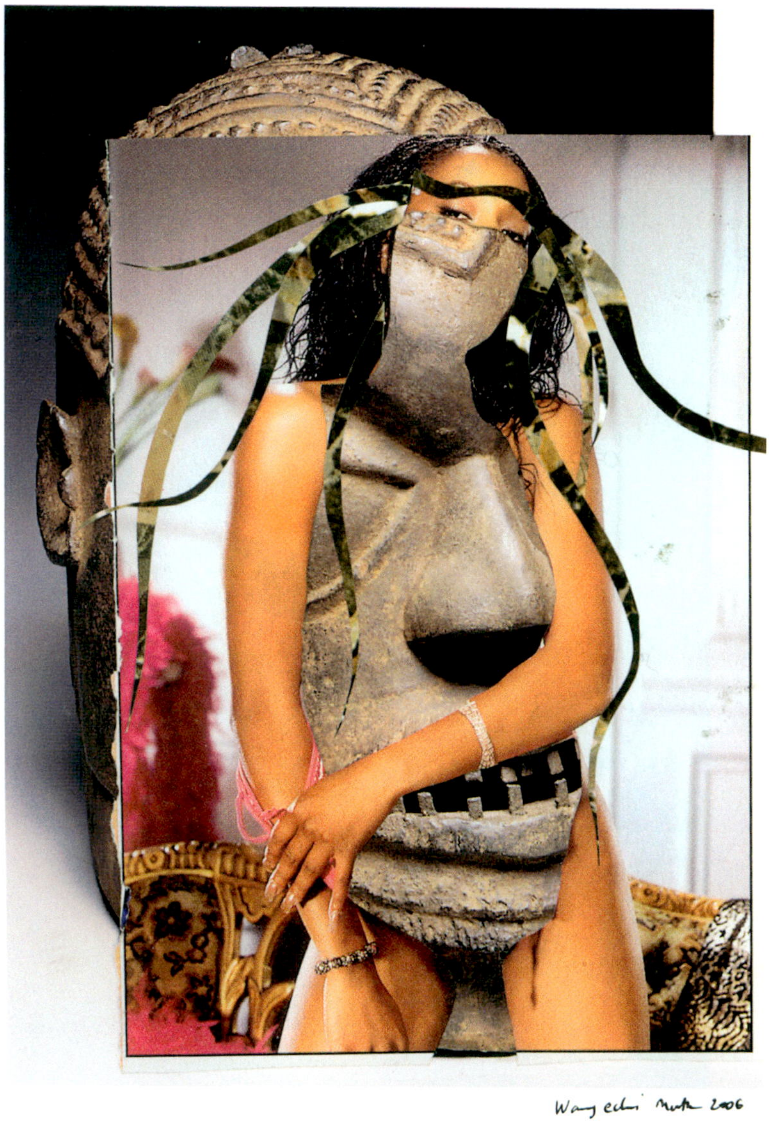

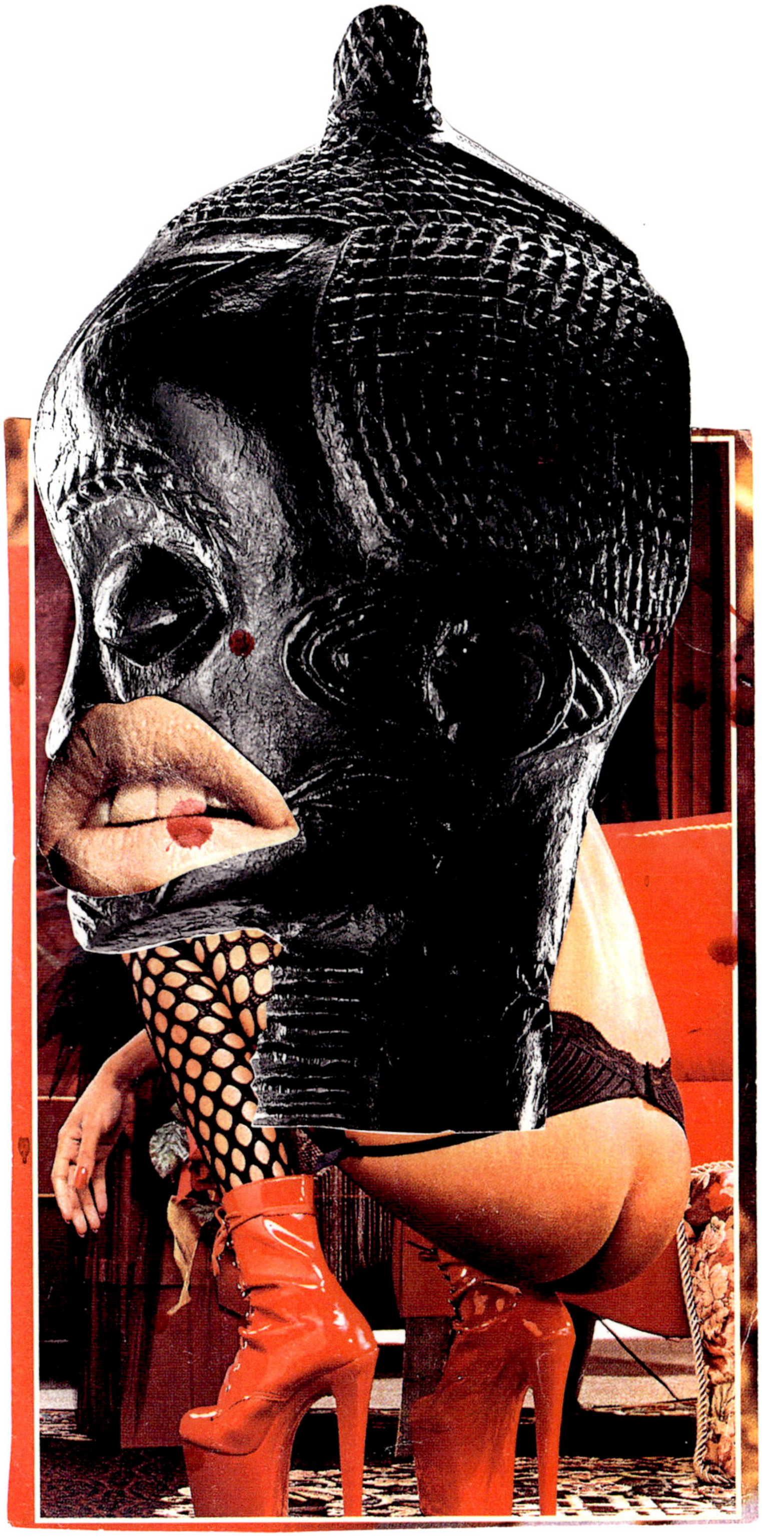

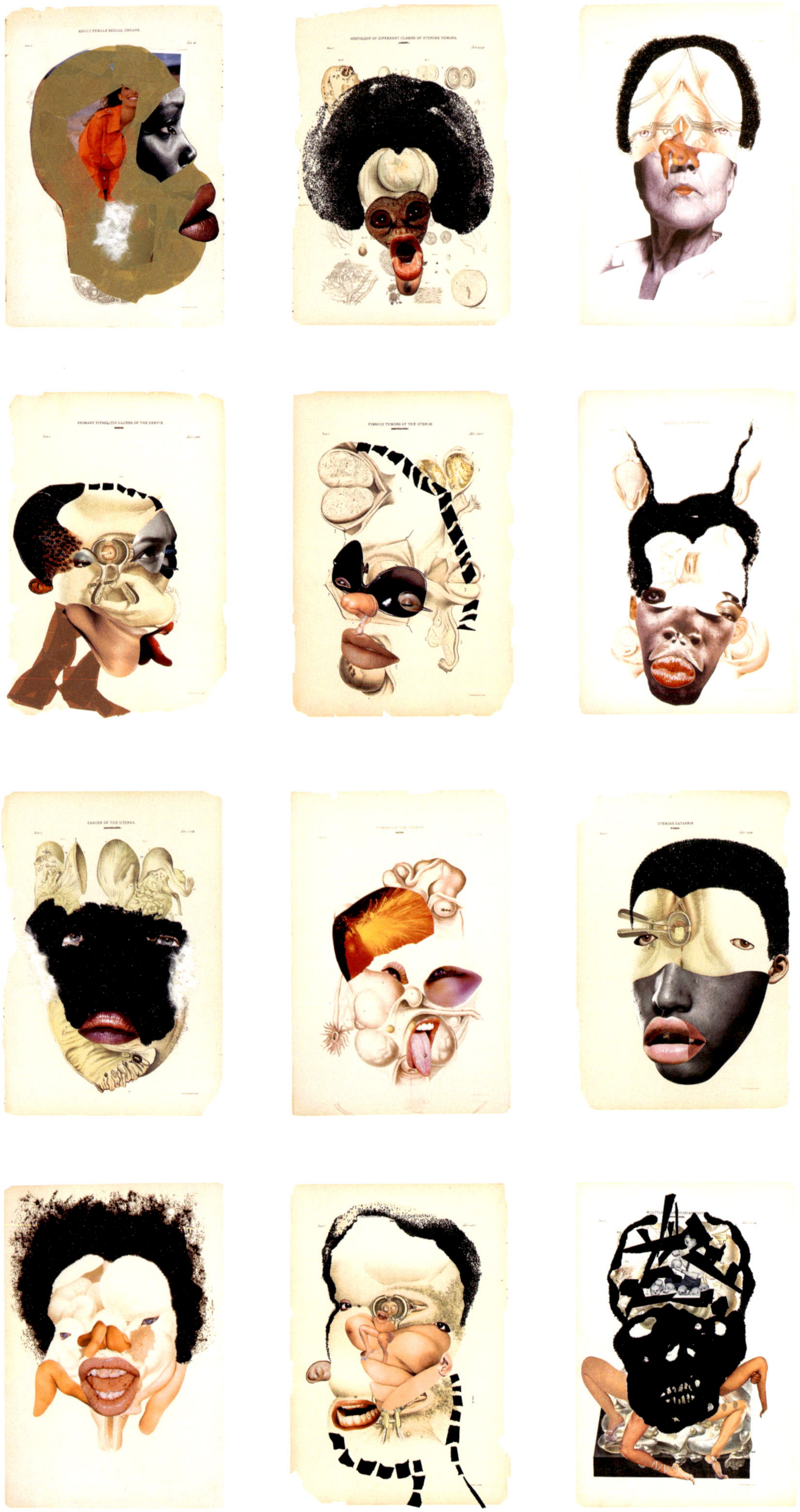

HISTOLOGY OF THE DIFFERENT CLASSES OF UTERINE TUMORS, 2006
GLITTER, INK, COLLAGE ON FOUND MEDICAL ILLUSTRATION PAPER
12 PARTS
EACH 58 X 43 CM

FLORAL INSIDEOUT I & II, 2018
WATERCOLOUR AND COLLAGE
ON PAPER
EACH 31 X 41 CM

Yet there is no question that the wanderings and reconfigurations of Mutu's figures do decolonial work. As curator Trevor Schoonmaker writes, Mutu's is a 'transformative aesthetic', where 'altered, fragmented, reassembled' materials perform a critique.[45] With wit and humour, these mobile and disidentificatory pieces disturb and seek to dismantle colonial taxonomies and ontologies.[46] One such series, *Histology of the Different Classes of Uterine Tumors* (2005), takes found vintage medical illustrations of female genital conditions and turns them into a dozen portraits. Glitter, ink, fur and body parts drawn from the same mix of fashion, skin and ethnographic magazines fill in facial features. In relying on watercolour, ink and paper here, Mutu also takes up the tools of those who charted the project of empire centuries earlier: 'geologists, archeologists, surveyors and mapmakers'.[47] Her humorous incongruities push against the notion of the incontrovertible evidence of medical science, and remind us that exactly because Black women were categorized as outside 'biopolitical calculations of personhood' gave white male doctors license to look, disfigure, debilitate.[48]

In the collages and her practice as a whole, Mutu conjures materials and figures that are wayward and willful. They exceed negation in their decolonial aims, and as Sarah Ahmed suggests, are 'heard as assertive'. She continues, 'some have to find voices because others are given voices; some have to assert their particulars because others have their particulars given a general expression'.[49] Mutu's characterization of the images as 'Female-ish' speaks to their intersubjectivity and transgender aspects.[50] This 'provocation and radical utterance' at the core of her practice bespeaks a commitment to plural and queer subjectivities.[51] The hyperbolic and excessive formations in her work are celebrations of the ecstasy in multiplicity that embellish what Nash identifies as 'paradoxes of pleasure rather than woundedness' that encompass and complicate: 'pleasures in looking, pleasures in being looked at, pleasures in performing racial fictions, pleasures in upending racial fictions'.[52]

At the same time, it is hard to overlook the torn flesh and spraying blood throughout Mutu's collages, often paired with references to consumption, as in *The Patrician's New Curse*, in which one being gnaws at the hand of another. Yet the violence that is so clearly on view is not just there to be dismantled; it effects resilience, claiming and embracing what the body has been through, scars and all.[53] Following Legacy Russell, we can see that what Mutu's visual technologies endeavour to bring into view is living as a 'machinery, that innovates, builds, resists'.[54] We might say it is based in a digital 'Black gooey',[55] the blur, stickiness, muck of disinformation with the potential to undermine gender as a hierarchy of specific social and cultural performances. The artist's gambols across and between media also expose shared spaces 'where pleasure and danger bleed into each other in messy ways'.[56]

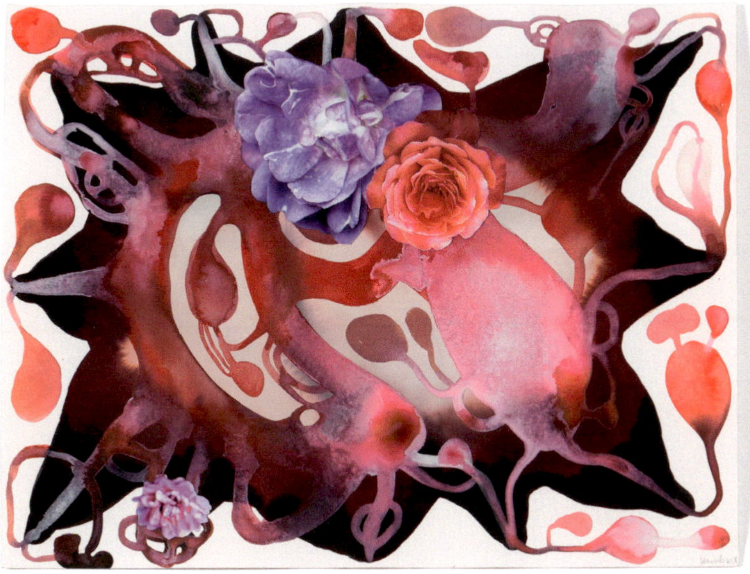

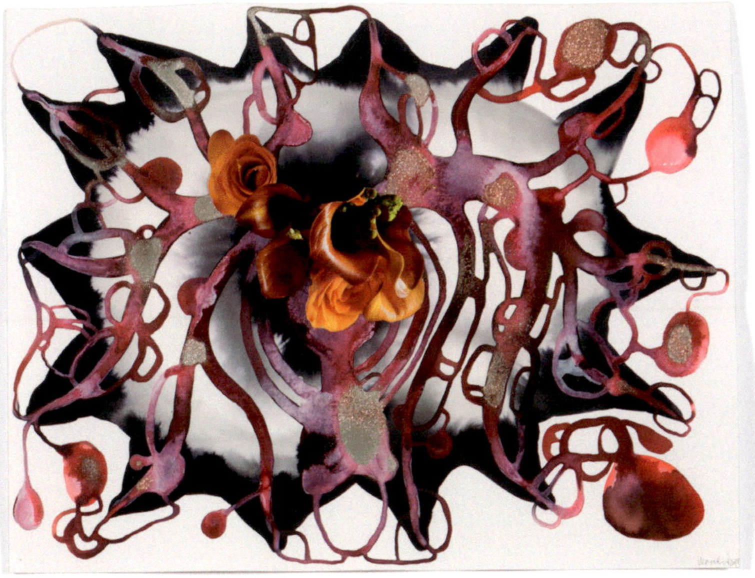

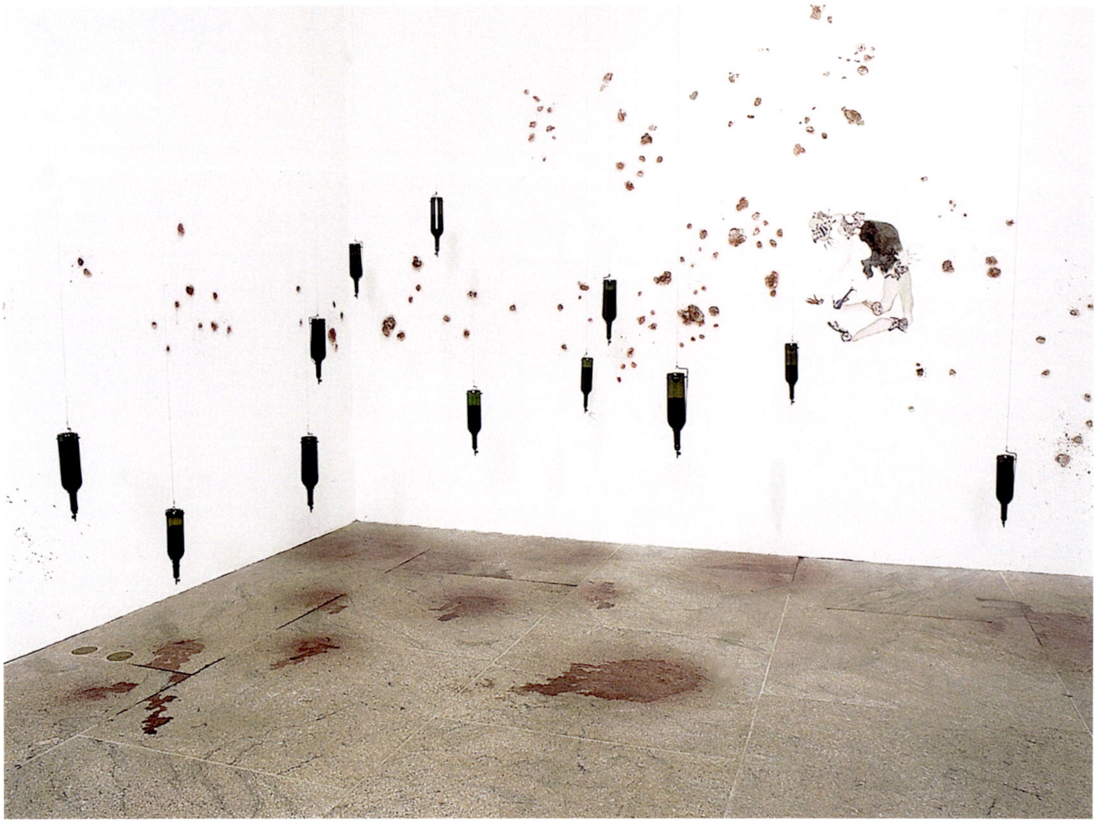

HANGIN' IN TEXAS, 2004
MIXED MEDIA
DIMENSIONS VARIABLE

INSTALLATION VIEW AT
ARTPACE, SAN ANTONIO, 2004

opposite,
ERASING INFESTATION: AN EXERCISE IN HISTORICAL FUTILITY (DETAIL), 2005
MIXED MEDIA
DIMESNIONS VARIABLE

ERASING INFESTATION: AN EXERCISE IN HISTORICAL FUTILITY, 2005
MIXED MEDIA
DIMESNIONS VARIABLE

INSTALLATION VIEW AT SUSAN VIELMETTER PROJECTS, LOS ANGELES, 2005

IV – Nguva

While Mutu's collages have always generated excitement, we should remember that she was trained as a sculptor, that her interest in the interface and intersection of things comes from three-dimensional thinking. Indeed, parallel to her pieces on paper she worked on room-scale installations, initially tying them to the wall and eventually moving into space. We can map the emergence of this idea in works created from 2004–06 under the title 'wounded wall'. Begun while she was in residence at San Antonio's ArtPace in 2004, Mutu bored into a wall using tools that punctured, scarred and tortured it. These markings are irregular lacerations, but also appear to ooze like infected sores. Freed from the rectangular, three of Mutu's figures bounce across the architectural surface in *Hanging in Texas* (2004). Arrayed with pelts, and less glamorous than her stand-alone beauties, one shoots into the head of another.[57] For Mutu, attacking the wall channelled her frustrations with war (in the world and on the continent of Africa), but was also triggered by scrimmages at the nearby US/Mexico border.[58]

In later iterations of the wounded-wall concept the artist replaces full bodies with the repetition of simpler forms. In Erasing Infestation – *An Exercise in Historical Futility* (2005), spiders composed of packing tape leave lesions across the surface, their limbs reaching around a corner and seemingly 'infecting' the large collage *Royal Blue Arachnid Curse* (2005), which bears the same markings. Or there is the portrait head, horizontal or falling, decapitated and decaying on the battlefield, as in *Sleeping Heads on Wounded Wall* (2006), shown in Toronto, their disfigurations and the oozing red gashes reverberating against a delicate sky-blue background. We might say the genre of portraiture is broadened, unnervingly so, by Mutu's practice, along the throughline between that work and the Histologies series created in this same moment, as well as the floating decapitation of the later and larger collage *Fallen Heads* (2010).

Scholars such as Rinaldo Walcott and Kristine Stiles have commented on the forensic facet of Mutu's art that Stiles sees as a scientific investigation unfolding across media and revealing 'the crime scenes of sexism, racism, classism, colonialism, and speciesism'.[59] For Walcott, Mutu sifts through and analyzes a colonial imaginary and its histories, scientific gazes and monstrous science.[60] Perhaps the most direct sense of this is found in the artist's *Our lost mind finding a heart in dutty water* (2007). A later conceptualization of the wounded wall, here a scrim eerily lit from behind features red punctures up above that become larger tumbling skulls as they reach the bottom. The floor itself is covered with a pool of liquid and sinuous lines of plastic tubing ending in various stilettos.

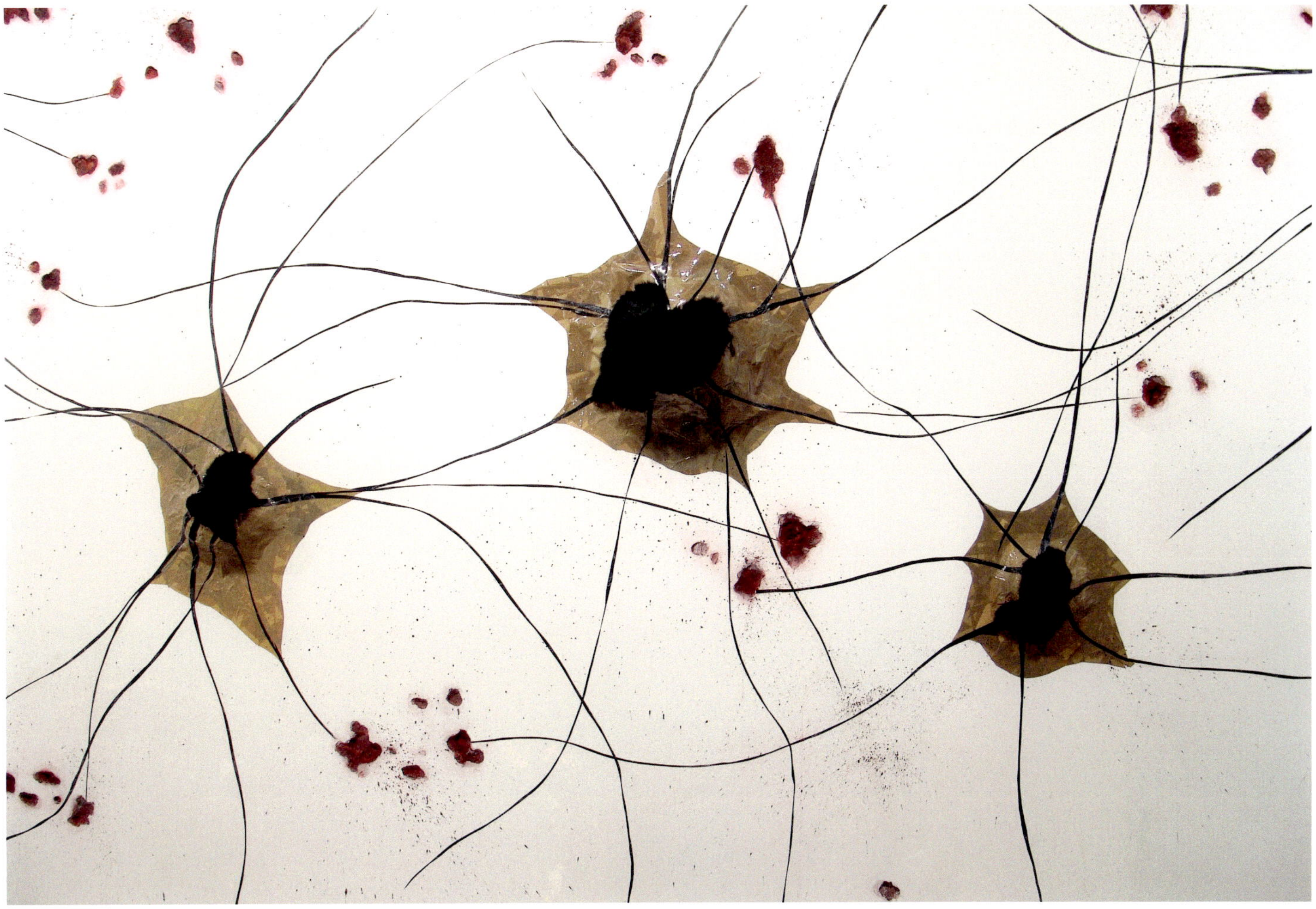

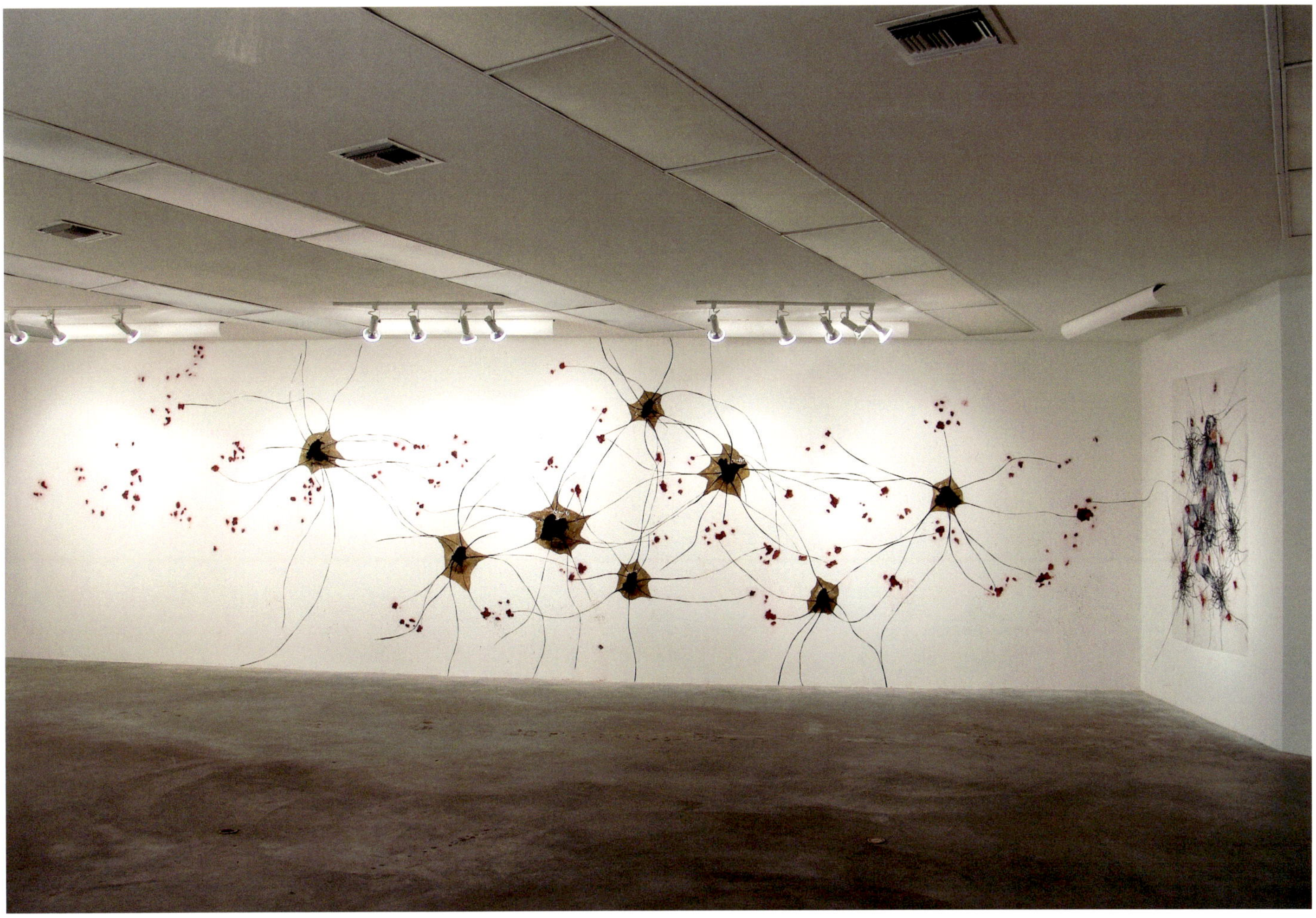

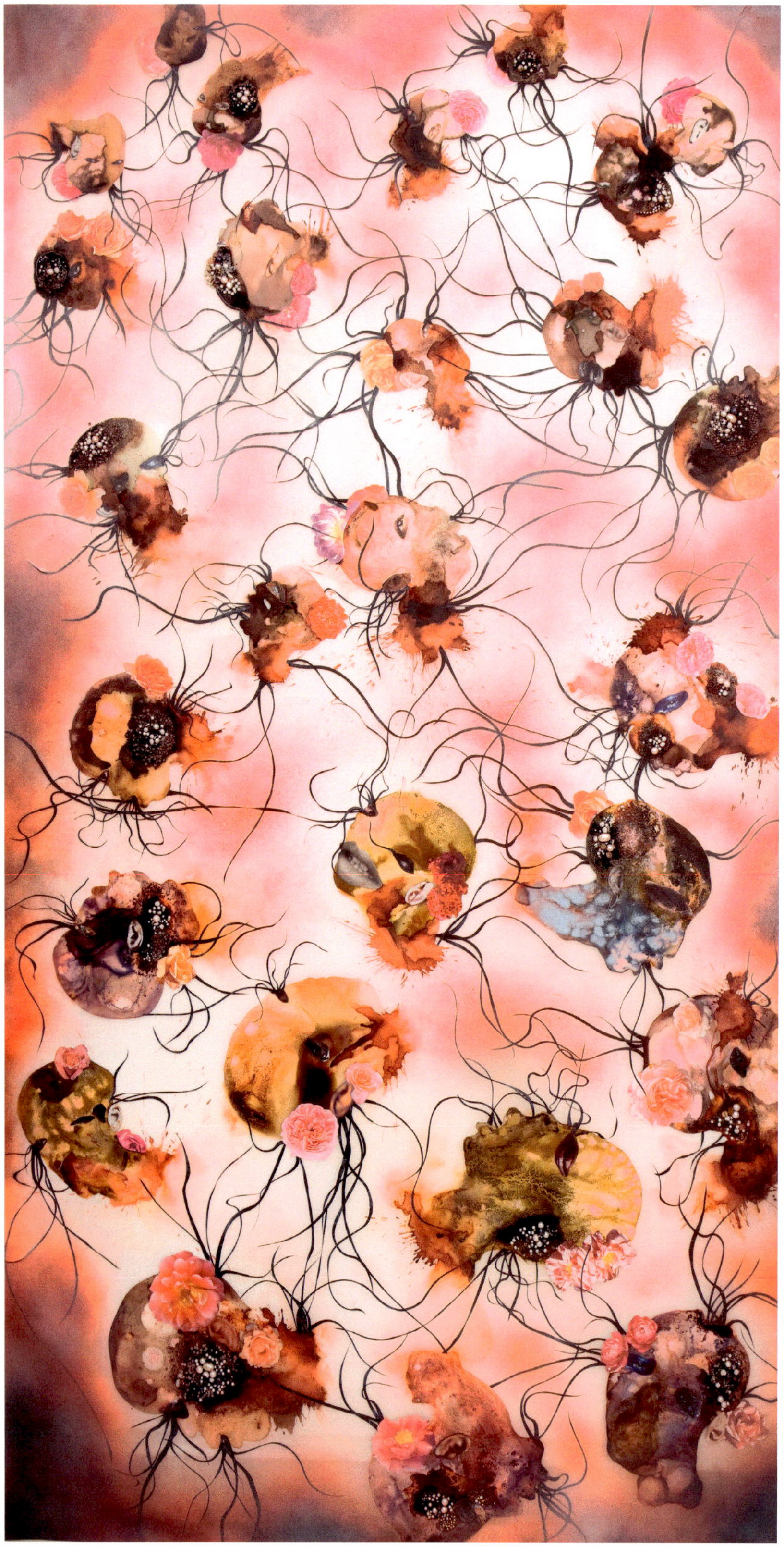

left,
FALLEN HEADS, 2010
PHOTO PRINTED CURTAINS,
COLLAGE VINYL TUBING,
ACRYLIC HEELS, WOOD, METAL
BASIN, LIGHT BULBS
DIMENSIONS VARIABLE

bottom,
ROYAL BLUE ARACHNID, 2005
INK, ACRYLIC, COLLAGE AND
CONTACT PAPER ON MYLAR
197 X 131 CM

opposite, from top,
OUR LOST MIND FINDING
HEART IN DUTTY WATER,
2007–09
PHOTO PRINTED CURTAINS,
COLLAGE VINYL TUBING,
ACRYLIC HEELS, WOOD, METAL
BASIN, LIGHT BULBS
DIMENSIONS VARIABLE

INSTALLATION VIEW AT
VICTORIA MIRO, LONDON, 2009

SLEEPING HEADS, 2006
MIXED MEDIA COLLAGES
ON MYLAR
WOUNDED WALL INSTALLATION
DONE ON SITE: LATEX WITH
HOLES
EACH APPROX 43 X 56 CM

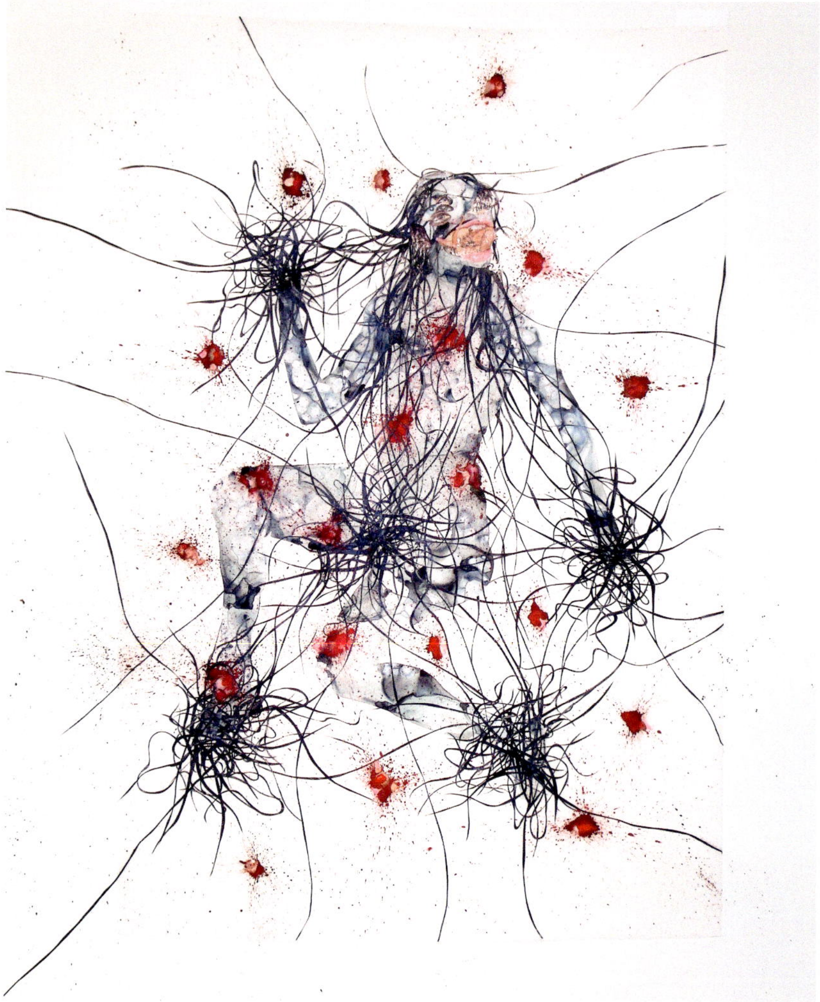

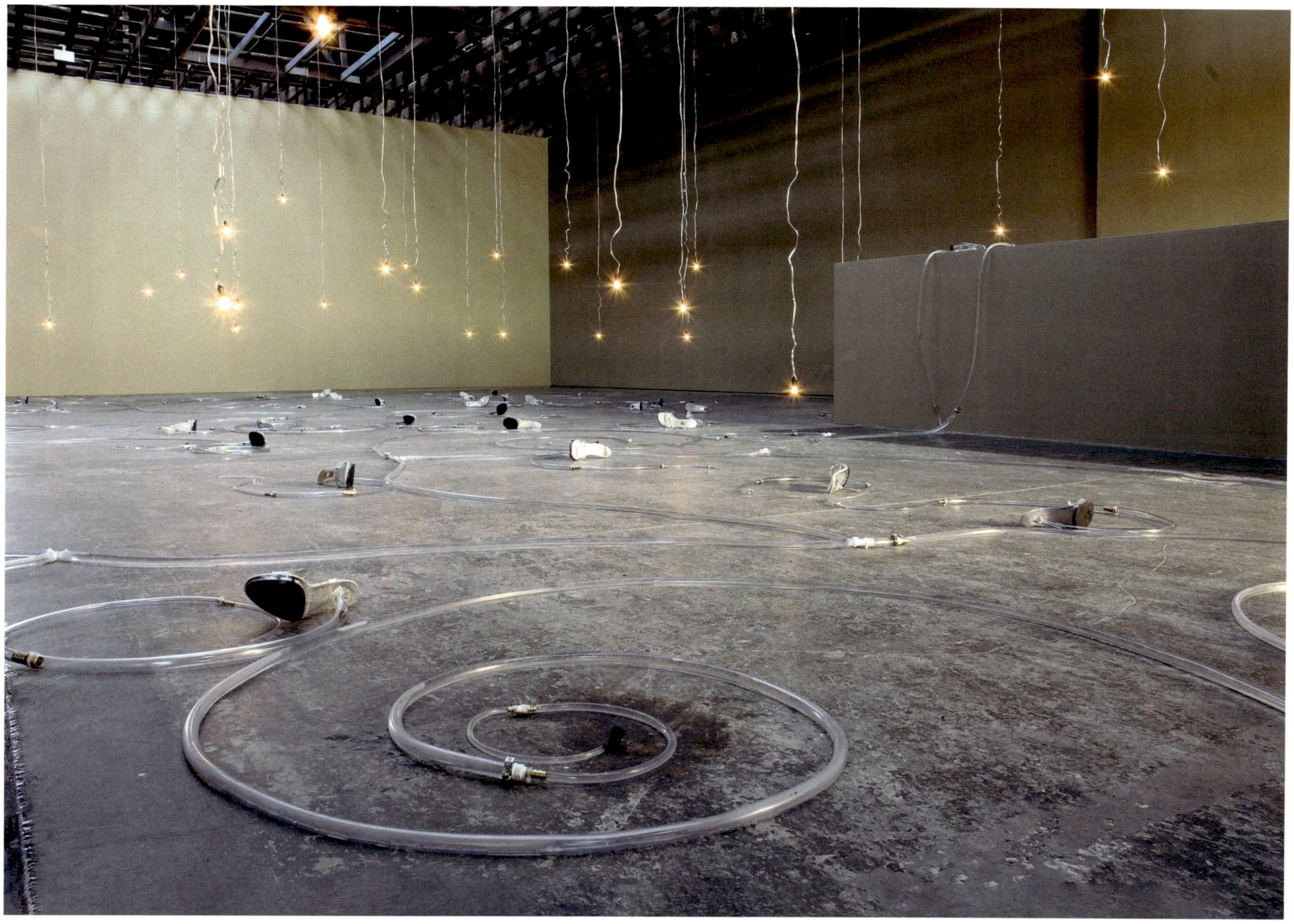

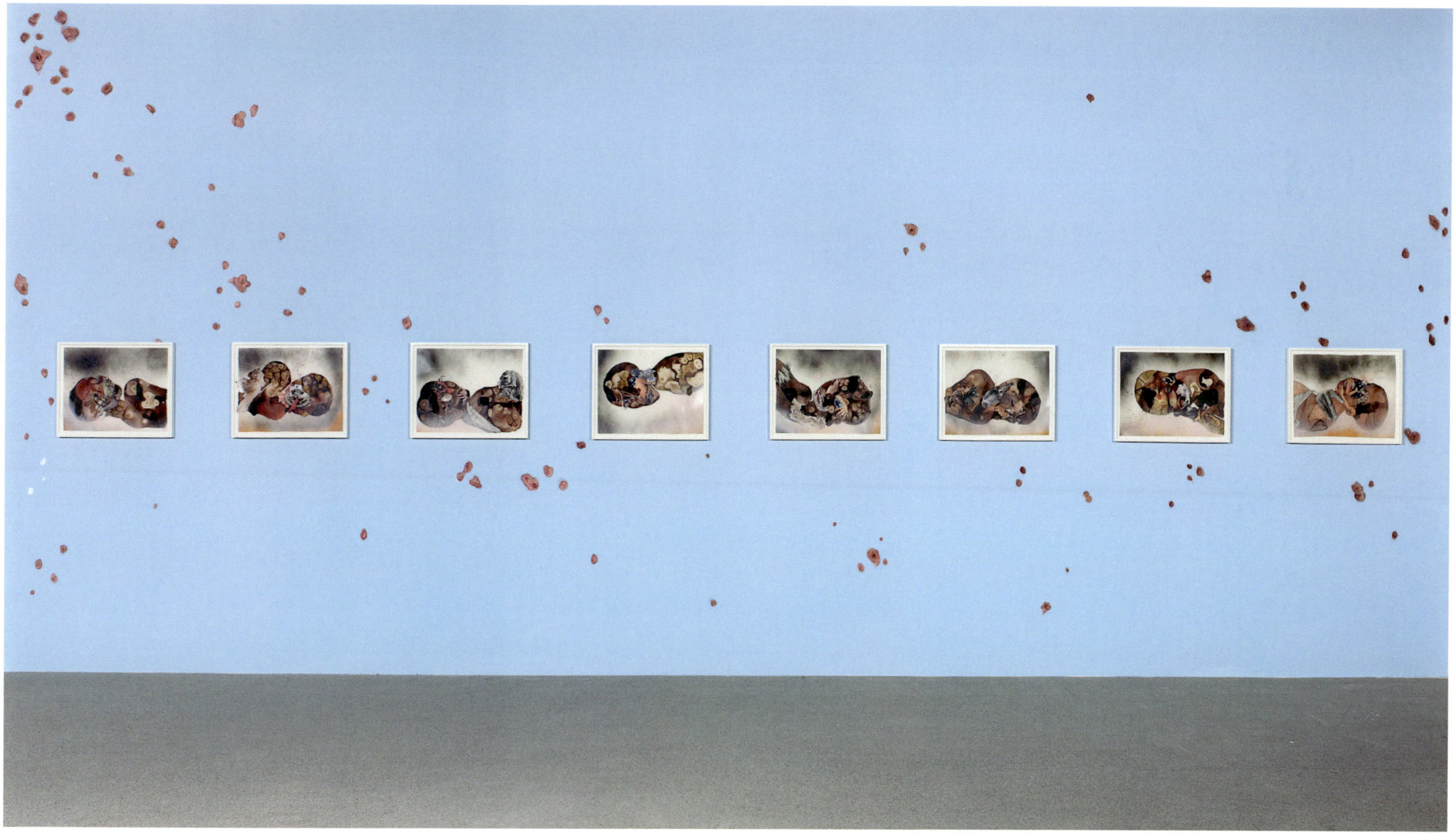

right,
SUSPENDED PLAYTIME, 2008
GARBAGE BAGS, TWINE
44 PARTS
SIZE VARIES FROM 8 TO 20 CM

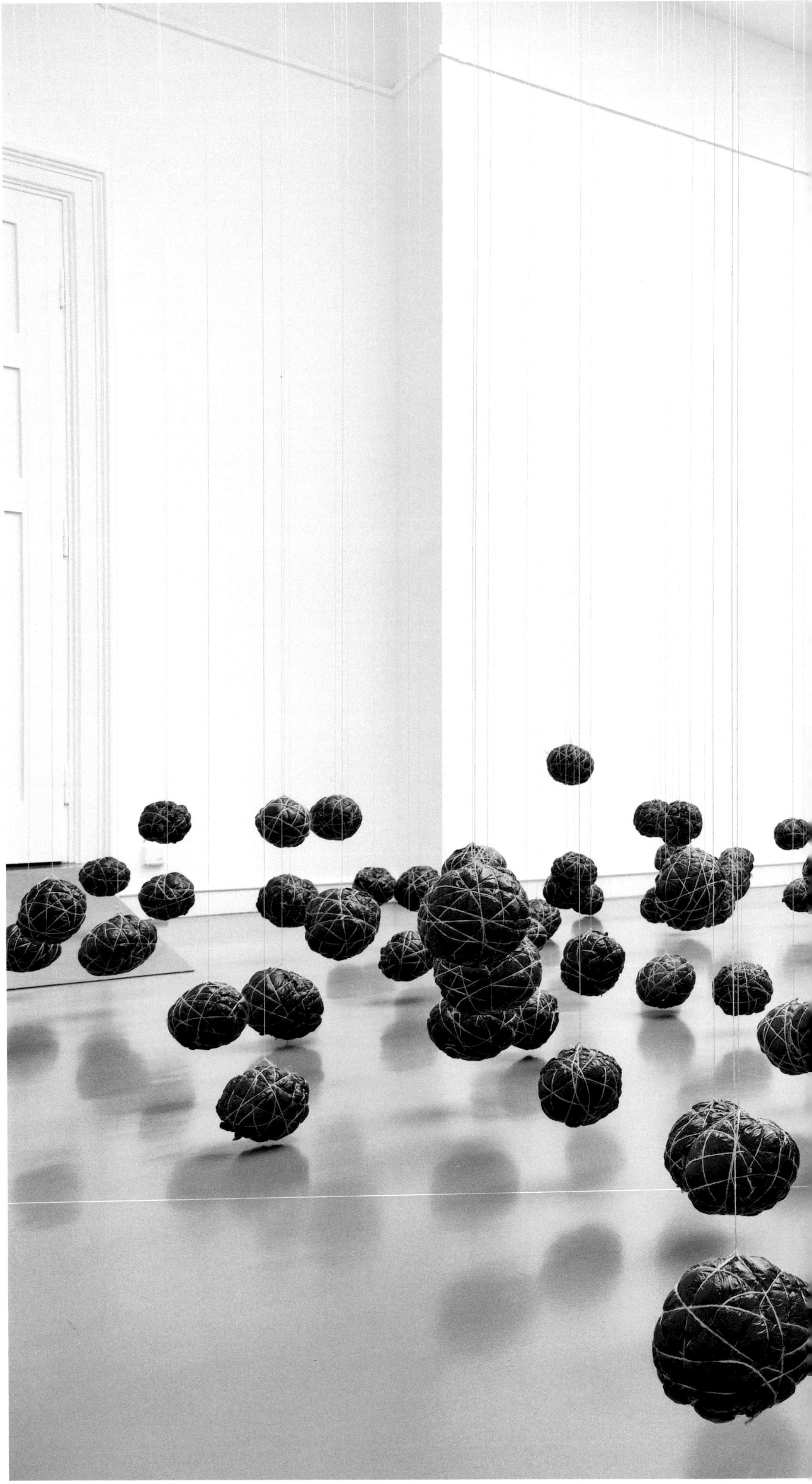

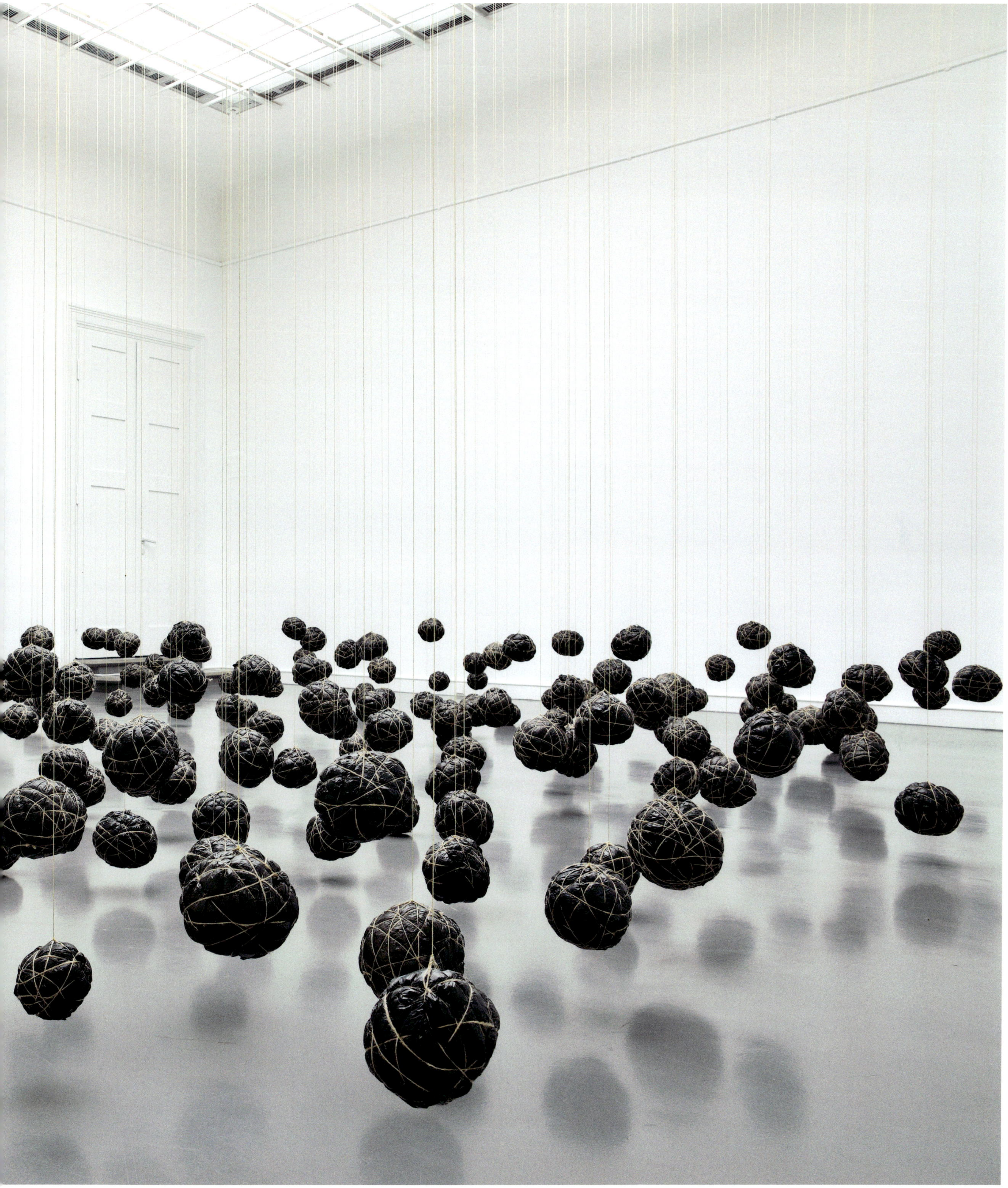

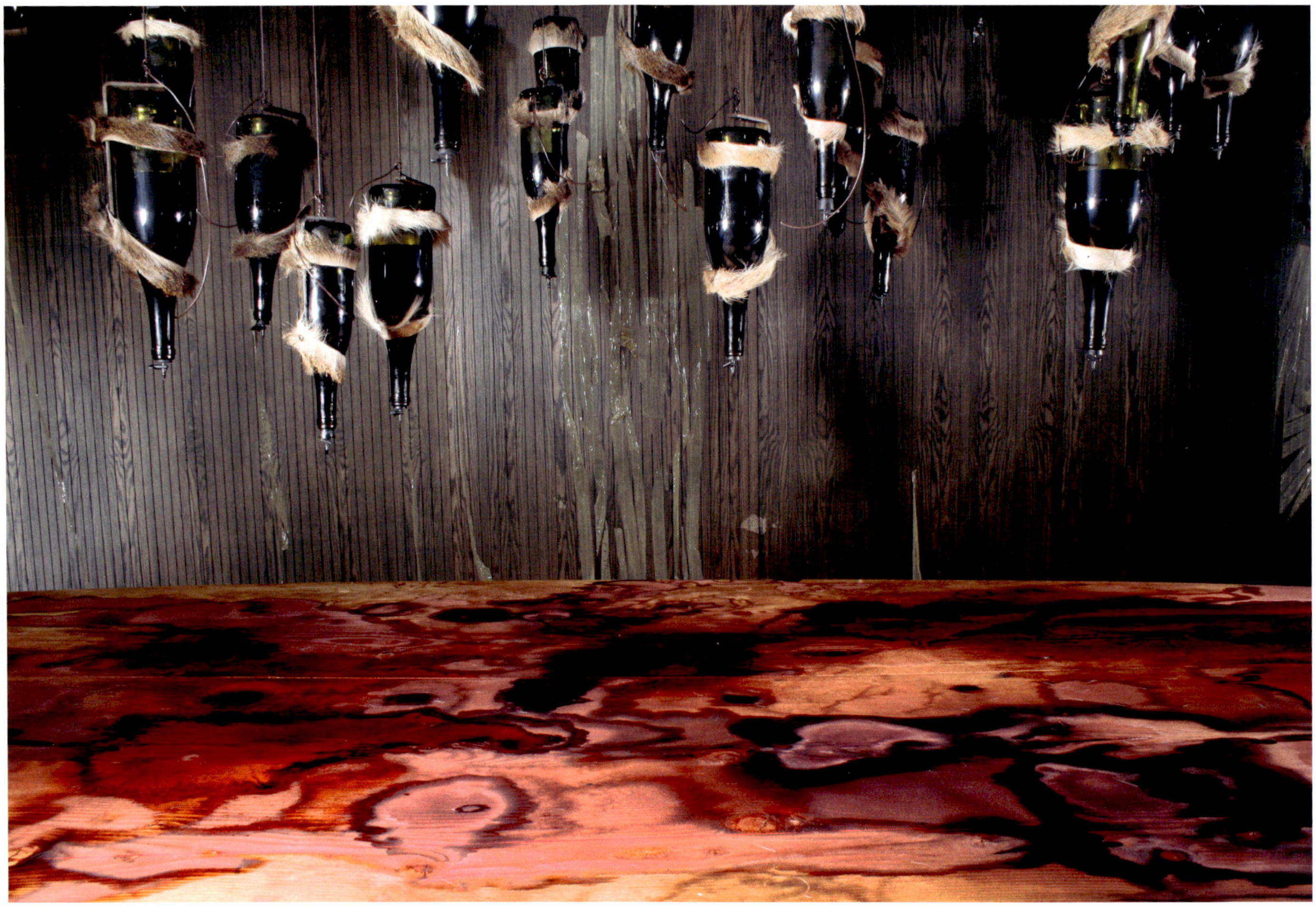

In other works, the artist jettisons walls and discrete objects for overpowering rooms. A 2006 collaboration in New York with Ghanaian-British architect David Adjaye, *Exhuming Gluttony: A Lover's Requiem,* and *The Cinderella Curse* in Atlanta the following year, both pivot on massive wine-soaked, table-like forms, piled high with or the setting for a parade of pelts. Through the central element of both these installations one can imagine and remap the so-called 'scramble for Africa' beginning in the early 1880s, in which the continent came increasingly under European domination, a power grab often represented by the continent laid flat on a table as Europeans carve out their slices. In his *Scramble for Africa* (2003), Yinka Shonibare, Mutu's Nigerian-British contemporary, offers his perspective on that late nineteenth-century era. While Mutu's pieces may have the same starting point in a similar strange feast, her reliance on sensory and visual overload along with abstraction pushes the narrative on war and imperial misadventures up to our current moment. These works are visual interpretations of human conflict and death, but equally about waste and environmental destruction.[61]

As we know, some of Mutu's earliest experiments in New York were sculptural; the joining of found things with the handmade in an assemblage practice was captivating in its challenge. She was impressed by the way in which things stubbornly held on to truths we recognize. There was excitement in pushing the syncretic properties of materials to, in her words, 'mutate meaning'.[62] Like many artists, Mutu has worked with a certain recurring constellation of materials over time that have led her towards the sculptural: bottles, pelts, felt and packing tape. All lead back to the body. The Bottle People was a series of discrete objects whose anthropomorphic qualities signalled the figurative cast of collage practice to come. By 2000, in a project curated by Trevor Schoonmaker, the three-dimensional as a proxy for the figure becomes abstracted in overturned bottles suspended from the ceiling and dripping red wine.[63]

In these very specific materials chosen by Mutu, we also find conversations with a Black art world in 1990s New York. If Mutu's teacher Fred Wilson explicated ideas of the spectatorial and coloniality in an installational practice, lessons from others were also grounded materially. David Hammons and Nari Ward, like Mutu, have also returned to certain elements over the years, including of course, bottles. Hammons' site-specific installations of bottle trees populated Harlem streets, while discrete objects made it indoors. They also served as things to be performed with. Ward's work with bottles since the 1990s was fuelled by scenography that he constructed for dancer Ralph Lemon's *Geography: Race* (1997), a floating column of glass that eventually became the stand-alone work *Geography: Bottle Messenger* (2002).[64]

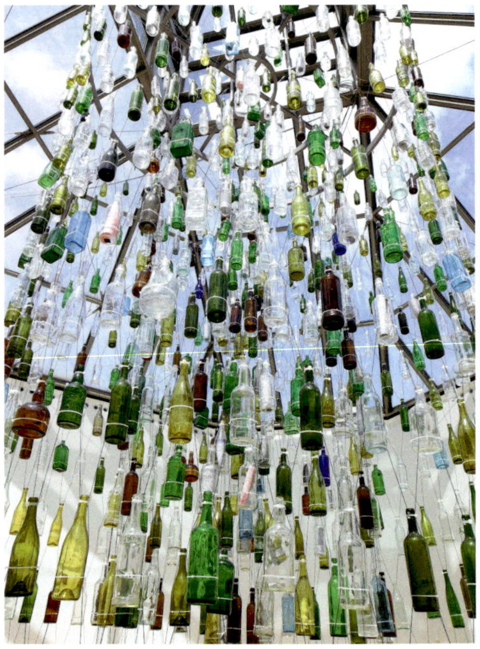

NARI WARD
GEOGRAPHY: BOTTLE MESSENGER, 2002
BOTTLES, LETTRES, WIRE AND METAL FRAME
900 X 400 CM

right and opposite,
EXHUMING GLUTTONY (ANOTHER REQUIEM), 2006–11
MIXED MEDIA INSTALLATION, ANIMAL PELTS, WOOD, BOTTLES, WINE, PACKING TAPE, AND BLANKETS
983 X 465 CM

INSTALLATION VIEW AT SALON 94, NEW YORK, 2006

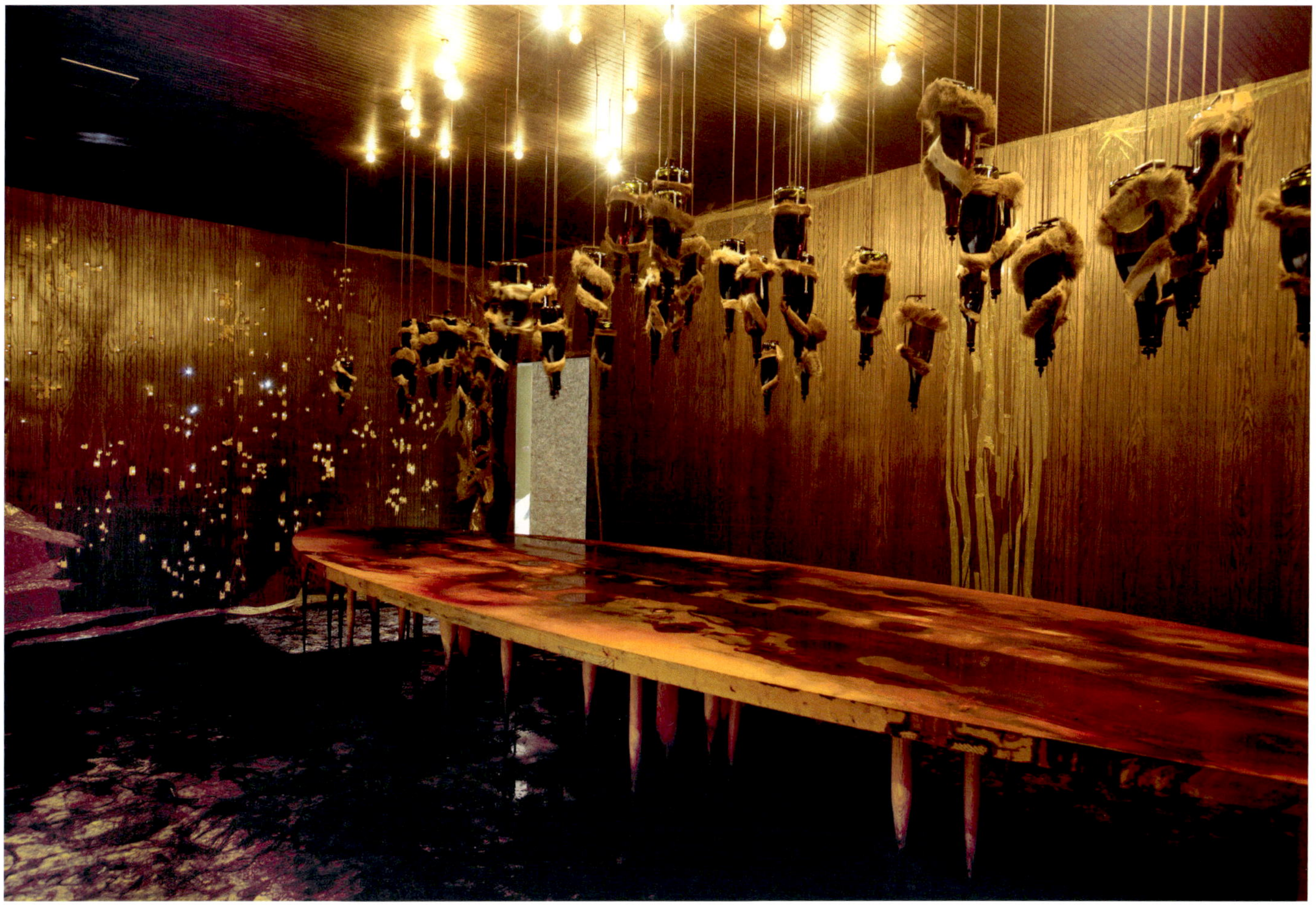

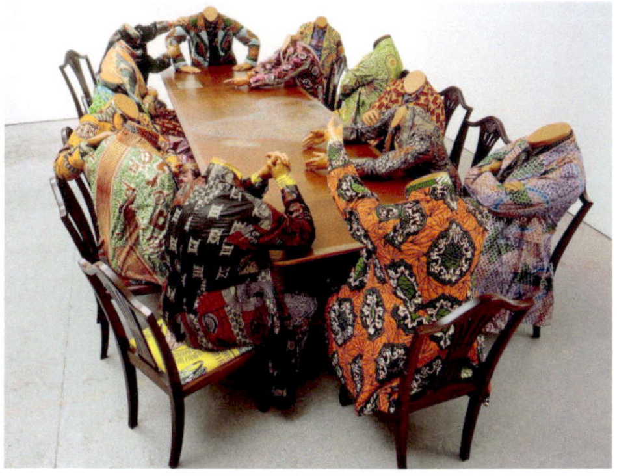

YINKA SHONIBARE
SCRAMBLE FOR AFRICA, 2003
14 LIFE-SIZE FIBREGLASS MANNEQUINS, 14 CHAIRS, TABLE, DUTCH WAX PRINTED COTTON

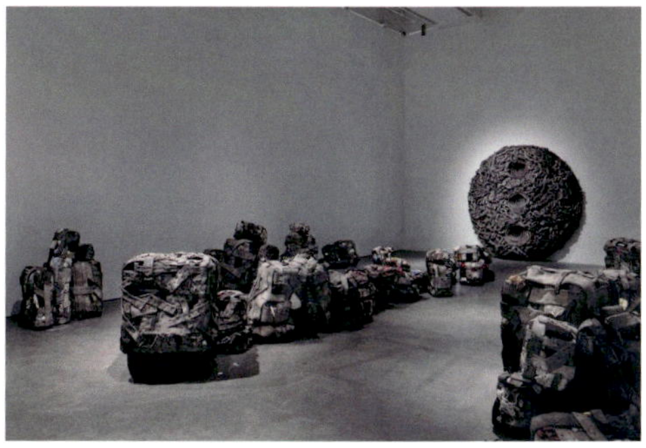

NARI WARD
EXODUS, 1993
MIXED MEDIA, TIRES AND FIRE HOSE

Ward was known for his immense found-object installations of urban detritus in the 1990s. Both artists took up things like plastic bags – in Ward's *Savior* (1996) and Mutu's *Suspended Playtime* (2008) – commenting on the cast-off culture of Western society. There was also a process of tying, wrapping and packing, exemplified by Ward's *Exodus* (1993), that spoke to an immigrant experience of mobility but also a diasporic configuration of binding of intention, prayers and will.[65] In Mutu's practice, this is signalled in her profligate use of packing tape. Many times she employs it to mimic living form, as with the spiders of *Erasing Infestation – An Exercise in Historical Futility*. She joins tape and felt packing blankets to create landscapes and trees. In this way, she follows the tradition of Maren Hassinger, whose creation of trees and bushes from wire rope also remarked on the misuse of natural resources. Mutu's turn to felt and pelts, to a sensuous tactility, is also a turn to the skin, and another substitution for the body. This is a shift seen in the practice of certain African American artists such as Hammons and Saar with their manipulation of leather in the 1970s. In the 1990s, marking a moment where she also removed the figure, Lorna Simpson printed on felt; decades earlier, Joseph Beuys celebrated the life-sustaining properties of that same material.

ONCE UPON A TIME SHE SAID, I'M NOT AFRAID AND HER ENEMIES BEGAN TO FEAR HER THE END, 2013
MIXED-MEDIA WALL DRAWING
DIMENSIONS

INSTALLATION VIEW AT BROOKLYN MUSEUM, NEW YORK, 2013

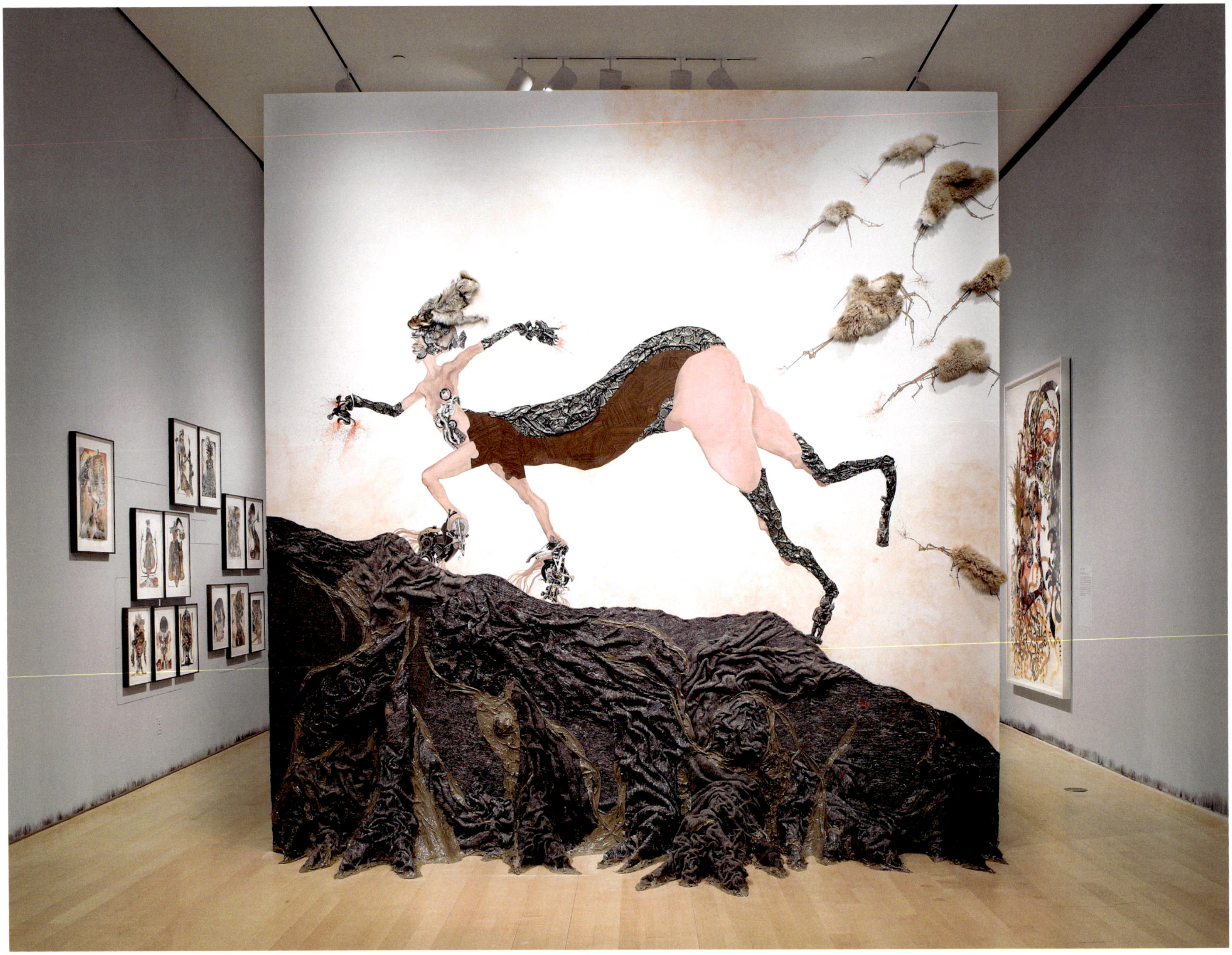

For Mutu, massive landscapes composed from artificial substances show up around 2007 in New York, Denver and Berlin. The most ubiquitous element in these configurations is the felt packing, or what she refers to as 'rescue' blankets, given to 'disaster victims back home'.[66] Among the most spectacular use of these materials was the commission by The Nasher Museum in 2013, *Once upon a time she said, I'm not afraid and her enemies became afraid of her The End*, where Mutu used them to bring trees and roots, a regenerated 'outside', inside, creating a landscape for the wall on which creatures clamber and float. This domain is extended to surfaces upon which collages also hang, transforming the architecture.

Mutu's interface with ecology in these wall pieces seems tied to what Steven Nathan Haymes refers to as 'relational ecologies': a sense of communal existence shared with the plant and animal world as kin. It is a consideration of the environmental that takes into account the social world and its displacements. If under white supremacy black as unhuman is anti-territorial, then Mutu performs what Chelsea M. Frazier sees as 'resistive notions of ecological relationality'.[66]

Mutu's work as a whole also ponders the essential topic of land in Kenya's recent history. By 1914, Europe controlled ninety percent of the African continent. Kenyan farmland was among the most productive for the British, who had moved in by 1885. Mutu's Gikuyu people lost sixty percent of their homeland. As anticolonial movements grew, people were imprisoned in internment camps in the 1950s and subjected to more barbarism. The militant Kenya Land and Freedom Army became renowned worldwide as the Mau Mau. Their activism to retrieve their territory became categorized as a psychotic state, similar in many ways to the nineteenth-century US condition identified as 'drapetomania', characterized by the desire to escape slavery.[68] From this vantage point, Mutu's entire practice grapples with the brutality that has characterized struggles against the colonial condition. As she writes: 'The bodies in my work are often wracked with the wounds of war yet keep on, despite missing or twisted limbs.'[69] Growing up after 1963 in an independent and postcolonial Kenya, she lived the process of remaking culture in the wake of carnage and uprooting, life interrupted by British intervention and convention.

Mutu's installational practices can thus be seen as assembling environments and placemaking as a way to signal new moral universes. What changes in 2013's *Once upon a time she said, I'm not afraid and her enemies became afraid of her The End* is the presence of 'a handful' of Kenyan soil that is added in the work.[70] This seemingly small addition asserts a turn towards new materials and approaches, one occasioned by the artist's growing opportunity to spend time in Africa. By 2016, Mutu would create a home in Kenya, and begin to divide her time between New York and Nairobi, simultaneously shifting her focus to Kenyan tales, imagery and fabulations.

Mutu has revisited her roots amongst the highlands Gikuyu people. Yet one of her first sustained explorations of Kenyan mythos looks to the Indian Ocean or Swahili Coast, its oceanic biologies and ecologies.[71] At London's Victoria Miro Gallery in autumn 2014, the artist presented the show 'Nguva na Nyoka', Kiswahili for 'Sirens and Serpents'. Through collage paintings, video and a single sculpture, Mutu explored the character of Nguva, an animal at once real and mythic. The manatee-like sea mammal of the genus Sirenia is known also as dugong, a creature at home in the warm waters of Africa's east coast. But Nguva also names a chimera, a water spirit that is half fish half woman, a sexual temptress and a beautiful singer. Nguva is a rebel who cannot be distinguished from a fully human 'real' woman, nor contained by patriarchy. Her mutability, her trans-ness, gives her 'limitless possibilities', along with 'terrifying yet seductive powers'.[72] In Mutu hands, Nguva also holds lessons for understanding our universe and generating empathy in our world.

Nguva is part of a constellation of African and African Diasporic water spirits collected under the name Mami Wata. As Henry Drewal observes, the deity has roots in more ancient guises of a 'hybrid human-aquatic' beauty, whose generosity is a sign of good fortune but who is also jealous and deadly, later symbolizing the tangled seductions of colonial and modern circuits of global exchange.[73] An early twentieth-century Liberian version could easily describe a Mutu collage: 'a fish body and tail, two human legs, and high-heeled shoes on her feet', with a luxurious mane of hair.[74] We see this in *Beneath lies the power* (2014). Here, the terrestrial beauty emerges from the water, birds alighting on her twiggy hair. Below the water line she rests on a submerged self, a serpent with fins and scales. In *The screamer island dreamer* (2014), much of the body of another aquatic beast is an enormous vagina, balancing on shapely legs in stilettos that morph into fins. Nguva might also lurk in *Yo Mama*, Mutu's 2004 femme posing with her serpent avatar and piercing it with her heel. As Ahmed suggests, stilettos as icons of femininity are also easily transformed into weapons against patriarchy, as are women's pleasure and laughter.[75]

Adopting Bearden's nomenclature, 'collage paintings', Mutu's 2014 works are larger and more painterly. They substitute heavier vinyl for Mylar, allowing for more commanding visions. Their collage substrate continues to signal the circulation of print media and print culture. We find that the artist's decade-long practice has its roots, not only in Europe's modernist collage and photomontage, but also in global circuits of the modern that Enwezor's Trade Routes hailed. The sheen of difference and foreignness that wraps Nguva, for instance, is embodied in a South Asian iconicity, snake charmers and Indian deities that flood colonial Africa into the mid-twentieth century, taking the form of chromoliths as well as film.[76] Like many female water spirits on the African continent, Nguva may also have a penchant for notebooks and paper.

BENEATH LIES THE POWER
2014
COLLAGE PAINTING ON VINYL
212 X 156 CM

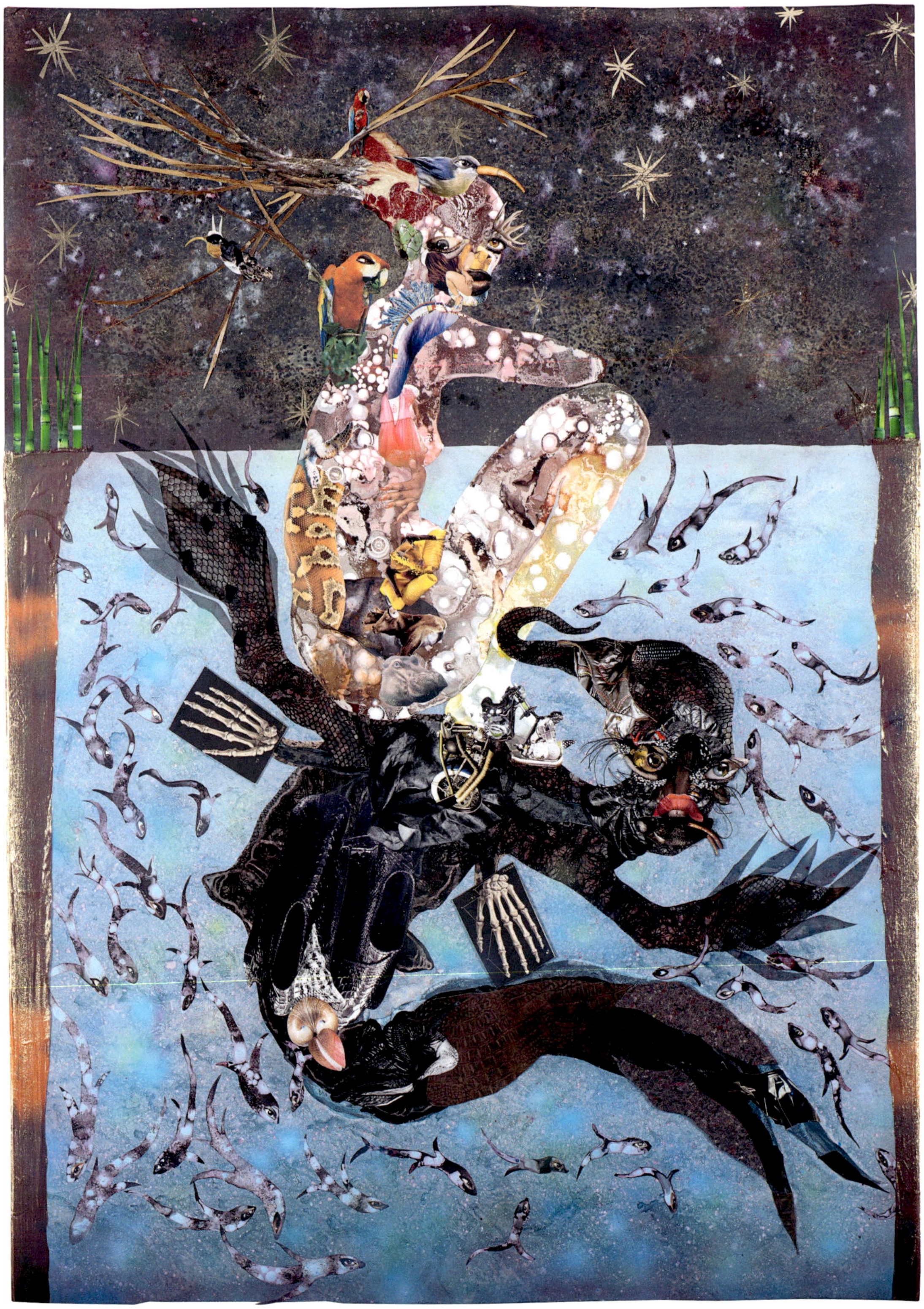

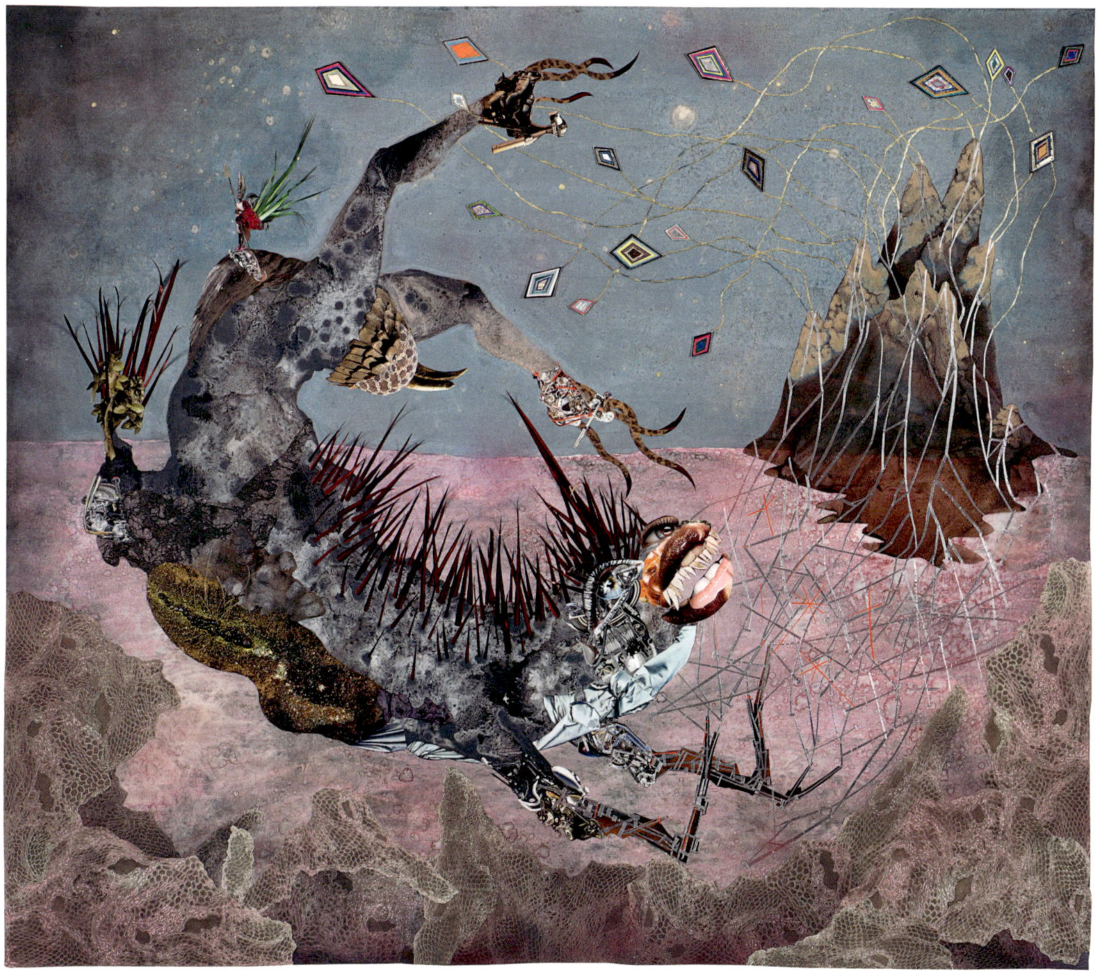

THE SCREAMER ISLAND DREAMER, 2014
COLLAGE PAINTING ON VINYL
185 X 155 CM

In the setting of Kenyan coastal culture, Mutu's project *Nguva na Nyoka* addresses other aspects of diaspora, migration and the mercantile. Indian Ocean global circuits have been active since at least the seventh century C.E., linking Africa with India, Asian and Arab states, and Muslim cultures of 'traders, slavers, and scholars' and associated with the development of a Swahili Islam.[77] In the Indian Ocean milieu, the mythology surrounding Nguva, the 'arch femininity' and ambiguity of the mermaid woman, offers morality tales in the 'context of Islam', speaking to ideals of sexual purity and consumption.[78] And as Heike Behrend further explains, in the midst of Muslim aniconics and proscriptions against the circulation of imagery of women, it is not surprising that Mutu takes up Nguva as an African and local feminist embodiment and figure of critique.[79]

Coming of age in Kenya of the 1970s the artist would have experienced first hand the growth of more doctrinaire Christian and Islamic religiosity, hinging on female chasteness and used also as a way to denigrate 'indigenous African faiths'.[80] In light of such history, it is not surprising that Mutu would embrace feminism by the early 1990s, remembering the exact moment when she realized that women seemed not to have any rights that the world might respect. With her growing consciousness as a woman and artist during that decade, Mutu was certainly part of Third Wave Feminism, her capacious notions of being and body embracing broad understandings of humanity, including gender non-conforming, queer, and what Nash calls 'sex-positive' facets.[81]

In East Africa, as elsewhere, there is divergence between cultures of the shoreline and those of the interior. This dynamic was further complicated by European colonial and Muslim Arab enslavement of inland peoples; in fact, slavery didn't officially end on the Kenyan coast until 1907.[82] Textiles and architecture were among the things that shaped these stratifications. Those of high rank were wrapped in yards of cloth. Upper-class women were veiled, masked, even covered by portable walls. Fabric of the lower classes was the dark *kaniki*, or *kanga*, a black and white cloth inscribed with text. The enslaved needed to appear almost naked, in doing so performing their lack of power. Freedom and transcending slavery was signified by the ability to cover, with the power to conceal signalling a certain respectability. Similarly, iconic white coral architecture announced patrician prerogatives while the more pervasive wattle and daub structures were marked as subordinate, even though all were 'part of the same spectrum of building technology'.[83]

In *Nguva na Nyoka*, Mutu thinks further about the marine environment and sirens that sound the alarm, not only grounding this particular series but even Mutu's oeuvre in its entirety. If Mutu warns us about misogyny, cruelty and war, her pieces imagining Nguva also reformulate the emergence of anti-Blackness in the context of slavery. In *Beneath Lies the Power*, Mutu's submerged Nguva is black, painted with the colour of the enslaved on the East African coast; they are figures thrown overboard by slavers or who have made their way to the water and are mythically/alchemically exacting their revenge. Perhaps even more to the point is *Long John Flapper*. Here our mermaid, similarly subaquatic, is covered with actual fringes of black fabric. Her figure is speckled with gold, strands dangling from her mouth, emblematic of the riches of the trade in human flesh. She floats among additional pieces of black and gold fabric, perhaps signs of other bodies, overboard.[84]

Black also makes a turn towards the more forthrightly sculptural. *Sleeping Serpent* (2014) seems taken from the deep, laid out as a specimen, its bulging body evidence of a human meal, whose crockery (along with a Dutch clog) is also displayed.[85] While the body is 'reptilian black vinyl', its ceramic human head, the colour of the ocean, lies in repose on a white pillow of delicate European lace.[86] Several years later, in *Water Woman* (2017) *Nguva*, rendered in velvety black bronze, returns to her glamorous aquatic self. 'As the artist writes of her growing embrace of Nairobi and her eventual return, 'I began collecting my fragments, my new family, my basket of spells and supplies. I moved towards my father's unrequited dream, to red soil, black cotton, and petrified roots.'[87]

If black cloth wraps the body of the enslaved at the coast, 'black cotton' also names a genus of East African soil. The red volcanic earth of the rolling highlands marks Mutu's inland homeland and Gikuyu roots. This 'earth and the soil that bred and fed me', in the artist's words, served as the basis for a show at New York's Barbara Gladstone Gallery in 2017.[88] Absent were her signature collages; instead, we found a field of sculpture. As critic Johanna Fateman remarked, 'The only paper on view was in the form of pulp' that mixed with 'wood glue and red soil' to form 'otherworldly' sculptural objects.[89] The show's Gikuyu title, 'Ndoro Na Miti' (Mud and Trees) indicated this changing materiality.

Virus and illness, along the lines of those highlighted in *Histology of the Different Classes of Uterine Tumors*, were now made three-dimensional. Spherical in shape, some were assembled into the form of a giant rosary or prayer beads, others imaging the likes of meningitis and smallpox, diseases brought with colonization. More showed off cicatrization, rituals performed on the skin that create a raised textured surface. Their earthy vermillion reflected the 'primordial goo of clay', fiery anthills, or the wattle and daub of the built

LONG JOHN FLAPPER, 2014
COLLAGE PAINTING ON VINYL
184 X 155 CM

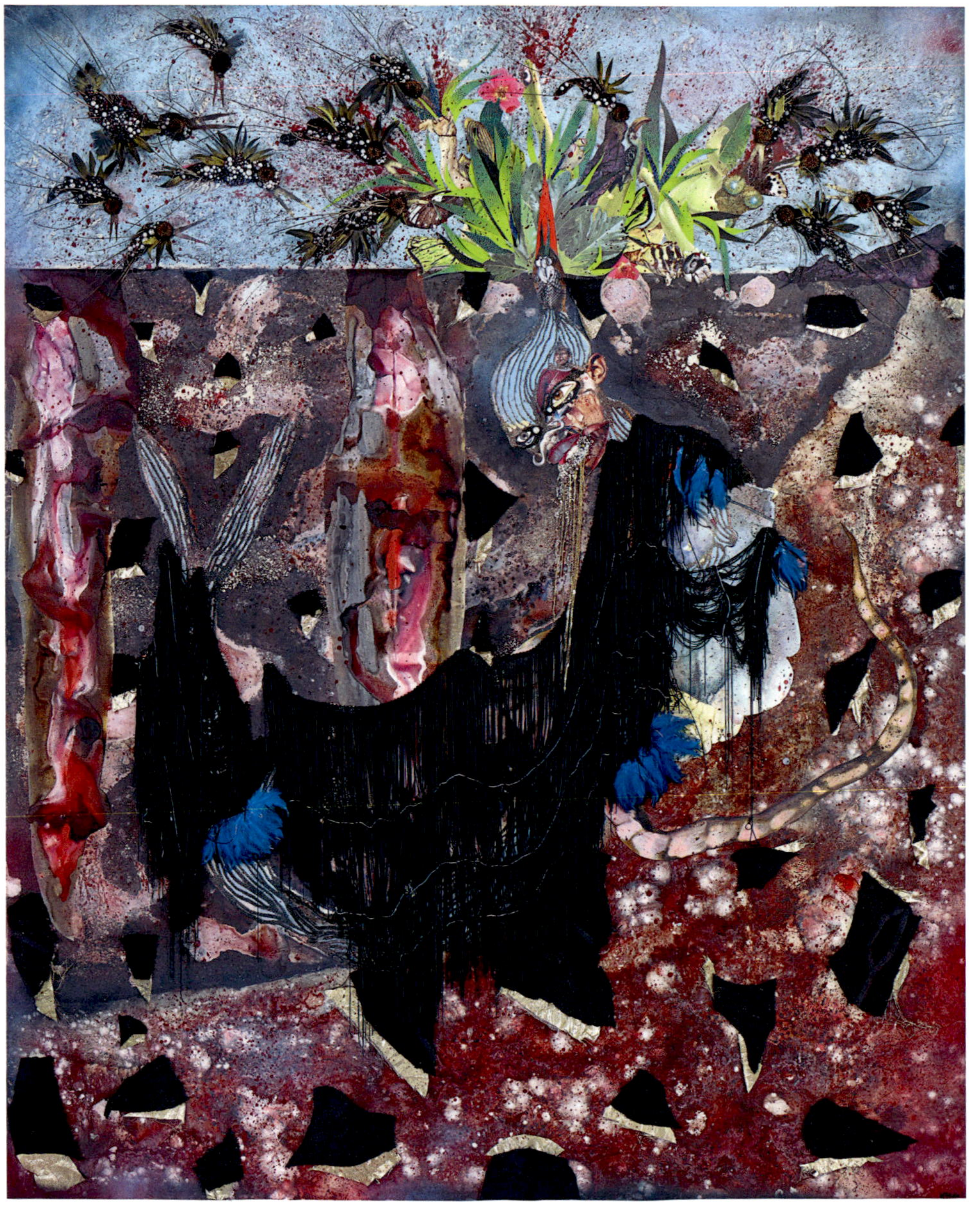

SLEEPING SERPENT, 2014
MIXED MEDIA FABRIC,
CERAMIC
91 X 91 X 945 CM

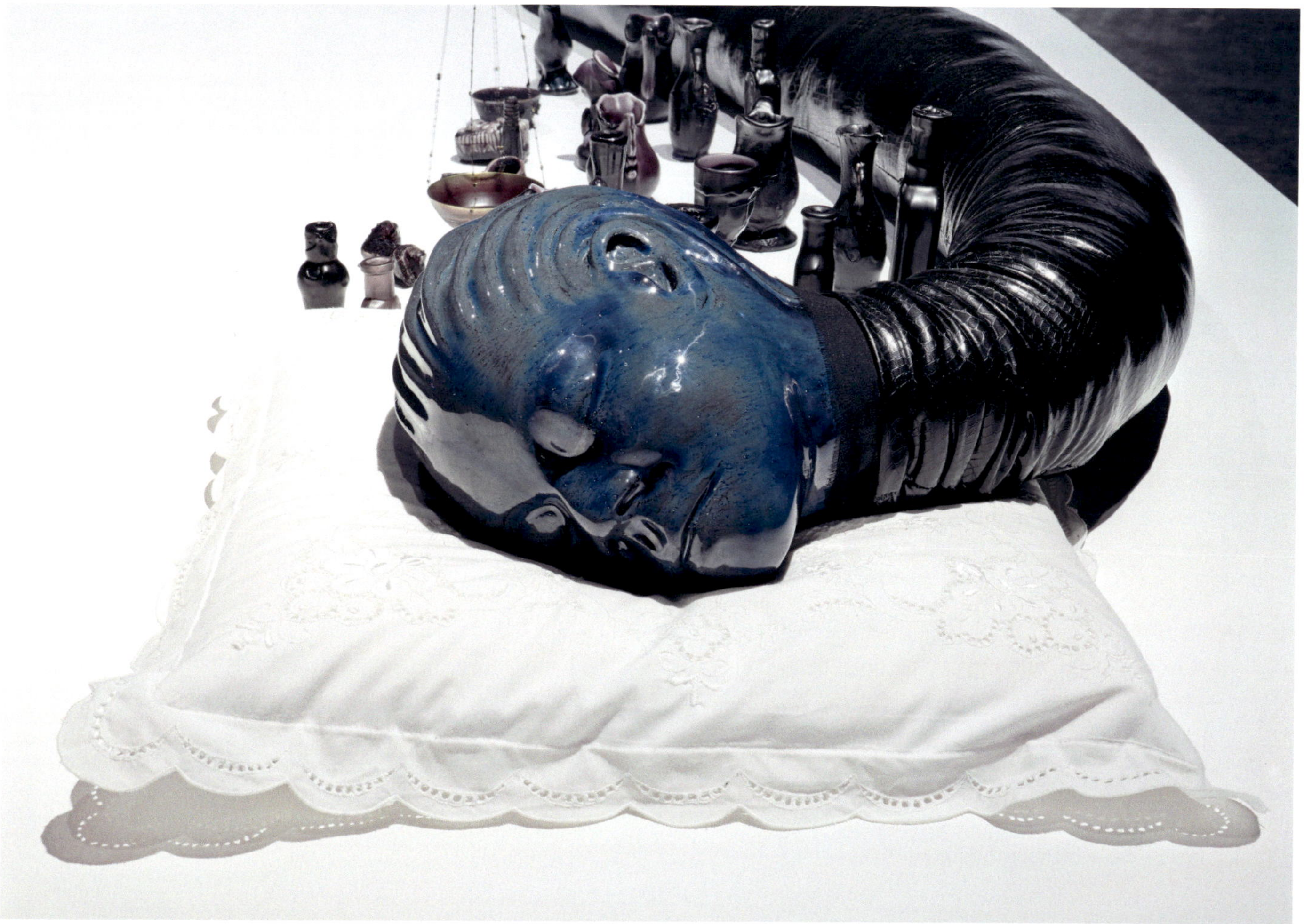

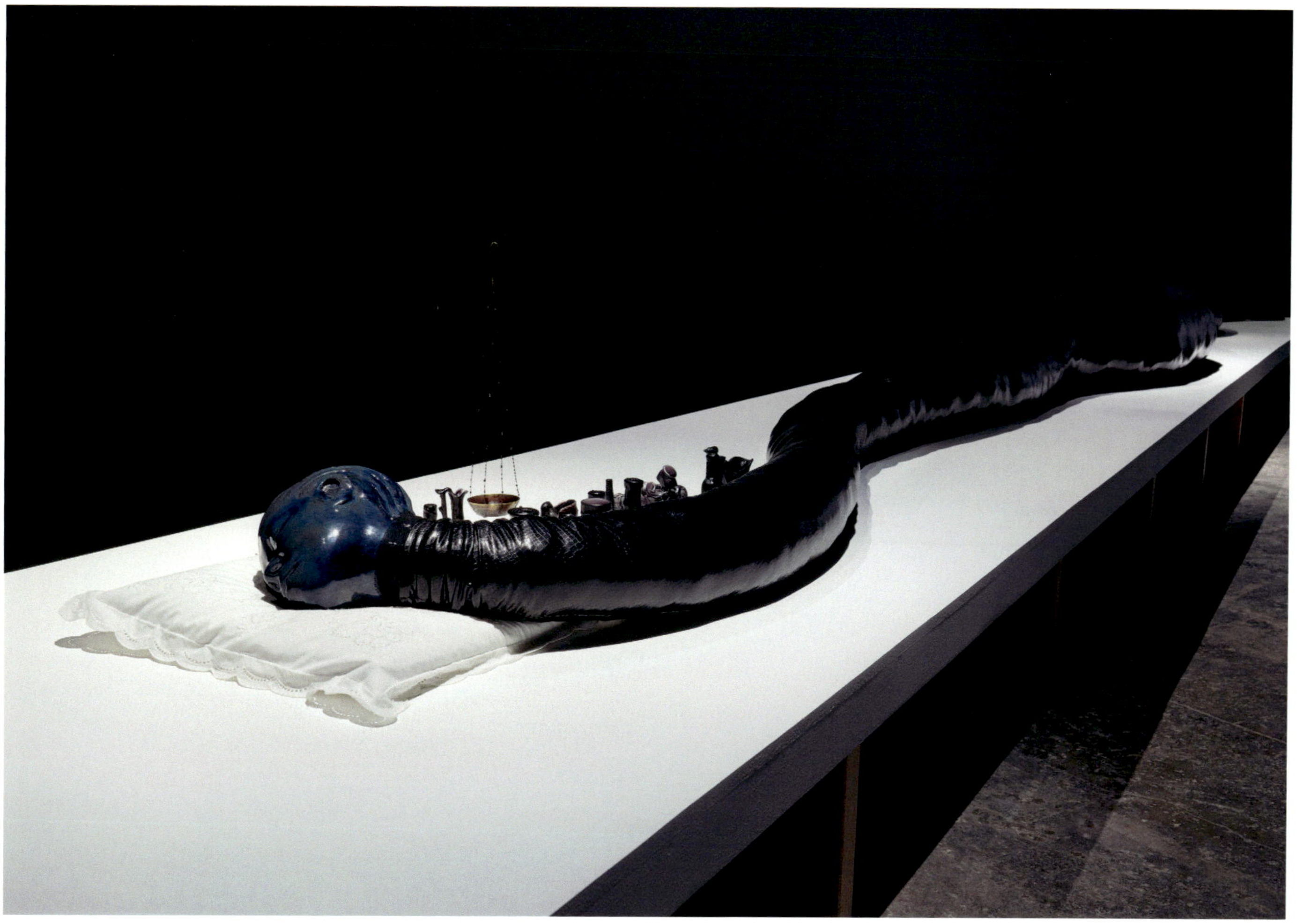

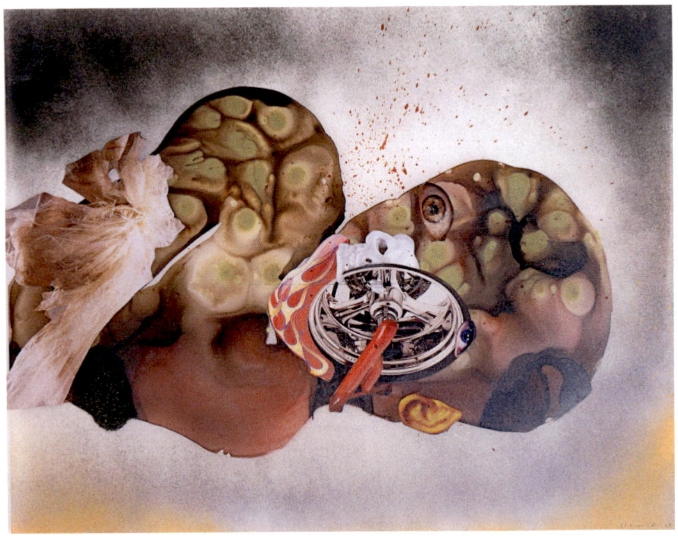

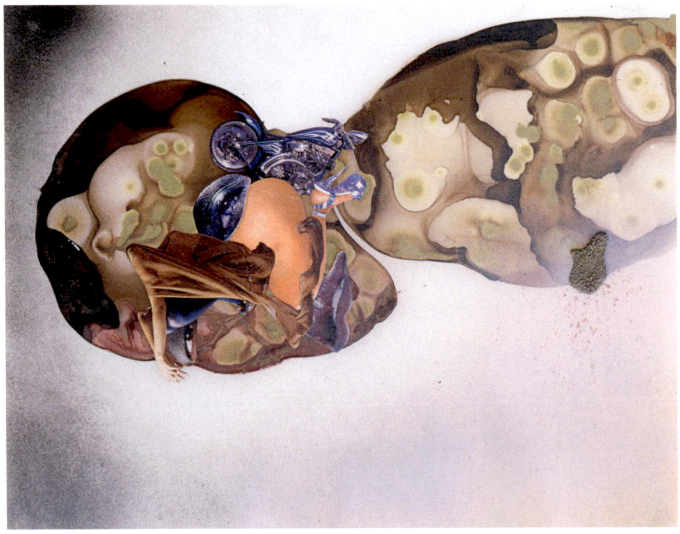

SLEEPING HEADS (DETAILS), 2006
MIXED MEDIA COLLAGES ON MYLAR
EACH 43 X 56 CM

environment in Kenya's highland interior.[90] Mounds of felt rescue blankets, their muted grey topped by the brilliant spheres, mirrored the structure, if not the colour, of anthills. Interspersed with these largely abstract elements were figurative pieces. Near life size, they emerged from/devolved into branches of actual wood: a standing figure in stilettos, whose hair exploded in twiggy styles, a seated figure also covered with raised marks of cicatrization and whose bushy topknot bore a resemblance to a tradition of men's wigs found in Western Kenya and Uganda formed using clay.[91] As Fateman noted, in this show Mutu presented things both ancient and futuristic, broaching ideas of extinction and creation, and a mythical, yet 'un-naïve passion for the glamour of the natural world'.[92]

Water Woman and *This Second Dreamer*, both 2017, signalled a further sculptural shift to the luxury and grandeur of bronze. However, with the latter, Mutu directs us towards the modern in a homage to the sculptor Constantin Brancusi, whose elegant volumes embraced a Romanian heritage and a passion for African sculptural form. Mutu's bronze head, laid horizontally, reimagined one of Brancusi's most recognizable pieces, *Sleeping Muse* (1910). Seemingly more naturalistic than built on an abstracted modernism, *This Second Dreamer* appears almost portrait-like, tracing the countenance of a Black woman with thick braids, similar to the ceramic visage of *Sleeping Serpent*. In the manner of Brancusi, the work's pedestal is part of the piece, joining the warmth of wood with the gleam of metal. In other ways, *This Second Dreamer* continues Mutu's own obsessions with horizontal, decapitated and expired bodies. Now we may never look at Brancusi again without considering the roots of European modernism, thinking not only on its 'appreciation' of African design but the cruelty of colonial domination veiled in this signature horizontality.[93] In Mutu's title, the Black figure is transformed from muse to one coveting her own wishes and desires, an apt description for young immigrants in the US, 'Dreamers' who continue to imagine and fight for their futures in America.

V – Glitch

While collage proved to be the most visible part of her oeuvre, it is clear that Mutu's sculptural practice had always continued apace and alongside. As the figure of Nguva moves about in Mutu's output, she helps us understand the larger spectrum of the artist's vision, one that reaches across media, from page to performance. Video unlocked dazzling 'sensory awareness', embodied knowledge that unleashed an empathetic and 'very active, visceral involvement' with her materials.[94]

At her 2014 Victoria Miro show, Mutu crowned her meditations on the shape-shifting mermaid with a seventeen-minute video. In *Nguva* (2014) the camera follows her slow, erratic and fraught movement from

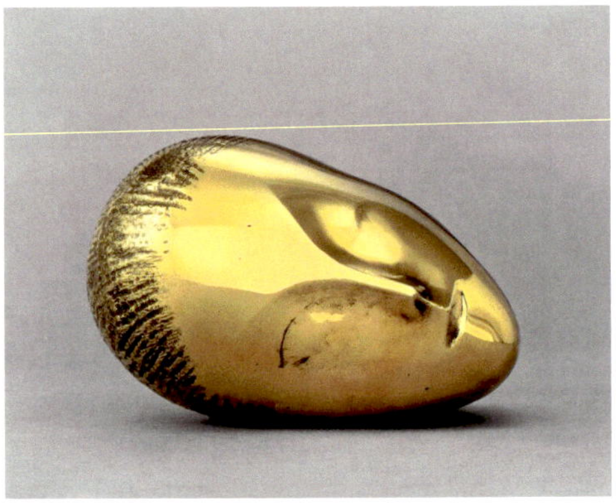

CONSTANTIN BRANCUSI
SLEEPING MUSE, 1910
BRONZE
17 X 24 X 15 CM

THIS SECOND DREAMER, 2017
PATINATED BRONZE AND WOOD
22 X 38 X 41 CM

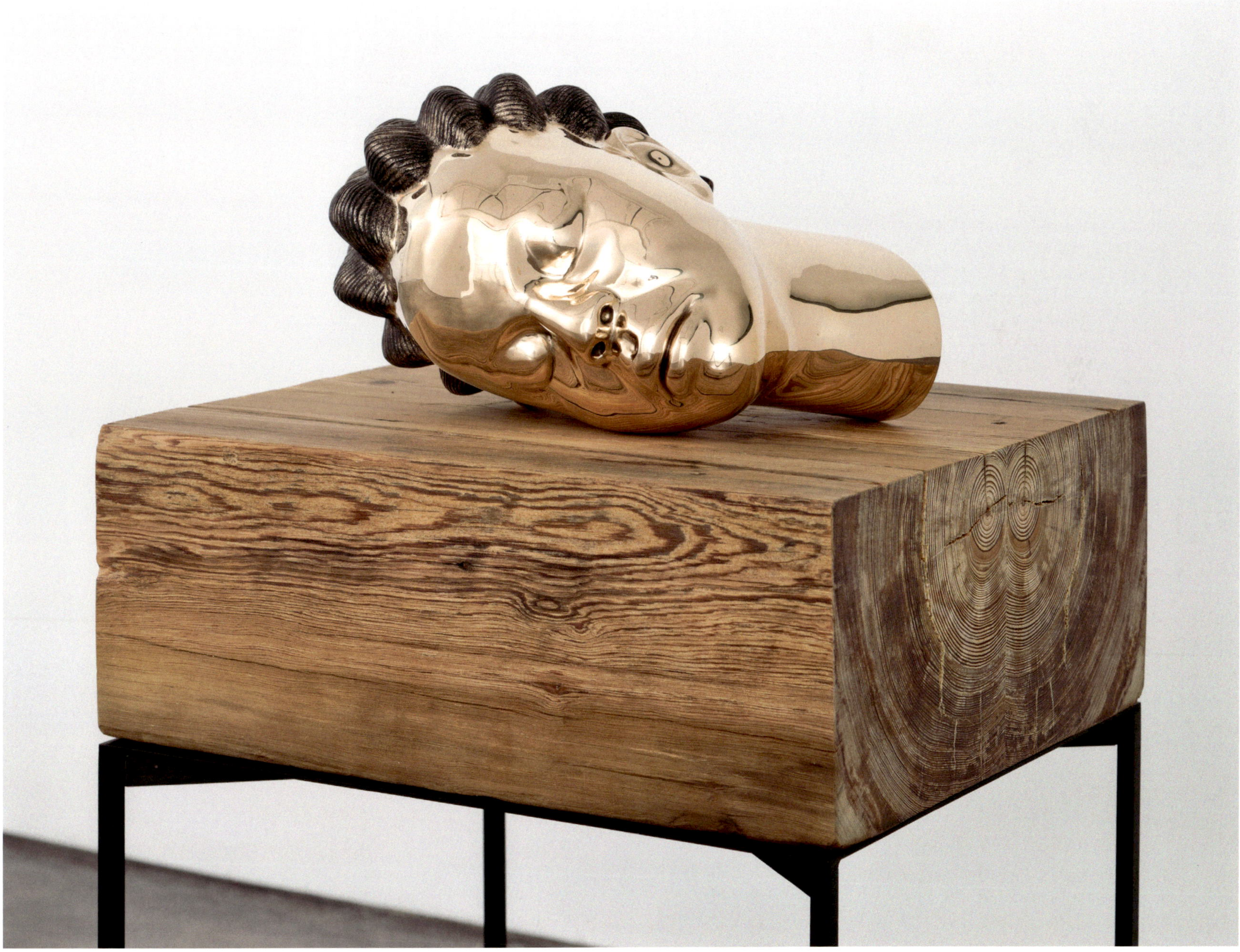

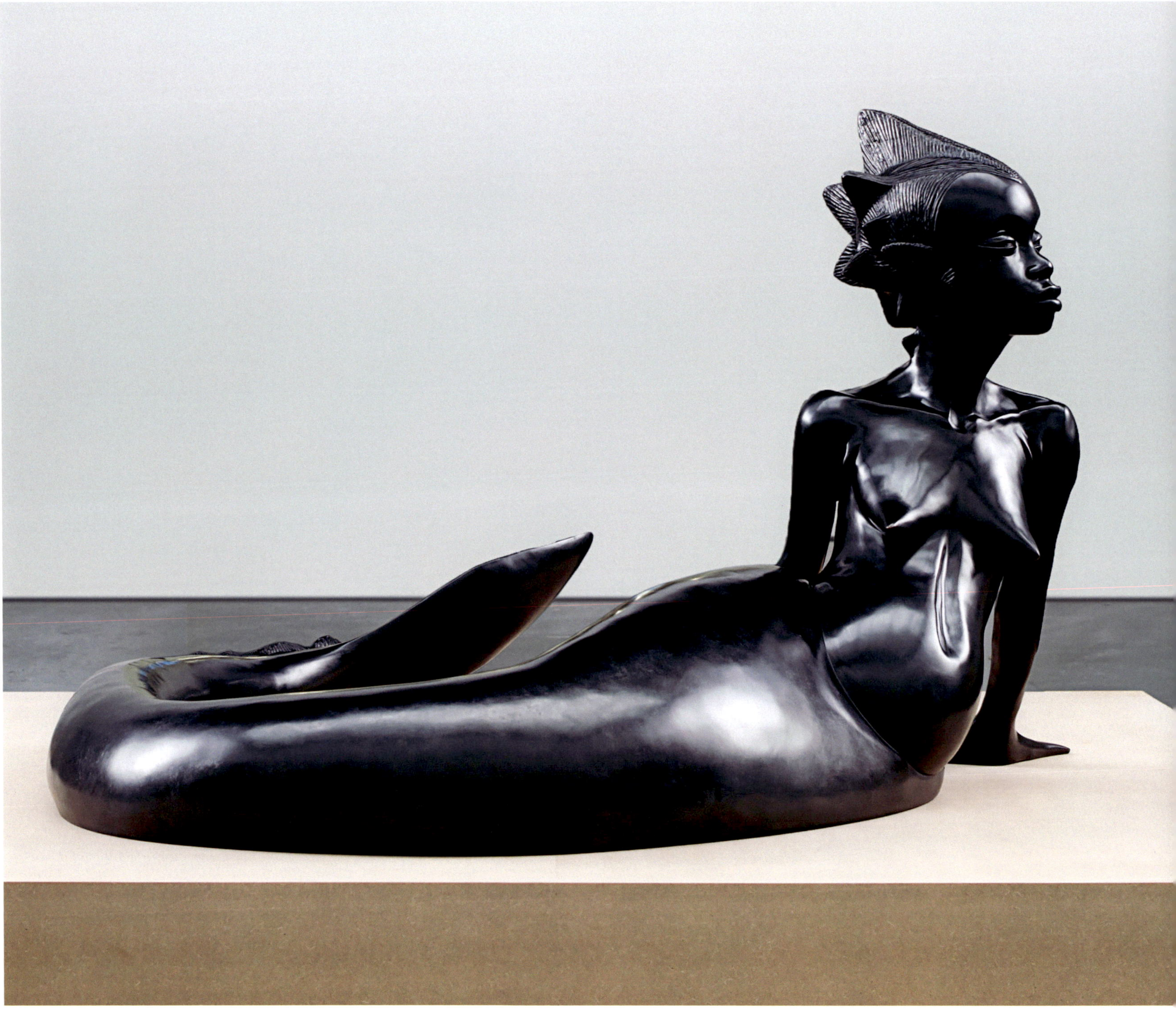

WATER WOMAN, 2017
BRONZE
91 X 165 X 178 CM

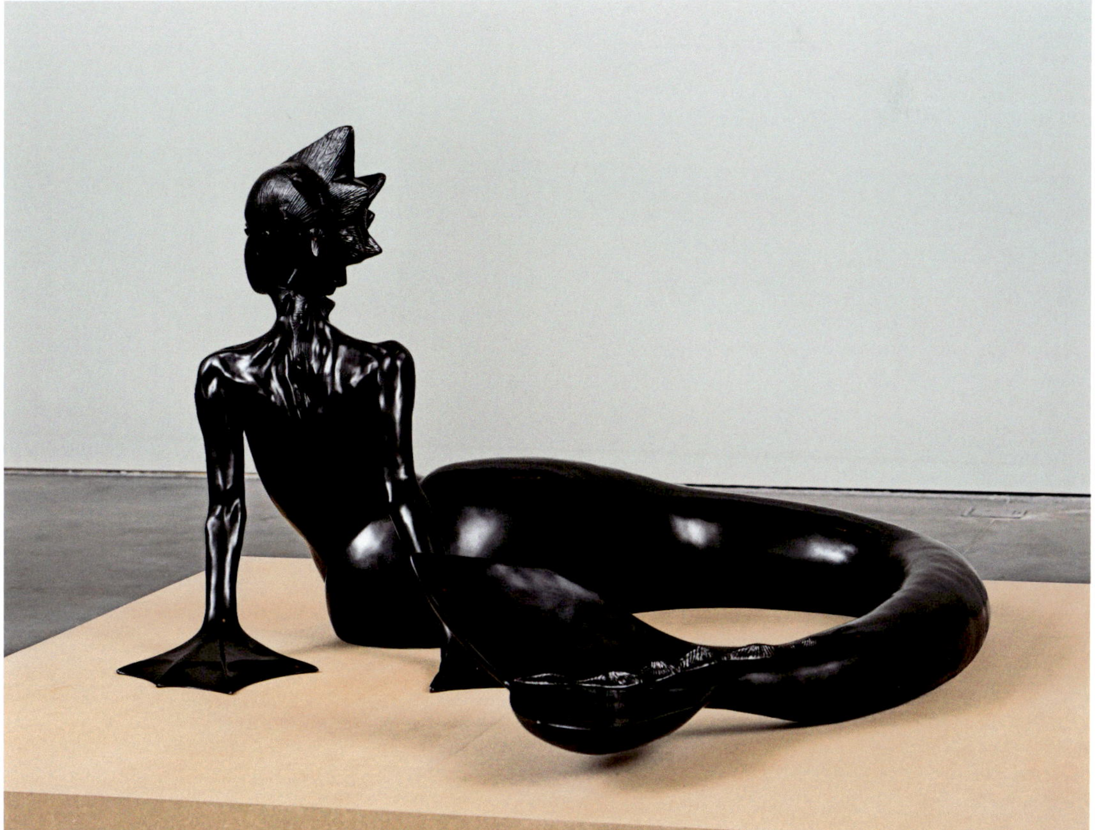

opposite,
AMAZING GRACE, 2005
SINGLE CHANNEL DVD
7 MIN. 6 SEC.

aquatic to terrestrial organism, bringing into greater relief the explorations of land/sea, culture/nature, dyads at the heart of much of Mutu's artmaking. In the earlier *Amazing Grace* (2005), for example, a figure walks along, into, and is eventually fully embraced by the ocean, against a delicate and haunting rendition of the hymn, sung in Gikuyu. The song's origins in the eighteenth-century British slave trade and employed as an emblem of colonization, takes on visual form. Water here, and the natural world in general, emerge as forceful characters. However, they also clash with a spirit realm that haunts a planet rent by myriad inequities; otherworldly beings seek justice, mirroring contemporary films such as *Atlantics* (2019) by the French-Senegalese filmmaker Mati Diop. Mutu's Nguva as video also engages discourses of technology as a contemporary spiritual tool on the East Africa coast. In that context, video is used by spirit mediums to attest to the workings of supernatural forces. Unlike the capture and apparent 'deadness' of the photograph, the vitality of spiritual forces can be deciphered through the moving digital image as luminosity – beaming, flashing or balls of light. Similarly, as Catherine Elwes observes, the liminal space of 'moving image installation embodies the perceptual doubleness of the spectator, the human ability to suspend disbelief and entertain two realities simultaneously'.[95]

One can consider Mutu a multimedia artist who thinks about different materials over time. However, she has always sited her practice in the intermedial, the space between an array of elements that transforms each one into a third. After M.J.W. Kings, we should also think of the transmedial, ideas of interaction, or the mutuality of collaboration among sources. Writing on the Kenyan context, Kings considers transmedia, a 'mode of storytelling that involves the interactive use of several media, seamlessly'; these include electronic, social media and content drivers like YouTube, along with older forms such a radio transmissions, comics and DVDs.[96] Transmedia is integral for Kenyan artists as a way to distribute work and generate income. In such examples, there is a celebration of the malleability and plurality of techne, and recognition of experimentation, occasioned by Africa's (and particularly Kenya's) access to digital technologies, which is unencumbered by outdated media infrastructure. It is also significant to the larger story that Mutu and her art tells about the will to continually supplement the local with other sources of news – with radio and publications from elsewhere – and the importance of paper to the circulation of information in the immediate postcolonial era.[97]

Like much art today, Mutu's work finds itself orbiting between things that exist as physical and performative objects in the world and those in digital space. This is an aspect of what curator Legacy Russell calls 'glitch feminism', whose digital life bespeaks a 'cyborgian turn', signalling a body that comes apart, dissolving material and creative boundaries and calcified gender roles.[98] Indeed, Mutu has been consistently working in the digital arena for over a decade. In videos such as *Cutting* (2004), *Cleaning Earth* (2006) and *Mud Fountain* (2010), the confrontation between woman, labour and the built or natural world, is imagined in single, medium to close-up shots that trace bounded, almost impregnable spaces; the lone figure is caught between heaven and earth, interminably cleansing a battered, earthen floor, and lingers, nude and indefinitely, in an underground dungeon. Containment in these pieces is reinforced with unadorned diegetic sound: a cutlass striking wood, a scrubbing rag, a cascade of mud, human breath. These pieces are specters of the durational, evincing repetition and a slow and deliberate kinesis, to which the body ultimately surrenders. In centring a recognizable human figure (the artist herself) in contradistinction to the fecund chimeras of her work in other media, these videos follow the path of 1970s feminist video and performance by the likes of Martha Rosler and Adrian Piper that takes up themes of domesticity and abjection.

Enwezor finds Mutu's early videos bleak, what Marianne Hirsch might call without recuperation, while after Russell we might understand the artist's protagonists as emblematic of the ways in which female bodies are seen as 'manufactured and commodified for capital'.[99] It is the starkness of such digital projects, however, that reveals their basis in environmentalism, their rootedness in a conscientious ecological practice that imagines human interconnectedness with the natural world. Amanda Renée Rico has referred to these as 'gendered ecologies', or an African ecofeminism, linking women, nature, and the political.[100] In many ways, this work is inspired by one of Mutu's heroes, Kenyan Nobel Laureate Wangari Maathai and her Green Belt movement, which joined earth justice to social justice and equity. Women's pain mirrored the earth's suffering and was parallel to 'transnational histories of colonialism and slavery where Black women's bodies were raped, sold, and objectified for profit', as was land.[101]

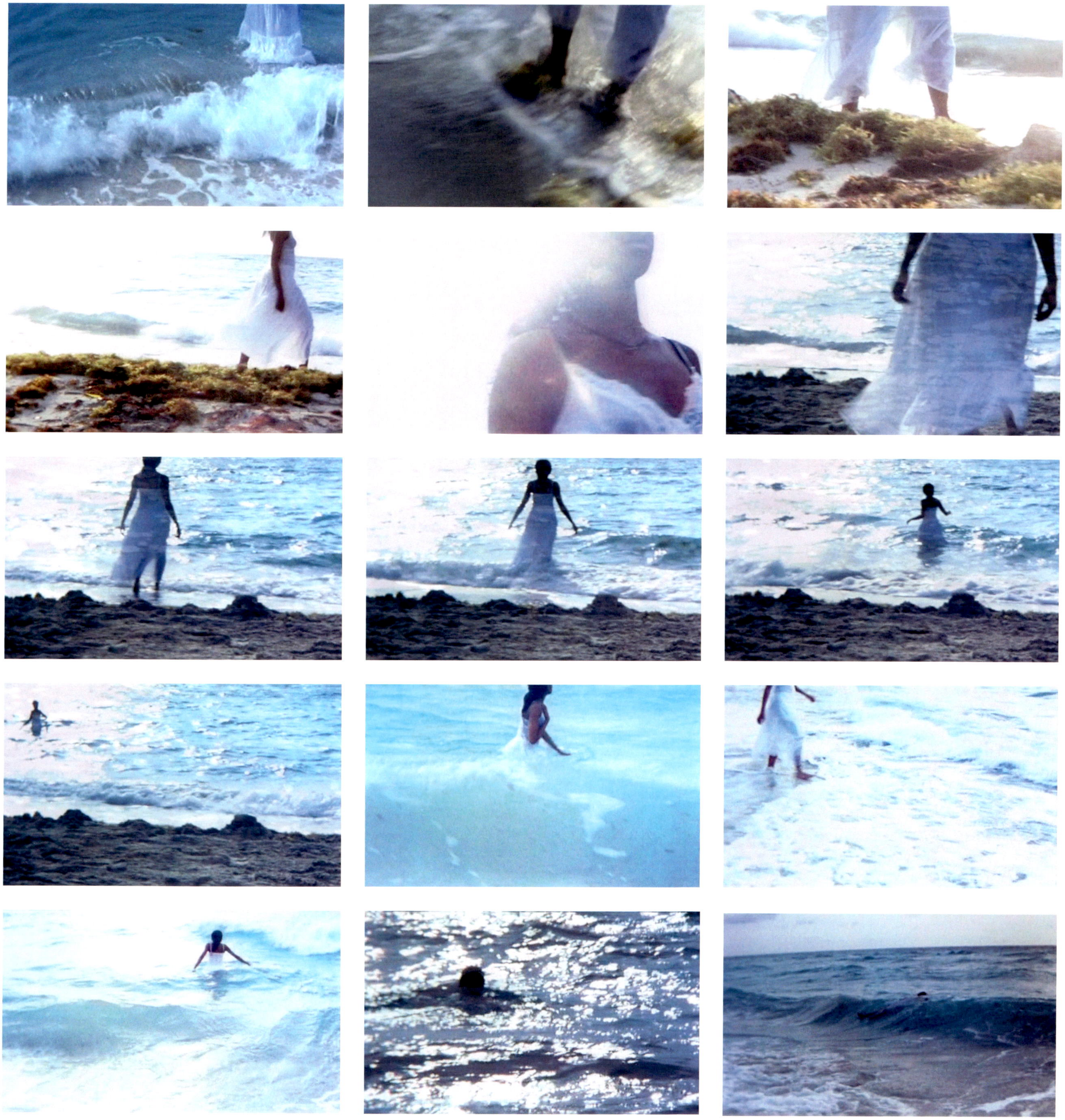

CUTTING, 2004
SINGLE-CHANNEL DIGITAL
VIDEO, SOUND
5 MIN. 45 MIN.

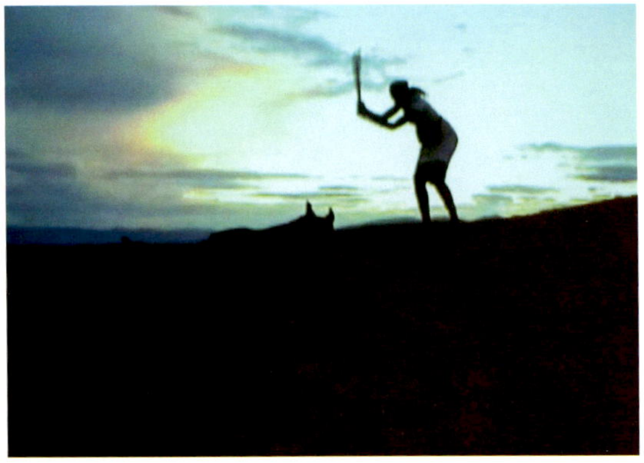

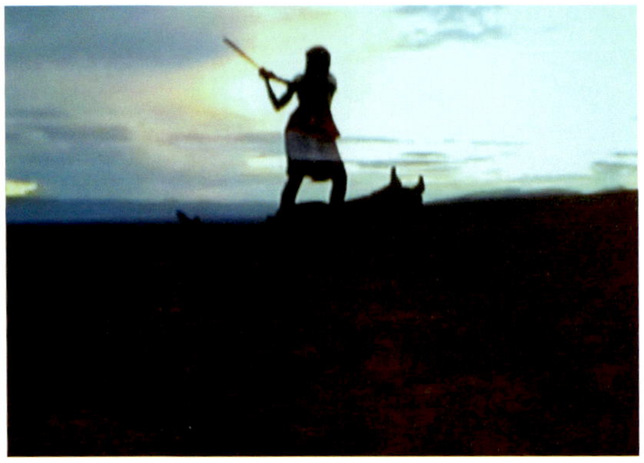

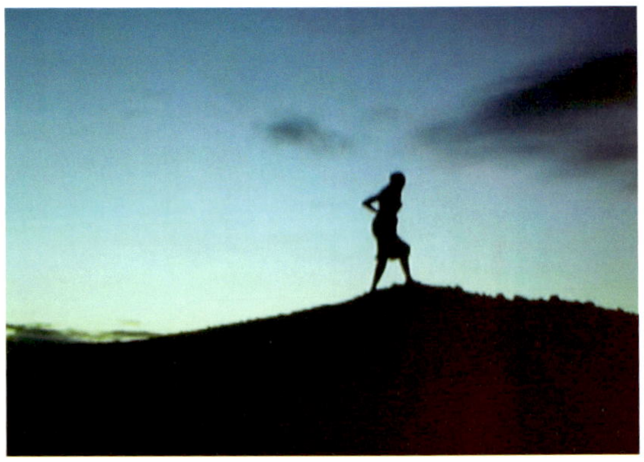

A shift to greater action and narrative in Mutu's video is concomitant with her exploration of live performance. Commissioned by Performa, New York's Biennial of Performance Art, *Stone Ihiga* (2009) was the first of her few public performances. Here recorded song, live vocalizations (some in Gikuyu), and paired movement by Mutu and singer Imani Uzuri took on women's executions by stoning, often for sexual infractions.[102] The piece highlighted the artist's continuing interest in the complexities of sexuality and pleasure as arenas that remain 'contingent and fraught', and which also open onto spacious terrains of desire and beauty.[103] Mutu's work invests in such concepts, encouraging the utterance of like sentiments by those who often haven't been allowed to own them.[104]

A mounting sense of repudiation of unworkable strictures is more evident in *Throw* (2016). Clad in a black gown and gloves, a barefoot Mutu repeatedly reaches into a bag and flings black viscous matter at a wall. While her early video and performance draws on legacies of such artists as Pope.L, Sherman Fleming, Hsieh/Montano, Acconci and Abramovic, who all created keen meditations on/through duration, with *Throw* there is a clear gesture and ritual of refusal. Mutu centralizes the Black woman protagonist as a surrogate for the viewer's own activism, building on Russell's glitch feminism, digital dissent, malfunction and failure to perform, instead enacting its survival. The kinesthetics of *Throw* develop from the earlier black and white video *Shoe Shoe* (2010), modelled on the tone of closed-circuit television and the surveillance of Black life. The figure, the urban un-homed, or perhaps simply the domestic worker that she is dressed as, slowly pushes a shopping cart down a city street toward the unseen camera, hurling footwear with increasing vigour, grunting with the exertion of disavowal.

This specific and deliberate gesture is one that Mutu has thought through over time and lingers at the core of her practice. It constitutes the refusal of sublimated status, of the colonized subject, or the bounds of sexuality and gender, and is empowered by figural complexity. It is an act tied to the emergence of the artist's own feminist consciousness, and protest actions like that of Maathai and the mothers who rejected police violence in 1992 by stripping naked to bear their own 'experienced' bodies as weapons of power and refutation. Over decades, this gesture has been used across the continent as an emblem of women's might, and meshes with myriad deeds throughout the globe where women raise their voices in dissent.[105]

Mutu's mark-making material in *Throw* is a stew of magazine pulp, to which she has often referred as the waste or fecal matter of Western society. Fermented, boiled and soaked, this refuse is effectively recycled in a method that glosses traditional dyeing processes, which she had used previously in early pieces like the 'Body Parts' series.[106] Creating an Action Painting in the grand performative motion of Gutai artist Saburo Murakami (*Passing Through,* 1955) Mutu transforms and seems to repudiate her earlier collage practice. Indeed, the pulpy materiality went hand in hand with her return to three-dimensions, its texture suggesting the sculptural possibilities of clay.[107]

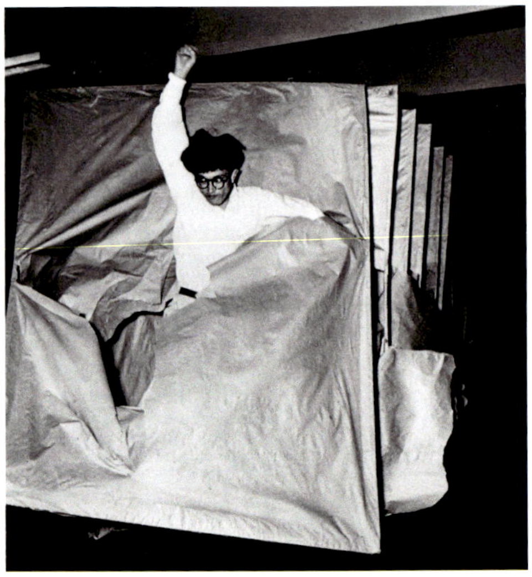

SABURO MURAKAMI
AT ONE MOMENT OPENING SIX HOLES, 1955
PERFORMANCE
OHARA HALL, TOKYO

STONE IHIGA, 2009
PERFORMANCE

PERFORMA, NEW YORK, 2009

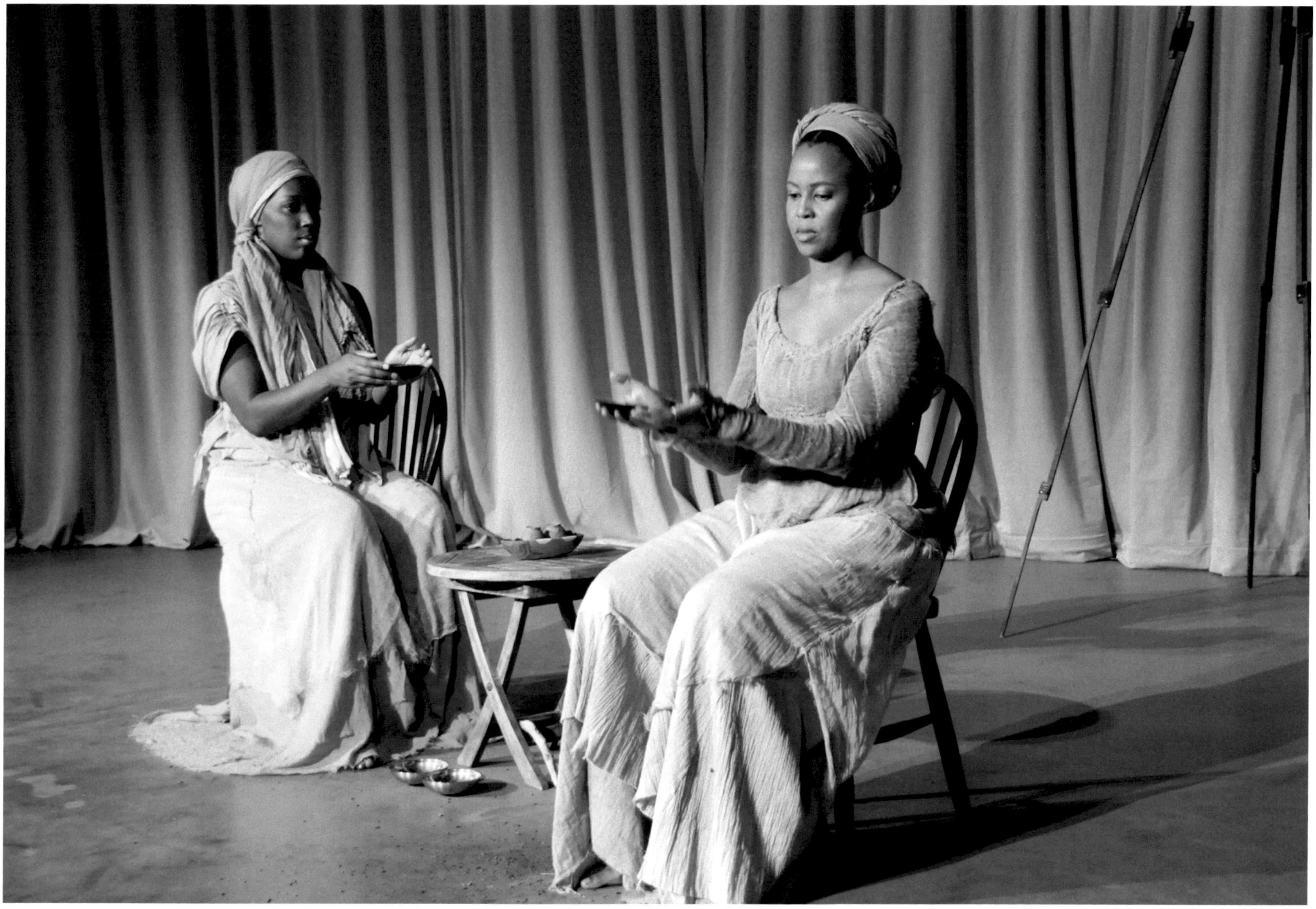

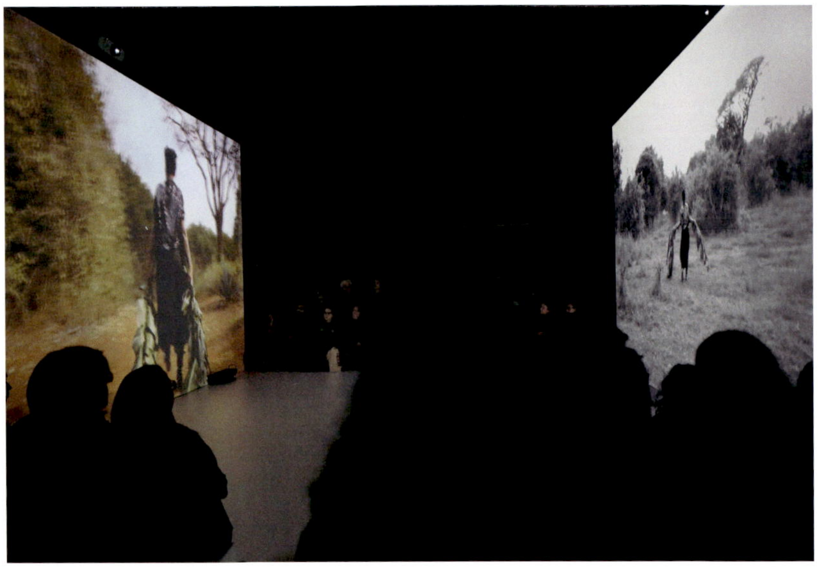
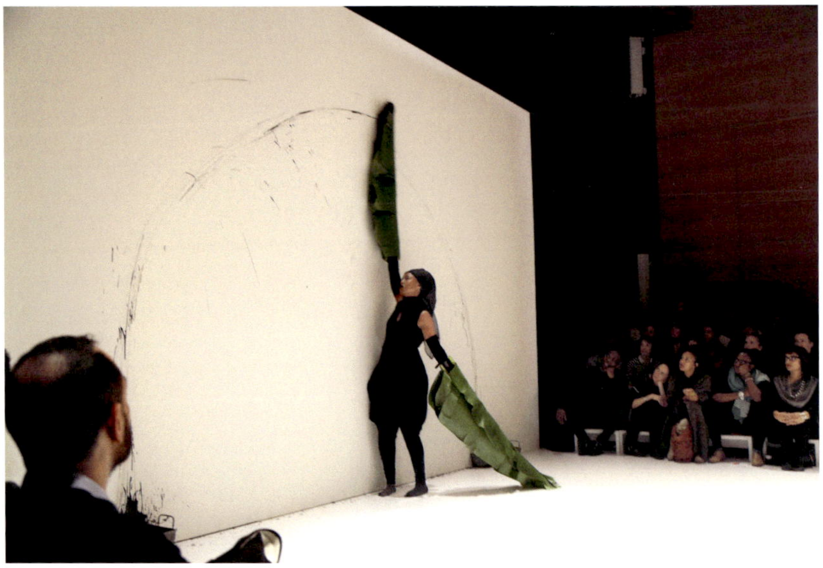
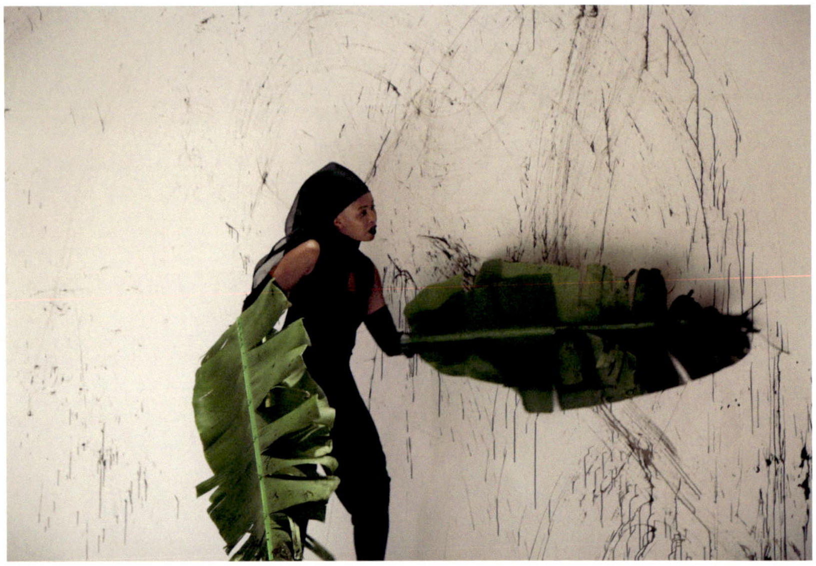
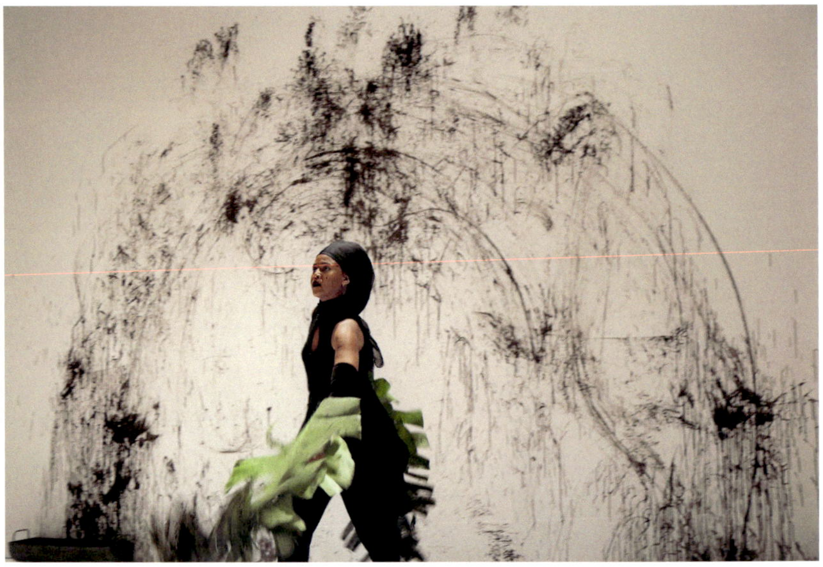
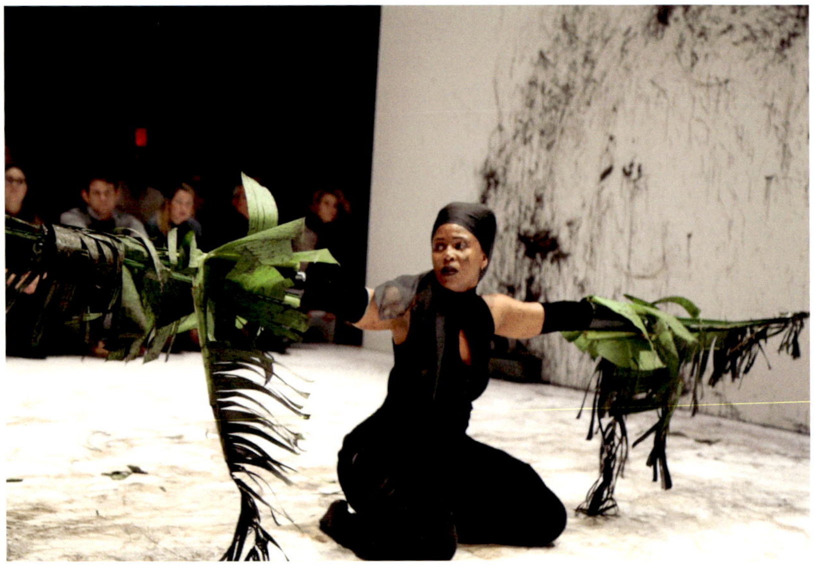
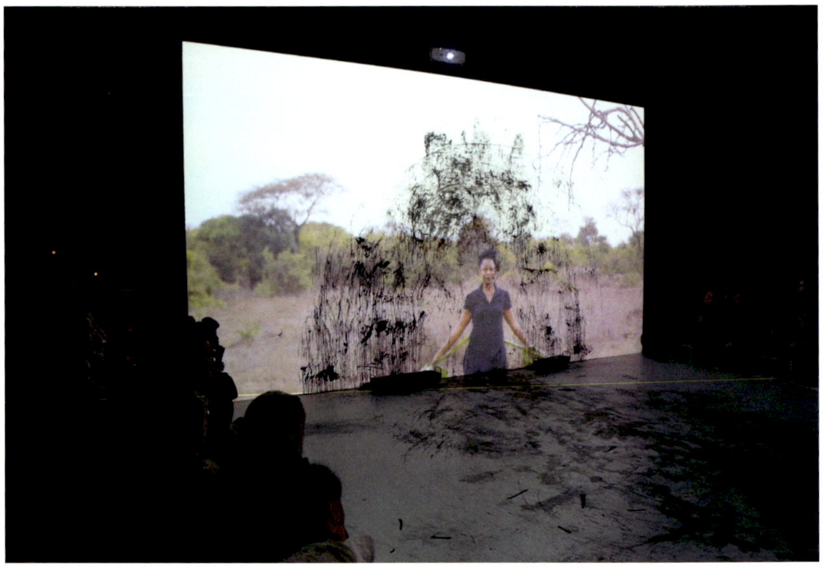

BANANA STROKE, 2017
SITE SPECIFIC ACTION
PAINTING

PERFORMA, NEW YORK, 2017

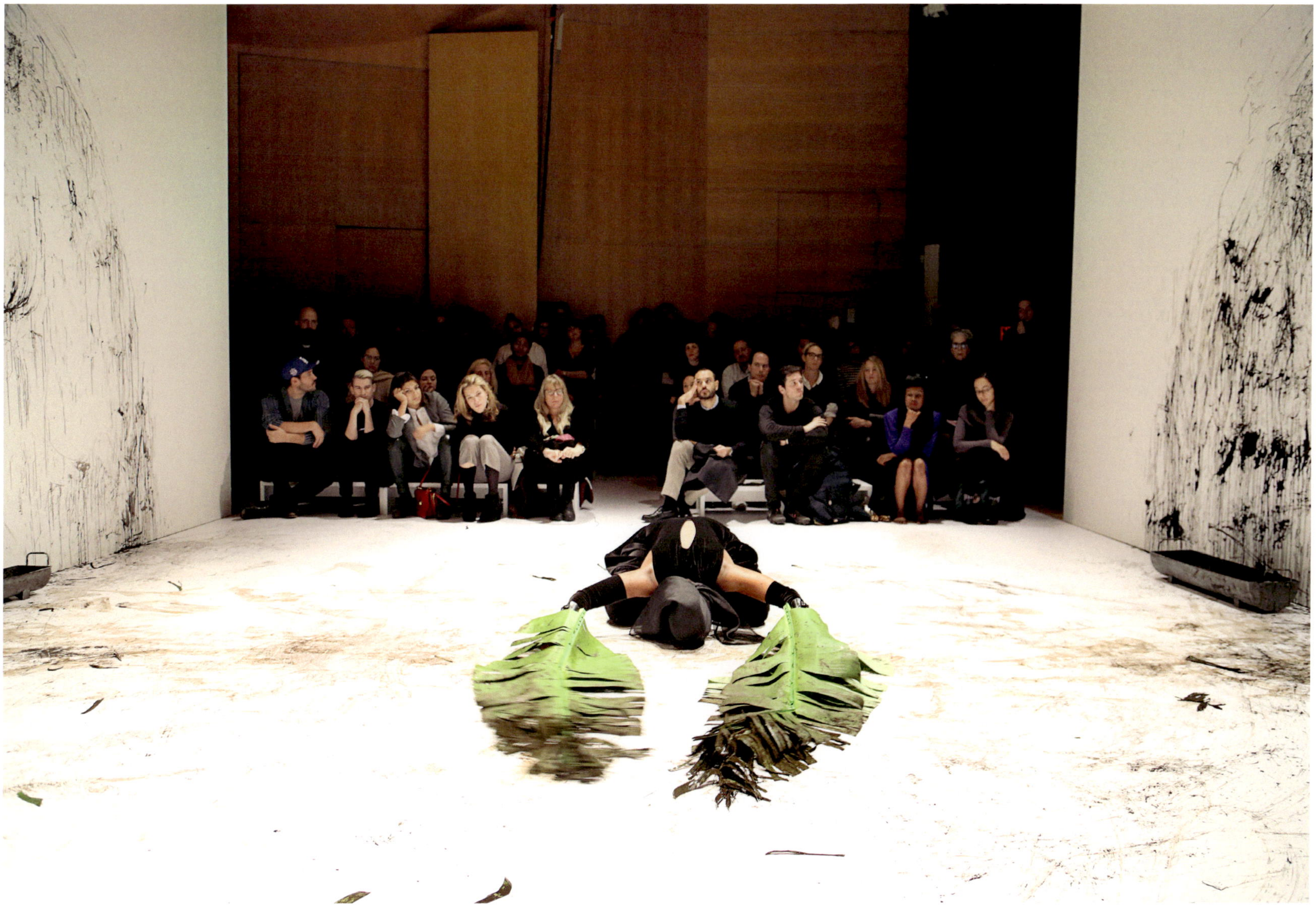

THROW, 2016
SITE-SPECIFIC ACTION
PAINTING AND PERFORMANCE

THE CONTEMPORARY AUSTIN,
AUSTIN, TEXAS

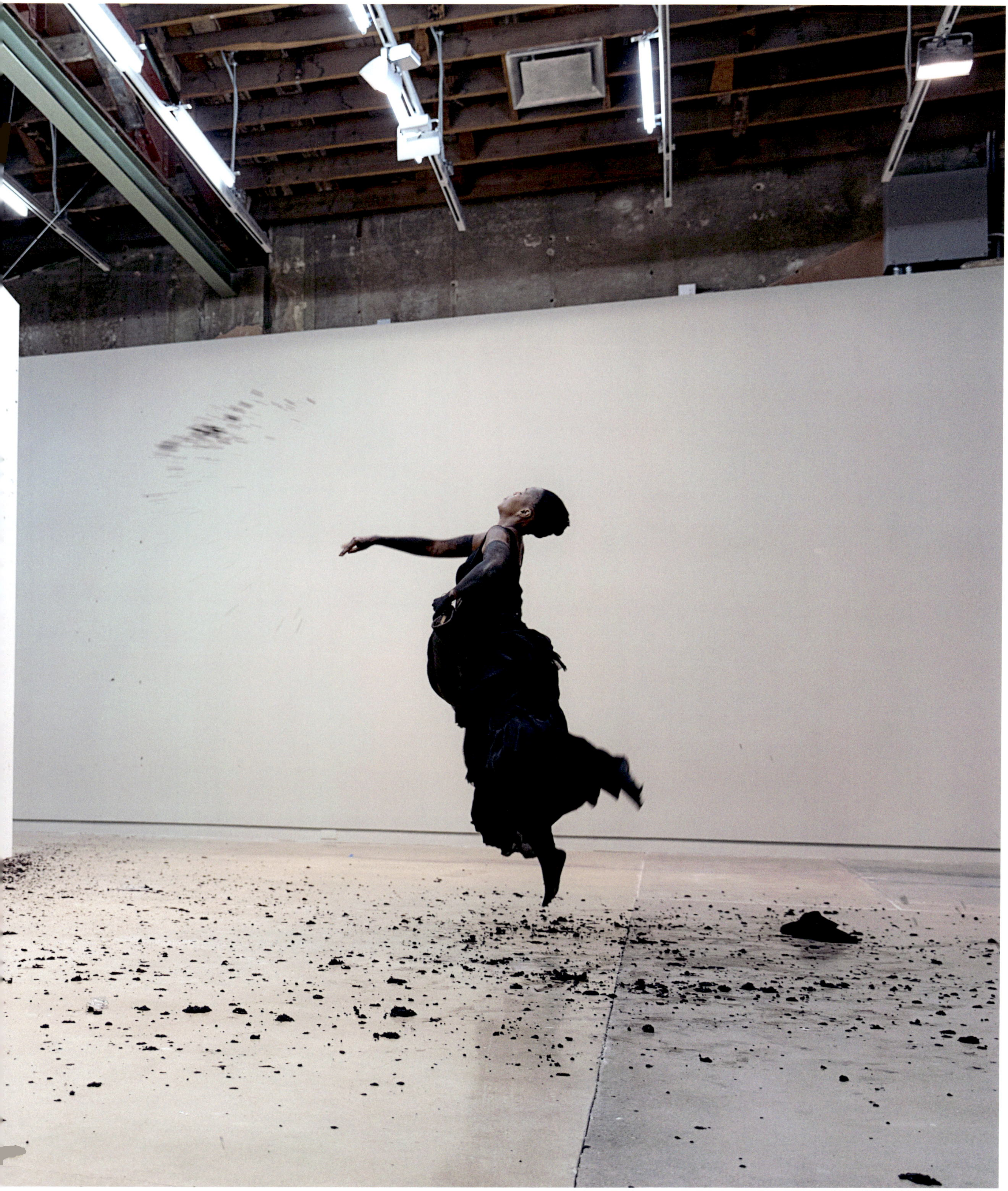

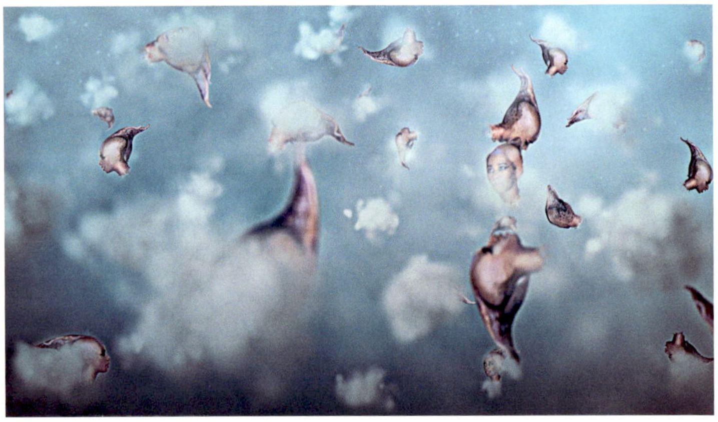

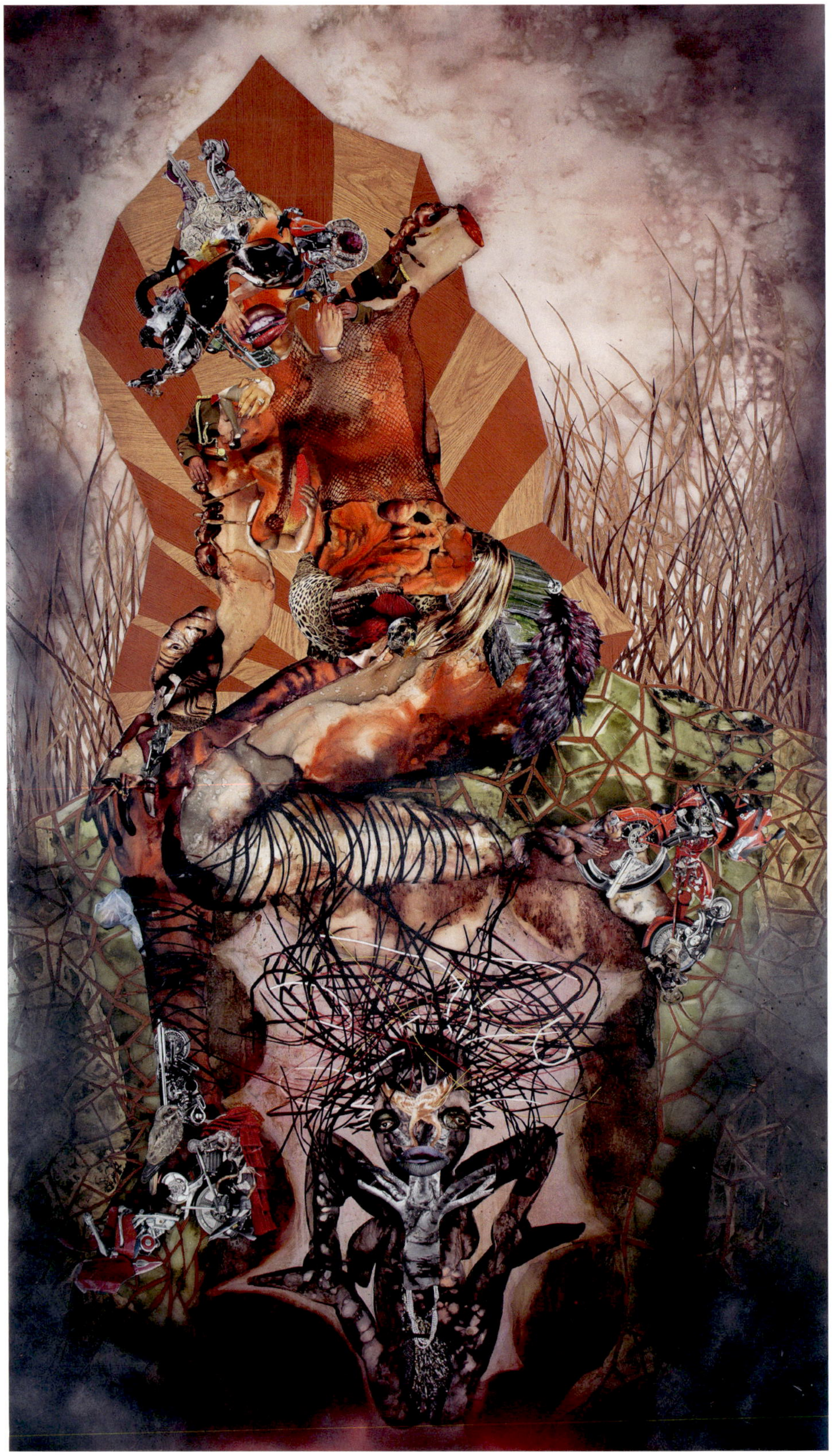

More complex camerawork and dense narratives are features of later digital projects, such as *Eat Cake* (2010). To the motley sounds of nature's birdcalls and the clank of costume jewellery, a siren in Lucite heels, nail and hair extensions, and other finery squats to eat her confection from a forest floor, frantically attempting to quell an insatiable hunger that is as much tactile as alimentary. Pleasure and erotics mingle with the apparent degradation of hyper-consumption. But we can also understand the protagonist's ritual feast as malleable, made over in the glitch, through electronic error signifying that things are not straightforward, questioning what or who is being consumed. The incoherence or wildness here is not a 'foil of civilization' but performs inconsistently, beside and beyond 'colonial epistemes'.[108]

Through animation and multichannel technology, *The end of eating everything* (2013) and *The End of carrying All* (2015) amplify contingent themes that turn our attention to 'consumptive neoliberal practices'.[109] In the earlier video, a floating figure (one Mutu sees as representing the earth as mother) consumes the 'discarded machinery' of humanity to the point of exploding, releasing diminutive living creatures into the world. Such motifs of renewal and rebirth visualize a Black feminist ecological turn, acknowledging human dependence on the environment and interconnectedness with it. The body becomes part of the land's

oppposite, from left,
THE END OF EATING EVERYTHING, 2013
ANIMATED VIDEO, COLOUR, SOUND
8 MIN. 10 SEC.

ROOT OF ALL EVES, 2010
MIXED MEDIA, INK, PAINT, COLLAGE ON MYLAR
246 X 147 CM

left,
SPROUT, 2010
MIXED MEDIA, INK, PAINT, FAKE PEARLS, GLITTER, COLLAGE ON MYLAR
137 X 130 CM

below,
EAT CAKE, 2012
VIDEO, BLACK-AND-WHITE, SOUND
12 MIN. 51 SEC.
INSTALLATION MATERIALS: NEWSPRINT, USED CARD-BOARD BOXES, WOOD, FELT, BLANKETS, RECYCLED PLASTIC, RECYCLED CARDBOARD

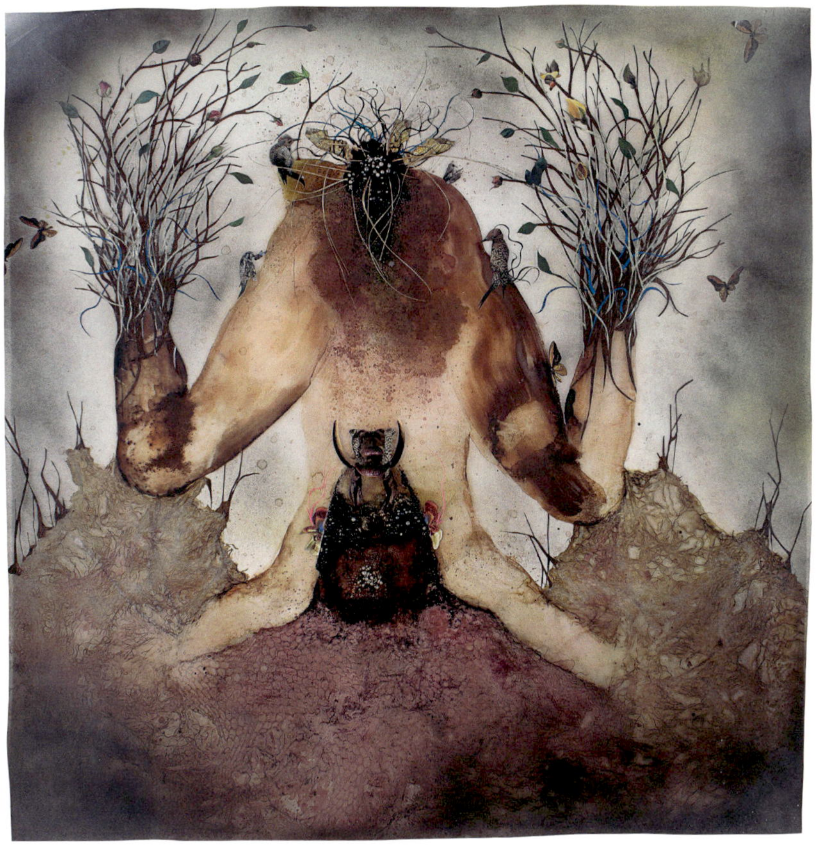

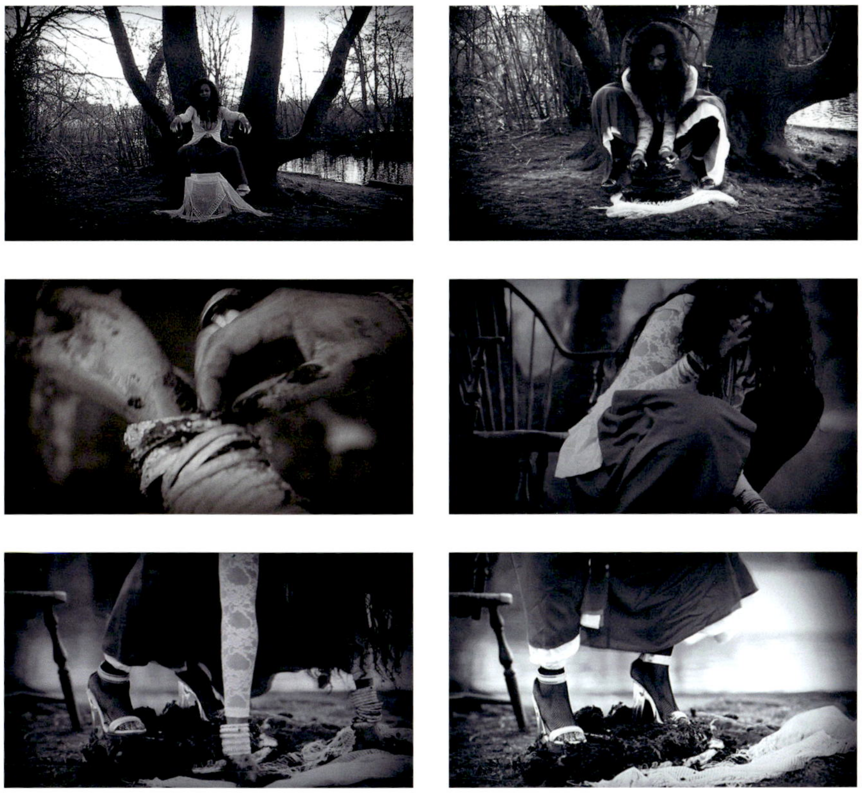

transformation by transmogrifying and repairing ecological abuse, actions mirrored in collages such as *Root of All Eves* (2010) and *Sprout* (2010) that cast Black women as a powerful generative force.

Hirsch reads the later *The End of Carrying All* (2015) as more apocalyptic. In this film commissioned by the 2015 Venice Biennale and its director Okwui Enwezor, Mutu's ever-present working woman moves incrementally across the foreground of three screens. A mountainous verdant landscape gives way to barren ground as the figure bends lower, carrying the weight of the world. Growing realms of technological refuse eventually consume its host, turning into a miasma that sends shock waves into the ground. The ambivalence or lack of closure is mitigated to a degree by the work's embeddedness in the installational, whose substance shuttles between sculpture, collage and filmic narrative, exemplifying Russell's concept of the infinite loop between our digital and physical worlds.

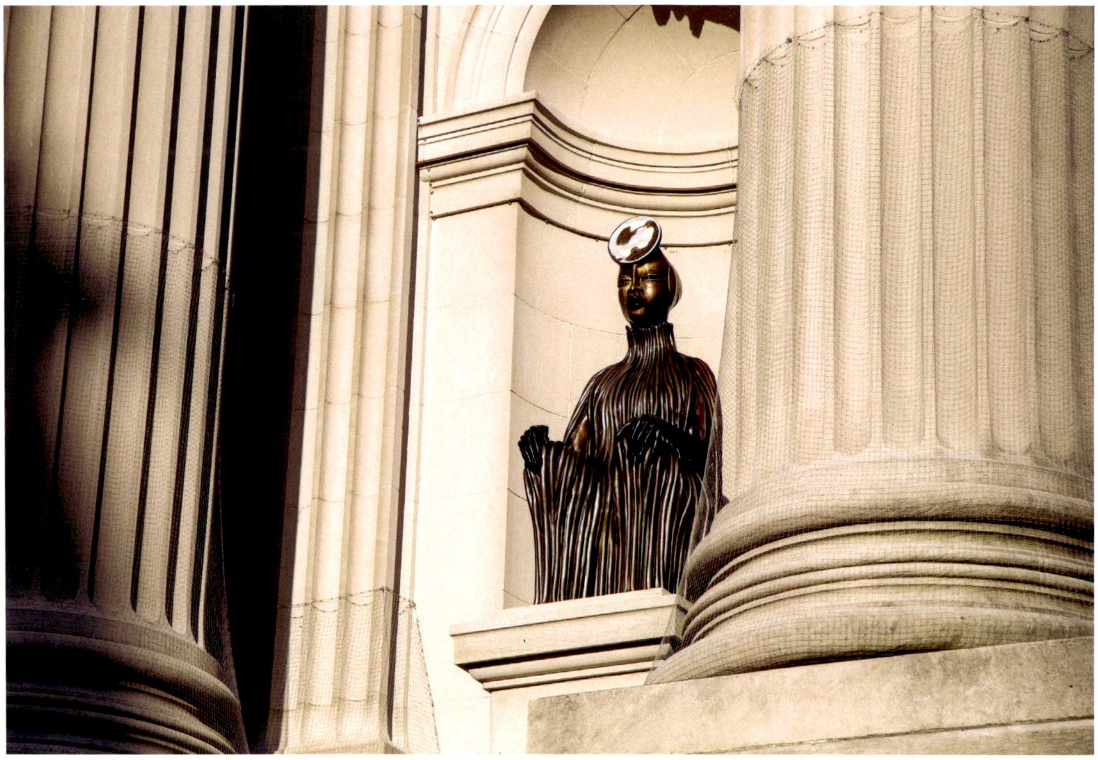

THE SEATED II, 2019
BRONZE
205 X 95 X 81 CM

INSTALLATION VIEW AT THE METROPOLITAN MUSEUM OF ART, NEW YORK, 2019

VI – Monuments

Monuments have been falling since at least 2015, when students at the University of Cape Town in South Africa insisted on the removal of a statue of British imperialist Cecil Rhodes, which for them stood as a testament to the inequities of education.[110] In 2020, in the wake of the deaths of George Floyd, Breonna Taylor, Amhaud Arbury, Tony McDade, and too many other victims of racial violence, such activities picked up in the United States and United Kingdom. Stone and metal statues of confederates and slavers were wrestled to the ground and picked apart or tossed into the waters to which they had unceremoniously consigned so many others. Sometimes, instead, these testaments to hatred and bigotry were just quietly and magically removed.

In announcing an initiative to rebuild the commemorative landscape of the United States, President of the Andrew W. Mellon Foundation and poet Elizabeth Alexander remarked on the 'vanishingly few' things celebrating the complex and vast array of US histories, instead commemorative spaces 'too often propagate menacingly incomplete accounts' of the past.[111] As Alexander called for a broader understanding of monuments, as video, as poetry, as place, as lived, scholar Ulrich Baer saw how artists could change the debate by reinventing the monument, stepping beyond representations of 'actual figures' to reset its terms and reinsert imagination while still addressing the vectors of history.[112] Baer looked to three artists whose 2019 projects made this turn toward reimagining the monument. While privately commissioned, all were public-facing and allied with museums. Kara Walker's *Fons Americanus* at London's Tate, and Kehinde Wiley's *Rumors of War* at the Virginia Museum of Fine Art both use classical European formulas – the grand fountain and equestrian statue respectively – reversing the objects of veneration from Confederate soldiers and European monarchs to the mostly unnamed, unrecorded Black bodies sacrificed in the name of Western power and dominance. Mutu's series of sculptures *The New Ones Will Free Us* (2019) occupied the niches on the Metropolitan Museum of Art's façade, spaces originally designed to house sculpture that had remained empty for over a century. The artist's monumental bronze female figures were seated, reversing the supportive role that caryatids usually play in such architectural detail, as elements that stand and appear to hold things up. But Mutu's endeavour also took structural and diagrammatic cues from African art rather than European tradition.

THE SEATED IV (DETAIL), 2019
BRONZE
205 X 93 X 85 CM

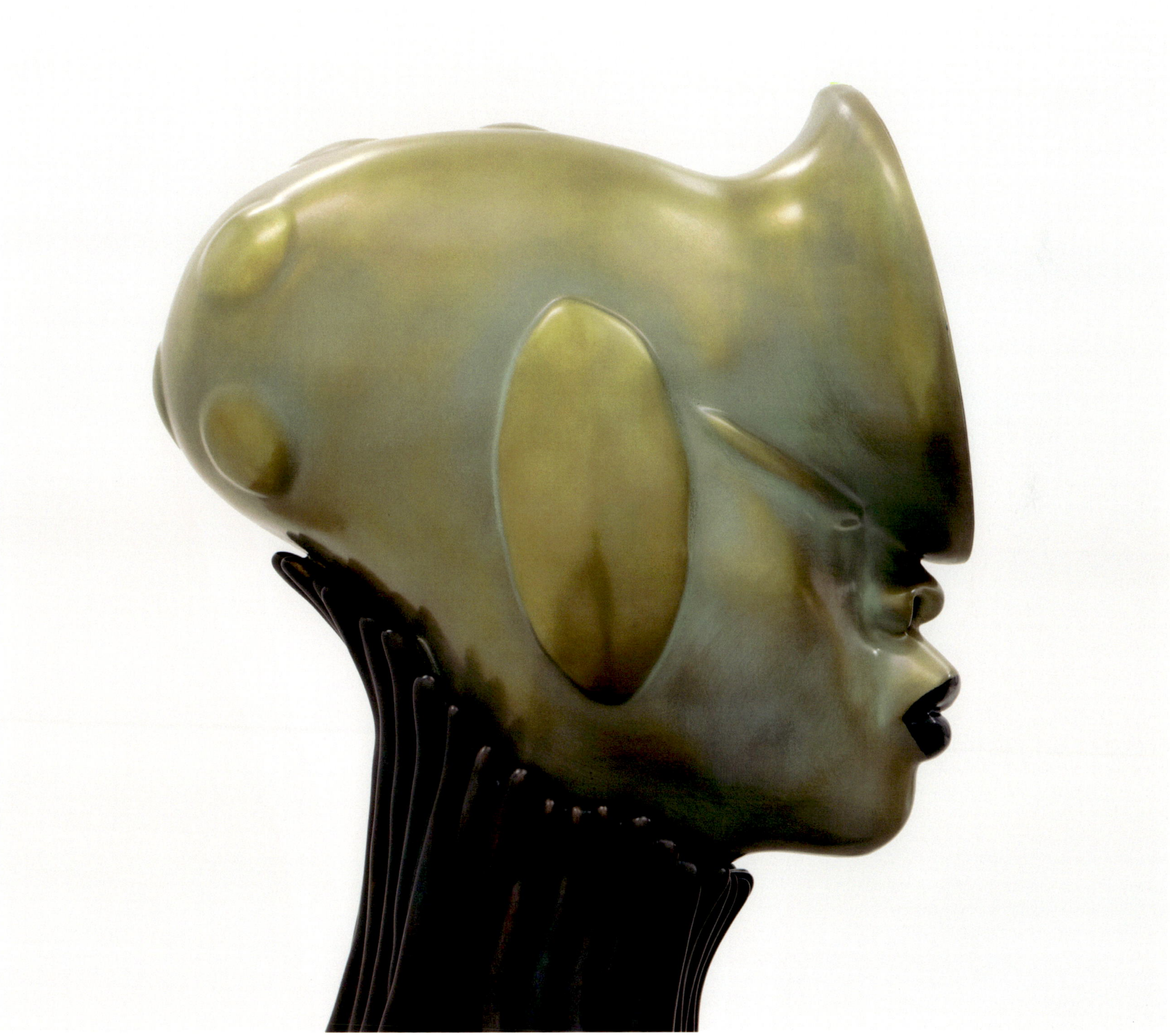

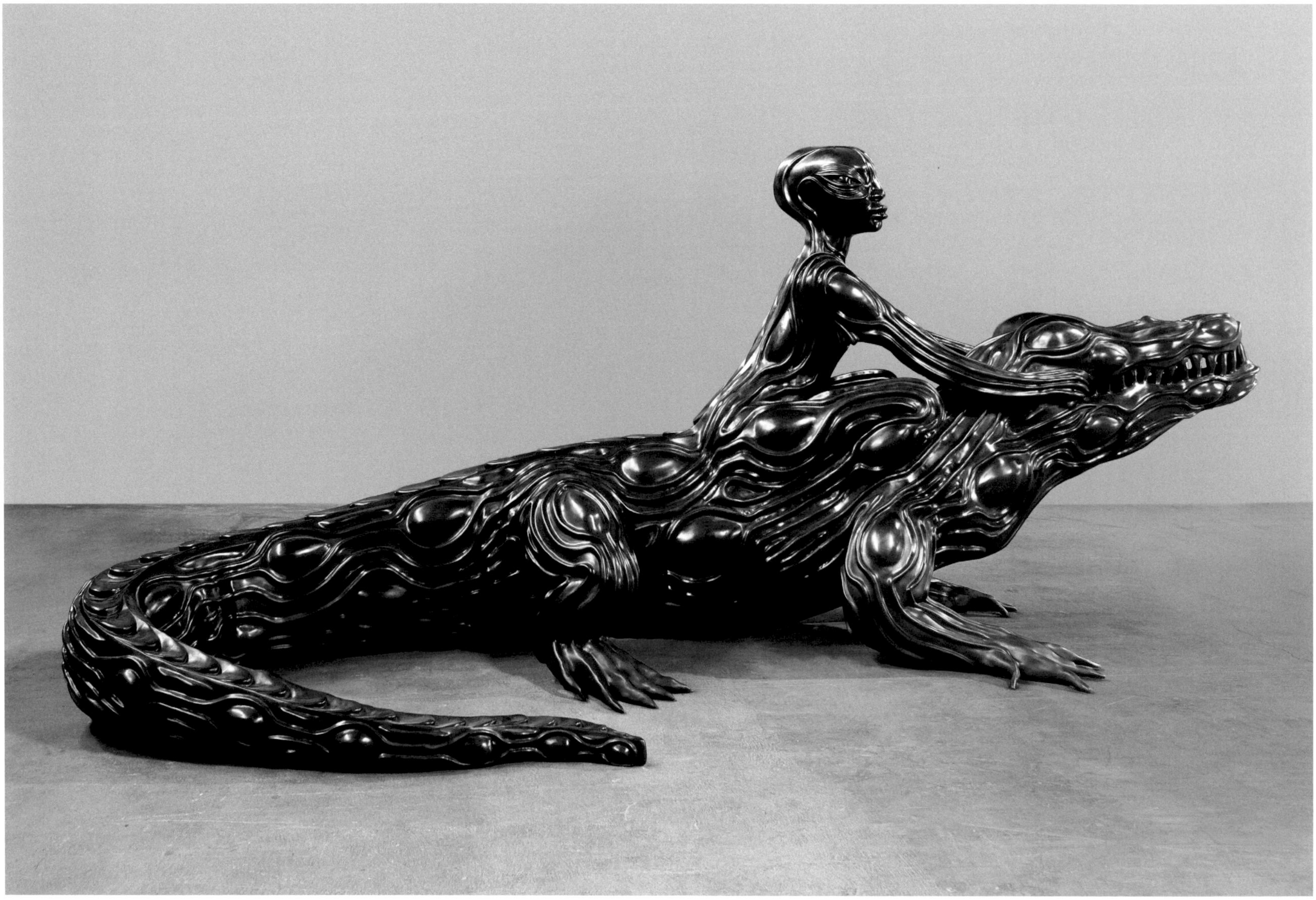

Mutu designed the *Seated, I–IV* (as they are identified), as conduits for the majesty of women of power and status. The heavy bronze coils of their garments are both protective armour and present a softness meant to imply fleshiness. Attenuated limbs and features give them a supernatural appearance. All four wear disks around their heads, polished to a brilliant shine, based on lip plates historically worn throughout East Africa (in Tanzania, Sudan, Ethiopia), and in *Seated III* worn as headdress in the manner of the Mangbetu of the Democratic Republic of Congo or Zulu in South Africa.[113] The coils encircling the bodies simulate those of the Sande women's society masks among the Mende of Sierra Leone, symbols of flourishing ascribed to water spirits that preceded Nguva and Mami Wata.[114] In the vertical orientation that covers *Seated II* and *Seated IV*, strands suggest raffia, the flora of masquerade adornment throughout the continent. We see Mutu working through some of these ideas in the extended digits and prominent lip plate of the earlier collage *Long Gold Fingerlings* (2012), done in the same year as two series in which she explores genealogy. *The Original Nine Daughters* creates experimental print portraits of women central to a Gikuyu origin story, while Family Tree, amongst Mutu's most abstract collages, meditates on the charting of ancestry, a mapping of kinship that is continually updating, and is always reconsidered and remade.

Ever more inspired by the natural world outside Mutu's Nairobi studio, *The New Ones Will Free Us* thinks through lineages that shape beauty and resilience. They are resplendent rather than subsidiary, and in that way reconfigure African sculptural tradition as well.[115] Rather than have them carry the weight of so many others, Mutu wanted to release these decidedly female figures from such worldly burdens. Instead as leaders and custodians, they are sentries for a new era, encouraging humans to do better. And as the artist remarks, 'They will be our redemption.'[116]

IN MEMORY OF SYLVIA BOONE AND OKWUI ENWEZOR.
WITH THANKS FOR RESEARCH ASSISTANCE TO MARCUS JAMISON AND DANA SUZANNE RODRIGUEZ.

THE ORIGINAL NINE DAUGHTERS, 2012
SERIES OF 9 ETCHING, RELIEF, LETTERPRESS, DIGITAL PRINTING, COLLAGE, POCHOIR, HAND COLORING AND HANDMADE CARBORUNDUM APPLIQUES, INK: JUSTIN ISRAELS, SARAH CARPENTER, KYLE SIMON
EACH 48 X 25 CM

opposite,
CROCODYLUS, 2020
BRONZE
424 X 221 X 185 CM

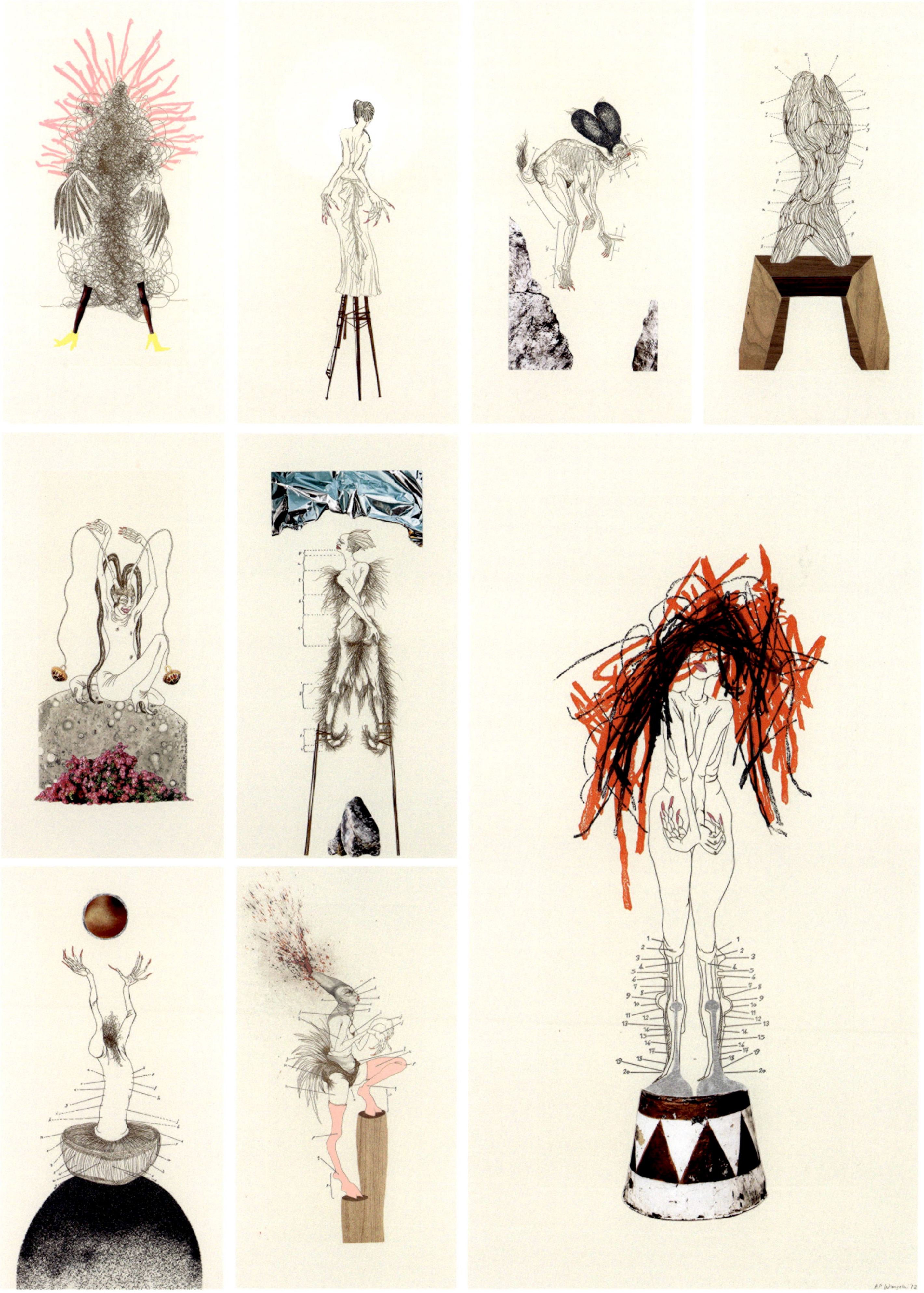

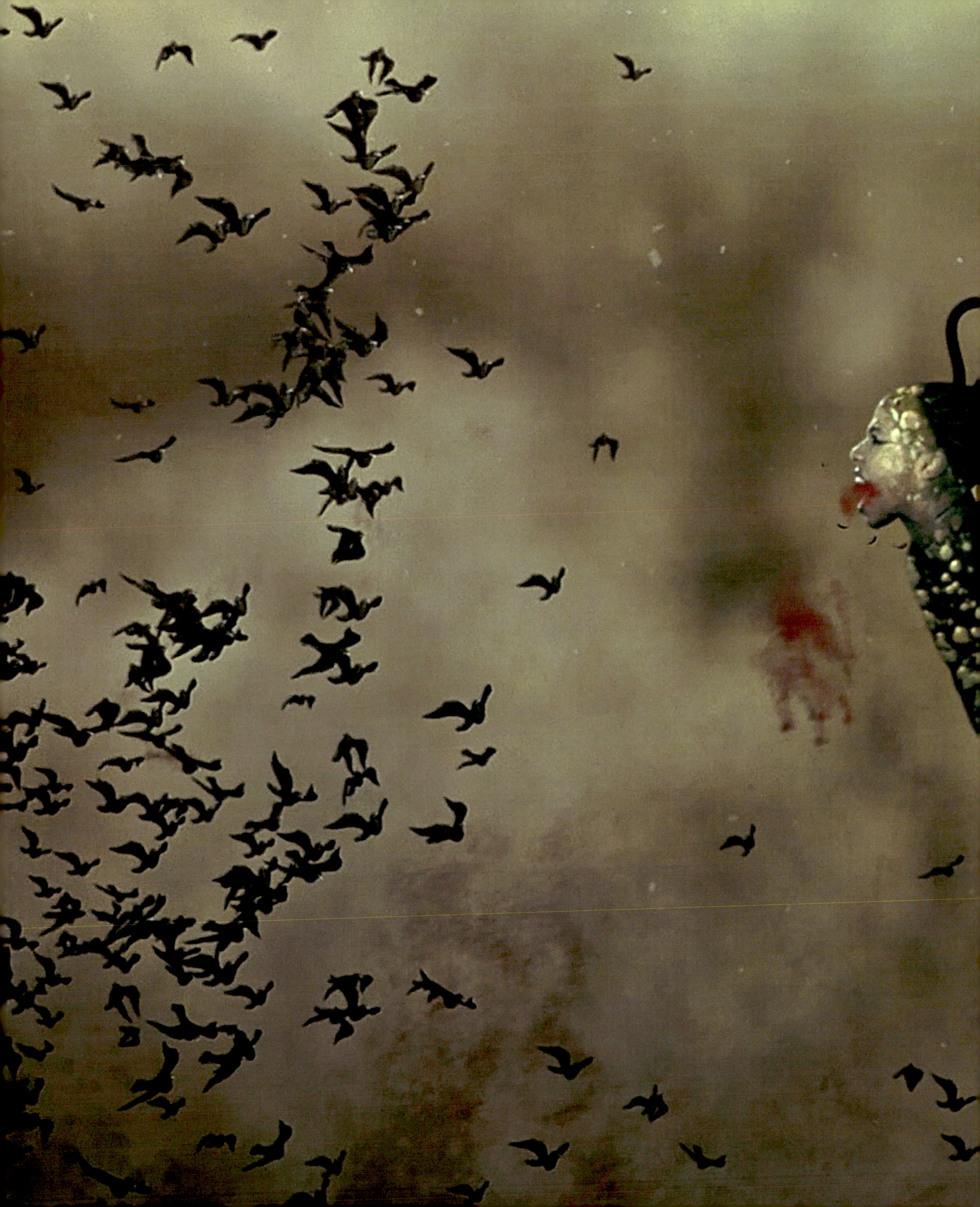

103 FOCUS

The End of eating Everything

Chika Okeke-Agulu

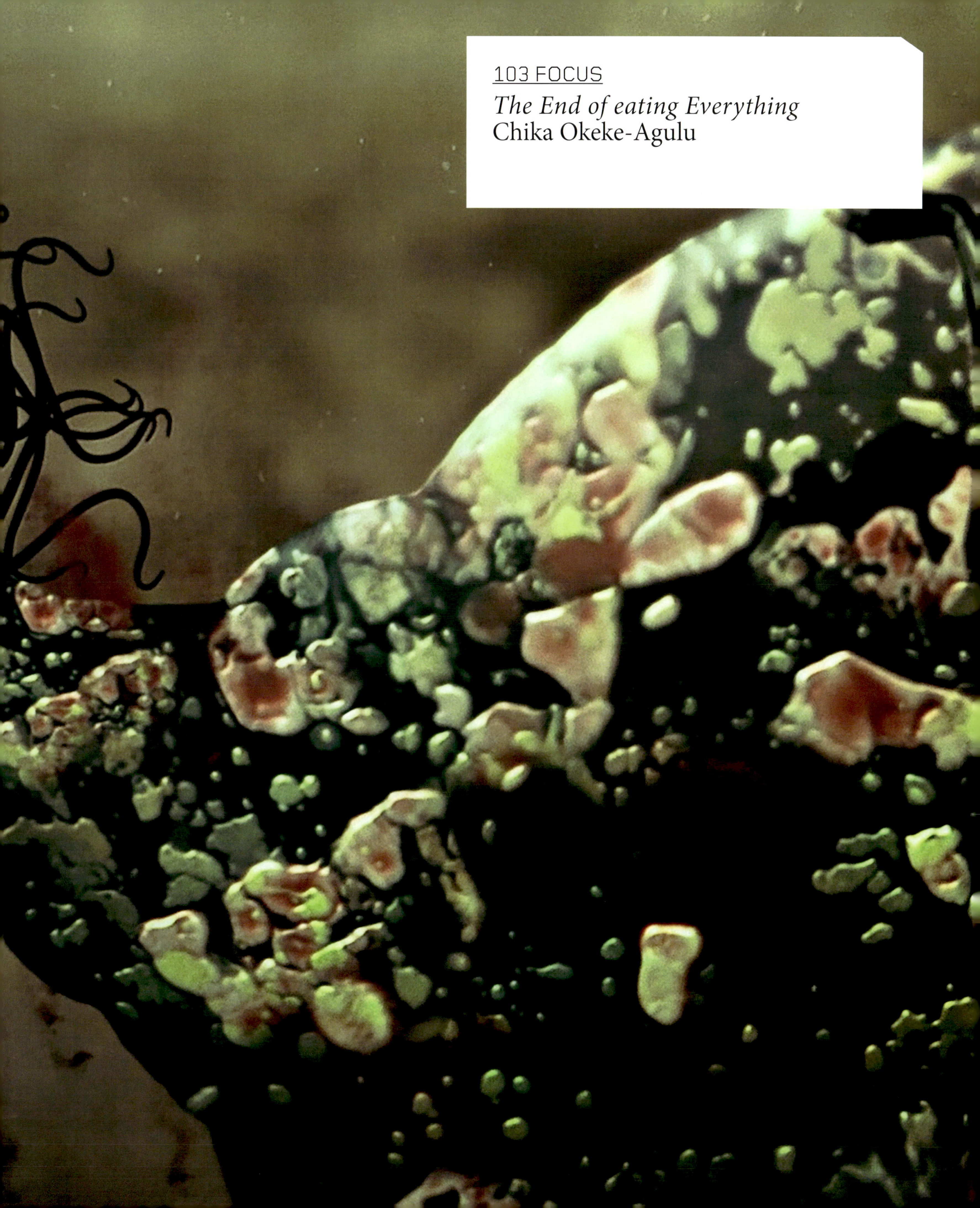

opposite and previous pages,
THE END OF EATING EVERYTHING, 2013
ANIMATED VIDEO, COLOUR, SOUND
8 MIN. 10 SEC

'Using land, either as subject matter or material in my work is a way for me to connect to and re-draw power from the fertile land of my childhood'.

– Wangechi Mutu[1]

Here is how Wangechi Mutu's video animation, The End of eating Everything (2013), plays out. Against a bloody skyscape, a horde of noisy black birds, slenderer and more agile than ravens, burst into the scene from the left, and dance their way forward. From the right emerges a woman's face, seen in profile and with striking pharaonic make up, her hairline pulsing with luminescent lesions. She might be royalty or mystic, someone with tremendous power. She casts her gaze in the direction of the birds, closes her eyes, sensing them. In this brief instant, a poem (written by the artist), one line at a time, flashes at the bottom of the screen:

I never meant to leave
I needed to escape
And now it's so far
Who knows where?
It's been like this for a very long time
It follows me, and I them
We've always been
Hungry, alone, together

From this moment on, the camera slowly and steadily pulls away, revealing the rest of the woman's gargantuan body. Her impossibly large, prehensile hair braids straighten, flutter gracefully and snap into menacing curls like a predator's tentacles as she sways and pulls her blob-body into view. She glowers at the birds, but they continue

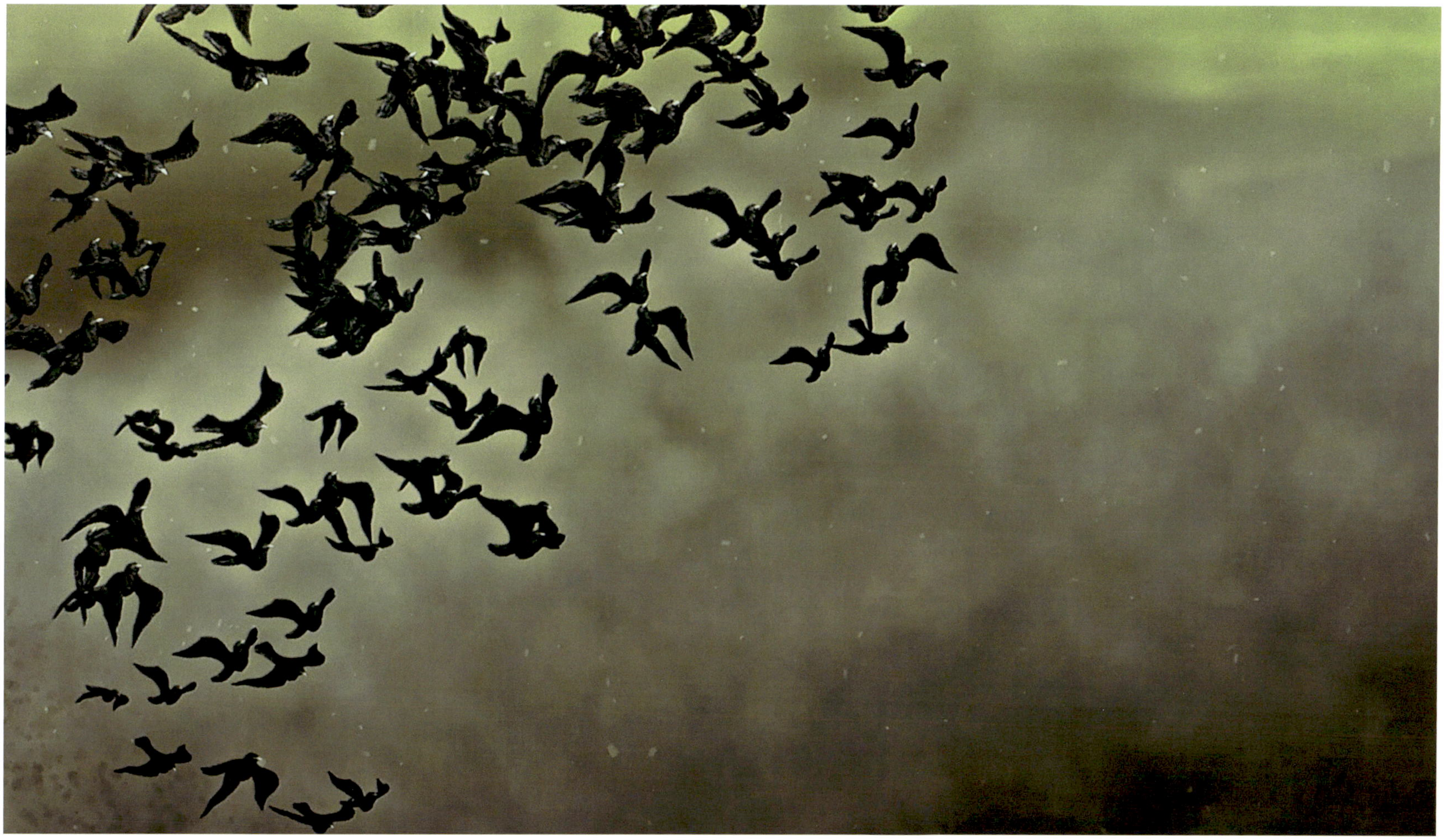

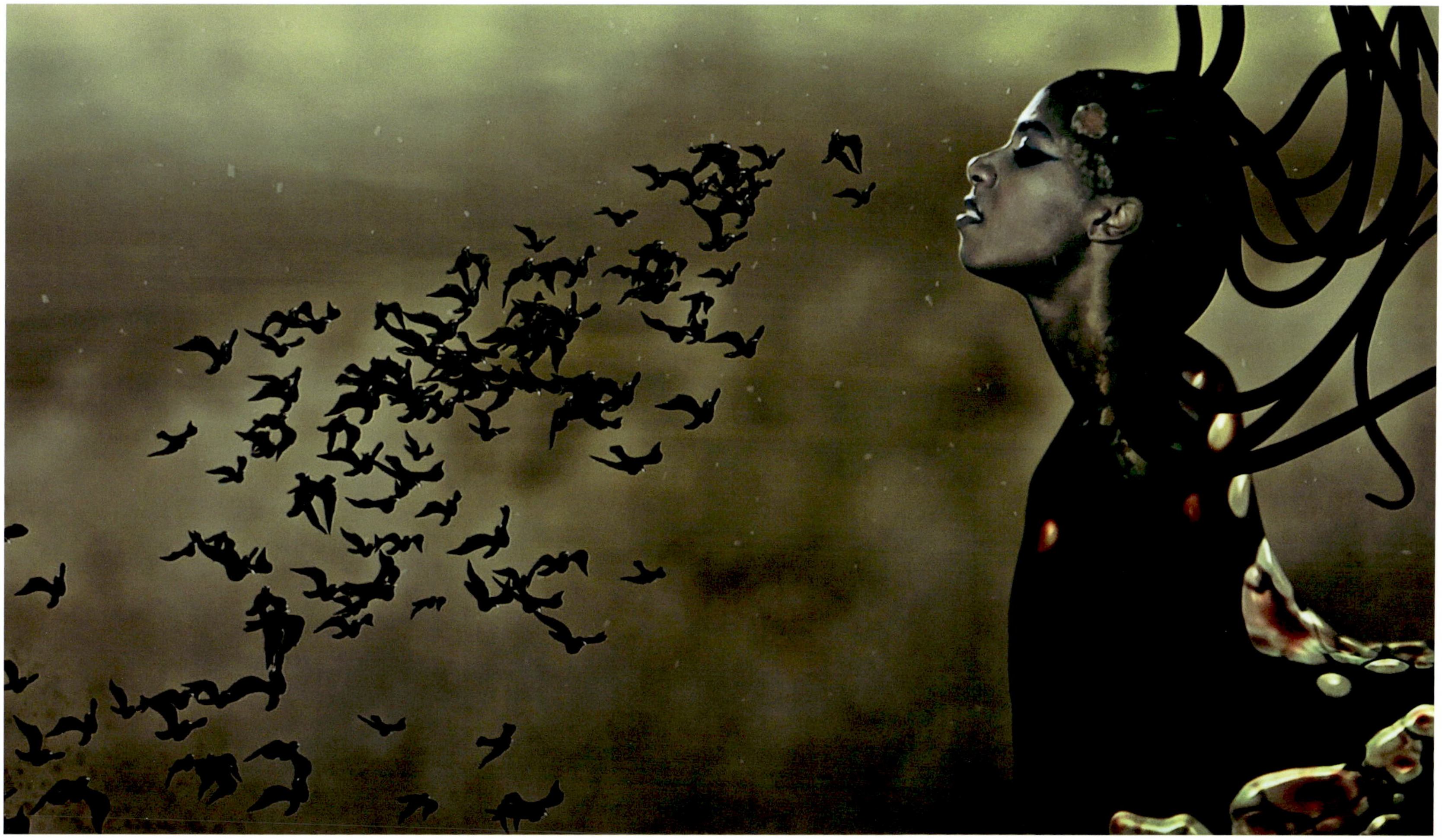

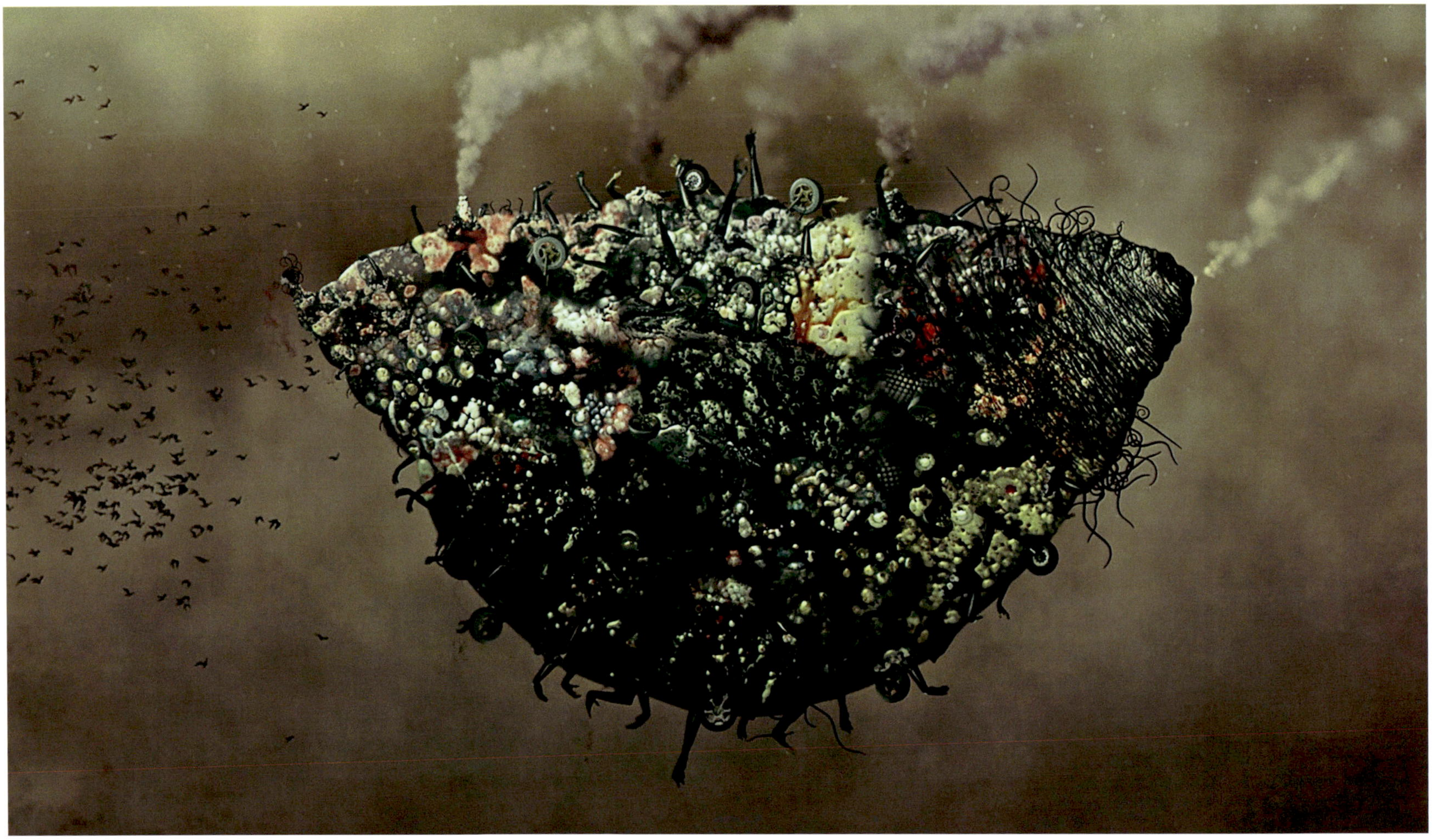

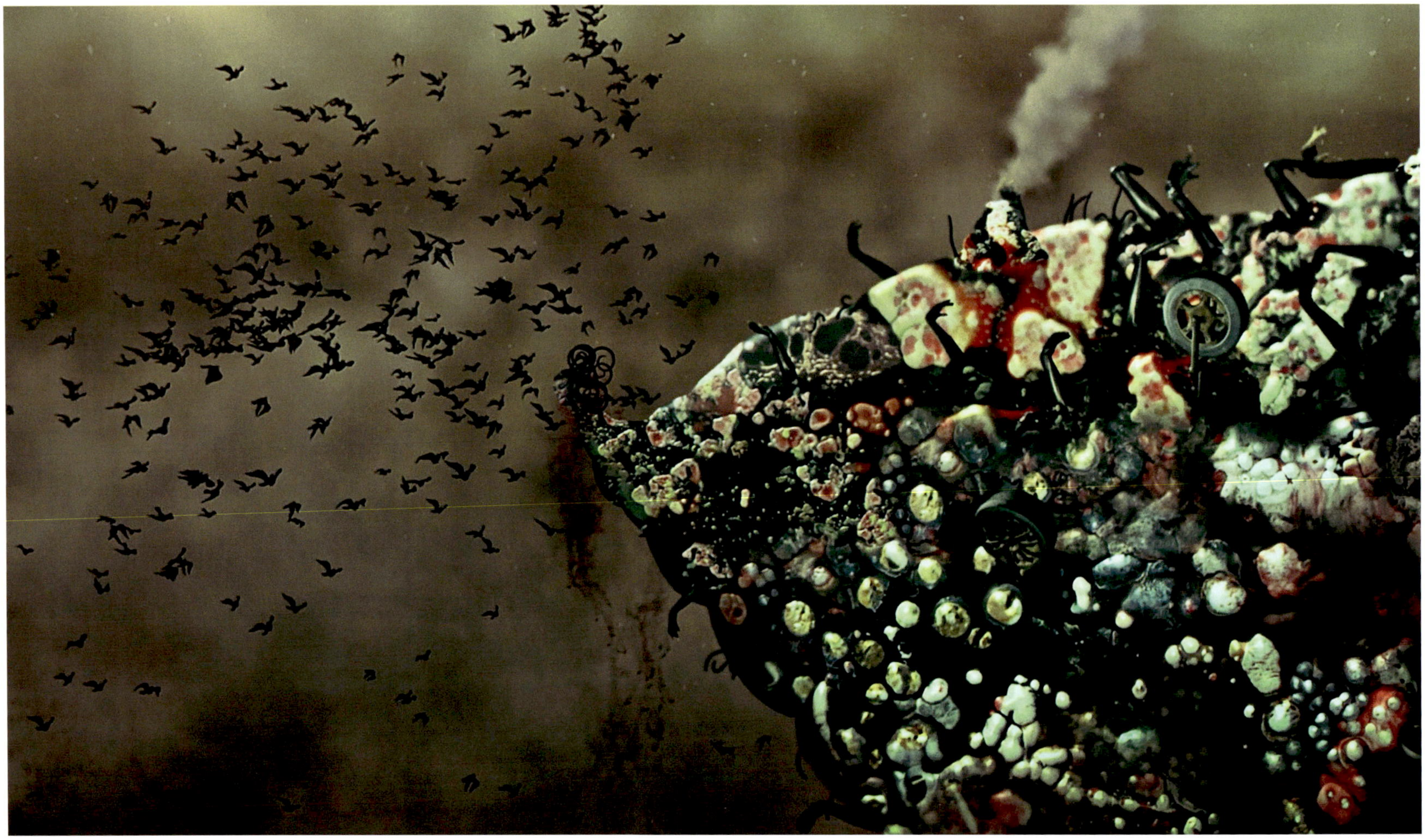

opposite,
THE END OF EATING EVERYTHING, 2013
ANIMATED VIDEO, COLOUR, SOUND
8 MIN. 10 SEC

their choreographed flight back and forth. She suddenly rears back, raises a mighty howl and pounces, leaving billows of blood. The birds, apparently unscathed, pull back then forward, continuing their aerial ballet. If this is a violent clash, we are not entirely sure whose blood has been spilled. In the meantime, as the camera pans away, we now see the woman's entire body. It is colossal and resembles a unicellular organism, without primary limbs or any other recognizable anatomical part. In its colourfulness, it reminds you of resplendent and populated coral reef; but it is also cacophonic with numerous rotating tyres, and other mechanical and organic rotting stuff that makes us think of a vast urban landfill. Her entire profile is punctuated by the tyres and numerous waving black arms that seem to paddle her, even as parts of her body heave like a subterranean Leviathan. On her dorsal side, several turrets belch white, red, grey and green smoke, while her anal orifice heaves volcanic clouds that soon swirl into a massive cyclone, which then overwhelms and obliterates her and her avian antagonists. In the wake of the cataclysm, numerous disembodied heads with cranial fins – multiples of the woman – pop up, tumble-floating, like galactic debris, in the blue, cumulus-filled sky. Then fade.

The affective and enigmatic power of this work lies not so much in its staging of this bloody and cataclysmic confrontation as in its mobilization and deployment of many paradoxes, its compression and stretching of the boundaries of the narrative and the poetic in such a way that the uncurious viewer might miss the big picture, enthralled by its secondary significations. I have been surprised by the general consensus in the scholarship that the film is a depiction of a gluttonous monster-woman with an insatiable appetite devouring hapless birds. She is, says one of the first critics to comment on the work, 'an extraordinary creature possessed of alarming power'.[2] That is, the video is an animated version of the often uncomfortable and dark pictorial drama featuring Afrofuturist humanimal women, at once beautiful and repulsive, that we see in Mutu's well known collage work. Maybe so. But I want to suggest that the essence, that is the fundamental concern, of The End of eating Everything is to be found in the artist's preoccupation since the early years of her career with the land and woman as founts and sustainers of life, both victims of anthropogenic and patriarchal subjection.

The figures in Mutu's work from early on, as Franklin Sirmans noted in 2003, 'are simultaneously abject and flamboyant, seductive and repulsive ... [They] tell a story of trauma and regeneration too often left out of our edited version of cultural history.'[3] Similarly, Claudia Schmuckli recently observed that 'Mutu's main concern has been with women's bodies as sites of ideological conflict but also as a loci of hope and renewal.'[4] For her part, Mutu has insistently alerted us to the incidence and meaning of land and earth as subject or material

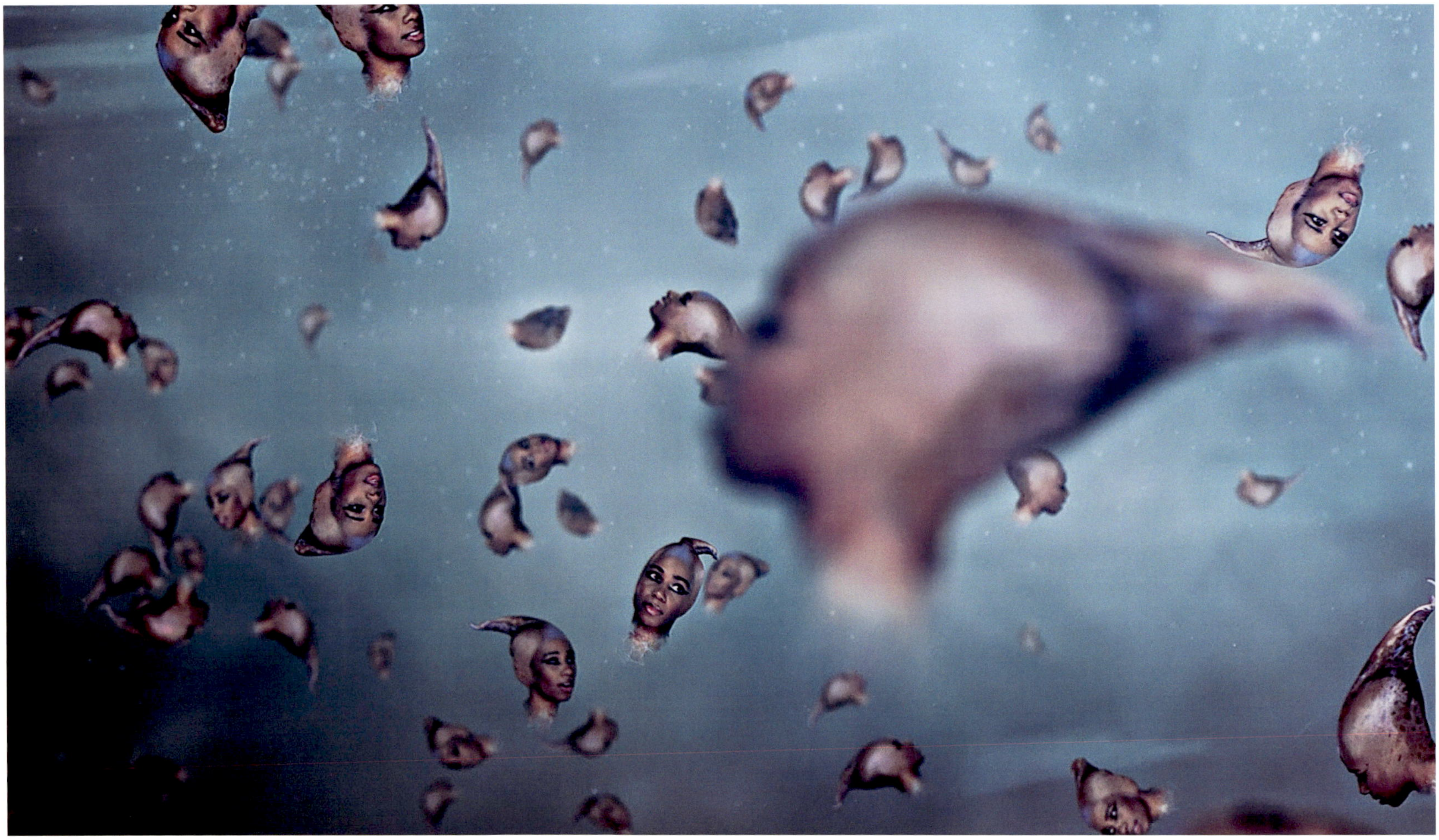

in her work, describing them as a means 'to connect and re-draw power from the fertile land of my childhood.'[5] And in 2014, shortly after completing The End of eating Everything, she described the work as about 'earth's predicament and present state of being. I feel like our illnesses are earth's illnesses. Our own lack of regard and respect for the earth is related to our lack of regard for our humanity.'[6] In other words, the woman in the video, with her beautiful face and rotting flesh, her Nefertiti neck and dump-yard body, is in fact Mutu's way of enfiguring – that is giving form to the idea of – the sick earth, the same earth whose sickness is co-extensive with the actions of post-industrial, hyper-consumptive humans. The figure's monstrosity, says Mutu is 'a culmination of all our illnesses'.[7] It becomes clear then, that the woman in The End of eating Everything, despite the terrifying beauty of her face, the bestial power she commands, and the repulsiveness of her distended, formless body, is indeed, a sympathetic, violated and justifiably enraged figure of the earth-land, whose natural capacity for generating and supporting life has been fatally compromised by anthropogenic forces.

CLEANING EARTH, 2006
SINGLE-CHANNEL DIGITAL
VIDEO, SOUND
25 MIN. 45 SEC.

opposite,
THE END OF EATING
EVERYTHING, 2013
ANIMATED VIDEO, COLOUR,
SOUND
8 MIN. 10 SEC.

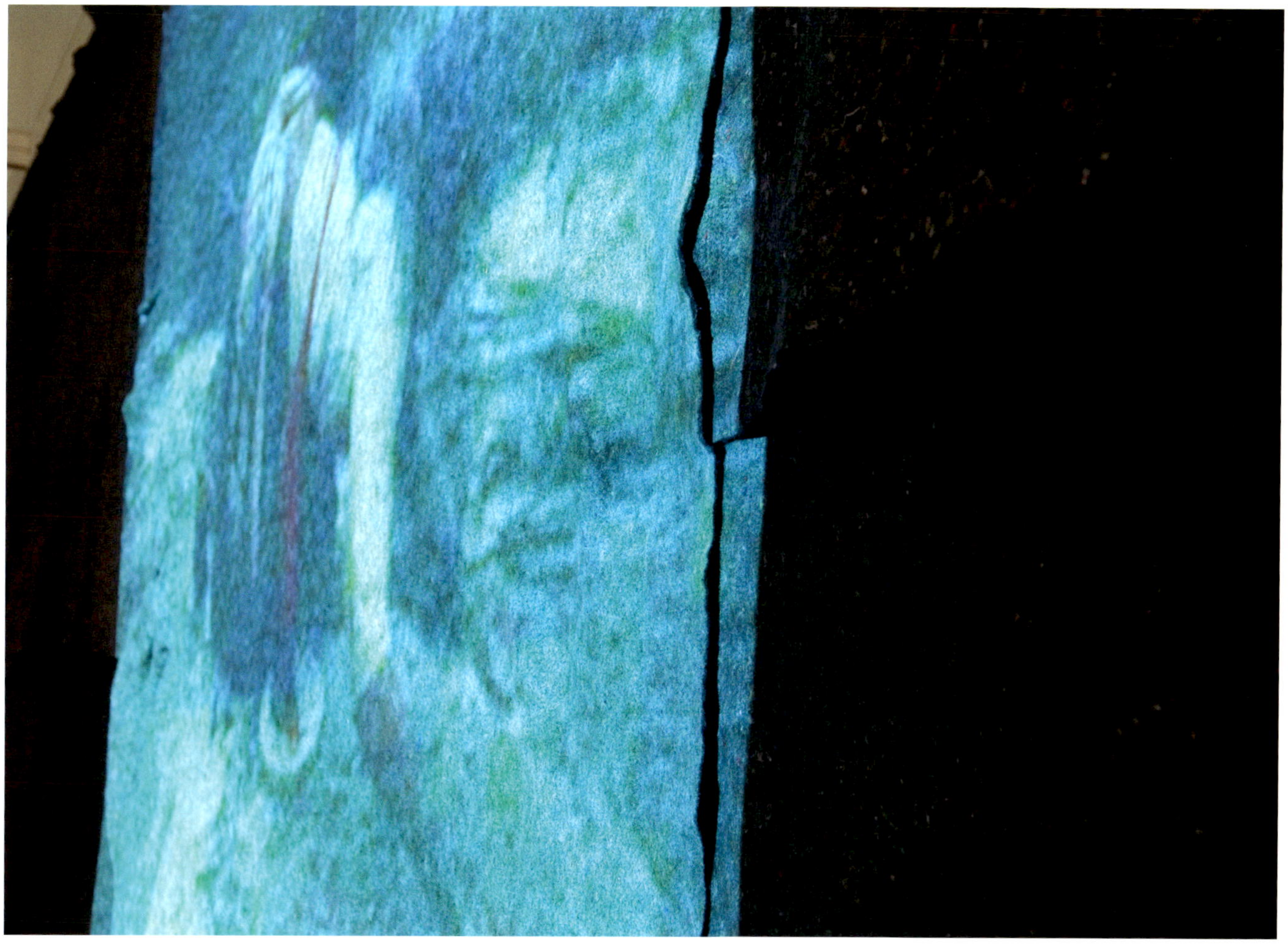

To be sure, Mutu had, in her previous video work, productively conflated both the value and status of the earth-land and woman-mother, and their fates under colonial/postcolonial and patriarchal regimes of subjection and exploitation. Consider, for instance, her Cleaning Earth (2006), in which a woman laboriously scrubs a dirty floor, overwhelmed by the enormity of her task. In a reading that seems to draw on religious traditions of women-shaming, Okwui Enwezor saw the woman's pointless cleaning as an act of penance and atonement.[8] However, as Mutu has indicated, her concern in this work has to do with the daunting and difficult work that often falls to women, and that is the task of 'restor[ing] a wounded land, be it a clear-cut forest or a war-torn town'.[9] I want to suggest, then, that there is a through line connecting Cleaning Earth and End of Eating Everything; the latter work, it seems to me, is Mutu's way of projecting what might happen in the event that the woman's work in Cleaning Earth – earth as a biospheric phenomenon – ultimately fails. The uncleanable dirt-wound festers, compounds, overwhelms the earth, which in its cataclysmic collapse takes with it everything it harbours.

CLEANING EARTH, 2006
SINGLE-CHANNEL DIGITAL
VIDEO, SOUND
25 MIN. 45 SEC.

If one returns to the video for a moment and pays closer attention to what might seem like its dramatological quirks, it soon becomes clear that these point to the fact that the supposedly carnivorous monster-woman might be the victim rather than the perpetrator of violence. Consider, for instance, that the black birds in their choreographed movement never really seem perturbed by her glower and roar, her savage rear and pounce. Not a single bird appears harmed, despite the blood-spray from her mouth. That is, the blood appears to hers. Which raises the question: are we witnessing the avatar of earth-woman – who because of her beauty and generosity, her natural disposition to nurture and support other life, was violated, exploited by these other agentive forces she once harboured – in her death throes? And are, then, the noisy and pestilential black birds her tormenters, the very beings whose actions and inactions caused her inexorable lurch to self-destruction? If she is overstuffed, as Schoonmaker noted years ago,[10] I am suggesting that it is not due to her supposed insatiable appetite; rather, her body is disfigured by what has been done to her. Moreover, the blood and smoke, rather than signifying her carnivorous impulse and mechano-digestive efficiency, signal internal systemic corruption and failure – which is how to understand the cataclysmic collapse that will soon follow.

Yet there is no clear sense of hard boundaries of victim and villain in this dramatic confrontation between the birds and the earth-woman. The back and forth, rather than unidirectional movement, suggests, perhaps, the existence of some prior beneficial relationship but which had long turned toxic, irreversible and deadly. Seen this way, the lines of verse flashing across the screen moments before an initial moment of lull invests the sudden change to the high-octane encounter with a new resonance. If, for a moment, we imagine the woman as the speaker of these lines, the melancholic tenor of her utterance – the insinuation of an existential distancing, of a long-broken bond, the mutuality of the ensuing dreadful loneliness, and the loss of what might have been a generative communitas – is telling. For it suggests that the explosive angst that overtakes her shortly is not so much due to a sinister intent or a will-to-violence on her part; rather, what we witness is a fiery reaction to an already done deed that disfigured her being, damaged her and that would lead inexorably to her auto-destruction. She is a tragic, anguished figure whose very body bears and is overburdened by all the signs and marks of her fatal violation.

There is a broader context for my reading of the woman in The End of eating Everything as Mutu's enfiguration of the abused, uncleanable, angry and death-bound mother earth, and this is not just the fact that, as noted earlier, she had herself drawn us to this conclusion with her previous work. In her discussion of a key influence on her critical environmentalism, Mutu has noted the impact of the radical disruption of her Kikuyu people's longstanding, harmonious relationship with

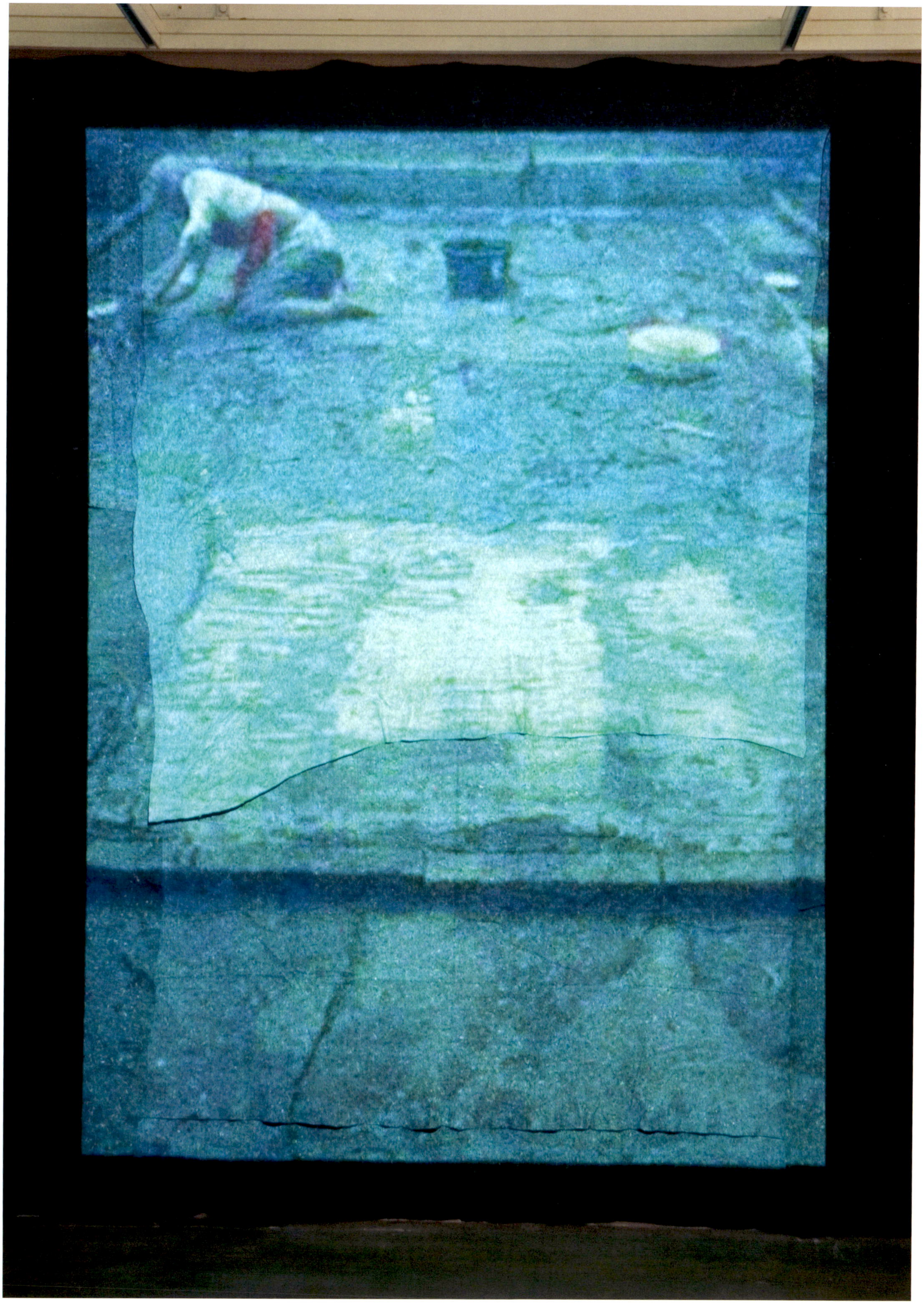

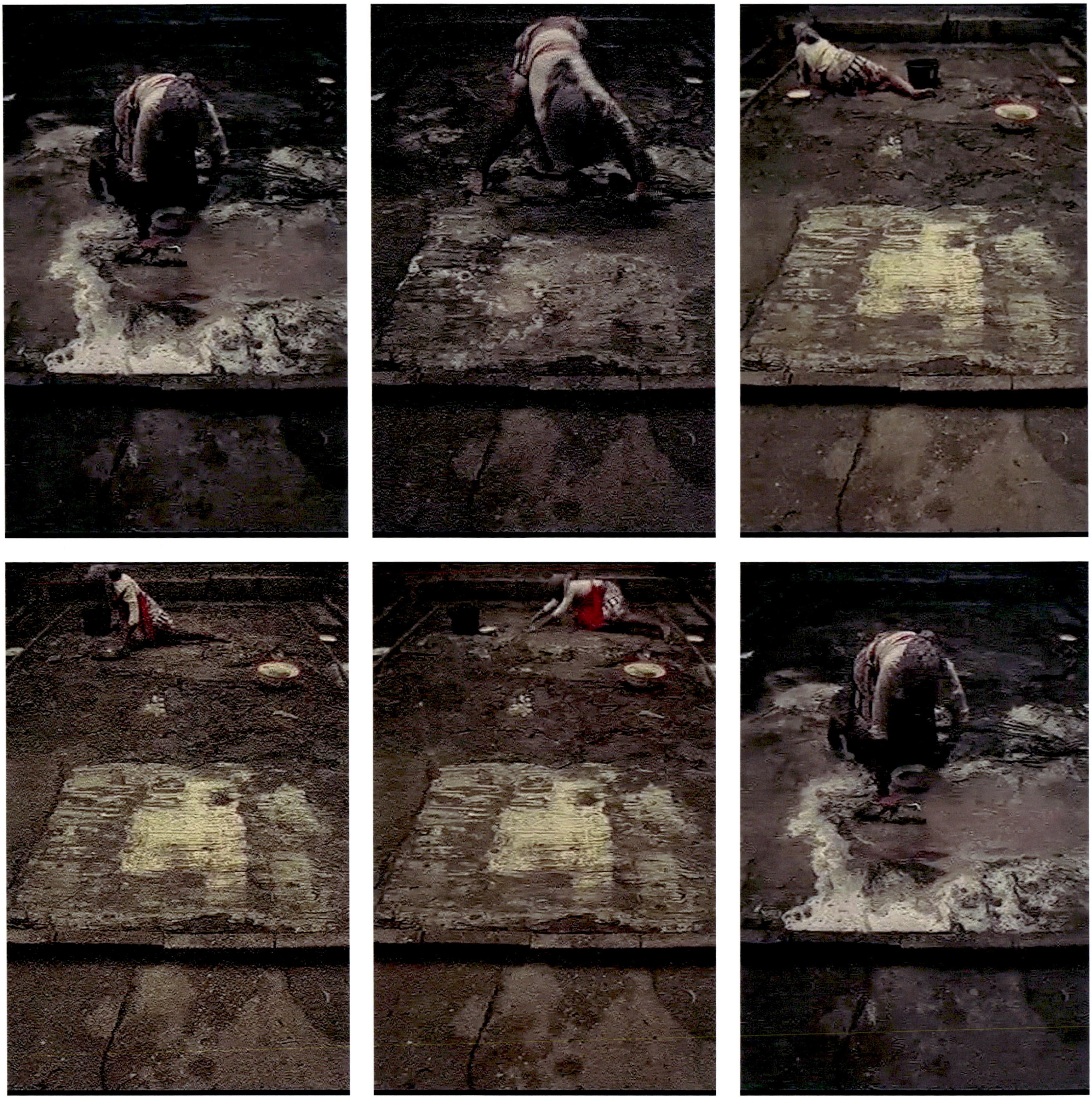

opposite,
CLEANING EARTH, 2006
SINGLE-CHANNEL DIGITAL
VIDEO, SOUND
25 MIN. 45 SEC.

land and nature in the verdant region around the foot of the Mount Kenya as a result of the introduction of colonial-era mechanized cash-cropping that both alienated the Indigenous populations and eventually impoverished the land. This invasive, colonial land exploitation, continuing beyond the age of empire, would later lead to deforestation and food crises that in turn posed an existential threat to East Africa's land, societies and peoples.

The unsustainable state of affairs discussed by Mutu was precisely the spur for the groundbreaking work of Wangari Maathai, the Kenyan ecofeminist whose Green Belt Movement began first as a massive tree-planting campaign – to heal and clean the wounded land – but soon turned into a drive for socio-political regeneration, that is the cleansing of the corrupted national body politic. The labouring woman in Cleaning Earth thus comes across as Mutu's Maathai, who in her work saw a direct connection between the restoration of natural environment, the land and social regeneration.

Stated differently, in Maathai's brand of African ecofeminism, a dirty, violated earth-land makes for a sick, impoverished, degraded society. Indeed, her work anticipated, as Nontando Hadebe has recently argued, Pope Francis' Laudato Si' (2015), in which he declared, that the world must heed 'both the cry of the earth and the cry of the poor', thus linking ecological crisis and social injustice. More pertinently, Hadebe also argues, through her reading of Maathai's Green Belt Movement, for what she calls a 'critical dialogue' between Laudato Si' and ecofeminism, asserting that 'the cry of the earth is the cry of women', as a way of centring the role of women in critical ecology.[11] What I am suggesting here, then, is that the woman-creature in The End of eating Everything must be seen within the context of Mutu's ecofeminist concerns. This character, in her melancholia that will become self-consuming rage, is not only an enfiguration of the crying earth-poor-woman of Laudato Si' and Maathai, it is Mutu's damning and dark prognostication of what is bound to happen to dirtied, uncleaned, abused earth-woman-us. The uncrackable existential question that this work raises is this: how to bring forth the clean, blissful world that briefly flashes at the end of the video, after the total destruction?

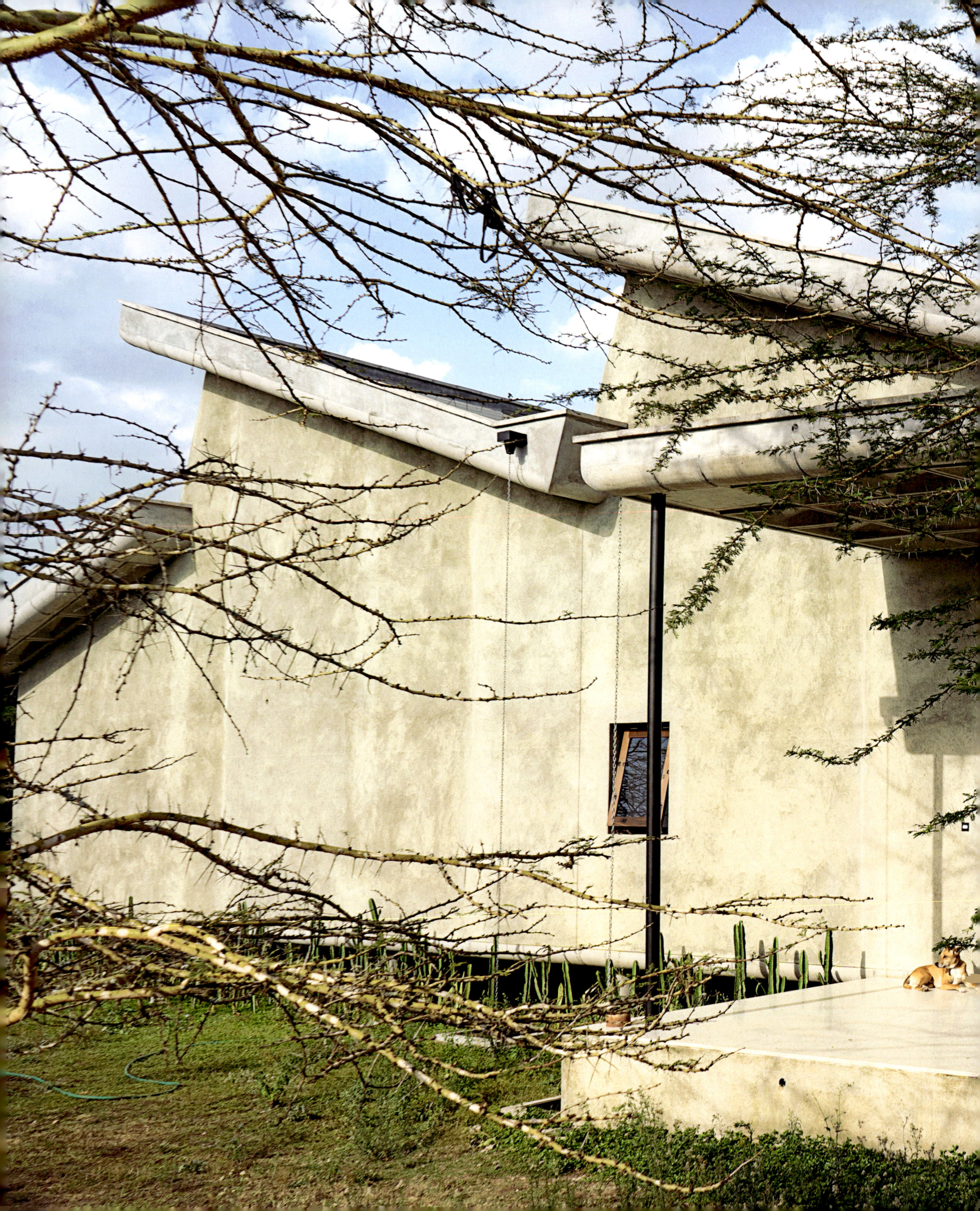

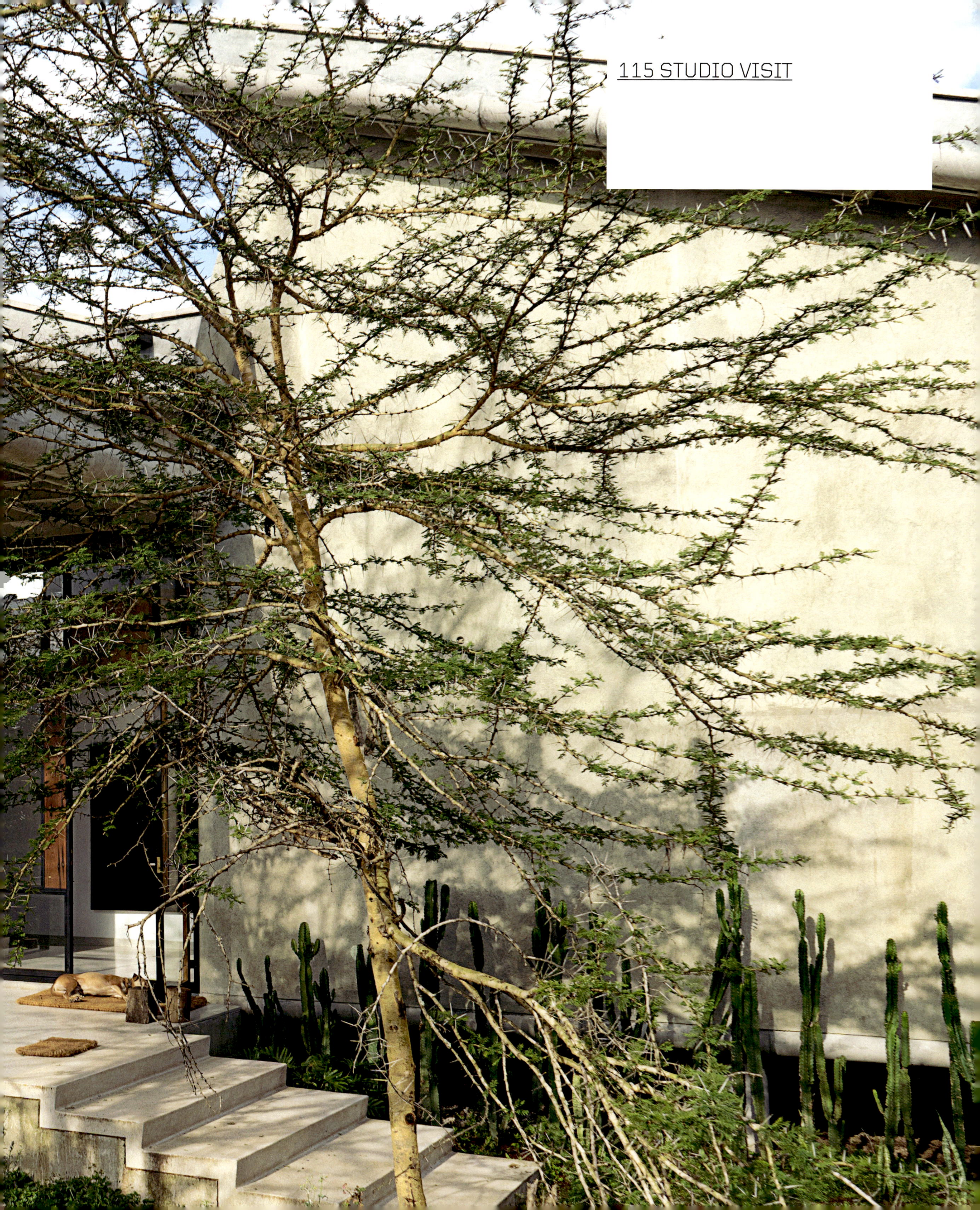

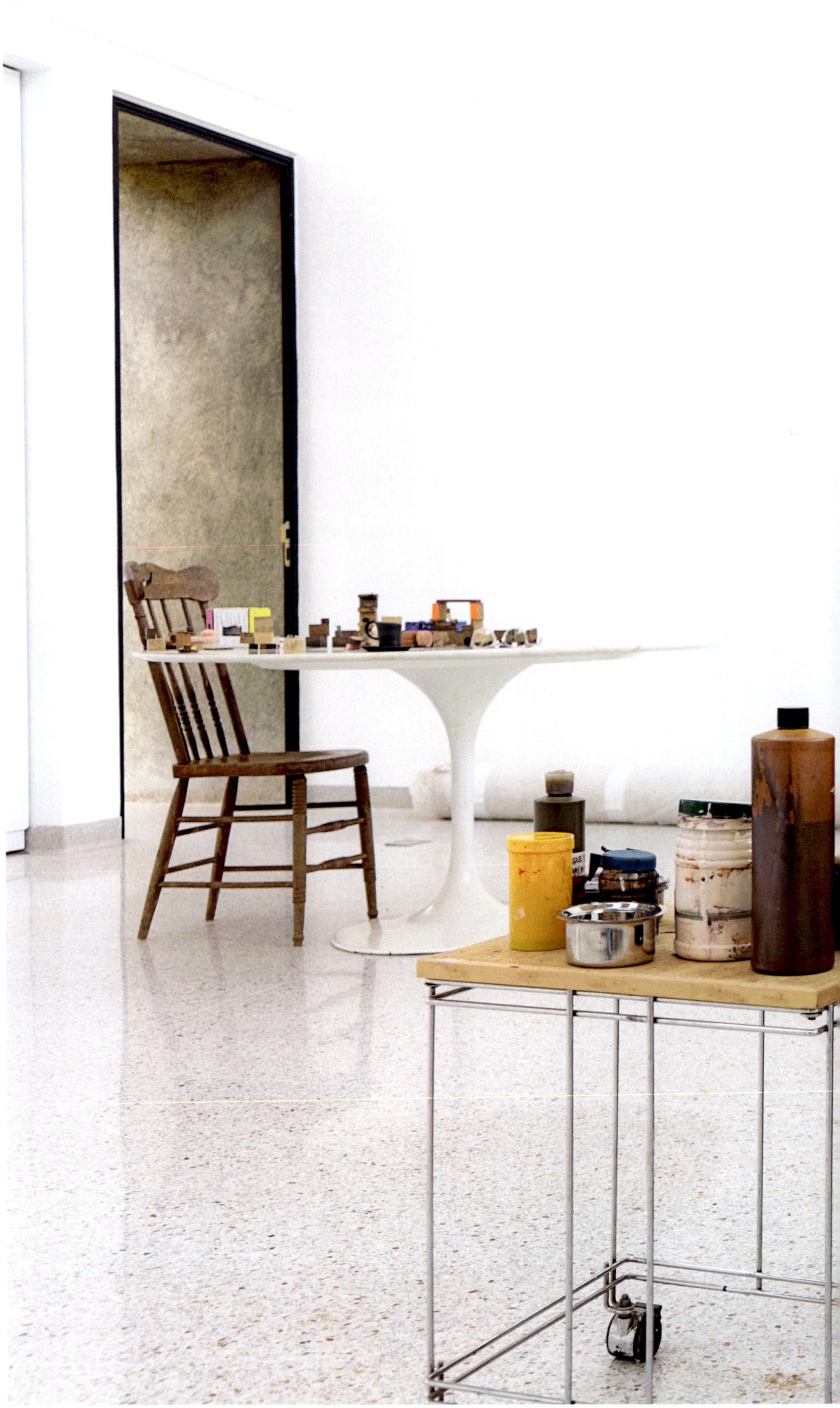

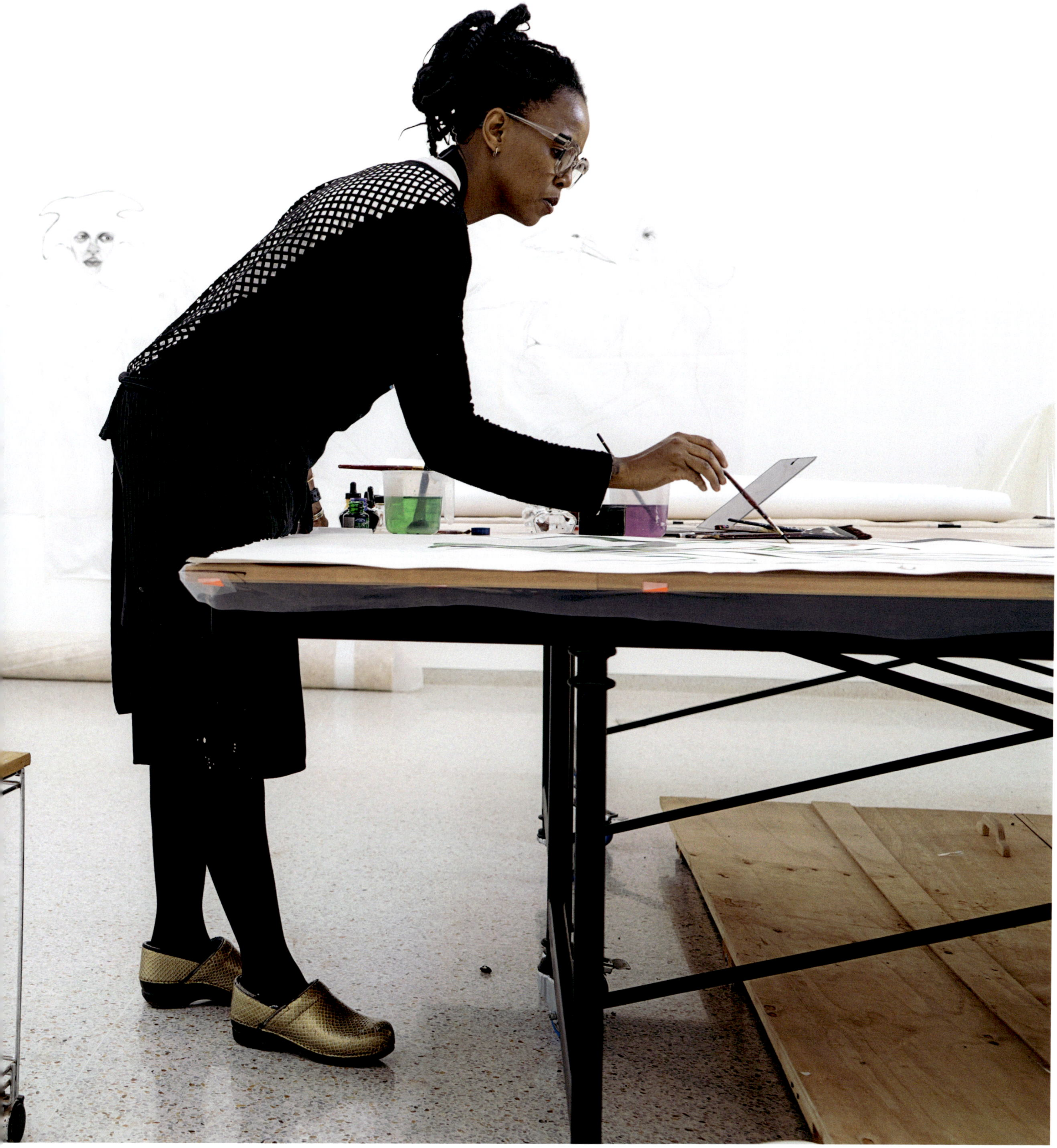

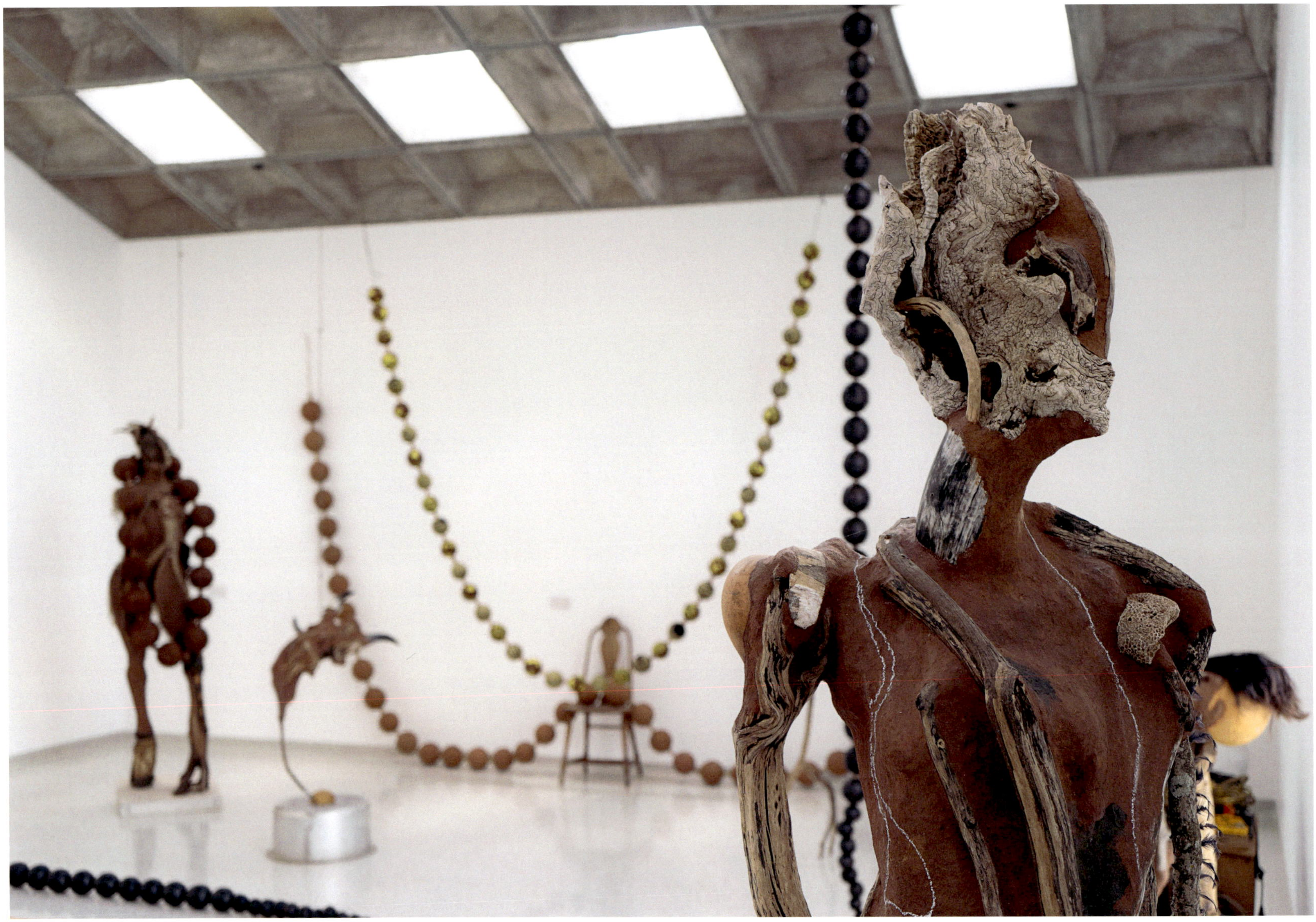

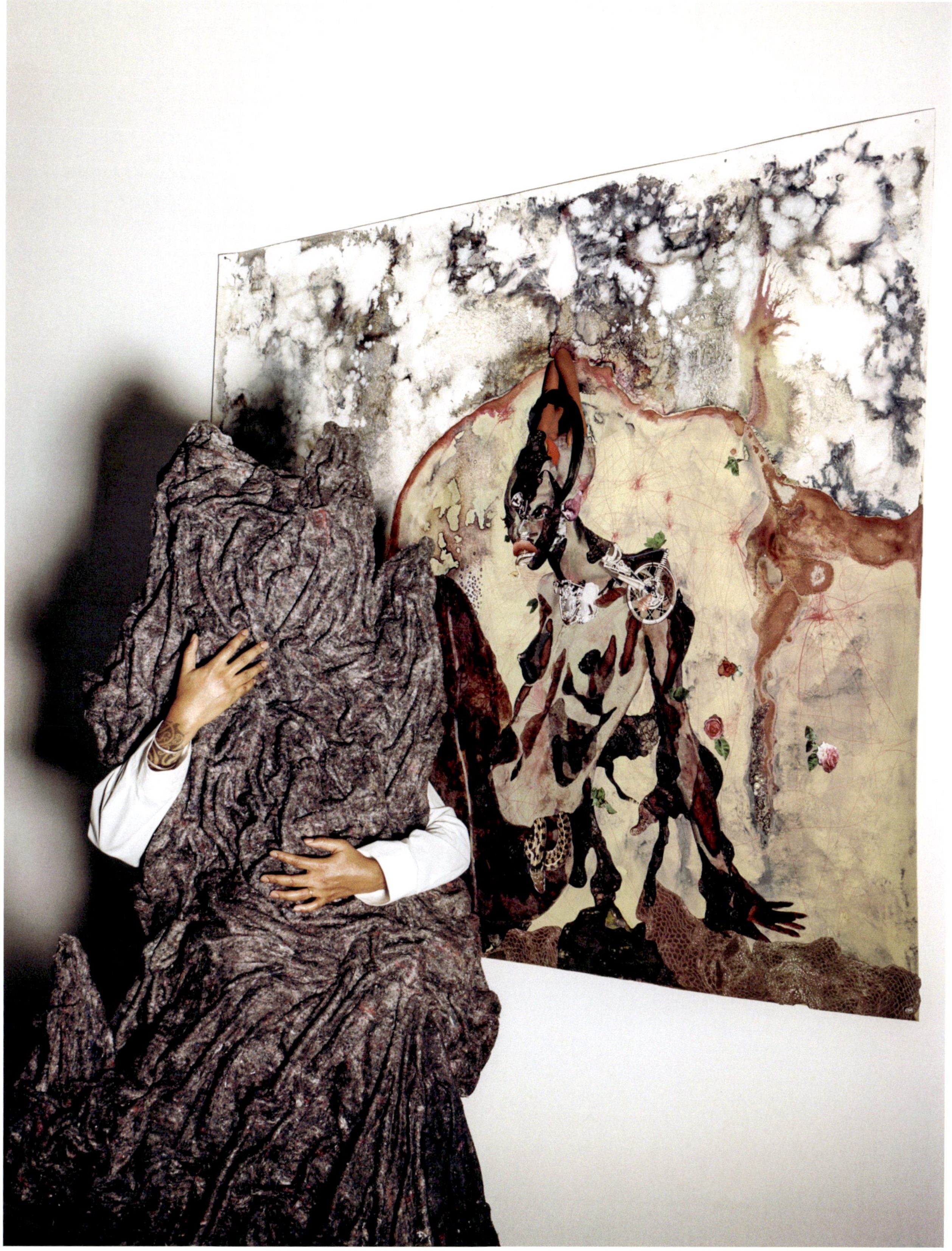

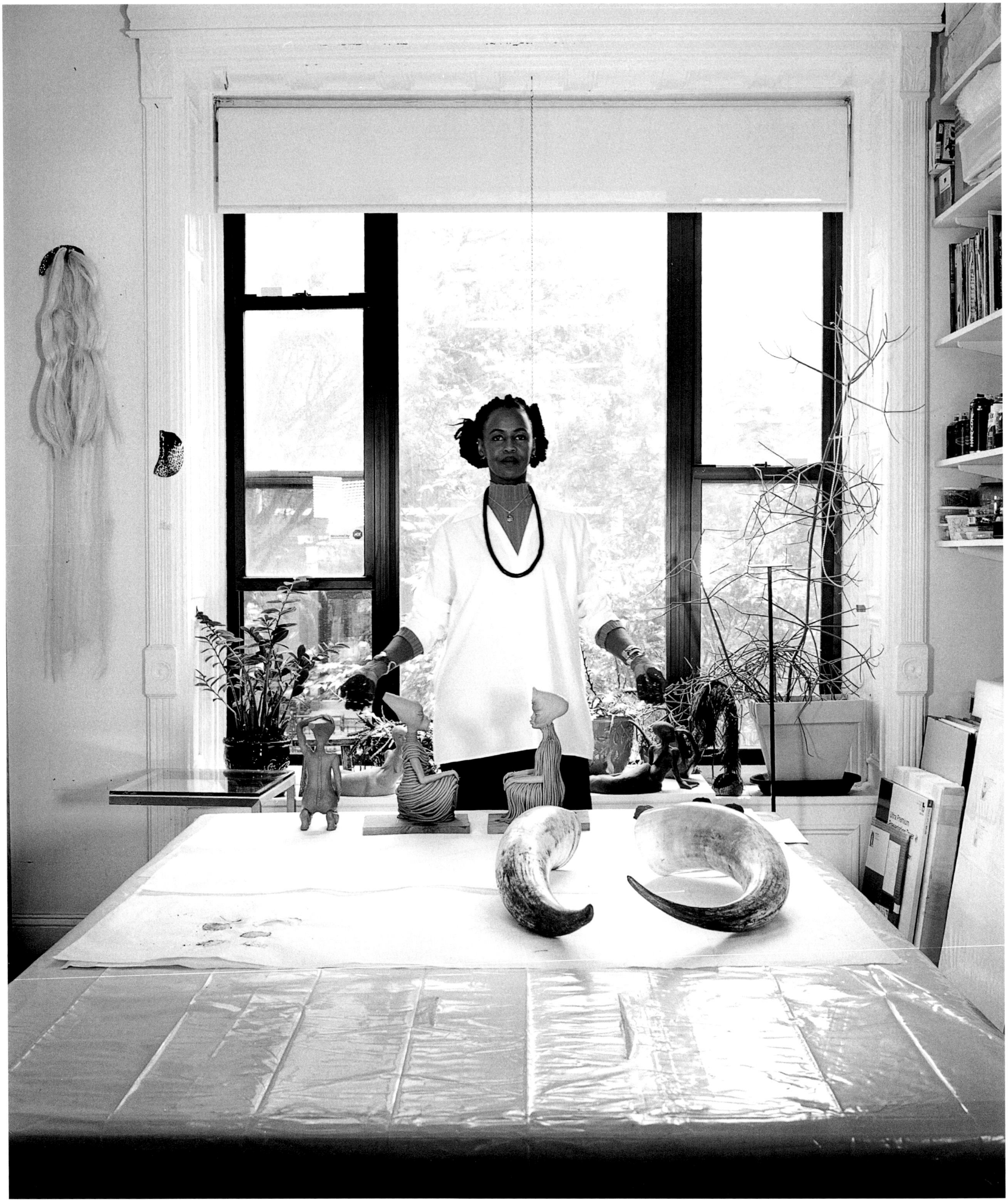

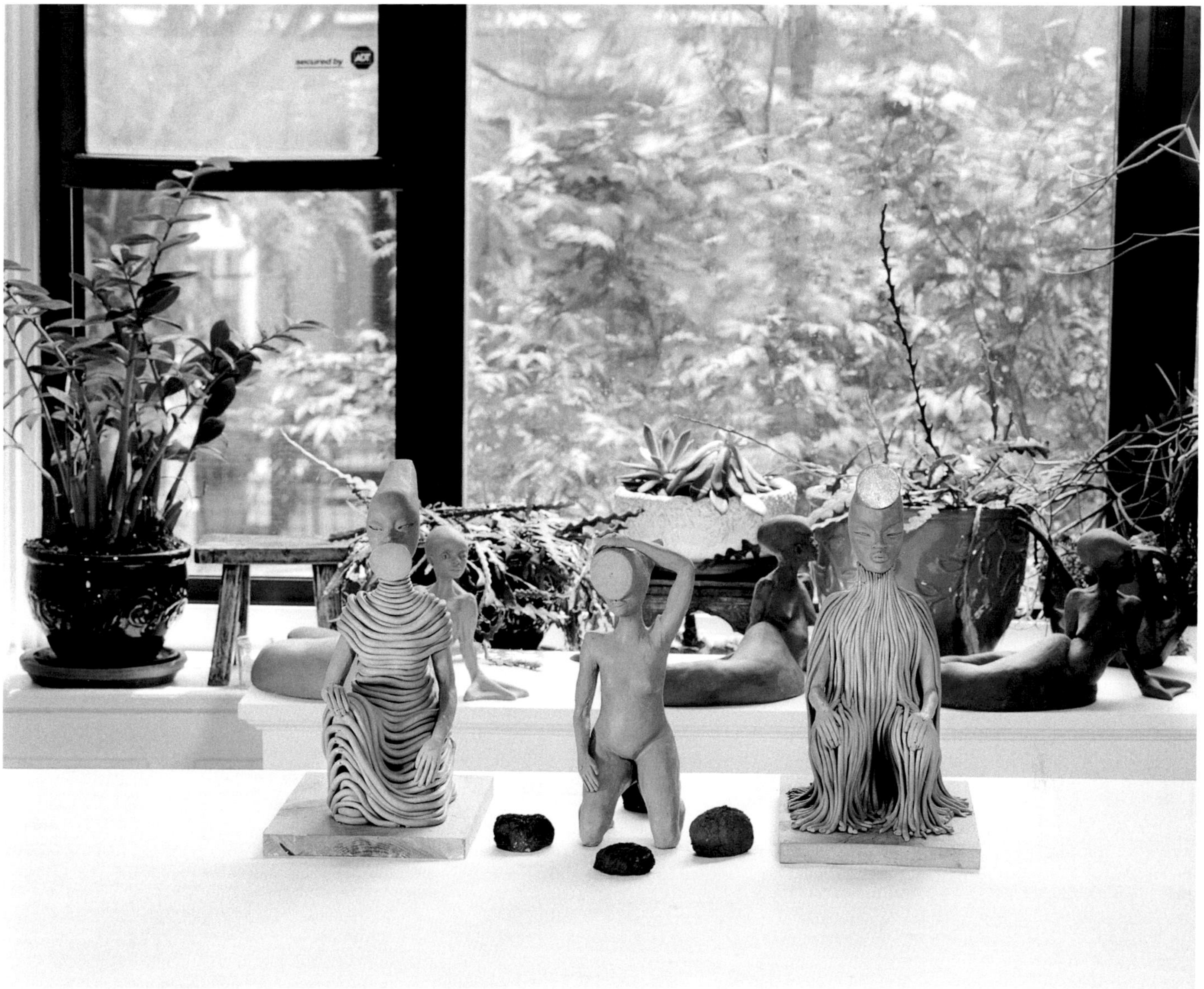
secured by

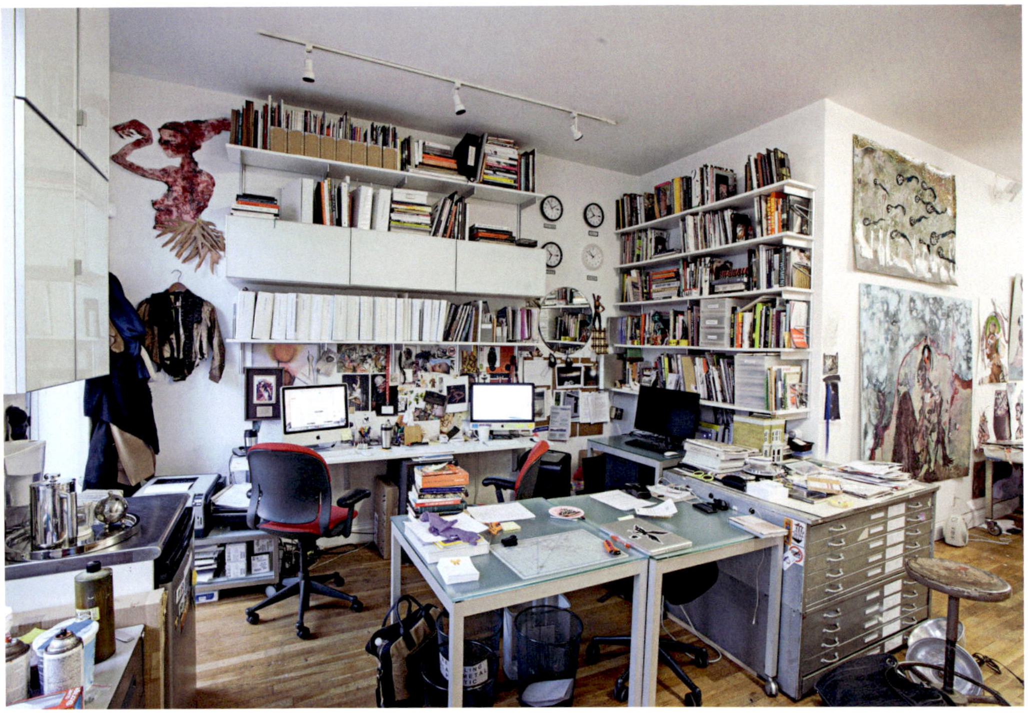

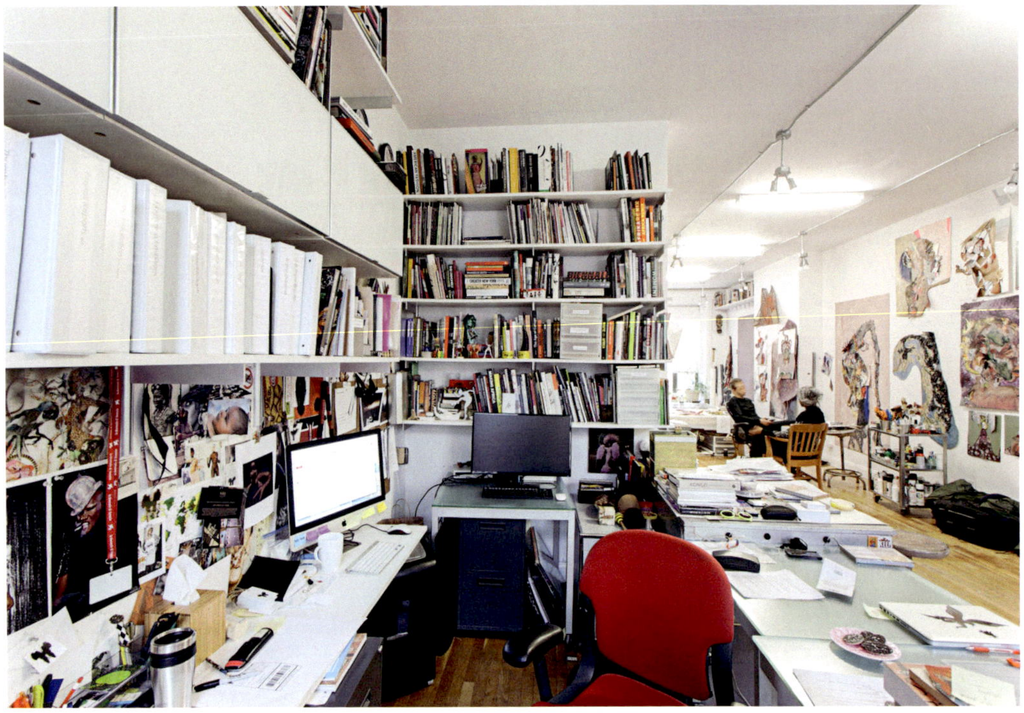

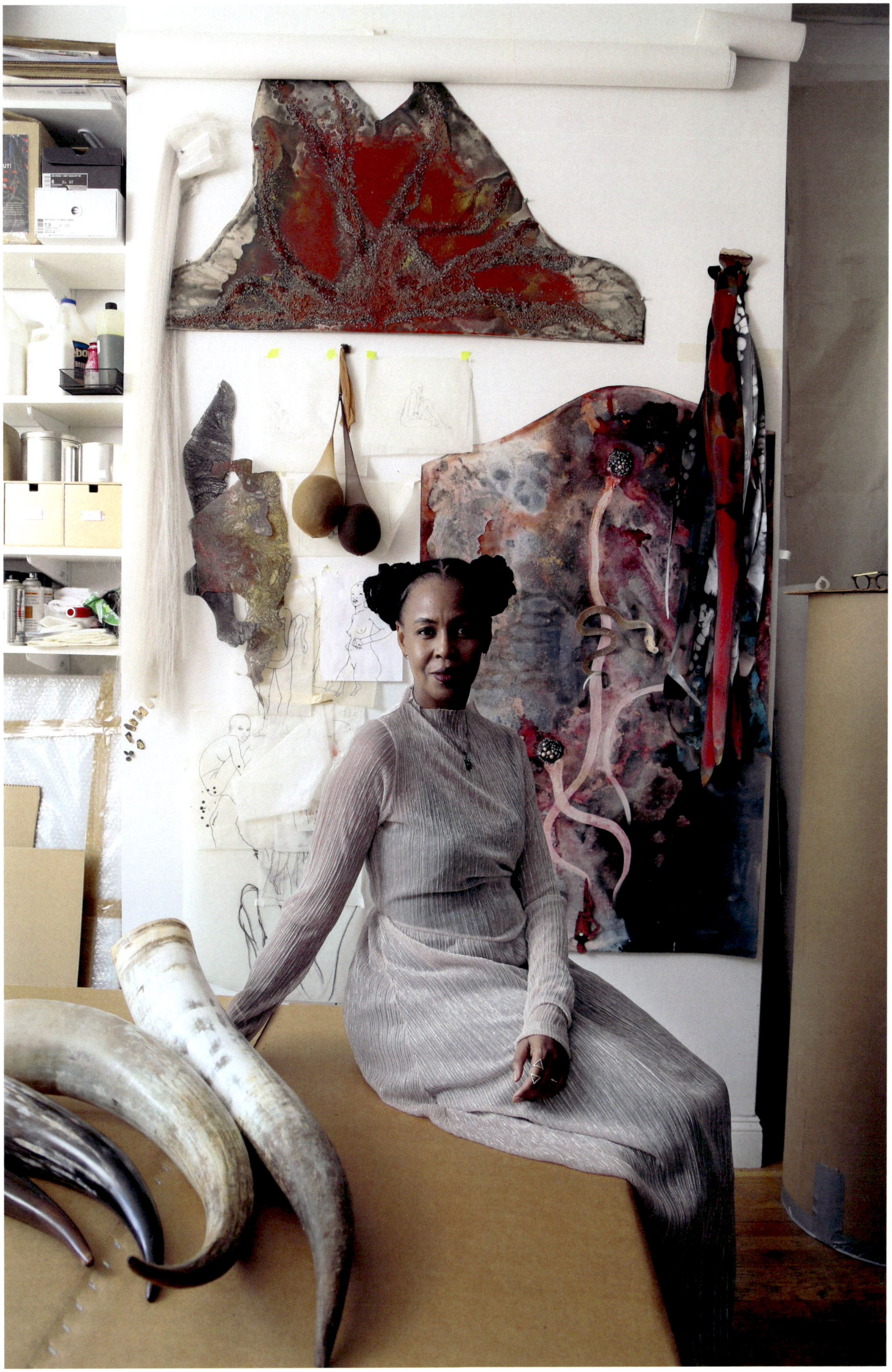

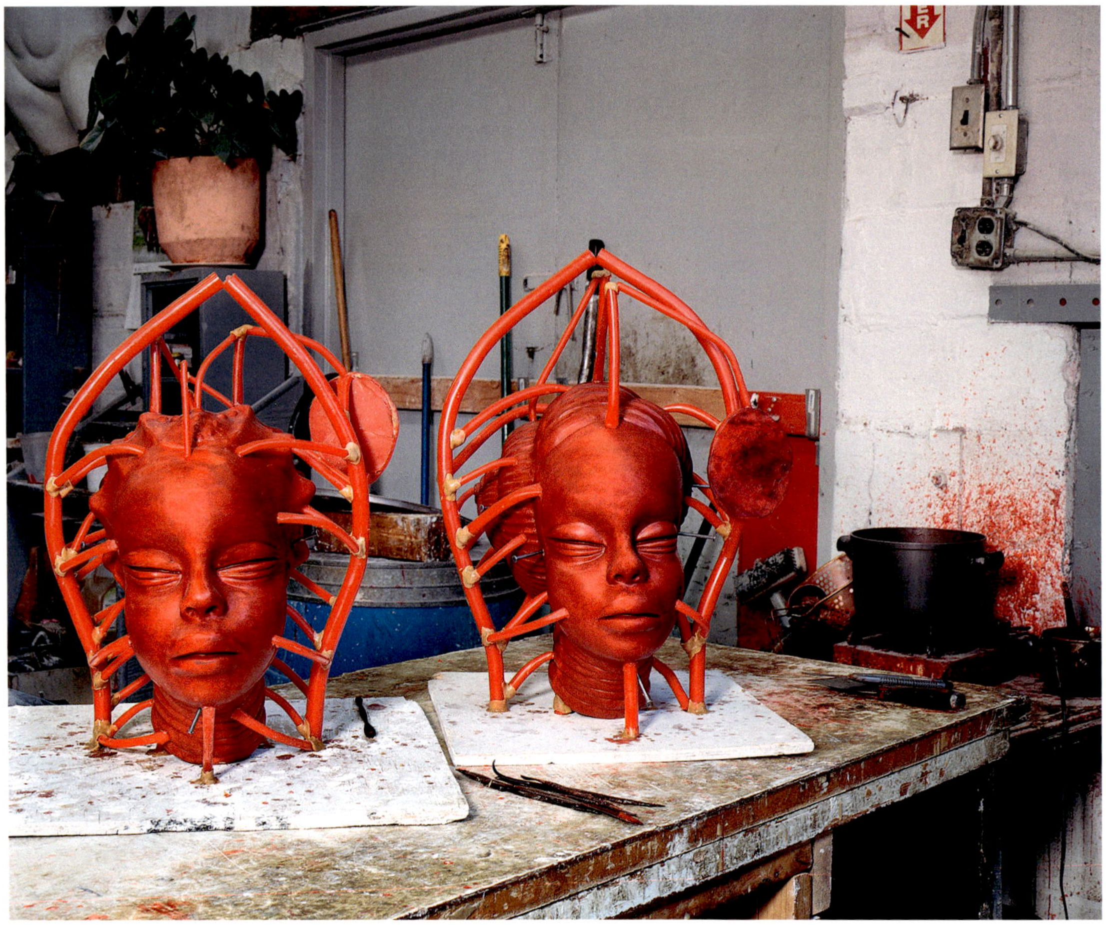

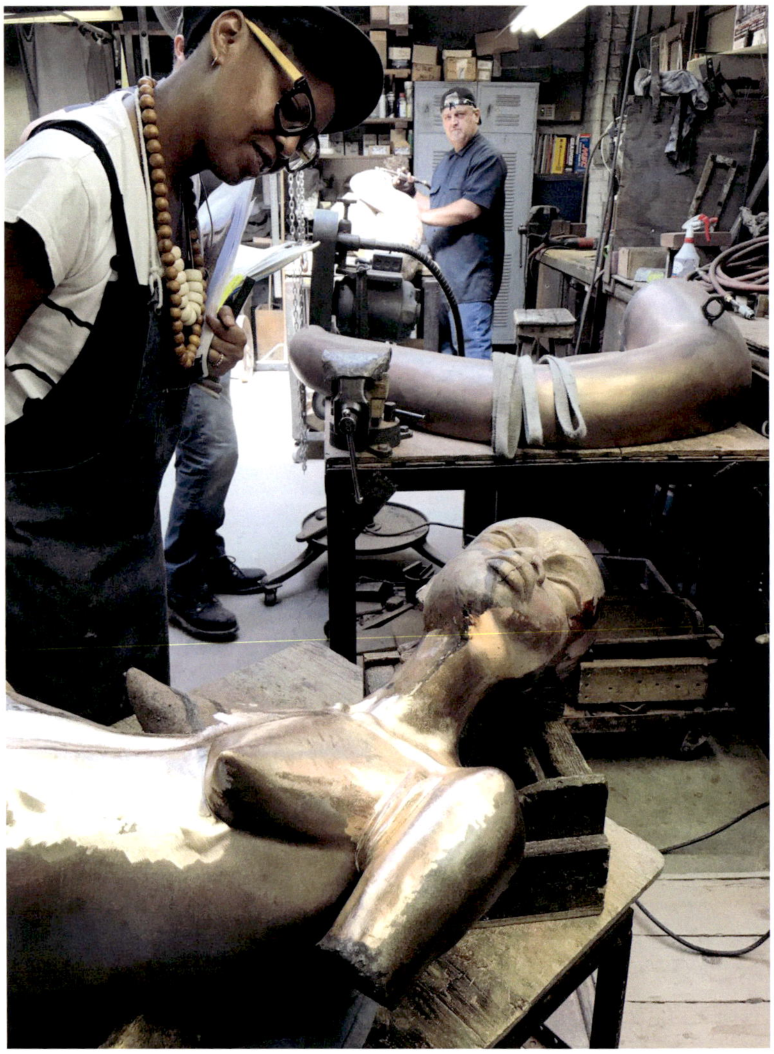

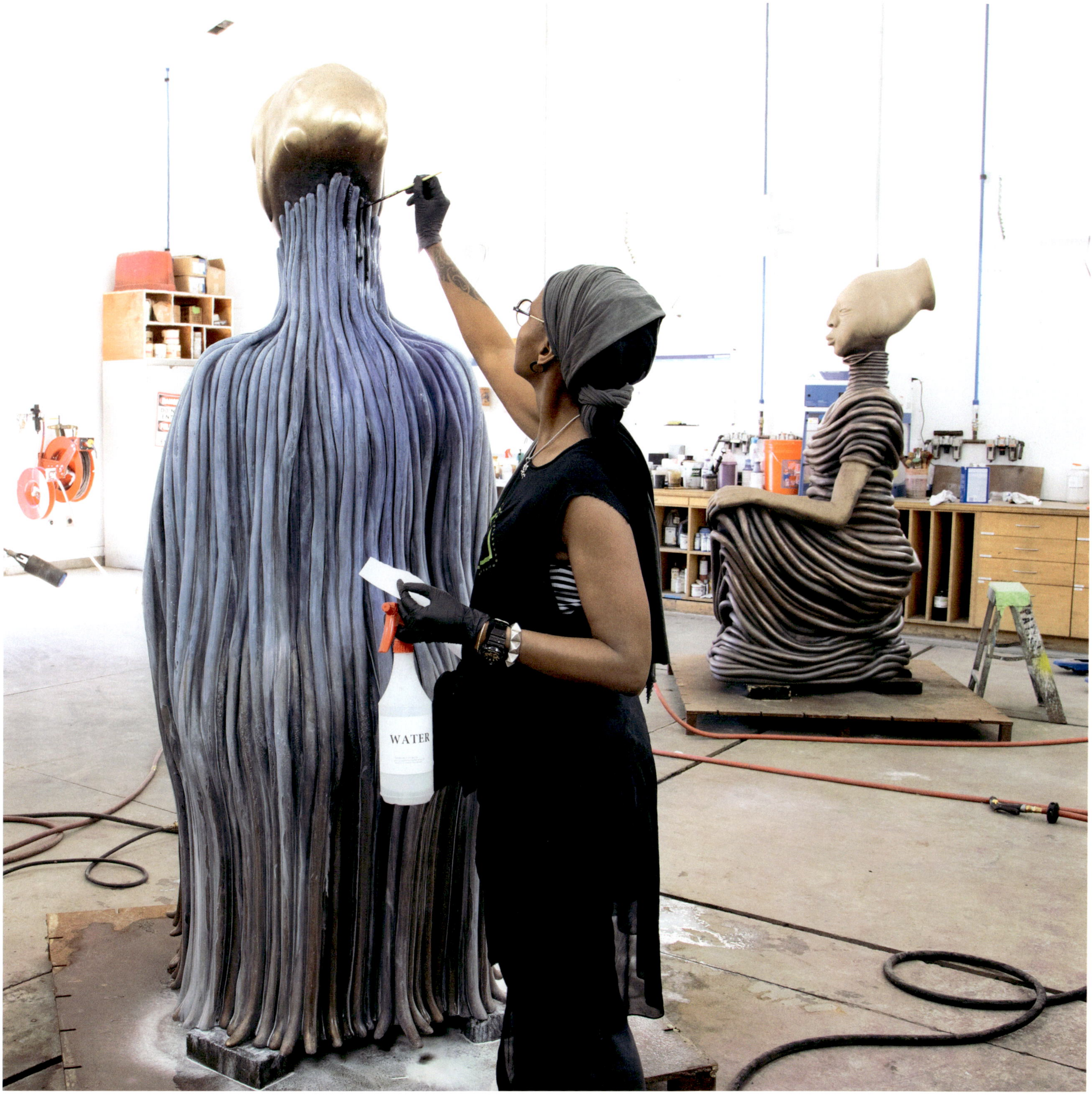
WATER

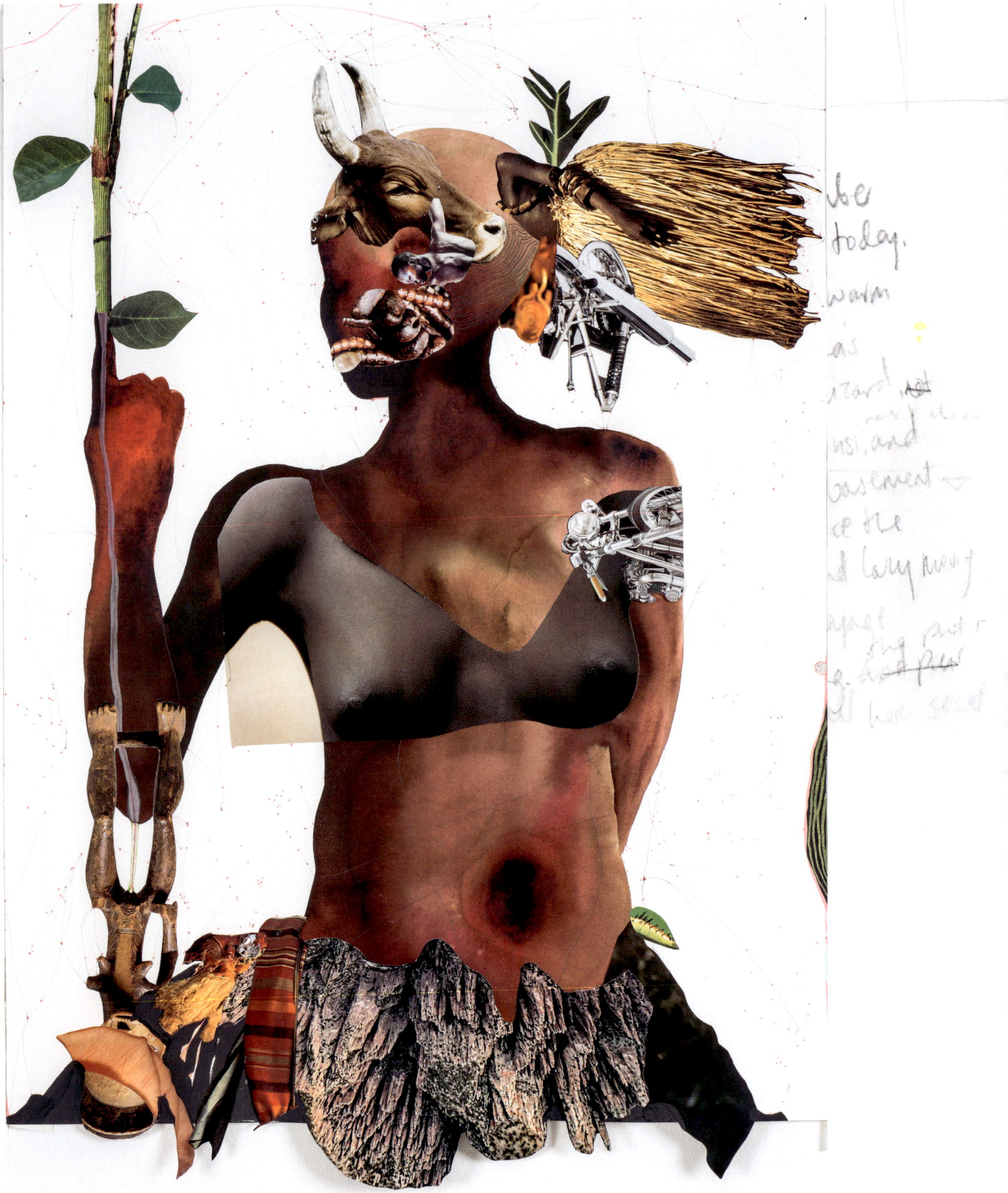
be
today.
warm
basement

endwisky – fixes Titi's kite

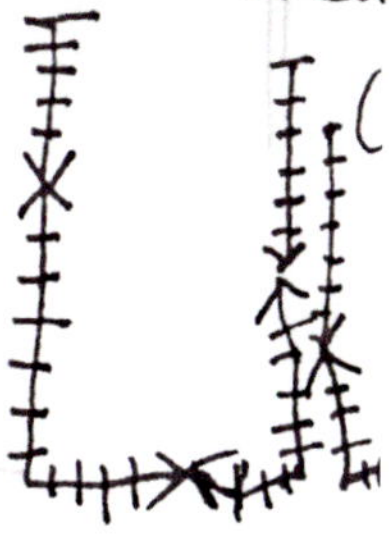

makes her wet happy
surrounds her with
friends

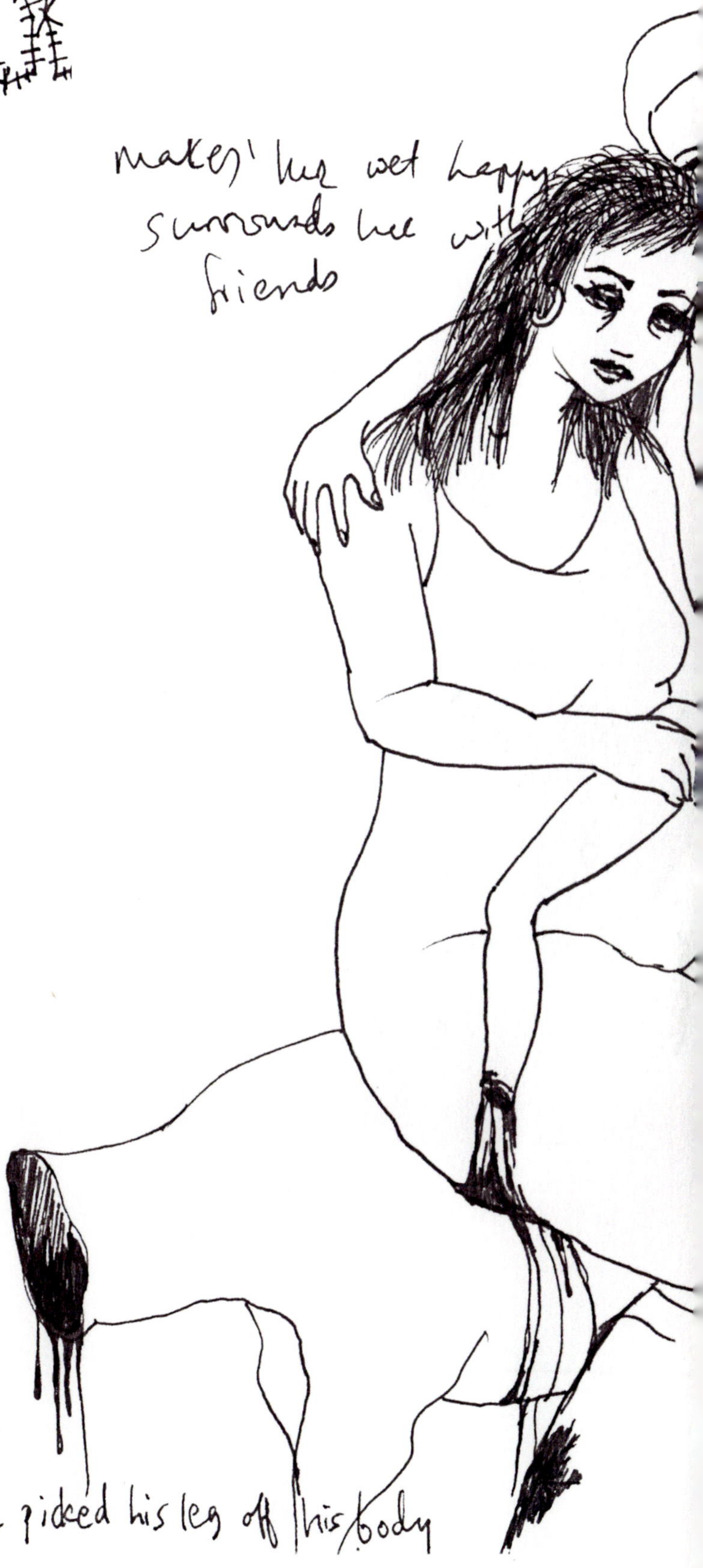

Problem

Ayana's day is dull and no one's around
It's summer, hot, bright, boring, lazy day
Ayana's played with all her toys, read all her books. Most of her friends have left for the summer.

Ayana's kite has just flown away.

Ayana's just had a fight with sister who calls a big bore

Ayana comes home distressed, unhappy
One late afternoon Ayana comes home distressed and unhappy, her summer school class went terribly and her favourite shoes have grown dull and old. To make it worse ~~her~~ today her favourite teacher just told her how dull her Art project is.

a gentle whore picked his leg off his body

Art, this old medicine, 2021

FAMILY TREE (BIRD PERCHED ON RIBCAGE) (DETAIL), 2012
MIXED-MEDIA COLLAGE ON PAPER
44 X 30 CM

previous pages, left,
A LONG QUESTION, 2015
COLLAGE PAINTING ON PAPER
66 X 46 CM

If I'm Afro-Futurism, then it's because, if still here, now, making, working and thinking and continuing a line of ideas that come from others who were here in the past asserting their now and preparing a future for me.

I'm here making art. The way I communicate is by creating, drawing, pulling, pushing forward materials, colours, pigments, questions about what it means to exist, to be human. It's through the making that I find out things, I find new ways to understand how we are all Africans. I discover by creating art how this entire human family born out of the mother-continent is related and belongs to one another and due to our wandering, nomadic, migratory habits we've moved further apart, forgetting each other and our common predecessors and believing myths about how much dissimilar we are.

It is through sculpting with soil and ash and water and tea that I am able to think that for over two hundred thousand years we've been walking, swimming, sailing, climbing further and further apart and away into the different landmasses and new continents to where we are today and where we claim we have now originated!

It is through art, I feel how distinct each human being is and how resilient we've been to have moved to this point and how we all, have a distinct role to play in curtailing this impulse to separate fracture and destroy each other, our bonds and our destinies. The making of art is a way of asserting my place in the present and mending the pained bodies and our shared wounds. It's my way of being clear that I am now and aware of being part of a shared future.

Art is one of our shared languages that's been around for a long long. We've been moving, dancing, scratching, carving, chipping, drawing, painting and engraving into skin, rock, walls in deserts, by river beds, up in the hills and mountains and near the ocean waves. All over the world, before there was writing, before we were an over-populated species we werepainting, annotating and recording our triumphs and anxieties and our existence for others to see, in order to connect, and in the hope of being remembered. Artmaking, regardless of what we call it, was always done to make a connection with others, with the spirits, with our ancestors, with those who hadn't been born, with the sun and the elements, with trees and the animals. We've always wanted to connect, and to be remembered and to remember things we cared for and believed in because, I believe, even when we don't consciously remember, we know that we all belonged and originated from one family, one group. Like the Universe we have moved further apart and expanded in numbers and distance from each other. How to re-assemble those fragments is my work, my challenge and my core task. I've worked with drawing to create images of trauma as a way to cry out for mine and our unspeakable wounds, I've used collage to unite fragmented ideas, to bring together unrelated images, to bridge together histories and ideas that have been positioned as separate.

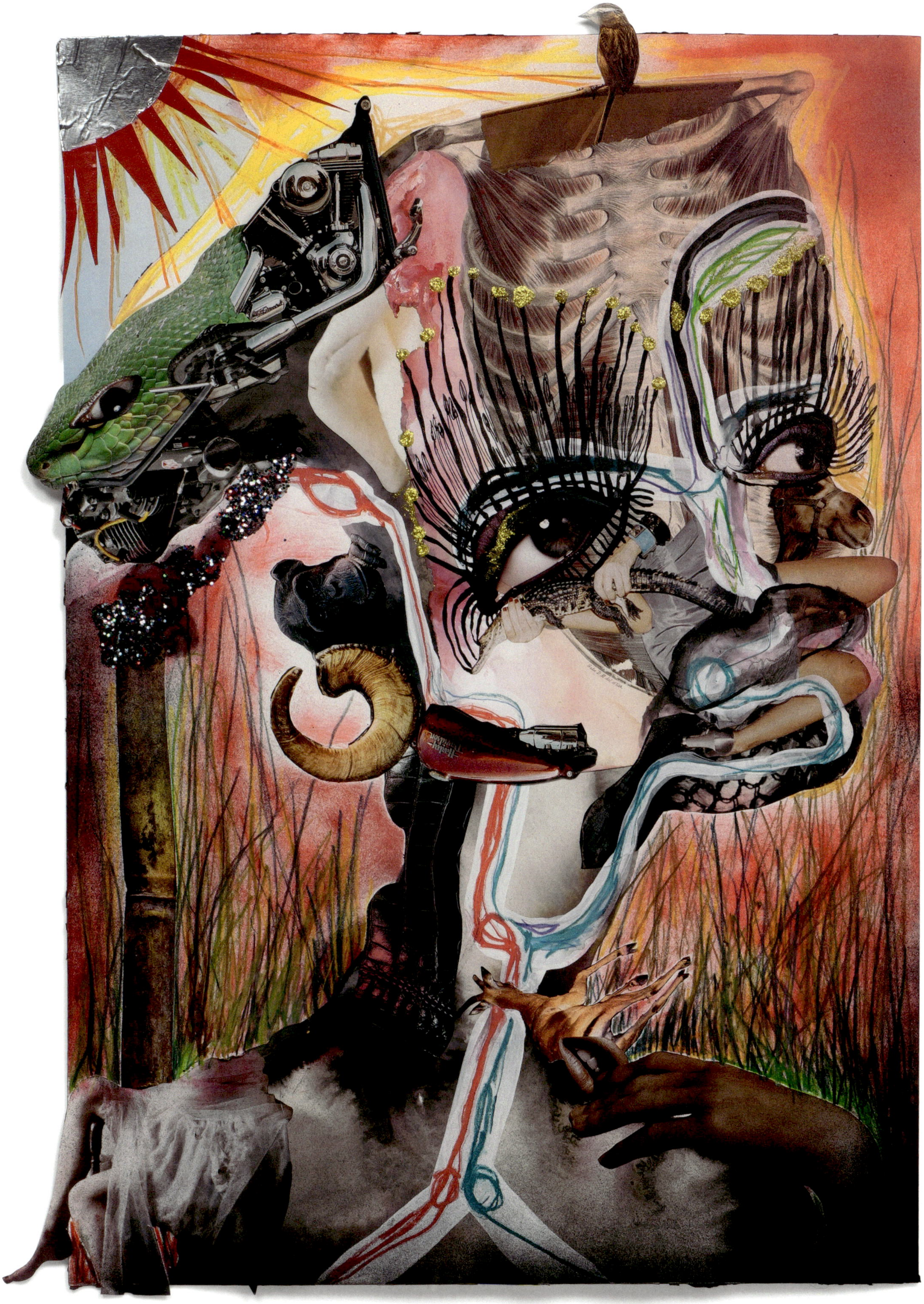

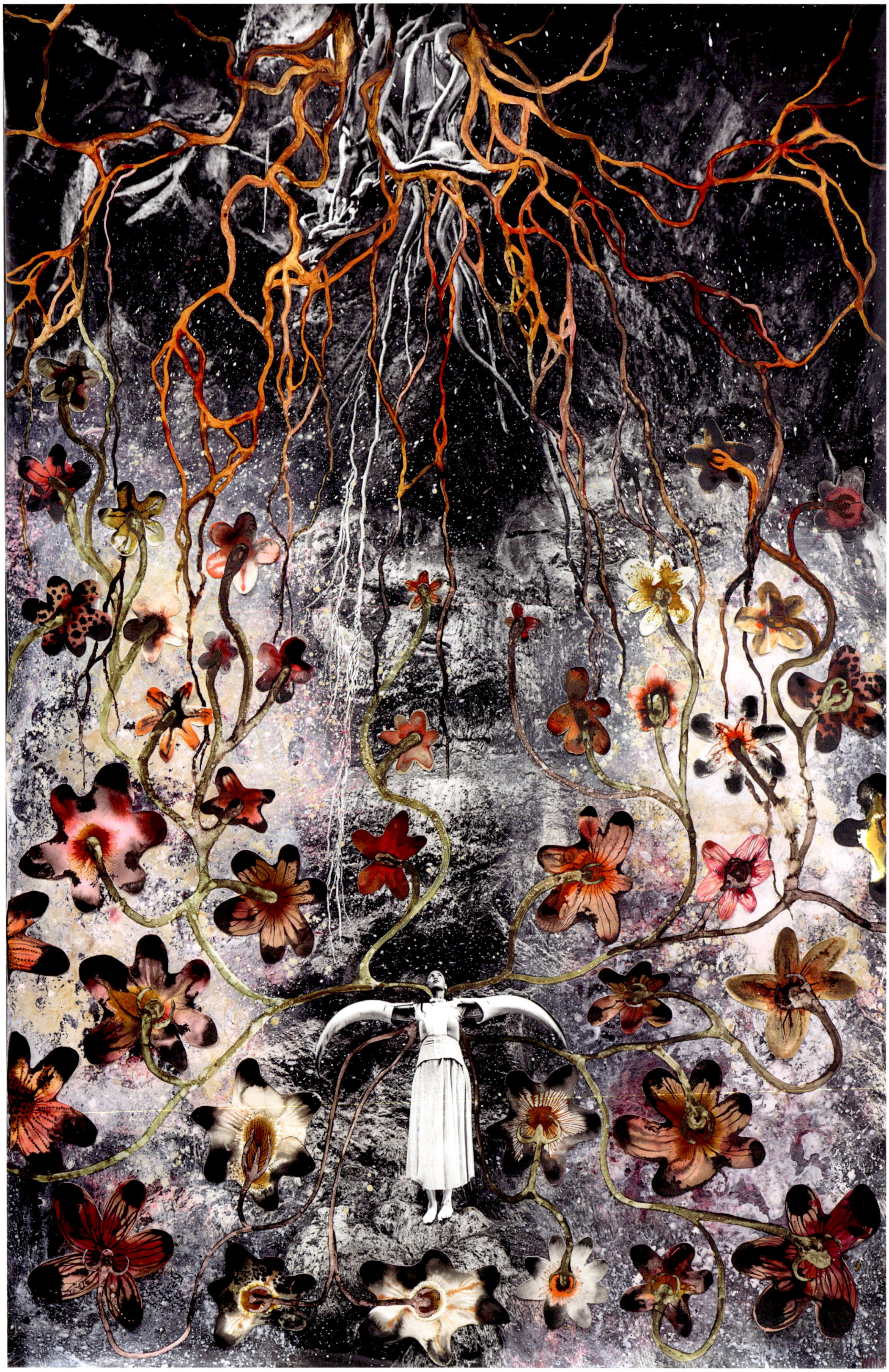

opposite,
SUBTERRANEA STEMMED, 2021
INK, EMULSION PAINT
AND WATERCOLOUR PAPER
ON PHOTOGRAPHIC PRINT
183 X 122 CM

This art that I make and is what I believe I am here to do, and all I believe and practicereligiously (no pun intended) is embodied in my ability to speak as with intuition about my experiences as I build new work. When I work, I feel the most human that I am. It's in that dance in the trenches of my studio-day that I'm able to read and intuit human behavior through the activity of mixing, sculpting, creating. I use my mind instinctually and as I play with all the stuff of art-making, I see how the divisiveness of our species, how it's separateness threatens our existence and moves us and many other species towards self-extinguishment.

I mostly work using very tactile methods.

Why? Because I just love the sensation and honesty of touching and handling what I'm working with. I compare it to eating with a fork or spoon, versus eating with your hands. The food seems to taste differently, and the chewing begins all the way from your fingertips and your palms before it even gets to your tongue.

I'm able to do deep dives into the substances, the materials using my hands first as my mind and my tools are there to enhance and strengthen what I see in my imagination and then I can truly listen and really hear. When I create, I'm actively tuning out fear, distractions and all the internal banter/noise, instead raising the volume for what is happening me to me as well as tapping into the most peaceful part of who I am and who we are and what we can be.

I call what I do my work, but it also feels even more innate and comforting uncontrollable, like a rhythmic ritual. It's never a singular gesture, things in the studio are never all done in one swing. One idea will seep into another, a new work helps give rise to the answers that I need for another work that's almost completed. Some works are permanently in the studio-space, like trees or landmarks of my journey, working time, they are reminders of lessons and stumbling blocks., They remind me where I've journeyed from and keep the lessons I've learntafresh. All said I make art to keep alert, to what it is to be alive and to be at peace and to love and be loved. I feel quite simply very fortunate to know how I most love spending my time here on earth day in day out.

opposite,
SUBTERRANEA FURY, 2021
INK, EMULSION PAINT ON
PHOTOGRAPHIC PRINT
183 X 122 CM

Art making is at its very core, an activity of empathy-enhancement. A human deliberately, slowly, decisively marking or carving or molding, or turning something into another thing, purposely giving material another way to exist. The way the universe was created by continuing to move energy into other forms of energy. We've practiced this art-thing, not just for centuries, but for millennia, using rock, minerals, fluids, clays, fabrics, simple tools, sophisticated technology, all to pass vibrant messages to each other.

In making art making I am vicariously and even adamantly reclaiming space for more women to be makers of decision, to be heard and to take on leadership roles. How so? By harnessing my energy and taking charge of how I speak, play and live. By guiding, leading, asserting, gently with ideas and by example, in my studio and out in the world through the art-sphere where my work ends up. In so many places women's contributions are healing and guiding the human-species with intelligence, using our abundant empathy and this gift of a much higher sensitivity to the anguish of our living earth.

I work as I said intuitively, I make things I sense, I listen to that part of me that is most in touch with others, with the earth, and those who have suffered human cruelty on this earth, those whose experiences have given them a deep reservoir of collective historical empathy and an enhanced consciousness. Of course, it begins with me, and an uncontrollable love of making and being imaginative, but for all who have ever made art, artmaking is calming, centring and creates a quiet focus that I call art-meditating, a way of defiantly finding a place of stillness where we tap into our familiarity and collective consciousness and the primal intelligence that all materials, all beings anything on earth share.

I feel that it is this intentionality what Afro-Futurism is grounded in and grown from. A desire to survive and heal and rectify the dangerous imbalance and disjointedness of humankind. All people are born and learn by playing and learn by making things and we all make something that is Art as children. All humans are therefore capable of making art and therefor probably capable of understanding the deeper reason for art.

However, like play and games and the formative activities that build our human brains, eventually, we're discouraged and talked out of artmaking. Even those who have a distinct predilection for art. We're encouraged to grow up and do things that are serious, lucrative, mature and proper.

I like to say that there are no bad-artists, just bad art teachers. Grown humans play less playful games and make less art. It seems harder to explain these types of activities and how much irrational joy they bring us the older you get. The kind of joy that heals trauma, keeps us from creating rifts and protects us from the fear inside our minds can be found in playing and in art and in doing what we're best at.

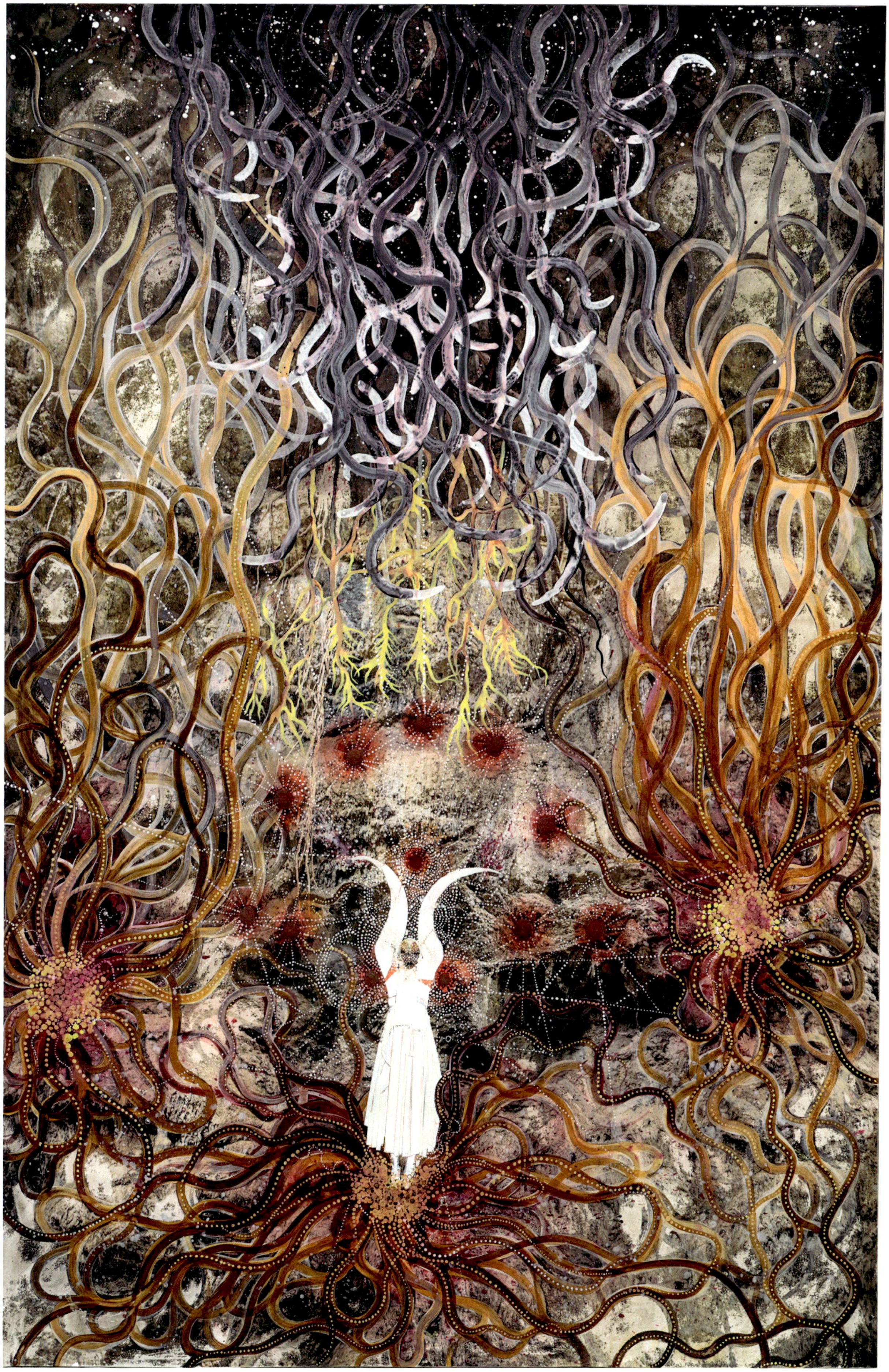

I return to the studio to make things, to be still and calm, to exercise the Art of being powerful in being simply present. That concentration is a ritual built from my love of being in such a focused state and my insatiable ability to be attentive for long hours. I am here now, there is proof that I was here in the past through all my predecessors and that we carry in our DNA inside our bodies. We are inside of our children and their children are in them. I don't feel compelled to proclaim how much I belong in the future because I carry the future, because I am with it inside of me, right here, right now.

The future is a projection and a hope of something less fractured and disjointed and that we need to step into through our work and our concentration and the connections we make, mine which happen through the Art. There is a clear connection between making art andbeing human and for me there's personal relevance in being a creative person and being a woman. I create within my body, and I also create from the outside of my body. I keep building that dignity and consciousness that we've lost, or that I've lost or forgotten. I love to make art because this old-ass language is our shared human behavior and as I return To it every day, it makes me willing to struggle to be here now and in tomorrow's now.

PREVIOUSLY UNPUBLISHED

MAMARAY, 2020
BRONZE
165 X 366 X 488 CM

opposite,
MAMARAY (DETAIL), 2020
BRONZE
165 X 366 X 488 CM

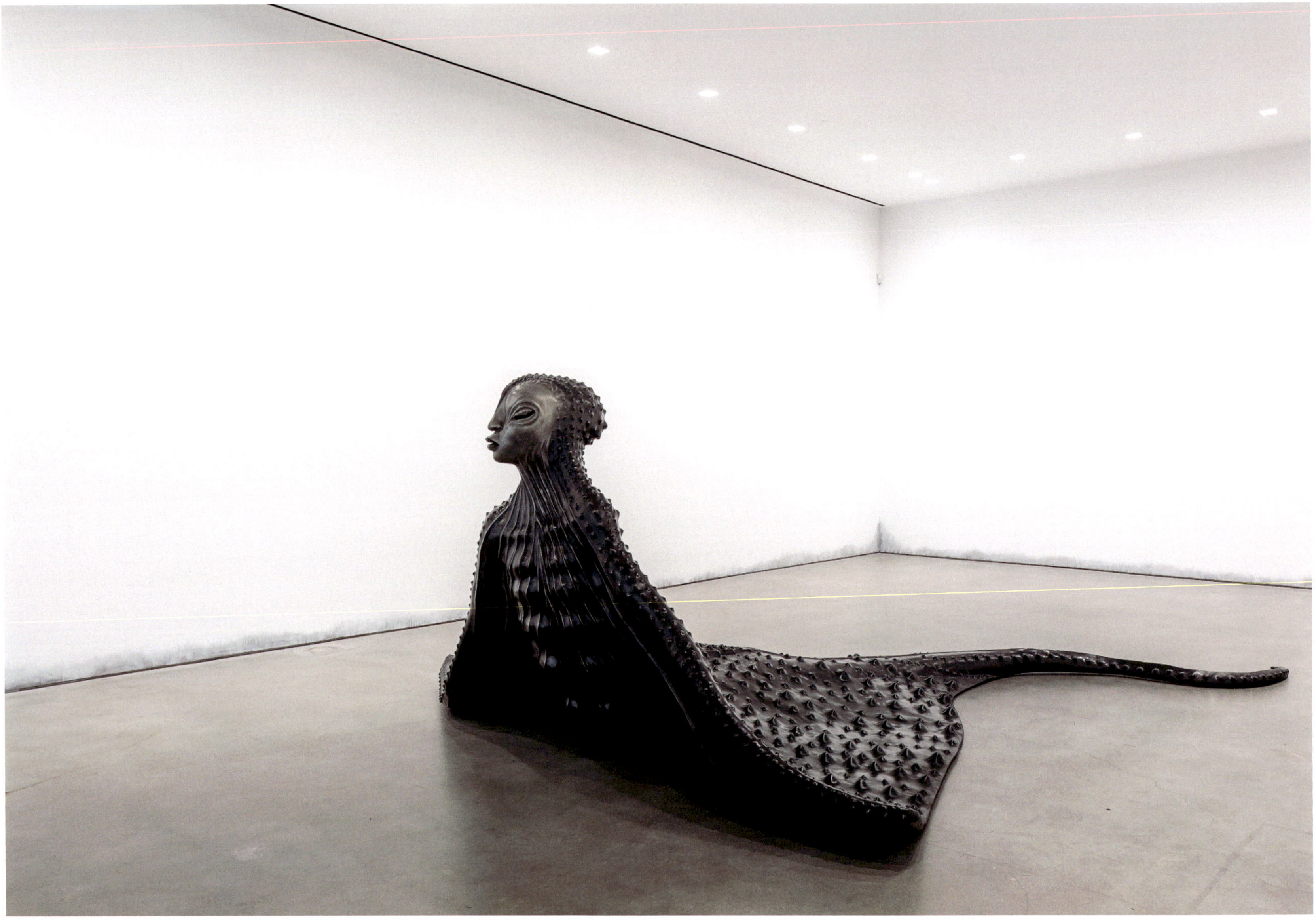

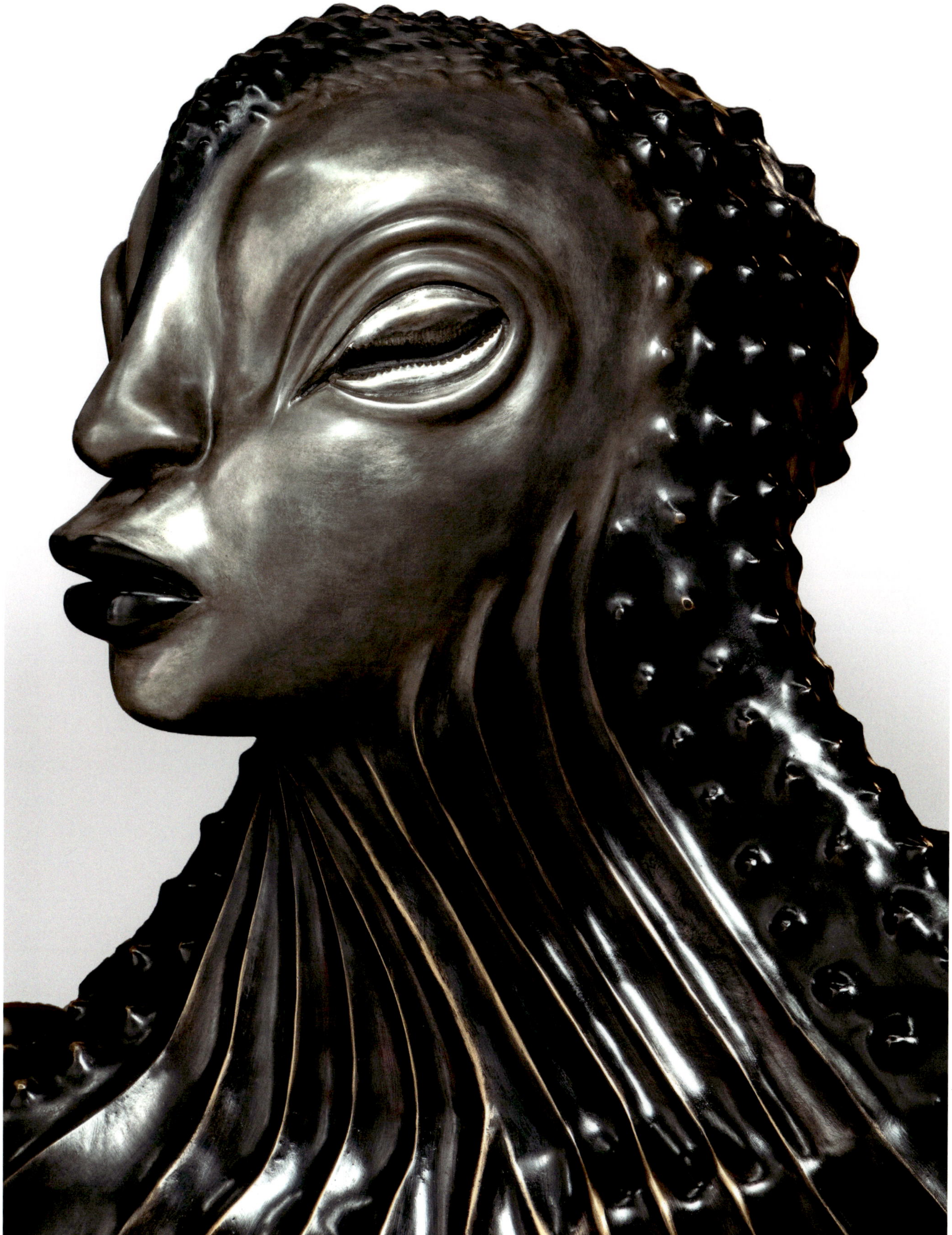

NOTES

INTRODUCTION PAGES 006–007

1 'A thin place' comes from the research and our conversations about the mami wata mythology Mutu has explored in her work. It is a liminal space that allows for crossing between the spiritual and human realm, the present and the afterlife. It also considers the artist's work existing between forms, mediums, as well as her life between New York and Nairobi.

INTERVIEW PAGES 009–049

1 Lamu is a small town on Lamu Island, a part of the Lamu Archipelago in the Indian Ocean, near the northern coast of Kenya.
2 A formerly active defense structure, the National Museums of Kenya and the Swedish International Development Cooperation Agency converted Lamu Fort (built 1813–21) into a museum and community site to preserve its historic character in 1993.
3 Rudolph Giuliani was mayor of the city of New York from 1994 to 2001.
4 Prospect.1, New Orleans, Louisiana, 1 November 2008–18 Januaury 2009.

SURVEY PAGES 051–101

1 Kellie Jones, 'Life's Little Necessities, Installations by Women in the Nineties', *Atlantica*, Winter 1998, p. 165. While this article has the same title as the catalogue essay, it is not the same piece. In fact it was written retrospectively, after the show was installed and gives a true sense of what was on view. Many thanks to Octavio Zaya for commissioning that article.
2 Okwui Enwezor, perhaps from an initial document sent to curators for the Johannesburg Biennale, cited in Kellie Jones, 'Life's Little Necessities, Installations by Women in the Nineties', *Atlantica*, p. 165, op. cit.
3 Okwui Enwezor, 'Travel Notes: Living, Working, and Travelling in a Restless World', in *Trade Routes, History and Geography* (Johannesburg: Greater Johannesburg Metropolitan Council, 1997), p. 8.
4 Tiffany E. Barber, Angela Naimou, and Wangechi Mutu, 'Between Disgust and Regeneration', *ASAP Journal* 1 (3), September 2016, pp. 341, 343, 351, 353. Wangechi wasn't able to come to South Africa for the installation due to US visa issues, as was the case with Cuban artist Magdalena Campos Pons. Other artists in 'Life's Little Necessities' included: Zarina Bhimji, Silvia Gruner, Veliswa Gwintsa, Glenda Heyliger, Berni (Bernadette) Searle, Lorna Simpson, Melanie Smith, Jocelyn Taylor, Fatimah Tuggar and Pat Ward Williams. The work by Valeska Soares could not be fabricated. On US immigration woes, see, Rachel Wolff, 'She'll Probably Cut Up This Magazine Too; How Wangechi Mutu snipped and clipped her way from Nairobi to the walls of the Brooklyn Museum', *New York* 46 (25), 26 August 2013.
5 What would eventually become the National Museums of Kenya came into being in 1909, when discrete ethnographic collections of various 'colonial British natural history enthusiasts' (Lagat, 26) were brought together. Since that time, the institution has witnessed a fitful transformation to a decolonial and national present. Kiprop Lagat, 'Representations of Nationhood in the Displays of the National Museums of Kenya (NMK): The Nairobi National Museum', *Critical Interventions* 11 (1), 2017, pp. 24–39; Rose Mwanga, 'Gourd Vessels: Women's Personal Objects', In Marion Arnold (ed.), *Art in Eastern Africa* (Dar es Salaam: Mkuki na Nyota Publishers, 2008): pp. 123–32; Elsbeth Joyce Court and Sylvester Okwunnodu Ogbechie (eds.), *Kenyan Art Worlds*, special issue *Critical Interventions* 11 (1) (2017). The Kenyan paleoanthropologist and one time director of the National Museum of Kenya, Richard Leakey, was also a mentor of Mutu's. See Deborah Willis, 'Wangechi Mutu' *Bomb Oral History Project* (14 February 2014).
6 Kellie Jones, 'Life's Little Necessities, Installations by Women in the Nineties' in *EyeMinded* (originally 1997), p. 132. Here Mutu references conflicts in central Africa from 1996 to 2006 in which millions of people lost their lives. See Carol Thompson, 'Sticks and Stones Will Break Your Bones, but Words Can Also Hurt You: Don't Let Sleeping Heads Lie', in David Moos (ed.), *Wangechi Mutu, This you Call Civilization?* (Toronto: Art Gallery of Ontario, 2010), p. 48, and Flip Reyntjens, *The Great African War: Congo and Regional Geopolitics 1996-2006* (Cambridge, UK: Cambridge University Press, 2009).
7 Okwui Enwezor, 'Travel Notes: Living, Working, and Travelling in a Restless World', in *Trade Routes, History and Geography* (Johannesburg: Greater Johannesburg Metropolitan council, 1997), p. 12.
8 Karen R. Good, 'Miss Mary Mack', *Village Voice*, April 1997, p. 59. Throwin' Tantrums was the name of rapper Da Brat's production company.
9 Uri McMillan, *Embodied Avatars, Genealogies of Black Feminist Art and Performance* (New York: New York University Press, 2015), p. 205.
10 Lindsay Zoladz, 'Megan Thee Stallion Contains Multitudes', *The New York Times*, 27 November 2020, C14.
11 Wangechi Mutu, 'Gender-based Violence Harms Us All', *The New York Times*, 6 December 2019; Megan Thee Stallion, 'Why I Speak Up for Black Women', *The New York Times*, 13 October 2020. See also Micha Cárdenas, 'Dark Shimmers: the Rhythm of Necropolitical Affect in Digital Media', in Reina Gossett, Eric A. Stanley and Johanna Burton, (eds.), *Trap door: trans cultural production and the politics of visibility* (Cambridge, Massachusetts: The MIT Press, 2017); Faka, 'On the Illusion of Safe Space,' in Kimberly Drew and Jenna Wortham (eds.), *Black Futures* (New York: One World, 2020), pp. 474–79. In *Pound The Alarm* (2012) Nikki Minaj revisits, revises and generally turns up the heat on Tenor Saw's *Ring the Alarm* (1985). An early Jamaican dancehall artist, Saw concentrated on the power of the beat, the song and the singer, while Minaj sets her video among the sensuality and ebullience of Trinidadian Carnival. A version by Beyoncé (*Ring the Alarm*, 2006) takes on the persona of the tough no-nonsense woman and not the sonics. Thanks to Tiona Nekkia McClodden for helping me unpack this idea.
12 It's safe to say that Mutu further developed her voice as an artist in two successive New York residencies, at Jamaica Center for Arts and Learning (2002) and The Studio Museum in Harlem (2003).
13 Danielle Knafo, 'Claude Cahun: The Third Sex', *Studies in Gender and Sexuality* 2 (1) (2001): pp. 29–61; Salomon Grimberg, 'Frida Kahlo's Still Lifes: "I Paint Flowers So They Will Not Die"', *Women's Art Journal* 25 (2) (Autumn 2004–Winter 2005), pp. 25–30. Leticia Alvarado, '... Towards a Personal Will to Continue to Being "Other": Ana Mendieta's Abject Performances,'*Journal of Latin American Cultural Studies* Volume 24, no. 1(1/2/2015): pp. 65-85.
14 Zoe Whitley, 'International Geographic: Wangechi Mutu on Paper, Print, and Printmaking', *Art in Print* 4 (4), November–December 2014, pp. 11–15.
15 Jennifer L. Morgan, '"Some Could Suckle over their Shoulder": Male Travelers, Female Bodies, and the Gendering of Racial Ideology, 1550–1770', *The William and Mary Quarterly* 54 (1), January 1997, pp. 167–92. Mutu's drawing dates from 1996.
16 Isolde Brielmaier, 'The Splendor of Our World', in Isolde Brielmaier (ed.), *Wangechi Mutu, A Shady Promise* (Bologna, Italy: Damiani, 2008), p. 13.
17 See Tiffany E. Barber, Angela Naimou and Wangechi Mutu, 'Between Disgust and Regeneration', *ASAP Journal* 1 (3), September 2016, p. 343. Okwui Enwezor and Chika Okeke-Agulu, *Contemporary African Art Since 1980* (Bologna: Damiani, 2009), p. 26.
18 Michael Veal, 'Enter Cautiously', in Isolde Brielmaier (ed.), *Wangechi Mutu, A Shady Promise* (Bologna, Italy: Damiani, 2008), p. 8. On the impact of Yale University professors, including Michael Veal, see Deborah Willis, 'Wangechi Mutu' *Bomb Oral History Project*, 14 February 2014. On the idea of the Postcolonial 'Big Man' see Achille Mbembe, *On the Postcolony* (Berkeley: University of California Press, 2001).
19 Anny Shaw, 'Why African women artists are bucking the market trend', *The Art Newspaper*, 3 October 2019.
20 Soraya Murray, 'Africaine,' *NKA Journal of Contemporary African Art*, Winter 2002, pp. 88–93. Okwui Enwezor, 'Weird Beauty: ritual Violence and Archaeology of Mass Media in Wangechi Mutu's Work', in *My Dirty Little Heaven* (2010), and Okwui Enwezor and Chika Okeke-Agulu, *Contemporary African Art Since 1980* (Bologna: Damiani, 2009), pp. 23, 30.Writing first in the late 1990s in the context of South Africa in the immediate post-apartheid moment, Enwezor was initially alarmed by the seemingly gratuitous approach to issues of power, access, race, sexuality and colonial legacy, particularly by white artists. Later, inspired by the approaches of Mutu and others, he reconsidered. Okwui Enwezor, 'Reframing the Black Subject, Ideology and Fantasy in Contemporary South African Representation', *Third Text* 40, Autumn 1997, pp. 21–40.
21 Courtney J. Martin, 'Fracture and Action: Wangechi Mutu's Collages 1999–2010', in *My Dirty Little Heaven*, 2010, op. cit.
22 Tiffany E. Barber, Angela Naimou and Wangechi Mutu,'Between Disgust and Regeneration', *ASAP Journal* 1 (3) September 2016, p. 340. See Kaira Cabañas, *The Myth of Nouveau Réalisme: Art and the Performative in Postwar France* (New Haven: Yale University Press, 2013); Brent Hayes Edwards, *The Practice of Diaspora: Literature, Translation, and the Rise of Black Internationalism* (Cambridge, MA: Harvard University Press, 2003).
23 Among the artist's major inspiration was Angela Fisher, *Women of the African Ark* (1990). The book features photographs of women in traditional rituals and settings by Carol Beckwith, images that were circulated widely in calendars and as postcards. Beckwith's photos date from as early as the 1970s in Kenya and Tanzania. On colonial postcard imagery, see Krista A. Thompson, *An Eye for the Tropics: Tourism, Photography, and Framing the Caribbean Picturesque* (Durham: Duke University Press, 2006).
24 David Moos, 'The Ark Collection: Disjunctive Continuity', in David Moos (ed.), *Wangechi Mutu, This you Call Civilization?* (Toronto: Art Gallery of Ontario, 2010), p. 16.
25 Jennifer C. Nash, *The Black Body in Ecstasy, Reading Race, Reading Pornography* (Durham: Duke University Press, 2014), p. 6.
26 Jillian Hernandez, 'The Ambivalent Grotesque: Reading Black Women's Erotic Corporeality in Wangechi Mutu's Work', *Signs* 42 (2), p. 434.
27 Jillian Hernandez, 'The Ambivalent Grotesque: Reading Black Women's Erotic Corporeality in Wangechi Mutu's Work', *Signs* 42 (2) 2017, p. 444.
28 Tiffany E. Barber, Angela Naimou, and Wangechi Mutu, 'Between Disgust and Regeneration', *ASAP Journal* 1 (3) September 2016, p. 347.
29 Brett M. Van Hoesen, 'Weimar Revisions of Germany's Colonial Past, The Photomontages of Hannah Höch and László Moholy-Nagy', in Volker Langbehn (ed.), *German colonialism, visual culture, and modern memory* (New York: Routledge, 2010), pp. 197–219.
30 Okwui Enwezor, 'Weird Beauty: Ritual Violence and Archaeology of Mass Media in Wangechi Mutu's Work', in *My Dirty Little Heaven* (2010), p. 28, op. cit.
31 Z.S. Strother, 'Looking for Africa in Carl Einstein's Negerplastik', *African Arts* 46 (4) Winter 2013, pp. 11, 9, 14.
32 Z.S. Strother, 'Looking for Africa in Carl Einstein's Negerplastik', *African Arts* 46 (4) Winter 2013, p. 14, and Okwui Enwezor, 'Weird Beauty: Ritual Violence and Archaeology of Mass Media in Wangechi Mutu's Work', in *My Dirty Little Heaven*, 2010, p. 28, op. cit.
33 Wangechi Mutu in Isolde Brielmaier (ed.), *Wangechi Mutu, A Shady Promise* (Bologna, Italy: Damiani, 2008), p. 85.
34 Trevor Schoonmaker, 'A Fantastic Journey', in Trevor Schoonmaker (ed.), *Wangechi Mutu: A Fantastic Journey* (Durham: Nasher Museum at Duke University, 2013), p. 26. Sketchbook drawings from 2010–11 as endpapers for this exhibition catalogue reveal Mutu's thinking here.
35 These days artists are more likely to use the more eco-friendly Yupo synthetic paper.
36 Ruth Fine, *The Art of Romare Bearden* (Washington, D.C.: National Gallery of Art, 2003), p. 105.
37 Judith Wilson, 'Getting Down to Get Over: Romare Bearden's Use of Pornography and the Problem of the Black Female Body in Afro-U.S. Art', in Gina Dent (ed.), *Black Popular Culture* (Seattle: Bay Press, 1992). Mutu's contemporary Mickalene Thomas also uses some of the same magazines, such as *Black Tail*, in composing her collage practice.
38 Romare Bearden, 'Encounters with African Art' (1987), in Robert G. O'Meally (ed.), *The Romare Bearden Reader* (Durham: Duke University Press, 2019), p. 165. MoMA's African Negro Art took place from 18 March–19 May 1935, and also made a great impression on Bearden's friend, painter Norman Lewis. See Kellie Jones, 'Mediterranean Conversations', in *Odyssey: Jack Whitten, Sculpture* 1963–2017 (Baltimore Museum of Art and the Metropolitan Museum of Art, 2018). With painter Ernest Crichlow, Bearden and Lewis would open Cinque Gallery in 1968 to support younger African American artists. It was named after a native of Sierra Leone who sued for his freedom in New Haven, Connecticut in 1839 and won, an event that set the stage for US abolition of slavery.
39 'Joshua Fit [or Fought] the Battle of Jericho' is a nineteenth century American Negro spiritual based on an Old Testament story in which that figure vanquishes his enemies through music.
40 The Nigerian Egungun is a Yoruba masquerade form that celebrates ancestors. Fang peoples live throughout Gabon, Cameroon and Equatorial Guinea.
41 Tiffany E. Barber, 'Cyborg Grammar?: Reading Wangechi Mutu's Non je ne regrette rien through Kindred', in Reynaldo Anderson and Charles E. Jones, *Afrofuturism 2.0, The Rise of Astro-Blackness* (Lanham, Maryland: Lexington Books, 2016), p. 3.
42 Tiffany E. Barber, 'Cyborg Grammar?: Reading Wangechi Mutu's Non je ne regrette rien through Kindred', in Reynaldo Anderson and Charles E. Jones, *Afrofuturism 2.0, The Rise of Astro-Blackness*, 2016), p. 12, op. cit.
43 Zakiyyah Iman Jackson, Becoming Human, Matter and Meaning in an Antiblack World (New York: New York University Press, 2019), p. 159. See also María Lugones, 'Methodological Notes Towards a Theory of Decolonial Feminism,' in Ada Maria Isasi-Diaz and Eduardo Mendieta, (eds), *Decolonizing Epistemologies: Latina/o Theology and Philosophy* (Fordham Scholarship Online, 2021), Hortense J. Spillers, 'Mama's Baby, Papa's Maybe: An American Grammar Book,' *Diacritics* 17 (2) Summer 1987, pp. 64-81; and Hazel V. Carby, 'Policing the Black Woman's Body in an Urban Context,' (1992) in *Carby, Cultures in Babylon, Black Britain and African America* (London and New York: Verso, 1999).
44 Tiffany E. Barber, 'Cyborg Grammar?: Reading Wangechi Mutu's Non je ne regrette rien through Kindred', in Reynaldo Anderson and Charles E. Jones, *Afrofuturism 2.0, The Rise of Astro-Blackness*, 2016), p. 13, op. cit.
45 Trevor Schoonmaker, 'A Fantastic Journey', in Trevor Schoonmaker (ed.), *Wangechi Mutu: A Fantastic Journey* (Durham: Nasher Museum at Duke University, 2013), p. 26.

46 Zakiyyah Iman Jackson, *Becoming Human, Matter and Meaning in an Antiblack World* (New York: New York University Press, 2019), 190. Sarah Jane Cervenak, 'Like Blood on Blossom: Wangechi Mutu's Resistant Harvests', *Feminist Studies* 42 (2) (2016), pp. 392–425; Elspeth VanVeeren, 'Layered wanderings: epistemic justice through the art of Wangechi Mutu and Njideka Akunyili Crosby', *International Feminist Journal of Politics* 21 (3) (2019), 488–98; Denise Ferreira da Silva, 'Toward a Black Feminist Poethics: The Quest(ion) of Blackness , Toward the End of the World', *The Black Scholar* 44 (2): 81–97; on limbs and prosthetics, see Sarah Ahmed, *Willful Subjects* (Durham: Duke University Press, 2014), pp. 99–101, 177–80.

47 Zakiyyah Iman Jackson, *Becoming Human, Matter and Meaning in an Antiblack World* (New York: New York University Press, 2019), p. 169.

48 Zakiyyah Iman Jackson, *Becoming Human, Matter and Meaning in an Antiblack World* (New York: New York University Press, 2019), p. 160.

49 Sarah Ahmed, Willful Subjects (Durham: Duke University Press, 2014), p. 160.

50 Wangechi Mutu in conversation with Rich Blint in David Moos (ed.), *Wangechi Mutu, This you Call Civilization?* (Toronto: Art Gallery of Ontario, 2010), p. 99.

51 Tiffany E. Barber, Angela Naimou and Wangechi Mutu, 'Between Disgust and Regeneration', *ASAP Journal* 1 (3) (September 2016), p. 342. Mutu's discusses her support for queer communities throughout this article. The artist developed the project Africa's Out as a mechanism to support queer lives in the African context in particular. Antwuan Sargent, 'Africa's Out! Let's Celebrate', *W Magazine* (8 June 2015). https://www.wmagazine.com/story/wangechi-mutu-africas-out/ (accessed 20 December 2020). On trans visibility see, Raquel Willis, 'Welcome to the Transvisibility Era', in Kimberly Drew and Jenna Wortham (eds), *Black Futures* (New York: One World, 2020), pp. 382–85.

52 Jennifer C. Nash, The Black Body in *Ecstasy, Reading Race, Reading Pornography* (Durham: Duke University Press, 2014), p. 3.

53 Tiffany E. Barber, 'Cyborg Grammar?: Reading Wangechi Mutu's Non je ne regrette rien through Kindred', in Reynaldo Anderson and Charles E. Jones, *Afrofuturism 2.0: The Rise of Astro-Blackness* (Lanham, Maryland: Lexington Books, 2016), pp. 3–25. Cyrée Jarelle Johnson and Carolyn Lazard in conversation, in Jenna Wortham (ed.), *Black Futures* (New York: One World, 2020), pp. 50–56. See also Farah Jasmine Griffin, 'Textual Healing: Claiming Black Women's Bodies, the erotic and resistance in contemporary novels of slavery', *Callalooo: A Journal African-American and African Arts and Letters* 19 (1996), pp. 519–36.

54 Legacy Russell, *Glitch Feminism* (New York: Verso, 2020), p. 7.

55 The Black Gooey Universe is a play on digital graphical user interfaces or GUI, pronounced as gooey. Legacy Russell, *Glitch Feminism* (New York,: Verso, 2020), pp. 113–17.

56 Jennifer C. Nash, *The Black Body in Ecstasy, Reading Race, Reading Pornography* (Durham: Duke University Press, 2014), p. 17. As Nash further elucidates, part of the development of Third Wave Feminism in the 1990s embraced a 'sex radicalism' that 'destabilized the tendency to view pornography as exclusively a site of women's subordination or a locus of women's agency … Rather than condemning particular sexual practices, sex-radicals challenged feminism to develop a politics that opens up sexual possibility.' (pp. 16, 17). In a recent dialogue, Shawné Michaelain Holloway and Tiona Nekkia Mcclodden discuss BDSM as a vessel or 'established form' (78) for desire and consent, where a mask doesn't conceal but reveals. Shawné Michaelain Holloway and Tiona Nekkia Mcclodden in conversation, in Kimberly Drew and Jenna Wortham (eds), *Black Futures* (New York: One World, 2020), pp. 72–81.

57 This installation travelled to The Whitney Museum at Altria.

58 Installed near the US/Mexico border, Hanging in Texas also remarked on the frustrations of immigrants. It was also a commentary on the Iraq War begun in 2003 with the U.S. invasion of that country. The conflict divided Kenyans, with Muslims Indian Ocean facing culture largely supporting Iraq and Christians siding with the United States, positions that had been staked out for a decade reflecting the ongoing tensions in the Persian Gulf. Interestingly, such postures were commemorated in the portrait photo studios along the East African Coast. See Heike Behrend, *Contesting Visibility, Photographic Practices on the East African Coast* (Bielefeld, Germany: Transcript Verlag, 2013), pp. 38-41, and Okwui Enwezor, 'Cut & Paste: Interview with Wangechi Mutu,' *Arise* 11 (2011).

59 Kristine Stiles, 'Wangechi Mutu's Family Tree', in Trevor Schoonmaker, (ed.), *Wangechi Mutu: A Fantastic Journey* (Durham: Nasher Museum at Duke University, 2013), p. 76.

60 Rinaldo Walcott, 'Repeating Histories, Black Bodies and Forensic Forms', in David Moos (ed.), *Wangechi Mutu, This You Call Civilization?* (Toronto: Art Gallery of Ontario, 2010), p. 40.

61 Wangechi Mutu in Isolde Brielmaier (ed.), Wangechi Mutu, *A Shady Promise* (Bologna, Italy: Damiani, 2008), p. 117. The olfactory plays a major part in these works.

62 Wangechi Mutu interviewed by Rich Blint in David Moos (ed.), *Wangechi Mutu, This you Call Civilization?* (Toronto: Art Gallery of Ontario, 2010), p. 101.

63 Trevor Schoonmaker, curator, *The Magic City*, Brent Sikkema, New York, NY, 2000.

64 *The Bottle Tree* also has vernacular and Black diasporic roots. See Robert Farris Thompson, *Flash of the Spirit, African and Afro-American Art and Philosophy* (New York: Random House, 1983), Chapter 2.

65 On wrapping and binding as a spiritual practice in Africa and the African Diaspora see Karen E. Milbourne, *Earth Matters, Land as Material and Metaphor in the Arts of Africa* (Washington: Smithsonian National Museum of African Art, and New York: Monacelli, 2013), pp. 82-87, and Kellie Jones, South of Pico, African American Artists in Los Angeles in the 1960s and 1970s (Durham: Duke University Press, 2017), pp. 103-108. Nari Ward was born in Jamaica, W.I.

66 Sarah Jane Cervenak, 'Like Blood on Blossom: Wangechi Mutu's Resistant Harvests,' *Feminist Studies* 42 (2) (2016), p. 400.

67 Stephen Nathan Haymes, 'An Africana Studies Critique of Environmental Ethics', in L. Nishime and K.D. Hester Williams, *Racial Ecologies* (Seattle: University of Washington Press, 2018. Disponível em: https://search-ebscohost-com.ezproxy.cul.columbia.edu/login.aspx?direct=true&db=e025xna&AN=1878366&site=ehost-live&scope=site.; Chelsea M. Frazier, 'Troubling Ecology, Wangechi Mutu, Octavia Butler, and Black Feminist Interventions in Environmentalism', *Critical Ethnic Studies* 2 (1), p. 43.

68 See Jonathan Metzl, *The Protest Psychosis: How Schizophrenia Became a Black Disease* (Beacon Press, 2010) and *Drapetomania, A Disease Called Freedom* (Fort Lauderdale: Bienes Center for the Literary Arts, 2000).

69 Wangechi Mutu, 'The Power of Earth in My Work', in Karen E. Milbourne, *Earth Matters, Land as Material and Metaphor in the Arts of Africa* (Washington: Smithsonian National Museum of African Art, and New York: Monacelli, 2013), p. 92.

70 Sarah Jane Cervenak, 'Like Blood on Blossom: Wangechi Mutu's Resistant Harvests', *Feminist Studies* 42 (2) (2016), p. 400.

71 Before moving to New York, Mutu spent time making art on Kenya's coast at Lamu Island. Deborah Willis, 'Wangechi Mutu', *Bomb Oral History Project* (14 February 2014).

72 Henry John Drewal, 'Beauteous Beast: The Water Deity Mami Wata in Africa' , in *The Ashgate Research Companion to Monsters and the Monstrous* (ed.), Asa Simon Mittman and Peter J. Dendle (Abingdon: Routledge, 15 August 2013), accessed 9 January 2021, Routledge Handbooks Online, p. 80. See also Adrienne Edwards, in Binyavanga Wainaina and Adrienne Edwards, *Wangechi Mutu: Nguva na Nyoka*. London, Victoria Miro, 2014, pp. 6-11.

73 Henry John Drewal, 'Beauteous Beast: The Water Deity Mami Wata in Africa' , in Asa Simon Mittman and Peter J. Dendle (eds), *The Ashgate Research Companion to Monsters and the Monstrous* (Abingdon: Routledge, 15 August 2013), accessed 9 January 2021, Routledge Handbooks Online, p. 87.

74 Henry John Drewal, 'Beauteous Beast: The Water Deity Mami Wata in Africa' , in Asa Simon Mittman and Peter J. Dendle (eds), *The Ashgate Research Companion to Monsters and the Monstrous* (Abingdon: Routledge, 15 August 2013), accessed 9 January 2021, Routledge Handbooks Online, p. 87.

75 This is exemplified in the film *A Question of Silence* (1982). Ahmed, pp. 153–54.

76 Henry John Drewal, 'Beauteous Beast: The Water Deity Mami Wata in Africa' , in Asa Simon Mittman and Peter J. Dendle (eds), *The Ashgate Research Companion to Monsters and the Monstrou,* op. cit., accessed 9 January 2021, Routledge Handbooks Online, pp. 88–96.

77 Prita Meier, *Swahili Port Cities, The Architecture of Elsewhere* (Bloomington: Indiana University Press, 2016), p. 9, and Heike Behrend, *Contesting Visibility, Photographic Practices on the East African Coast* (Bielefeld, Germany: transcript Verlag, 2013), p. 29. Elsbeth Joyce Court and Sylvester Okwunnodu Ogbechie have located the beginning of such Indian Ocean interaction to as early as 45 C.E. Elsbeth Joyce Court and Sylvester Okwunnodu Ogbechie, 'Editor's Desk, Kenyan Art Worlds', in Elsbeth Joyce Court and Sylvester Okwunnodu Ogbechie (eds), *Kenyan Art Worlds*, special issue *Critical Interventions* 11 (1) (2017), p. 1.

78 Eileen Moyer, 'Death of the Mermaid and Political Intrigue in the Indian Ocean', in Henry John Drewal (ed.), *Sacred Waters: Arts for Mami Wata and Other Divinities in Africa and the Diaspora* (Bloomington: Indiana University Press, 2008), pp. 452, 453, 460.

79 Heike Behrend, *Contesting Visibility, Photographic Practices on the East African Coast* (Bielefeld, Germany: transcript Verlag, 2013), Chapter 1 and Chapter 4.

80 Henry John Drewal, 'Beauteous Beast: The Water Deity Mami Wata in Africa', in Asa Simon Mittman and Peter J. Dendle (eds), *The Ashgate Research Companion to Monsters and the Monstrou,* op. cit., (Abingdon: Routledge, 15 August 2013), accessed 9 January 2021, Routledge Handbooks Online, p. 97. During the late 1980s and early 1990s, there was a rise in the establishment of Islamic schools particularly for women, Heike Behrend, *Contesting Visibility, Photographic Practices on the East African Coast* (Bielefeld, Germany: transcript Verlag, 2013), p. 31.

81 Jennifer C. Nash, The Black Body in Ecstasy, Reading Race, Reading Pornography (Durham: Duke University Press, 2014), p. 15. On Mutu and feminism see Deborah Willis, 'Wangechi Mutu' *Bomb Oral History Project* (14 February 2014); Okwui Enwezor, 'Cut & Paste: Interview with Wangechi Mutu,' *Arise* 11 (2011); Rebecca Walker , 'Becoming the Third Wave' Ms. Magazine (January 1992), pp. 39-41.

82 Prita Meier, *Swahili Port Cities, The Architecture of Elsewhere* (Bloomington: Indiana University Press, 2016), p. 14, op. cit. See also Chapurukha M. Kusimba, 'Archaeology of Slavery in East Africa', *The African Archaeological Review* 21 (2) (June 2004), pp. 59–88.

83 Prita Meier, *Swahili Port Cities, The Architecture of Elsewhere* (Bloomington: Indiana University Press, 2016), p. 13, op. cit. Heike Behrend, *Contesting Visibility, Photographic Practices on the East African Coast* (Bielefeld, Germany: transcript Verlag, 2013), op. cit. Chapter 4.

84 An alternative reading understands fabric remnants as mediators of blessings in the Muslim tradition. Heike Behrend, *Contesting Visibility, Photographic Practices on the East African Coast* (Bielefeld, Germany: transcript Verlag, 2013), pp. 67–71, op. cit.

85 With the addition of the clog, Mutu calls attention to the workings of the Dutch East India company along the Indian Ocean and East African coast, and its imbrication in imperialism and the slave trade beginning in the seventeenth century. See Matthias Van Rossum, 'Global Slavery, Local Bondage? Rethinking Slaveries as (Im)Mobilizing Regimes from the Case of the Dutch Indian Ocean and Indonesian Archipelago Worlds.' Journal of World History, vol. 31 no. 4, 2020, pp. 693-727. Project MUSE, doi:10.1353/jwh.2020.0049.

86 Adrienne Edwards,, *Wangechi Mutu: Nguva na Nyoka*, op. cit., pp. 6-11.

87 Wangechi Mutu, 'Making Through Motion', in Deborah Willis, Ellyn Toscano and Kalia Brooks Nelson (eds), *Women and Migration: Responses in Art and History*. Cambridge: Open Book Publishers, 2019 (accessed 9 January 2021). <http://books.openedition.org.ezproxy.cul.columbia.edu/obp/7954>, p. 76.

88 Wangechi Mutu, 'Making Through Motion, in Deborah Willis, Ellyn Toscano, and Kalia Brooks Nelson (eds), *Women and Migration: Responses in Art and History*. Cambridge: Open Book Publishers, 2019 (accessed 9 January 2021). <http://books.openedition.org.ezproxy.cul.columbia.edu/obp/7954>, p. 77.

89 Johanna Fateman, 'Wangechi Mutu', *Artforum* (April 2017), p. 206.

90 Karen E. Milbourne, *Earth Matters, Land as Material and Metaphor in the Arts of Africa* (Washington: Smithsonian National Museum of African Art, and New York: Monacelli, 2013), p. 25.

91 Karen E. Milbourne, *Earth Matters, Land as Material and Metaphor in the Arts of Africa* (Washington: Smithsonian National Museum of African Art, and New York: Monacelli, 2013), pp. 27–28, op. cit.

92 Johanna Fateman, 'Wangechi Mutu', *Artforum* (April 2017), p. 207, op. cit.

93 In this regard I continue to be fascinated by Brancusi's, *White Negress I* (1923) and *Blonde Negress II* (1933), as part of the artist's response to the Black presence in Europe, whether in colonial fairs or as performers in Jazz Age Paris like Josephine Baker. https://www.moma.org/collection/works/80936

94 Interestingly, as Behrend argues, in Islamic visual tradition decapitated humans and animals (sometimes represented by a line drawn disconnecting head from body) are not proscribed since their apparent lack of wholeness does not mimic God's work. Additionally, two-dimensional images, ones that throw no shadows, are already lifeless, and are also not problematic. Heike Behrend, *Contesting Visibility, Photographic Practices on the East African Coast* (Bielefeld, Germany: transcript Verlag, 2013), p. 79, op. cit.

95 Wangechi Mutu in conversation with Rich Blint in David Moos (ed.), Wangechi Mutu, *This you Call Civilization?* (Toronto: Art Gallery of Ontario, 2010), p. 101.

96 Catherine Elwes, Installation and the Moving Image (London and New York: Wallflower Press, 2015), 2. Heike Behrend, 'Space of Refusal: Photophobic Sprits and the Technical Medium of Photography', in Heike Behrend, Anja Dreschke and Martin Zillinger (eds), *Trance Mediums and New Media: Spirit Possession in the Age of Technical Reproduction* (New York: Fordham, 2014), pp. 201–220.

97 M.J.W. Kings, 'Jongo Love: A Self-Reflective Movies Shot on a Mobile Phone', *Critical Interventions* 11 (1) (2017), 73. See also Irina O. Rawjewsky, 'Intermediality, Intertextuality, and Remediation: A Literary Perspective on Intermediality', *Intermédialities* 6 (Autumn 2005), pp. 43-64, and Dick Higgins, 'Intermedia,' (1966) in Richard Kostelanetz, (ed.), *The Young American Writers* (New York: Funk & Wagnalls, 1967), pp. 191-196.

98 Zoe Whitley, 'International Geographic: Wangechi Mutu on Paper, Print, and Printmaking', *Art in Print* 4 (4) (November–December 2014), 12. On press suppression see Okwui Enwezor, 'Cut & Paste: Interview with Wangechi

opposite and next pages,
THE GLIDER, 2021
SOIL, CHARCOAL, PAPER PULP, WOOD GLUE, CHARCOAL, INK, WOOD, GOURD, SHELL, BRASS BEAD
72 X 75 X 278 CM

Mutu,' *Arise* 11 (2011), and Ruha Benjamin, Race After Technology, *Abolitionist Tools for the New Jim Code* (Cambridge, UK: Polity Press, 2019).

99 Legacy Russell, *Glitch Feminism* (New York: Verso, 2020), 45. On spectres of disintegration and Amazing Grace see Sarah Jane Cervenak, 'Like Blood on Blossom: Wangechi Mutu's Resistant Harvests', Feminist Studies 42 (2) (2016), p. 424.

100 Legacy Russell, 9. Marianne Hirsch, 'Carrying Memory', in Deborah Willis, Ellyn Toscano and Kalia Brooks Nelson (eds), *Women and Migration: Responses in Art and History*. Cambridge: Open Book Publishers, 2019 (accessed 9 January 2021). <http://books.openedition.org.ezproxy.cul.columbia.edu/obp/7954>, p. 62. Okwui Enwezor, 'Cut & Paste: Interview with Wangechi Mutu,' *Arise* 11 (2011).

101 Amanda Renée Rico, 'Gendered Ecologies and Black Feminist Futures in Wanuri Kahiu's Pumzi, *Wangechi Mutu's The End of Eating Everything*, and Ibi Zoboi's 'The Farming Gods', *Wagadu: A Journal of Transnational Women's and Gender Studies* 18 (Winter 2017), p. ?.

102 Amanda Renée Rico, 'Gendered Ecologies and Black Feminist Futures in Wanuri Kahiu's Pumzi, *Wangechi Mutu's The End of eating Everything*, and Ibi Zoboi's 'The Farming Gods', *Wagadu: A Journal of Transnational Women's and Gender Studies* 18 (Winter 2017), p. 87.

103 Carol Thompson, 'Sticks and Stones Will Break Your Bones, but Words Can Also Hurt You: Don't Let Sleeping Heads Lie', in David Moos (ed.), *Wangechi Mutu, This you Call Civilization?* (Toronto: Art Gallery of Ontario, 2010), p. 55, and Matt Cornish, 'The Future, Unhurried,' *PAJ: A Journal of Performance Art* 32 (2) (May 2010), pp. 40–50.

104 Jennifer C. Nash, *The Black Body in Ecstasy, Reading Race, Reading Pornography* (Durham: Duke University Press, 2014), p. 18

105 Renée Mussai and Zanele Muholi in conversation, in Kimberly Drew and Jenna Wortham (eds), *Black Futures* (New York: One World, 2020), pp. 304–11.

106 Kristine Stiles, 'Wangechi Mutu's Family Tree', in Trevor Schoonmaker, (ed.), *Wangechi Mutu: A Fantastic Journey* (Durham: Nasher Museum at Duke University, 2013), p. 68; Okwui Enwezor and Chika Okeke-Agulu, *Contemporary African Art Since 1980* (Bologna, Italy: Damiani, 2009), 8, 45; Hazel Carby,'White Woman Listen! Black feminism and the boundaries of sisterhood' in Centre for Contemporary Cultural Studies, *Empire Strikes Back, Race and Racism in 1970s Britain* (1982), pp. 211–234; Kellie Jones, 'AK.A. Saartjie, The Hottentot Venus in Context (Some Recollections and a Dialogue) 1998–2004' in *EyeMinded, Living and Writing Contemporary Art* (Durham: Duke University Press, 2011), p. 64 n. 3.

107 Karen E. Milbourne, *Earth Matters, Land as Material and Metaphor in the Arts of Africa* (Washington: Smithsonian National Museum of African Art, and New York: Monacelli, 2013), pp. 29–30; Tiffany E. Barber, Angela Naimou and Wangechi Mutu, 'Between Disgust and Regeneration', *ASAP Journal* 1 (3) (September 2016), pp. 353, 355. Alanna Martinez, 'Why Artist Wangechi Mutu Chooses to Perform in Secret', *Observer.com* (18 July 2016) https://observer.com/2016/07/why-artist-wangechi-mutu-chooses-to-perform-in-secret/ (accessed 20 December 2020).

108 Ian Borland interviews Wangechi Mutu, *Artforum online* (12 July 2016); Tiffany E. Barber, Angela Naimou, and Wangechi Mutu, 'Between Disgust and Regeneration', *ASAP Journal* 1 (3) (September 2016), 356; Elements of ground and earth reappear through this digital work and can be related back to some of Mutu's earliest use of actual mud in her Pin Up Series. The comparison with Kazuo Shiraga, *Challenging Mud*, 1955 might also be apropos.

109 Jack Halberstam and Tavia Nyong'o, 'Theory in the Wild', in Jack Halberstam and Tavia Nyong'o (eds), *Wildness Special Issue, South Atlantic Quarterly* 117 (3) (July 2018), pp. 453–54. See also Shawné Michaelain Holloway and Tiona Nekkia Mcclodden in conversation, in Kimberly Drew and Jenna Wortham (eds), *Black Futures* (New York: One World, 2020), pp. 72–81.

110 Rico 'Gendered Ecologies and Black Feminist Futures in Wanuri Kahiu's Pumzi, *Wangechi Mutu's The End of Eating Everything*, and Ibi Zoboi's 'The Farming Gods', *Wagadu: A Journal of Transnational Women's and Gender Studies* 18 (Winter 2017), p. 91.

111 Pontsho Pilane, '#FEESMUSTFALL', in Kimberly Drew and Jenna Wortham (eds), *Black Futures* (New York: One World, 2020), pp. 238–41; Tamar Garb, 'Falling and Rising in the Wake of Cecil John Rhodes,' *NKA: Journal of Contemporary African Art* 44 (May 2019), pp. 24-37.

112 Elizabeth Alexander, 'The Monuments Project: Building the commemorative landscape 21st-century needs', *Salon* (October 11, 2020).

113 Ulrich Baer, 'Kehinde Wiley, Wangechi Mutu, and Kara Walker Upstage the Monuments Debate', (15 January 2020) https://hyperallergic.com/536619/kehinde-wiley-wangechi-mutu-and-kara-walker-upstage-the-monuments-debate/ (accessed 20 December 2020). See also Paul B. Preciado, 'When Statues Fall,' *Artforum* 59 (3) (December 2020).

114 This type of head gear has been the subject of fascination throughout the western world for decades, beginning in the twentieth century with Malvina Hoffman's *Mangbetu Woman*, c. 1930s, imagined by costume designer Ruth E. Carter for Angela Bassett's Queen Ramonda in the film *Black Panther* (2018), and seen in Beyonce's *Black is King* (2020) project.

115 See Sylvia Ardyn Boone, *Radiance from the Waters, Ideals of Feminine Beauty in Mende Art* (New Haven: Yale University Press, 1986).

116 Like the Congolese and Nigerian examples Mutu found at the Met with kneeling or standing women holding up powerful men and state power. https://www.metmuseum.org/exhibitions/listings/2019/facade-commission-wangechi-mutu

117 Wangechi Mutu in Nancy Princenthal, 'Wangechi Mutu: A New Face for the Met', *The New York Times* (5 September 2019). https://www.nytimes.com/2019/09/05/arts/design/wangechi-mutu-metropolitan-museum.html (accessed 20 December 2020).

FOCUS: PAGES 103–113

1 Wangechi Mutu, 'The Power of Earth in My Work', in Karen E. Milbourne, *Earth Matters: Land as Material and Metaphor in the Arts of Africa* (Washington: Smithsonian National Museum of African Art, and New York: Monacelli, 2013), p. 95.

2 Trevor Schoonmaker, 'A Fantastic Journey', in *Wangechi Mutu: A Fantastic Journey* (Durham: Nasher Museum at Duke University, 2013), p. 21. My emphasis.

3 Franklin Sirmans, 'Wangechi Mutu', *Grand Street*, 72 (Autumn, 2003), p. 161.

4 Claudia Schmuckli, 'Art as a Weapon of Mass Construction', in *Wangechi Mutu: I am Speaking, Art You Listening?* (New York: Delmonico Books, 2021), p. 23.

5 Mutu, 'The Power of Earth in My Work', p. 95.

6 See Jan Garden Castro, 'Wangechi Mutu's Fantastic Journey', *Black Renaissance* 14, 1 (Spring 2014), p. 85.

7 Castro, 'Wangechi Mutu's Fantastic Journey', p. 85.

8 Okwui Enwezor, 'Weird Beauty: Ritual Violence and Archaeology of Mass Media in Wangechi Mutu's Work', in *Wangechi Mutu: My Dirty Little Heaven* (Ostfildern: Hatje Cantz, 2010), p. 32.

9 Mutu, 'The Power of Earth in My Work', p. 95.

10 Schoonmaker, 'A Fantastic Journey', p. 38.

11 See, Nontando Hadebe, 'The Cry of the Earth Is the Cry of Women: Ecofeminisms in Critical Dialogue with Laudato Si', in Sophia Chirongoma and Esther Mombo (ed.), *Mother Earth: Postcolonial Liberation Theologies* (London: Lexington Books, 2021), pp. 83–98.

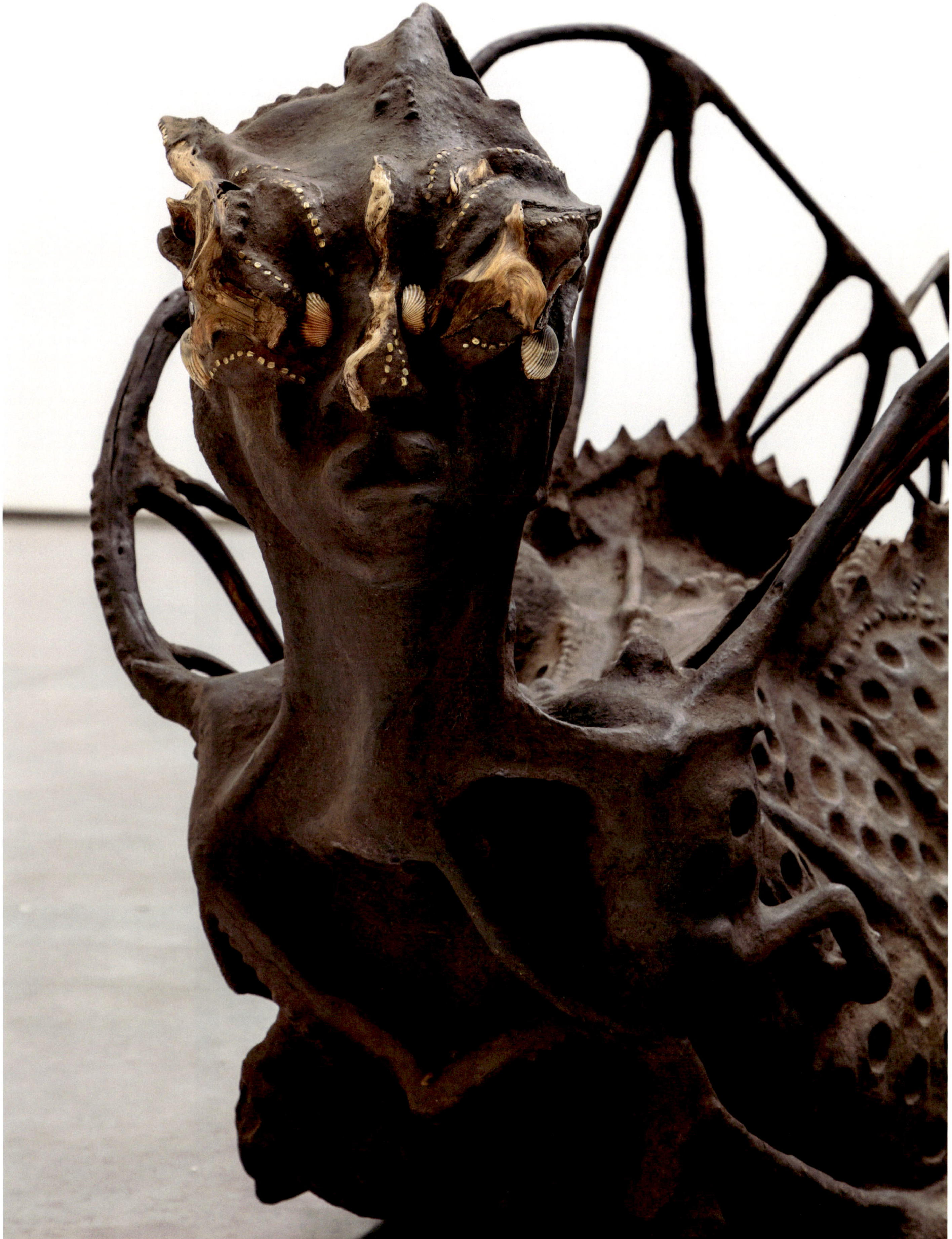

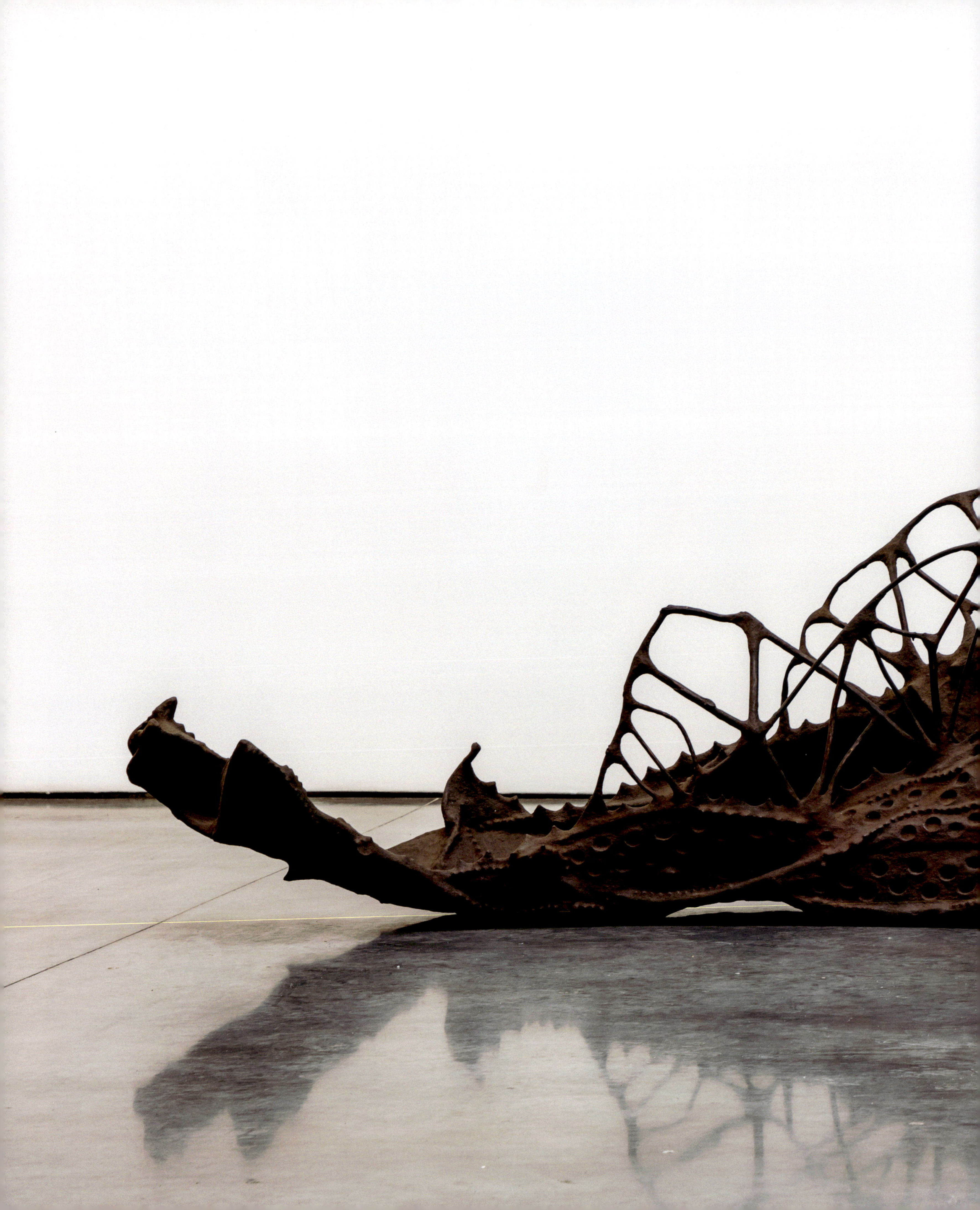

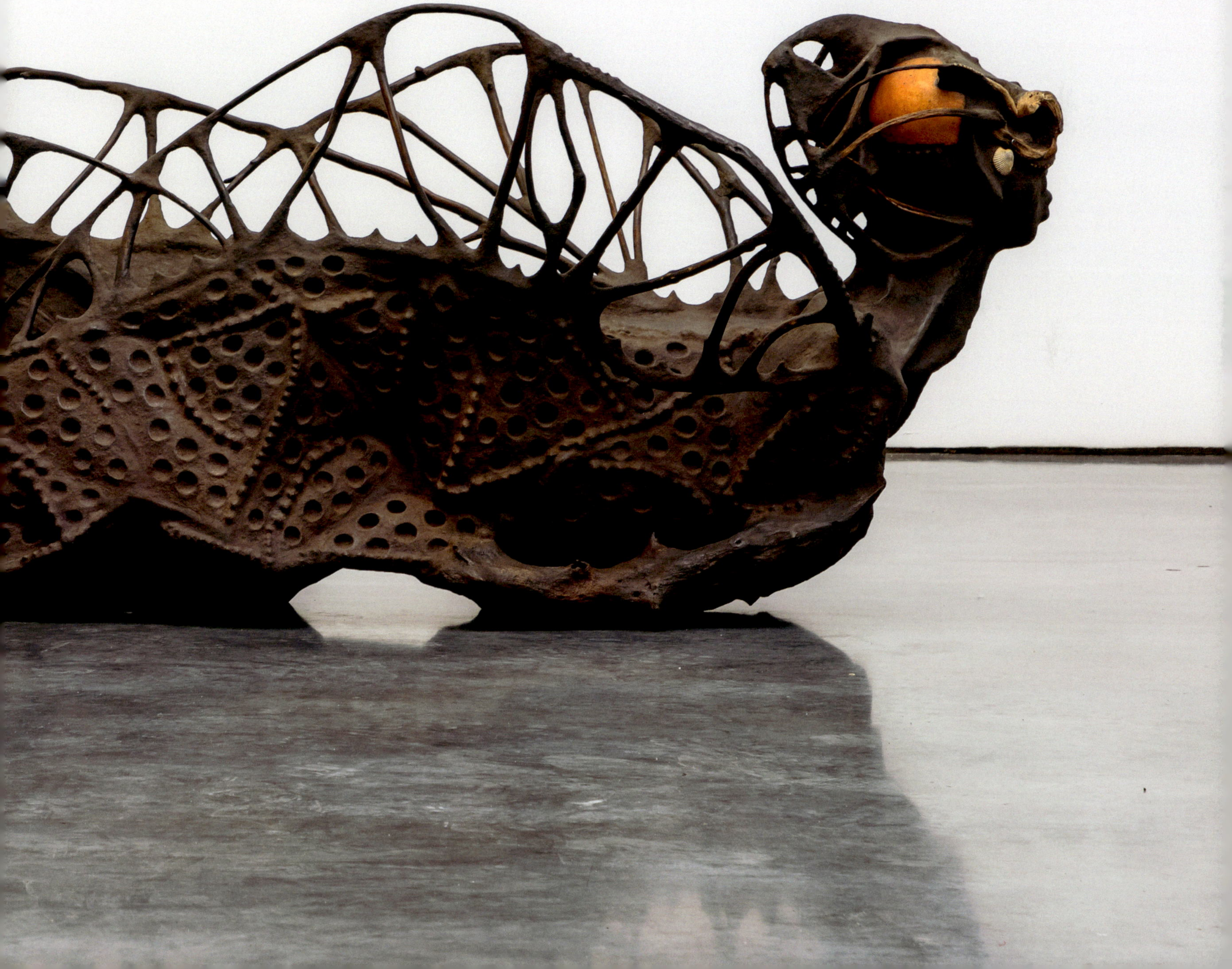

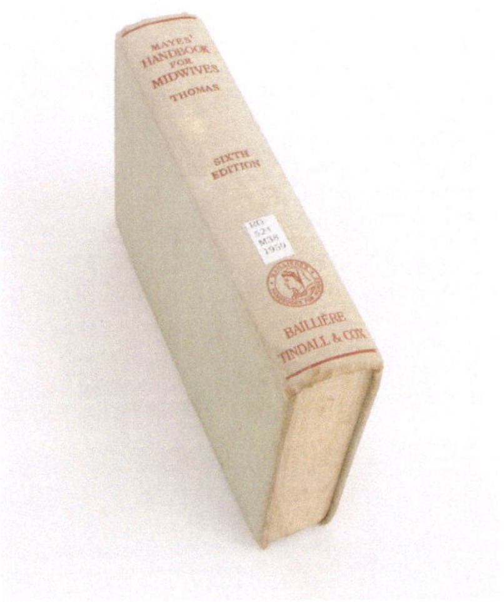

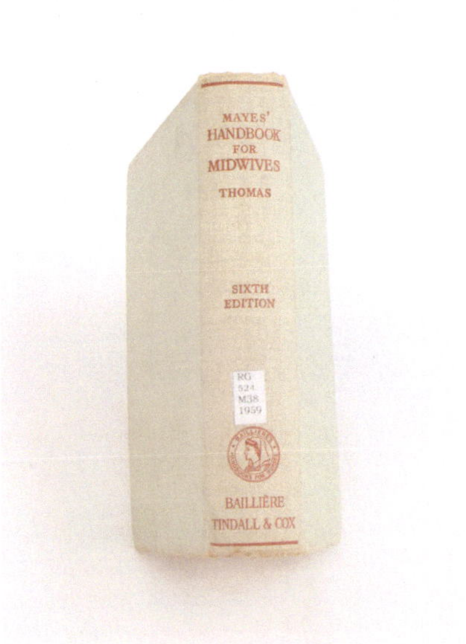

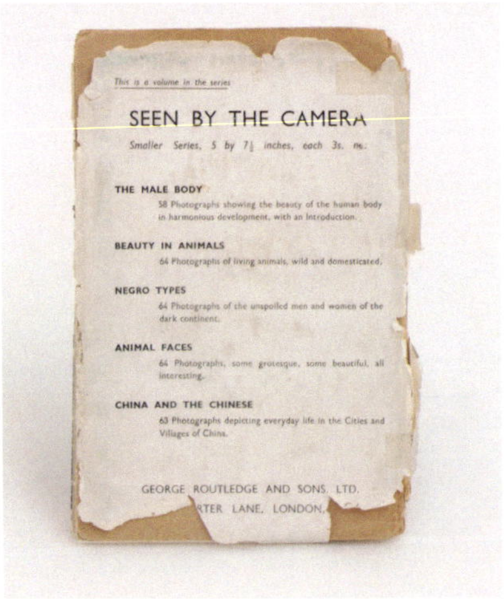

CHRONOLOGY: Wangechi Mutu, born 1972 in Nairobi, lives and works in Nairobi and New York.

SELECTED EXHIBITIONS AND PROJECTS
1991–2003

SELECTED ARTICLES AND INTERVIEWS
1991–2003

1991
Obtains I.B. at United World College of the Atlantic, School in Llantwit Major, Wales

---

1994
Receives the Richard Leakey Merit Award, Nairobi

1996
'One Voice',
7TH GALLERY, COOPER UNION, New York

Obtains a BFA at Cooper Union for the Advancement of the Arts and Science, New York

---

1997
'Life's Little Necessities',
THE CASTLE, Cape Town (group)

1998
'In Coming',
ART & ARCHITECTURE GALLERY, New Haven, Connecticut (group)

'Fusions',
IMARISHA GALLERY, New York (group)

1999
'Surely it Cannot Burn so Long',
RUSH ARTS GALLERY, New York (solo)

RUSH ARTS GALLERY, New York (group)

1999
Sirmans, Franklin, 'Surely it Cannot Burn so Long', Time Out New York, 25 November–2 December

---

2000
'The Magic City',
BRENT SIKKEMA, New York (group)

Obtains a MFA in Sculpture at Yale University School of Art, New Haven

2000
Johnson, Ken, 'The Magic City', The New York Times, August 4
Brockington, Horace, 'After Representation', The International Review of African American Art, no. 1

Ziolkowski, Thad, 'The Magic City', Artforum, October

2001
'Fusion',
MOCADA, New York (group)

'Challenge',
SKYLIGHT GALLERY, New York (group)

'Out of the Box',
QUEENS MUSEUM, New York (group)

2001
Sonkin, Rebecca, 'Good Rap', ARTnews, April

'African Art Exhibit', Daily News, 25 November

2002
'Scratch',
ARENA GALLERY, New York (group)

'Culture In A Jar',
LONGWOOD ARTS PROJECT, New York (group)

'Africaine',
THE STUDIO MUSEUM IN HARLEM, New York

2002
Cotter, Holland, 'From the Ferment of Liberation Comes a Revolution in African Art', The New York Times, 17 February

Hazlewood, Carl E., 'Hot Shows From the Edge: Summer in the City', NYArts, September

Murray, Soraya, 'Africaine', NKA Journal of Contemporary African Art, Fall–Winter

---

2003
'Creatures',
JAMAICA CENTER FOR THE ARTS AND LEARNING, New York (solo)

2003
McKanic, Arlene, 'Mutu's Disturbing "Creatures" at JCAL', Q.Guide, 13 March

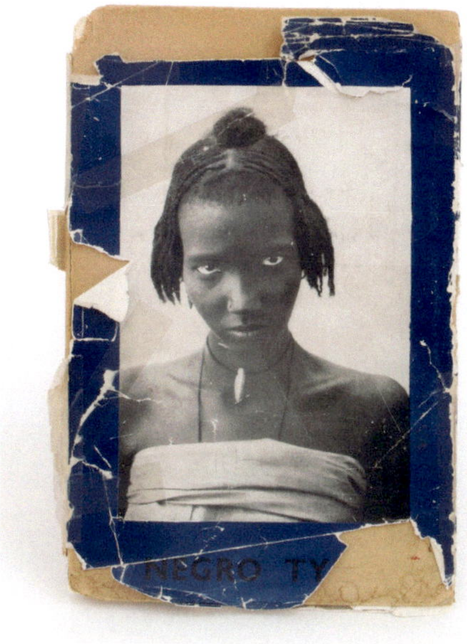

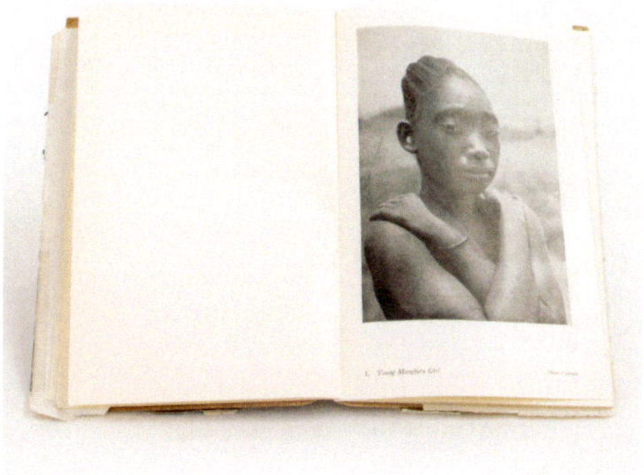

SELECTED EXHIBITIONS AND PROJECTS
2003–04

2003 (cont.)
'Pagan Poetry',
SUSANNE VIELMETTER, Los Angeles (solo)

'Wangechi Mutu/Carl Scholz',
MOMENTA ART, New York (solo)

'Only Skin Deep',
INTERNATIONAL CENTER OF PHOTOGRAPHY, New York (group)

'Looking Both Ways: Art of the Contemporary African Diaspora',
MUSEUM FOR AFRICAN ART, Long Island City, New York (group)

'New Art Wave',
BROOKLYN ACADEMY OF MUSIC, New York (group)

MUSEUM CALOUSTE GULBENKIAN, Lisbon (group)

MUSEUM OF THE AFRICAN DIASPORA, San Francisco (group)

'Off the Record ,
SKYLIGHT GALLERY, New York (group)

'The Broken Mirror',
LEROY NEIMAN GALLERY at COLUMBIA UNIVERSITY, New York (group)

'Studio Museum Exhibition',
PARRISH ART MUSEUM, Southhampton, New York (group)

'Open House: Working in Brooklyn',
BROOKLYN MUSEUM OF ART, New York (group)

'Creatures',
JAMAICA CENTER FOR THE ARTS AND LEARNING, New York (group)

'7 Walls, 8 Views',
ARENA GALLERY, New York (group)

'Next Next Visual Art',
BROOKLYN ACADEMY OF MUSIC, New York (group)

'Black President: The Art and Legacy of Fela Anikulapo-Kuti',
THE NEW MUSEUM OF CONTEMPORARY ART, New York, toured to THE CONTEMPORARY ARTS CENTER, Cincinnati; THE YERBA BUENA CENTER FOR THE ARTS, San Francisco; BARBICAN CENTRE, London (group)

2004
'Hangin' in Texas',
ART PACE, San Antonio, Texas (solo)

'Fight or Flight: Kristin Baker, Amy Gartrell, Rico Gatson, Wangechi Mutu, Marc Swanson and Ivan Witenstein',
WHITNEY MUSEUM OF AMERICAN ART at ALTRIA, New York (group)

'Pin-Up: Contemporary Collage and Drawing',
TATE MODERN, London (group)

5th GWANGJU BIENNALE, South Korea (group)

'I Feel Mysterious Today: 25 International Emerging and Established Contemporary Artists',
PALM BEACH INSTITUTE OF CONTEMPORARY ART, Lake Worth (group)

'Looking Both Ways: Art of the Contemporary African Diaspora',
CANBROOK ART MUSEUM, Bloomfield Hills, Michigan (group)

SELECTED ARTICLES AND INTERVIEWS
2003–04

2003 (cont.)
Ashford, Doug, 'Off The Record', Time Out New York, 8–15 May

Cotter, Holland, 'Wangechi Mutu', The New York Times, 14 March

Koirala, Snigdha, 'Black President', BOMB, Fall

Sirmans, Franklin, 'Portfolio', Grand Street, Fall

Martin, Courtney J., 'Black President: The Art and Legacy of Fela Anikulapo-Kuti', Flash Art, no. 132, October

Fleey, Peter, 'Black President', Frieze, no. 78, October

Pagel, David, 'Harrowing, Hallucinatory Visions: Wangechi Mutu at Susanne Vielmetter Los Angeles Projects', Los Angeles Times, 24 October

Cotter, Holland, 'Redefining the African Diaspora', The New York Times, 21 November

Williamson, Sue, 'Looking Both Ways', Artthrob, December

2004
Martin, Courtney J., 'Looking Both Ways', Flash Art, no. 232, January–February

Smith, Roberta, 'Emerging Talent and Plenty of It', The New York Times, 12 March

Saltz, Jerry, 'Borough Hall', Village Voice, 3 May

Kerr, Merrily, 'Extreme Makeovers', Art on Paper, July–August

Ribas, João, 'She's Come Undone', Time Out New York, 8–15 July

Johnson, Kenneth, 'She's Come Undone', The New York Times, 9 July

Kelly, Kevin, 'Reward for Creative Touch', Daily Nation, 11 August
Cotter, Holland, 'Black comes in Many Shadings', The New York Times, 13 August

Leitzes, Cary Estes, 'Body Politic'; Daniel Kunitz, 'US Editor's Letter', Art Review, September

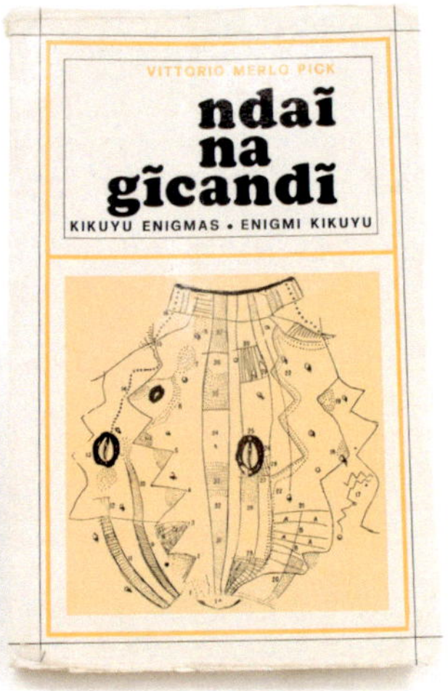

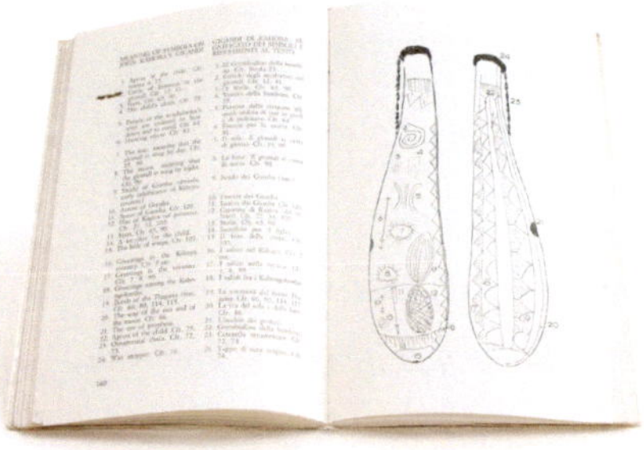

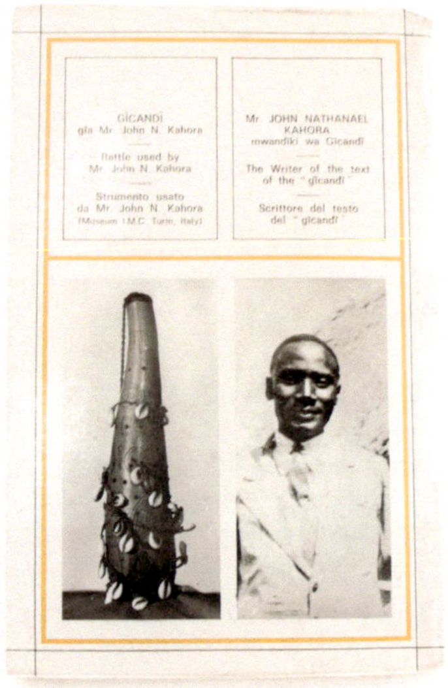

SELECTED EXHIBITIONS AND PROJECTS
2004–06

2004 (cont.)
'Figuratively',
THE STUDIO MUSEUM IN HARLEM, New York (group)

'Gio Ponti: Furnished Settings and Figuration',
ACME, Los Angeles (group)

'Open House: Working in Brooklyn',
BROOKLYN MUSEUM OF ART, New York (group)

'Africa Remix',
KUNSTPALAST DÜSSELDORF, toured to CENTRE POMPIDOU, Paris; HAYWARD GALLERY, London; MORI ART MUSEUM, Tokyo; JOHANNESBURG ART GALLERY (group)

'Art on Paper',
WEATHERSPOON MUSEUM, Greensboro (group)

The Raw and the Cooked',
CLAREMONT UNIVERSITY, California (group)

'Only Skin Deep Changing Visions of the American Self',
SEATTLE ART MUSEUM, toured to INTERNATIONAL CENTER OF PHOTOGRAPHY, New York City (group)

2005
'Problematica',
SUSANNE VIELMETTER, Los Angeles (solo)

'Wangechi Mutu: Amazing Grace',
MIAMI ART MUSEUM (solo)

'The Chief Lair's A Holy Mess',
SAN FRANCISCO MUSEUM OF MODERN ART (solo)

'Linkages & Themes in the African Diaspora: Selections from the Eileen Harris Norton and Peter Norton Art Collections',
MUSEUM OF THE AFRICAN DIASPORA, San Francisco (group)

'After Cézanne',
MUSEUM OF CONTEMPORARY ART, Los Angeles (group)

'Matisse and Beyond: The Painting and Sculpture Collections',
SAN FRANCISCO MUSEUM OF MODERN ART (group)

'Drawing from The Modern 1975-2005',
MUSEUM OF MODERN ART, New York (group)

'African Queen',
THE STUDIO MUSEUM IN HARLEM, New York (group)

'Figures of Thinking: Convergences in Contemporary Cultures',
RICHARD A. PEELER ART CENTER, DEPAUW UNIVERSITY, Indiana (group)

'Greater New York 2005',
P.S.1 CONTEMPORARY ART CENTER, Long Island City, New York (group)

'Follow Me: A Fantasy,
ARENA 1, Santa Monica (group)

'Rewind/Re-Cast/Review',
BERRIE ARTS CENTER at RAMAPO COLLEGE GALLERIES, New Jersey (group)

2006
'Sleeping Heads Lie',
POWER HOUSE, Memphis (solo)

SELECTED ARTICLES AND INTERVIEWS
2004–06

2004 (cont.)
Ciuraru, Carmela, 'Cutting Remarks', ARTnews, November

'A-Z London', The Art Newspaper, no. 153, December

Cripps, Charlotte, 'Work at the Cutting Edge', The Independent Review, 2 December

Graham-Dixon, Andrew, 'All Stuck and Scribbled', The Sunday Telegraph, 19 December

Muhammad, Dalya Erica, 'Wangechi Mutu', The Studio Museum in Harlem, July

2005
Biro, Matthew, 'Midwest', Art Papers, January–February

Harrison, Sara, 'Pin-Up: Contemporary Collage and Drawing', Art Monthly, February

De La Forterie, Maud, 'Africa Remix Continental', Art Actuel, no. 38, May–June

Lo, Melissa, 'Wangechi Mutu', Flash Art, no. 242, May–June

Brielmaier, Isolde, 'Wangechi Mutu: Re-Imagining The World', Parkett, no. 74

Kapferer, Roland, 'Africa Remix', Frieze, no. 92, June–August

Heartney, Eleanor, 'Return to the Real?', Art in America, June–July

Suarez de Jesus, Carlos, 'Mutu's Mojo', The Miami New Times, 21 July

Oliveira, Filipa, 'Wangechi Mutu', W-Art, no. 8

Fricke, Kirsten, 'Wangechi Mutu', Beautiful/Decay, August

Luis, Carlos M., 'Wangechi Mutu y su "Amazing Grace"', Artes & Letras, 7 August

Turner, Elisa, 'Going Solo: Wangechi Mutu Finds Inspiration In Her Native Africa', The Miami Herald, 11 September

Trellis, Emma, 'Mutable Mutu', South Florida Sun-Sentinel, October

Adjaye, David, 'Top Ten', Artforum, November

Smith, Roberta, 'Where Issues of Black Identity Meet the Concerns of Every Artist', The New York Times, 18 November

2006
Helfand, Glen, 'Voluptuous Horror: Wangechi Mutu Harnesses the Power of Violence and Beauty', San Francisco Bay Guardian, 4–10 January

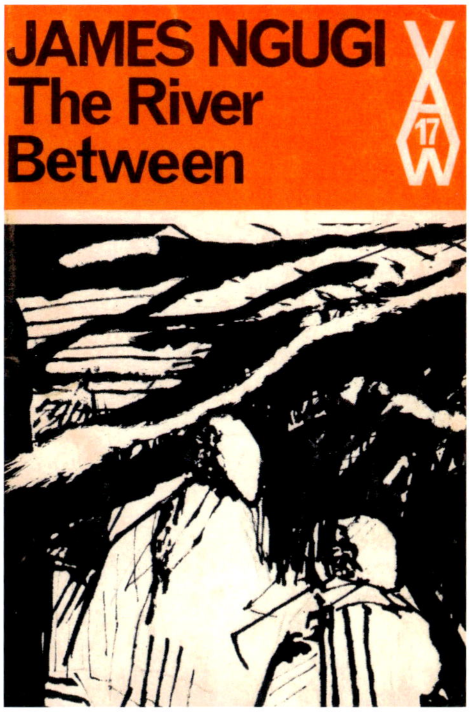

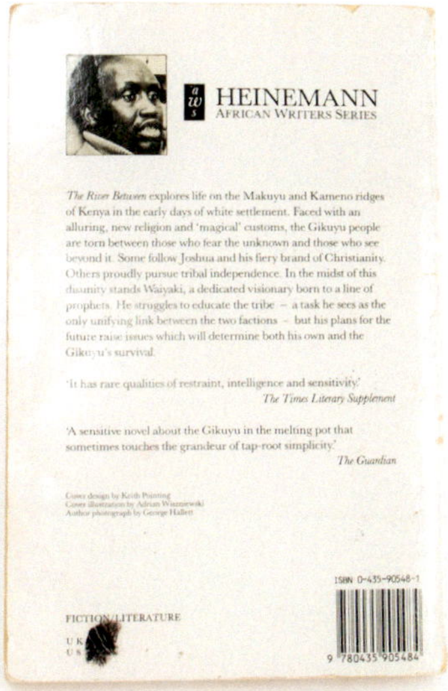

SELECTED EXHIBITIONS AND PROJECTS
2006–07

2006 (cont.)
'Exhuming Gluttony: A Lover's Requiem',
SALON 94, New York (solo)

'An Alien Eye and Other Killah Anthems',
SIKKEMA JENKINS & CO., New York (solo)

'(Re)Volver',
PLATAFORMA REVOLVER, Lisbon (group)

'USA Today',
ROYAL ACADEMY OF ARTS, London (group)

2nd BIENNIAL CONTEMPORARY ART, Sevilla (group)

'Land Mine',
THE ALDRICH MUSEUM, Ridgefield, Connecticut (group)

6th SITE SANTA FE, New Mexico (group)

'If a cat gives birth to kittens in an oven, are they kittens or biscuits?',
ROEBLING HALL, New York (group)

'The Triumph of Painting',
THE SAATCHI GALLERY, London (group)

'Having New Eyes',
ASPEN ART MUSEUM (group)

'Infinite Painting: Contemporary Painting and Global Realism',
VILLA MANIN CENTRE FOR CONTEMPORARY ART, Passariano, Italy (group)

'New African Art',
SEATTLE ART MUSEUM (group)

'The F-Word: Female Vocals',
THE ANDY WARHOL MUSEUM, Pittsburgh (group)

'Figures of Thinking: Convergences in Contemporary Cultures',
MCDONOUGH MUSEUM OF ART, YOUNGSTOWN STATE UNIVERSITY, Ohio (group)

Receives the Chrysalis Award, The Museum of Contemporary African Diaspora Arts, New York

2007
'The Cinderella Curse',
ATLANTA COLLEGE OF ART GALLERY AT WOODRUFF ART CENTRE, SAVANNAH COLLEGE OF ART AND DESIGN (solo)

'Cleaning Earth',
FRANKLIN ARTWORKS, Minneapolis (solo)

'Yo.n.I',
VICTORIA MIRO, London (solo)

'Every Revolution is a Roll of the Dice',
BALLROOM, Marfa, Texas (group)

'Fractured Figure',
DESTE FOUNDATION, Athens (group)

'Star Power: Museum as Body Electric',
MUSEUM OF CONTEMPORARY ART, Denver (group)

'Global Feminisms: New Directions in Contemporary Art',
BROOKLYN MUSEUM, New York (group)

'Interstellar Low Ways: Sun Ra',
HYDE PARK ART CENTER, Chicago (group)

SELECTED ARTICLES AND INTERVIEWS
2006–07

2006 (cont.)
Goodyear, Sarah, 'Wangechi Mutu: An Artist Comes into Her Own', Bklyn, Spring

Murinik, Tracy, 'Afro-Alien Exquisite Corpses'; Sandra Klopper, 'Distant Relatives/Relative Distance', Art South Africa, Spring

Pollack, Barbara, 'Wangechi Mutu: An Alien Eye and Other Killah Anthems'; Paul Miller, 'A Gathering of the Tribes #11', Time Out New York, 25–31 May

Kazanjian, Dodie, 'Fierce Creatures', Vogue, June

Smith, Roberta, 'Wangechi Mutu: An Alien Eye and Other Killah Anthems', The New York Times, 9 June

Morris, Tom, 'Still Points of the Turning World'; Angela Roberts, 'Infinite Painting: Contemporary Painting and Global Realism', Art Review, July

Vogel, Carol, 'Where Bel Canto Meets Paintbrush', The New York Times, August 15

Black, Ezrha Jean, 'Labyrinths of SITE: Ottmann scales down numbers and theme, but stays big on art', Artillery, September

Murray, DC, 'Wangechi Mutu at SFMOMA', Art in America, October

Auricchio, Laura, 'Wangechi Mutu', Art Papers, September–October

Martin, Courtney J., 'Site San Fe 6th International Biennial: 'Still Points of the Turning World', Contemporary, no. 86

Carver, Jon, 'Still Points of the Turning World', Art Papers, November–December

Blumenstein, Ellen, 'L.A. Confidential', Monopol, November–December

Korotkin, Lindsay, 'Reviews', Tema Celeste, November–December

2007
Spaulding, David, 'New York, Interrupted', Artforum, January

Oguibe, Olu, 'Looking Back: The Most Significant Shows of 2006', Frieze, no. 104, January

Cotter, Holland, 'Feminist Art Finally Takes Center Stage', The New York Times, 29 January

Abbie, Mary, 'Feminism Revisited: Art by two African-born women revitalizes feminist issues in a handsome Franklin Art Show', Star Tribune, March

Koenig, Wendy, 'Wangechi Mutu: Memphis', Art Papers, March–April

Nolan, Joe, 'Wangechi Mutu: Sleeping Heads Lie', Number Independent Arts Journal, no. 58, Spring

Kruger, Barbara, 'Wangechi Mutu', Interview Magazine, April

Cecilia Aldarondo, 'Ghada Amer + Wangechi Mutu', Art Papers, May–June

Heartney, Eleanor, 'Worldwide Women', Art in America, June–July

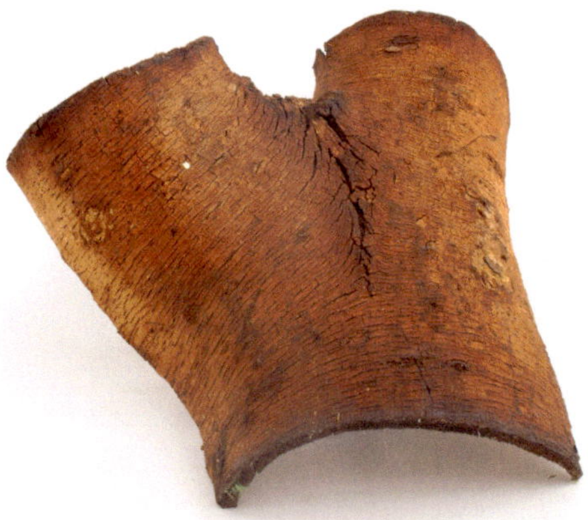

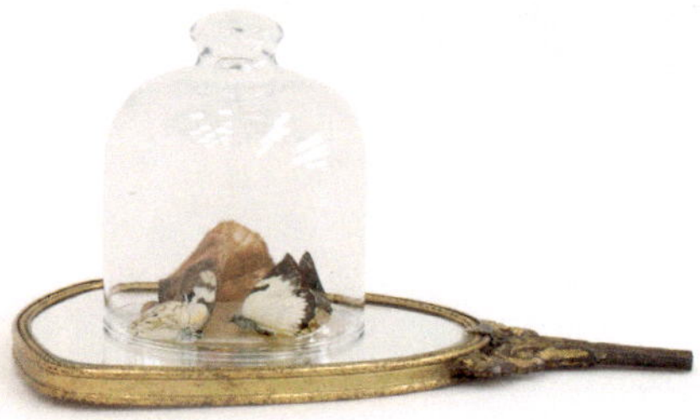

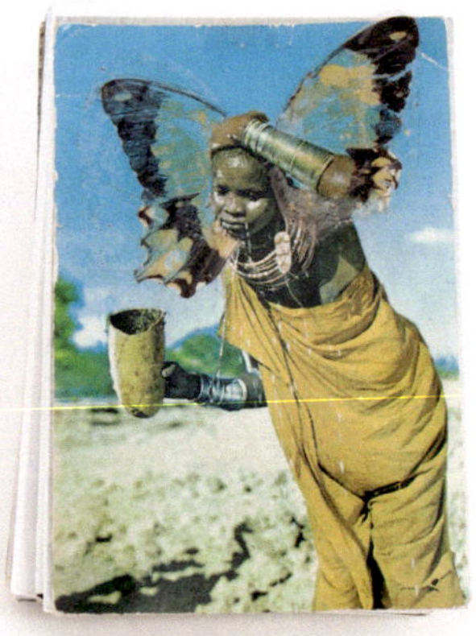

SELECTED EXHIBITIONS AND PROJECTS
2007–08

2007 (cont.)
'Heroines',
SCHWARTZ GALLERY, METROPOLITAN OPERA, New York (group)

'Out of Time: A Contemporary View',
MUSEUM OF MODERN ART, New York (group)

Receives the Joan Mitchell Foundation Painters & Sculptors Award, New York

2008
'Little Touched',
SUSANNE VIELMETTER, Los Angeles (solo)

'Wangechi Mutu: In Whose Image?',
KUNSTHALLE WIEN PROJECT SPACE, Vienna (solo)

'30 Americans',
THE RUBELL FAMILY COLLECTION, Miami, toured to NORTH CAROLINA MUSEUM OF ART, Raleigh; CHRYSLER MUSEUM OF ART, Norfolk, Virginia; CINCINNATI ART MUSEUM; TACOMA ART MUSEUM, Washington; McNAY ART MUSEUM, San Antonio, Texas; TUSCON MUSEUM OF ART; JOSLYN ART MUSEUM, Omaha, Nebraska; NELSON-ATKINS MUSEUM OF ART, Kansas City; BARNES FOUNDATION, Philadelphia; HONOLULU MUSEUM OF ART; ALBUQUERQUE MUSEUM, New Mexico; COLUMBIA MUSEUM OF ART, South Carolina; CORCORAN GALLERY OF ART, Washington, DC (group)

'Objects of Value',
MIAMI ART MUSEUM (group)

'Videostudio',
THE STUDIO MUSEUM IN HARLEM, New York (group)

PROSPECT.1, New Orleans (group)

'Body Memory',
PRINCETON UNIVERSITY ART MUSEUM (group)

'Excerpt: Selections from the Jeanne Greenberg Rohatyn Collection',
THE FRANCES LEHMAN LOEB ART CENTER, VASSAR COLLEGE, Poughkeepsie, New York (group)

1st U-TURN QUADRENNIAL, Copenhagen (group)

'Damaged Romanticism: A Mirror of Modern Emotion',
BLAFFER GALLERY, THE ART MUSEUM OF THE UNIVERSITY OF HOUSTON, toured to PARRISH ART MUSEUM AND THE GREY ART GALLERY, New York University (group)

'In the Land of Retinal Delights: The Juxtapoz School',
LAGUNA ART MUSEUM, California (group)

'Pandora's Box',
DUNLOP ART GALLERY, Regina, Saskatchewan, toured to PLUG IN INSTITUTE OF CONTEMPORARY ARTS, Winnipeg, Manitoba; KITCHENER-WATERLOO ART GALLERY, Ontario (group)

'Black Woman Hood: Images, Icons and Ideologies of the African Body',
HOOD MUSEUM OF ART, DARTMOUTH COLLEGE, Hanover, New Hampshire (group)

'Collage: The Unmonumental Picture',
NEW MUSEUM OF CONTEMPORARY ART, New York (group)

Receives the Emerging Talent Award, Cooper Union, New York

SELECTED ARTICLES AND INTERVIEWS
2007–08

2007 (cont.)
Volzke, Daniel, 'Ab dem 22. November: Wangechi Mutu zeigt opulente Collage in London', Monopol, December

Eshun, Ekow, 'The Art of Darkness', Vogue, November
Steinberg, Claudia, 'Aufbruchstimmung an der Lower East Side', Kunstzitung, December

2008
Martin, Courtney J., 'Wangechi Mutu: Yo.n.l', Artkrush, no. 75, January

Enright, Robert, 'Resonant Surgeries: The Collaged World of Wangechi Mutu', Border Crossings, no. 105, February

Shaw, Alex, 'More Flavor: Lecture, Wangechi Mutu', Flavorpill, 13 March

Watson, Simon, 'Wangechi Mutu: Mass in the Time of War', Whitewall, Spring

Catherine Wagley, 'Destroying Prettiness: Wangechi Mutu and Kara Walker', Daily Serving, 31 March

Heartney, Eleanor, 'Make It New', Art in America, April
Pagel, Daniel, 'Boldly Linking all the Pieces: Wangechi Mutu at Vielmetter', Los Angeles Times, 11 April

Pagel, David, 'Wangechi Mutu: Boldly Connecting the Dots', Los Angeles Times, 20 April

Fong, Phyllis, 'Wangechi Mutu: A Shady Promise', Modern Painters, May

Lieberman, Paul, 'Artist Transforms Trailer into a Mobile Art Studio', Los Angeles Times, 13 June

Casadio, Maruccia, 'Colorful', Vogue Italia, July

Berwick, Carly, 'Encouraging Wards', ARTnews, October

Browne, Alix, 'Cuff Love', The New York Times, 3 October

Bookhardt, Eric D., 'The Big Easel', Gambit Weekly, 28 October

Dewan, Shaila, 'New Orleans Rising, by Hammer and Art', The New York Times, 29 October

Ellwood, Mark, 'Our Man In: New Orleans', GQ Magazine, November

Robinson, Walter, 'Bleeding-Heart Biennale', Art Net Magazine, November

Kimani, Martin, 'The Historical Future of a Contemporary Artist', Juxtapoz Art and Culture Magazine, November

Drohojowska-Philp, Hunter, 'Los Angeles: Wangechi Mutu', ARTnews, November

Britt, Douglas, 'Blaffer Exhibit Finds Beauty in the Bleak', The Houston Chronicle, 5 November

Mueller, Kurt, 'Houston: Damaged Romanticism at the Blaffer Gallery', Art Lies, no. 60, Winter

Wilson, Risë, 'All Hail the Queen', Black Renaissance Noire, no. 1, Winter–Spring

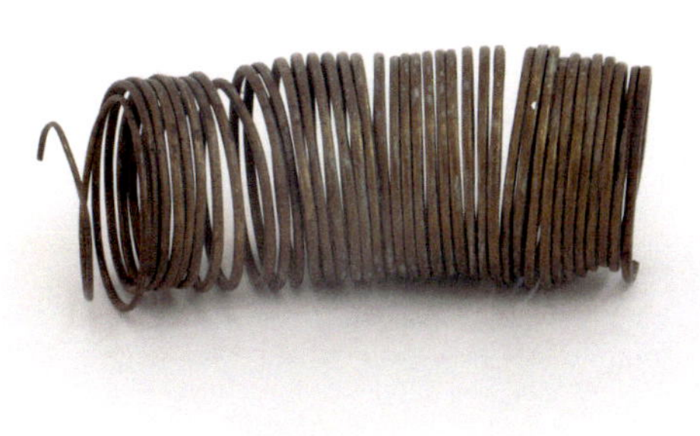

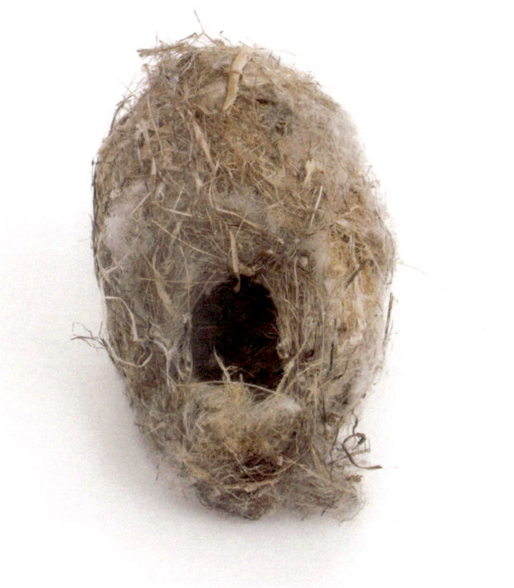

SELECTED EXHIBITIONS AND PROJECTS
2009–11

2009
'Rebelle: Art and Feminism 1969-2009',
MUSEUM OF CONTEMPORARY ART, San Diego, toured to MUSEUM VOOR MODERNE KUNST ARNHEM, the Netherlands (group)

'Sortilège',
FOUNDATION FOR CONTEMPORARY ART CLAUDINE AND JEANMARC SOLOMON, Château d'Arenthon, France (group)

'Off the Beaten Path: Violence, Women and Art',
STENERSEN MUSEUM, Oslo, toured to UNIVERSITY ART GALLERY, San Diego; CENTRO CULTURAL TIJUANA; MUSEO UNIVERSITARIO DEL CHOPO, Mexico; CHICAGO CULTURAL CENTER; DAVID J. SENCER CENTERS FOR DISEASE CONTROL MUSEUM, Atlanta; NEW ORLEANS CENTER FOR CREATIVE ARTS; NEWCOMB GALLERY, TULANE UNIVERSITY, Louisiana; REDLINE, Denver; THE ART GALLERY OF CALGARY; FUNDACIÓN CANAL DE ISABEL II, Madrid; JOHANNESBURG ART GALLERY; THE WINNIPEG ART GALLERY, Manitoba (group)

3rd ICP TRIENNIAL OF PHOTOGRAPHY AND VIDEO, New York (group)

10th BIENNALE D'ART CONTEMPORAIN DE LYON (group)

'Paint Made Flesh',
FRIST CENTER OF VISUAL ARTS, Nashville, toured to THE PHILLIPS COLLECTION, Washington DC; MEMORIAL ART GALLERY, UNIVERSITY OF ROCHESTER, New York (group)

'Black Womanhood: Images, Icons and Ideologies of the African Body',
SAN DIEGO MUSEUM OF ART (group)

2010
'This You Call Civilization?',
ART GALLERY OF ONTARIO (solo)

'My Dirty Little Heaven',
DEUTSCHE GUGGENHEIM, Berlin, toured to WIELS, Brussels (solo)

'Hunt Bury Flee',
GLADSTONE GALLERY, New York (solo)

'Disquieted: Contemporary Voices from Out of the Shadows',
PORTLAND ART MUSEUM, Oregon (group)

'Until Now: Collecting the New 1960–2010',
MINNEAPOLIS INSTITUTE OF ARTS (group)

'Afro Modern: Journeys Through the Black Atlantic',
TATE LIVERPOOL, toured to CENTRO GALEGO DE ARTE CONTEMPORÁNEA, Santiago de Compostela, Spain (group)

'Collection: MOCA's First Thirty Years (1980–Now)',
THE GEFFEN CONTEMPORARY at the MUSEUM OF CONTEMPORARY ART, Los Angeles (group)

'Visceral Bodies',
VANCOUVER ART GALLERY (group)

Receives the Artist of the Year Award, Deutsche Bank, Berlin

2011
'Wangechi Mutu',
GALLERIA IL CAPRICORNO, Venice (solo)

'The Bearden Project',
THE STUDIO MUSEUM IN HARLEM, New York (group)

SELECTED ARTICLES AND INTERVIEWS
2009–11

2009
Ligon, Glenn, 'Civic Engagement: To Miss New Orleans', Artforum, January

Stern, Steven, 'Looking Back: Prospect.1 New Orleans', Frieze, no. 120, January

Perrée, Rob, 'Femme Vileine', Africa Magazine Zam, 13 January
Halpern, Ashlea, 'Out of Africa', Time Out New York, 15–21 January

Mirov, Ben, 'Art: Pretty Ugly: Wangechi Mutu, A Shady Promise', The Brooklyn Rail, February

Wei, Lilly, 'New Orleans Report: Deliverance: The Biennial', Art in America, February

Bernoni, Giorgia, 'Un Corpo Mutante e Ambiguo', Insideart, March

Wolff, Zoe, 'Motherlode', Tar Mag, Spring

Sweeney, Eve, 'A Fertile Mind', Vogue, April

Cotter Holland, 'Art: The Week Ahead', The New York Times, 26 April

Smith, Roberta, 'Dress Codes: Beyond a Simple Fashion Statement', The New York Times, October

2010
Milroy, Sarah, 'Amid the Games, Artists Dissect the Body', The Globe and Mail, 19 February

Crow, Kelly, 'Wangechi Mutu is Deutsche Bank's Artist of the Year 2010', Wall Street Journal, 22 February

Evans, Matthew, 'Wangechi Mutu: Between Beauty and Horror', ArtMag, no. 57

Cash, Stephanie, 'Wangechi Mutu: Terrible Beauty', Art in America, May

Clarke, Bill, 'Wangechi Mutu at the Art Gallery of Ontario', Modern Painters, Summer

Smith, Roberta, 'Art? Life? Must We Choose?', The New York Times, 2 July

Yablonsky, Linda, 'Artifacts: Moths and Mercenaries', T: The New York Times Style Magazine, 4 November

Rosenberg, Karen, 'Art in Review: Wangechi Mutu', The New York Times, 12 November

Wehr, Anne, 'Wangechi Mutu: Hunt Bury Flee', Time Out New York, 18–24 November

2011
Sandals, Leah, 'Questions and Artists: Wangechi Mutu's Beauty Riff Collages', National Post, 25 February

Karcher, Eva, 'Wangechi Mutu', Vogue Deutsch, April

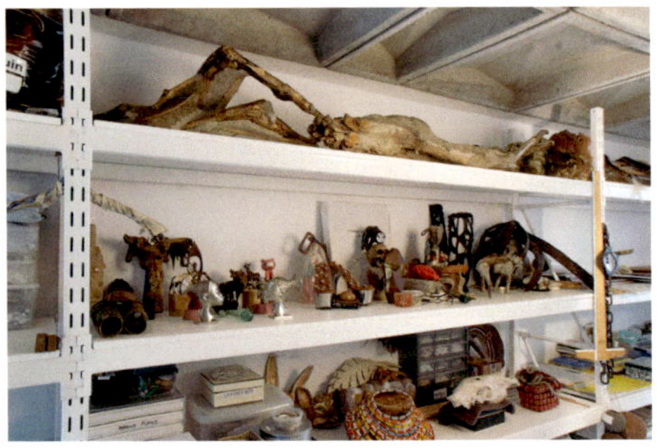

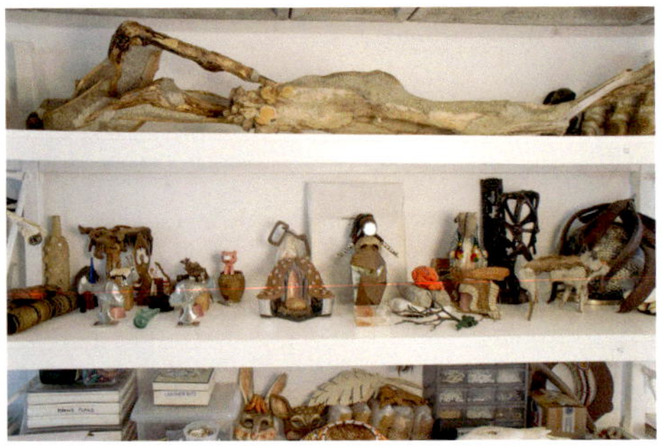

SELECTED EXHIBITIONS AND PROJECTS
2011–12

2011 (cont.)
'Taguchi Art Collection: Global New Art',
SOMPO JAPAN MUSEUM OF ART, Tokyo (group)

'The Power of Doubt',
MUSEO COLECCIONES ICO, Madrid (group)

'The African Continuum',
UNITED NATIONS, New York (group)

4th INCHEON WOMEN'S BIENNALE, South Korea (group)

'15 x 15 Rush Arts 15th Anniversary Edition',
RUSH ARTS GALLERY, New York (group)

'Alles Kannibalen?',
ME-COLLECTOR'S ROOM/STIFTUNG OLBRICHT, Berlin (group)

'Contemporary Magic: A Tarot Deck Project',
THE ANDY WARHOL MUSEUM, Pittsburgh (group)

'The Hybrid Fuels',
KUNST + PROJEKTE, Sindelfingen, Germany (group)

'The Luminous Interval',
GUGGENHEIM BILBAO (group)

'On the Occasion of the Publication of Basics: A Celebration of Revolution and a New World',
HARLEM STAGE, New York (group)

'Paper Cuts',
FULLERTON COLLEGE ART GALLERY, California (group)

'The Power of Doubt',
TIMES MUSEUM, Guangzhou, China (group)

'Twisted Selves',
CALIFORNIA MUSEUM OF PHOTOGRAPHY, Riverside (group)

'Seeing is a Kind of Thinking: A Jim Nutt Companion',
MUSEUM OF CONTEMPORARY ART, Chicago (group)

'Stargazers: Elizabeth Catlett in Conversation with 21 Contemporart Artists',
BRONX MUSEUM, New York (group)

'Tous cannibals',
LA MAISON ROUGE, Paris (group)

Receives the Augustus St. Gaudens Distinguished Artist Award,
Cooper Union, New York

2012
'Blackthrones',
GLADSTONE GALLERY, Brussels (solo)

'Wangechi Mutu',
MUSÉE D'ART CONTEMPORAIN DE MONTRÉAL (solo)

'This Undreamt Descent',
STAATLICHE KUNSTHALLE BADEN-BADEN, Germany (solo)

'Nitarudi Ninarudi I plan to return I am returning',
SUSANNE VIELMETTER, Los Angeles (solo)

'The Soul of a City: Memphis Collects African American Art',
BROOKS ART MUSEUM, Memphis (group)

'All That Glitters',
PALAZZO CONTARINI MICHIEL, Venice (group)

SELECTED ARTICLES AND INTERVIEWS
2011–12

2011 (cont.)
Rylance, David, 'Bold New Bodies for a Brave New World: David Altmejd's The Index and Wangechi Mutu's This you call civilization?', Transductions, 4 April

Reed, Aimee, 'Interview with Wangechi Mutu', Daily Serving, 12 April

Spence, Rachel, 'The Power of Instinct', Financial Times, 15 April

Cotter, Holland, 'Under Threat: The Shock of the Old', The New York Times, 17 April

Lapp, Axel, 'Wangechi Mutu', Art Review, May

Woeller, Marcus, 'Sex und Gewalt (Vorsicht, Falle!)', TAZ, 12 May

Mumo, Angela, 'Wangechi Mutu: Portrait of an Artist', Weekend Star, 21–22 May

Hove, Jan Van, 'Droombeelden Uit Afrika', De Standard, July

Rohr-Bongard, 'Schreckensschoene Schnippelei', Manager Magazin, August

Kunitz, Daniel, 'Wangechi Mutu', Modern Painters, September
Saro-Wiwa, Zina, 'Interview with Wangechi Mutu', Kilimanjaro Magazine, no.11, Autumn–Winter

Herndon, Lara Kristin, ''Wangechi Mutu', ArtPapers, March–April
Enwezor, Okwui, 'Cut & Paste: Interview with Wangechi Mutu', Arise Magazine, No. 11

Tate, Greg and LaTasha Diggs, 'Wangechi Mutu', Coon Bidness: The Critical Ass Issue, no.82

Wehr, Anne, 'Wangechi Mutu: Hunt Bury Flee', Time Out New York, 18-24 November

Stern, Melissa, 'Hunt, Bury, Flee: Drawings By Wangechi Mutu', CityArts, 20 November

2012
Goldberg, RoseLee, 'Shirin Neshat and Wangechi Mutu', Flash Art, no. 282, January–February

Arbus, Miriam, 'Artists Rethink Black History Month in 28 Days', The Art Newspaper, January

Schechter, Fran, 'For 28 Days Only: Top Artists Fuel Black History Show', Now Toronto, 1 February

Pohl, John, 'The Beauty of Body Language', Montreal Gazette, 3 February

Bynoe, Holly, 'Museum of Fine Arts Houston and Glassell School of Art presents "There is no archive in which nothing gets lost"', ARC Magazine, September

Pagel, David, 'Past, present collide in Wangechi Mutu's "Nitarudi Ninarudi"', The Los Angeles Times, 29 November

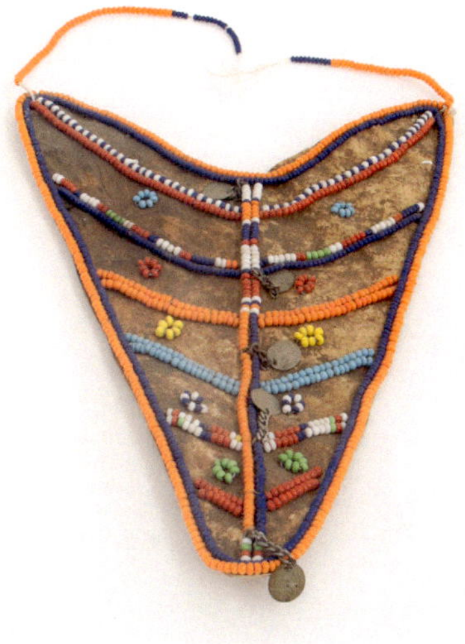

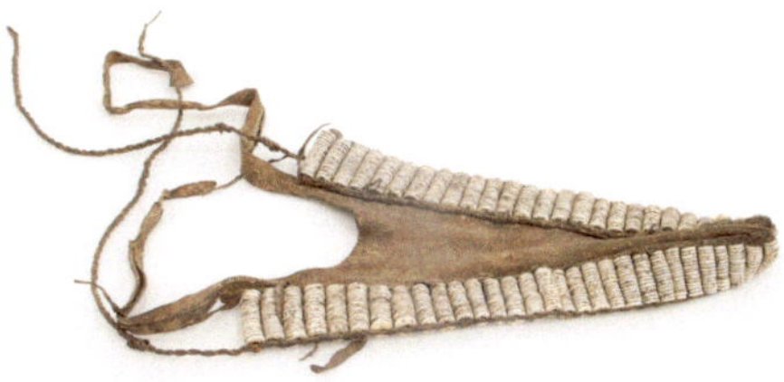

SELECTED EXHIBITIONS AND PROJECTS
2012–13

2012 (cont.)
1st PARIS TRIENNALE (group)

'Earth Matters Exhibit',
SMITHSONIAN INSTITUTION, New York (group)

'The Virgins Show',
FAMILY BUSINESS, New York (group)

'28 Days: Reimagining Black History Month',
JUSTINA M. BARNICKE GALLERY at UNIVERSITY OF TORONTO (group)

2013
'Wangechi Mutu',
LEONARD PEARLSTEIN GALLERY at DREXEL UNIVERSITY, Philadelphia (solo)

'Wangechi Mutu',
MUSEUM OF CONTEMPORARY ART, Sydney, toured to ORANGE COUNTY MUSEUM, Santa Ana, California (solo)

'Wangechi Mutu: A Fantastic Journey',
NASHER MUSEUM OF ART at DUKE UNIVERSITY, Durham, North Carolina, toured to BROOKLYN MUSEUM OF ART, New York; MUSEUM OF CONTEMPORARY ART, North Miami; MARY AND LEIGH BLOCK MUSEUM, Northwestern University, Evanston, Illinois (solo)

'The Shadows Took Shape',
THE STUDIO MUSEUM IN HARLEM, New York (group)

5th MOSCOW BIENNIAL OF CONTEMPORARY ART (group)

'African Contemporary Art',
CENTRO CULTURAL BANCO DO BRASIL, Rio de Janeiro (group)

SOUTH AFRICAN NATIONAL GALLERY, Cape Town (group)

'Aquatopia: The Imaginary of the Ocean Deep',
NOTTINGHAM CONTEMPORARY, toured to TATE ST. IVES (group)

'Migrating Identities',
YERBA BUENA CENTER FOR THE ARTS, San Francisco (group)

'Sakahàn: International Indigenous Art',
NATIONAL GALLERY OF CANADA, Ontario (group)

4th ICP TRIENNIAL OF PHOTOGRAPHY AND VIDEO, New York (group)

'Broken Memories',
MUSEU AFROBRASIL, São Paulo (group)

'Earth Matters: Land as Material and Metaphor in the Arts of Africa',
NATIONAL MUSEUM OF AFRICAN ART, Washington, DC (group)

'Seismic Shifts: 10 Visionaries in Contemporary Art and Architecture',
NATIONAL ACADEMY MUSEUM, New York (group)

'Visions of Our 44 th President',
WRIGHT MUSEUM, Detroit (group)

'Following the Line',
THE GIRL'S CLUB, Fort Lauderdale, Florida (group)

'There is No Archive in Which Nothing is Lost',
GLASSELL SCHOOL at the MUSEUM OF FINE ARTS, Houston (group)

SELECTED ARTICLES AND INTERVIEWS
2012–13

2012 (cont.)
Richardson, Jared, 'Attack of the Boogeywoman: Visualizing Black Women's Grotesquerie in Afrofuturism', Art Papers, November–December

Yablonsky, Linda, 'Women In Art 2012: Wangechi Mutu', Elle Magazine, December

2013
Lax, Thomas J, 'Preview: Wangechi Mutu: A Fantastic Journey at the Nasher Museum of Art', Artforum, January

Schad, Ed, 'Wangechi Mutu at Susanne Vielmetter Los Angeles Projects', Art Review, January–February

Gandy, Mira, 'A conversation with Kenyan artist Wangechi Mutu on art, power and returning home', Beacon, February

Boucher, Brian, 'Mutu's Enchanted Forest', Art In America, March

Kumar, Sudhir, 'The Dirty Picture', New Indian Express: March 7
Buck, Louisa, 'Mutable Montage', The Art Newspaper, no. 244, March

Grannum, Sean J., 'Santigold collaborates with Wangechi Mutu for experimental animation "The End of Eating Everything"', Soul Culture, March

Akintoye, Dotun, 'Art: Wangechi Mutu at new Leonard Pearlstein Gallery', The City Paper, 7 March

Menconi, David, 'Wangechi Mutu takes Nasher on "A Fantastic Journey"', News Observer, 23 March

Vilensky, Mike, 'Brooklyn Art Is Now Served', Wall Street Journal, 27–28 April

Garnett, Adrienne, 'Mutu exhibit at Nasher "Otherworldy"', The Durham News, 30 April

Preston, Sammy, 'Wangechi Mutu's Mysterious World', Broadsheet, 28–30 May

Wolff, Rachel, '50 Under 50: The Next Most Collectible Artists', Art + Auction, June

Hansen-Bundy, Benjy, 'A Fantastic Journey Into the Mind of Collage Artist Wangechi Mutu', Mother Jones, October

Karefa-Johnson, Gabriella, 'Wangechi Mutu's "Fantastic Journey' Opens at the Brooklyn Museum,' Vogue, October

Mutu, Wangechi, 'The Women', Art In America, October

Cotter, Holland, 'A Window, Not a Mirror', The New York Times, 11 October

Plagens, Peter, 'Passion and Talent in Large Doses: Exhibitions of Wangechi Mutu, Thomas Eggerer and Karl Wirsum', The Wall Street Journal, 25 October

Rosenberg, Karen, 'The Future is African', The New York Times, 8 November

Kaitano, Chiwoniso, 'The Afrofuturism of Wangechi Mutu', The Guardian, 13 November

SELECTED EXHIBITIONS AND PROJECTS
2013–15

SELECTED ARTICLES AND INTERVIEWS
2013–15

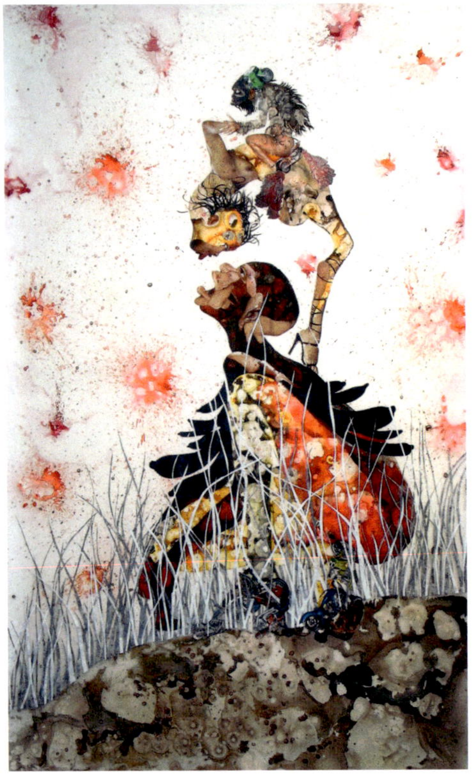

2013 (cont.)
1st KOCHI-MUZIRIS BIENNALE, India (group)

Receives the BlackStar Film Festival Audience Award for Favourite Experimental Film, Philadelphia

Receives the Asher B. Durand Artist of the Year Award, Brooklyn Museum, New York

Receives the African Diaspora Awards, Society for Africans in the Diaspora, New York

2013 (cont.)
Odidi, Bill, 'Wangechi Grabs World Attention with Rare Art', Daily Nation, 17 November

Budick, Ariella, 'Wangechi Mutu: A Fantastic Journey, Brooklyn Museum, New York', Financial Times, 26 November

Weaver, A.M., 'The End of Eating Everything', Art South Africa, December

2014
'Nguva na Nyoka (Sirens and Serpents)',
VICTORIA MIRO, London (solo)

'Herland',
DEUTSCHE BANK, New York (group)

'Made by Brazilians',
CIDADE MATARAZZO, Sáo Paulo (group)

'Divine Comedy',
MUSEUM FÜR MODERNE KUNST, Frankfurt, toured to
The SAVANNAH COLLEGE OF ART AND DESIGN, Georgia;
SMITHSONIAN NATIONAL MUSEUM OF AFRICAN ART,
Washington, DC (group)

'Death is Your Body',
FRANKFURTER KUNSTVEREIN, Frankfurt (group)

'Unbound: Contemporary Art After Frida Kahlo',
MUSEUM OF CONTEMPORARY ART, Chicago (group)

'Conflict: Contemporary Responses to War',
UNIVERSITY OF QUEENSLAND ART MUSEUM, Brisbane, toured
to UNIVERSITY OF QUEENSLAND ART MUSEUM, St. Lucia,
Australia (group)

'Interrupting Entropy',
SANTA CLARA UNIVERSITY, California (group)

11th DAKAR BIENNIAL (group)

'Broadway Billboard: A Sunset Satire',
SOCRATES SCULPTURE PARK, New York (group)

'Haute Africa',
FOTOFESTIVAL KNOKKE-HEIST, Belgium (group)

'Pace Gems: Selections from the Linda Pace Foundation's
Permanent Collection',
SPACE GALLERY, San Antonio, Texas (group)

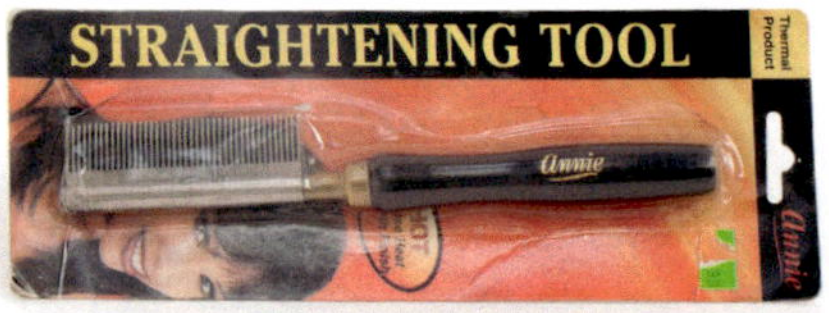

2014
Willis, Deborah 'Wangechi Mutu', BOMB, February

Tschida, Anne 'Mutu show at Museum of Contemporary Art in North Miami is a fantastic journey', Miami Herald, 23 May

Grillo, Gina, 'Artist turns African female stereotypes into symbols of power', Evanston Review, 23 September

Okeke-Agulu, Chika, 'Dak'Art 2014', Artforum, October

Nduta, Beth,'Kenya's Queen of Collage exhibits in London', The Star, 2 October

Bell, Caroline, 'Five Minutes with Wangechi Mutu', Chicago Sun Times, 13 October

Sheffler, Daniel, 'Brooklyn Inspires African Artists', The New York Times, 14 October

Conway, Megan, ' Renaissance Women', Wall Street Journal, 29 October

2015
'Wangechi Mutu',
GALLERIA IL CAPRICORNO, Venice (solo)

'No Man's Land: Women Artists from the Rubell Family Collection',
RUBELL FAMILY COLLECTION, Miami (group)

'Picasso.mania',
GRAND PALAIS, Paris (group)

'Us is Them',
PIZZUTI COLLECTION, Columbus, Ohio (group)

'European Ghosts: The Representation of Art from Africa in the 20th Century',
KUNSTMUSEUM AANZEE, Ostend, Belgium (group)

2015
De Jesus, Carlos Suarez, 'Art Mirrors Life in Wangechi Mutu's MOCA Show', Miami Times, 1 May

Wullschlager, Jackie, 'A Global "Parliament of Forms"', Financial Times, 9–10 May

Sangweni, Yolanda, 'Artist Wangechi Mutu Celebrates 'Africa's Out!' Campaign, with a Little Help from Solange', Essence, June

Sargent, Antwaun, 'Africa's Out! Let's Celebrate', W Magazine, June

Scher, Rob, 'This New Arts Endeavor Hopes to "Change the Way We Engage with Africa"', New York, 5 June

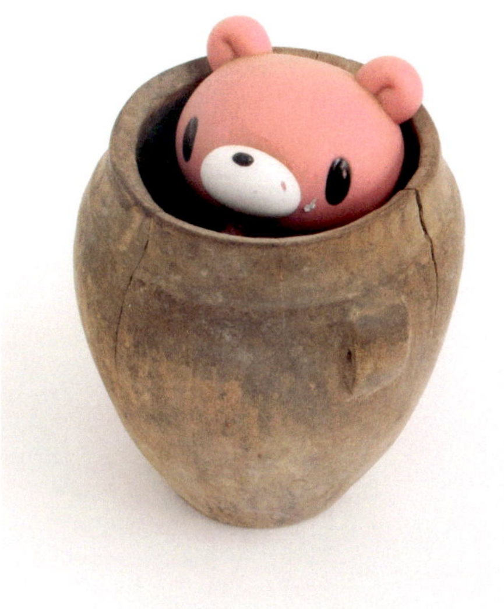

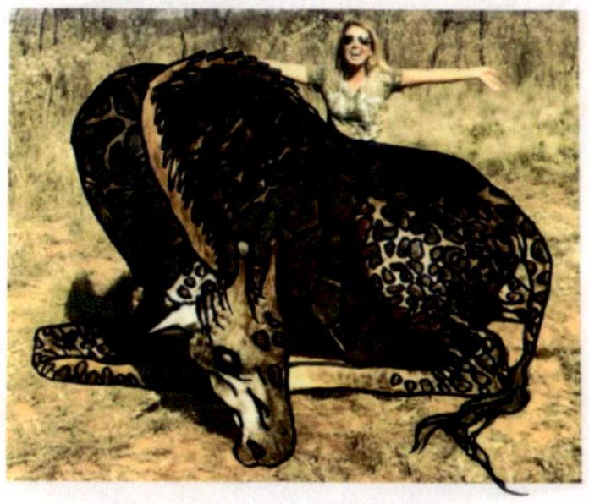

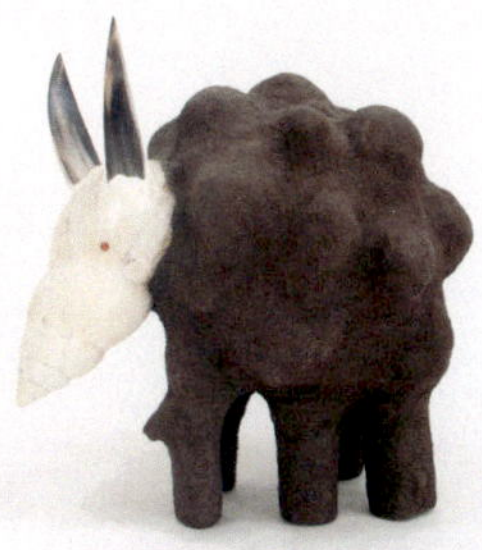

SELECTED EXHIBITIONS AND PROJECTS
2015–16

2015 (cont.)
1st KYIV BIENNIAL (group)

56th VENICE BIENNALE (group)

'Africa: Architecture, Culture and Identity',
LOUISIANA MUSEUM OF MODERN ART, Humblebaek, Denmark (group)

'Portraits and Other Liknesses from SFMoMA',
MUSEUM OF THE AFRICAN DIASPORA, San Francisco (group)

'The Divine Comedy: Heaven, Purgatory, and Hell Revisited by Contemporary African Artists',
NATIONAL MUSEUM OF AFRICAN ART, Washington, DC (group)

'Open This End: Contemporary Art from the Collection of Blake Byrne',
NASHER MUSEUM at UNIVERSITY URBAN ARTS SPACE, Colombus, Ohio, toured to THE MIRIAM AND IRA D. WALLACH ART GALLERY, COLUMBIA UNIVERSITY, New York; THE RONNA AND ERIC HOFFMAN GALLERY OF CONTEMPORARY ART, Lewis & Clark College, Vancouver (group)

'Making Africa: A Continent of Contemporary Design',
VITRA DESIGN MUSEUM, Weil am Rhein, Germany, toured to GUGGENHEIM MUSEUM, Bilbao; CENTRE DE CULTURA CONTEMPORÀNIA DE BARCELONA (group)

'Spatial Stories: Topographies of Change in Africa',
CENTER FOR VISUAL ART, THE METROPOLITAN STATE UNIVERSITY OF DENVER (group)

2016
'The Hybrid Human',
ARLENE AND HAROLD SCHNITZER CENTER FOR ART AND DESIGN, PACIFIC NORTHWEST COLLEGE OF ART CENTER FOR CONTEMPORARY ART AND CULTURE, Portland (solo)

'SITE 20 Years: Wangechi Mutu',
SITE SANTA FE, New Mexico (solo)

YALE UNIVERSITY ART GALLERY, New Haven (solo)

'The End of Carrying All',
MUSEUM OF FINE ARTS, Houston (solo)

'Regarding Africa: Contemporary Art and Afro-Futurism',
TEL AVIV MUSEUM OF ART (group)

'Beyond Mammy, Jezebel, & Sapphire: Reclaiming Images of Black Women',
ALEXANDRIA MUSEUM OF ART, Virginia, toured to the INTERDISCIPLINARY EXPERIMENTAL ARTS SPACE at COLORADO COLLEGE, Colorado Springs (group)

3rd BIENNALE INTERNATIONALE DE L'ART CONTEMPORAIN DE CASABLANCA (group)

'Making & Unmaking',
CAMDEN ART CENTRE, London (group)

'L'image volée',
FONDAZIONE PRADA, Milan (group)

'I Prefer Life',
WESERBURG BREMEN, Germany (group)

'Belief + Doubt: Selections from the Francie Bishop Good and David Horvitz collection',
NSU ART MUSEUM FORT LAUDERDALE, Florida (group)

SELECTED ARTICLES AND INTERVIEWS
2015–16

2015 (cont.)
'Five Artists, Five Book Reviews; Wangechi Mutu', The New York Times, 28 June

Whitley, Zoe, 'International Geographic: Wangechi Mutu on Paper, Print and Printmaking', Art in Print, November–December

Waxman, Lori, 'Seductive Hells', Chicago Tribune, 26 November
'Wangechi Mutu: Nuguva na Nyoka, Victoria Miro, London', Aesthetica Magazine, 2 December

2016
Hernandez, Jillian, 'The Ambivalent Grotesque: Reading Black Women's Erotic Corporeality in Wangechi Mutu's Work', Signs: Journal of Women in Culture and Society, no. 2

Lequeux, Emmanuelle, 'De New York a Paris La Folie Des Artistes Africains', Beaux Arts, March

Kook-Anderson, Grace, 'Wangechi Mutu and the revolt of the female form', Oregon Artswatch, 9 March

Jadrnak, Jackie, 'The End of 20/20', Albuquerque Journal, 18 March

Buck, Louisa, 'The Making of Duro Olowu: Designer's Camden Arts Centre Show confounds curatorial convention', The Telegraph, 24 June

Battaglia, Andy, 'Dark Matter at Pace Gallery', Wall Street Journal, 26 June

Mutu, Wangechi, '500 Words', Artforum, July

Martinez, Alanna, 'Why Artist Wangechi Mutu Chooses to Perform in Secret', New York Observer, 18 July

Molefe, Ayana, '5 Women whose work you must see at FNB Joburg Art Fair', Elle South Africa, September

Tate, Greg, 'Wangechi Mutu: Collagist and 'cultural anomaly' is returning home after 20 years', Mail & Guardian: Africa's Best Read, 6 September

Samaha, Barry, 'Ippolita Links Up with Seven Artists on a Charm Bracelet that Celebrates Female Unity', Forbes, 9 November

Hyland, Veronique, 'Cindy Sherman and Fellow Artist Teamed Up to Design a Haute Charm Bracelet', New York Magazine, 11 November

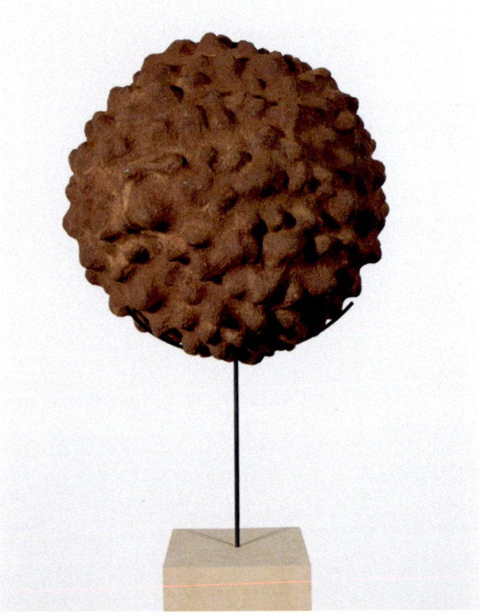

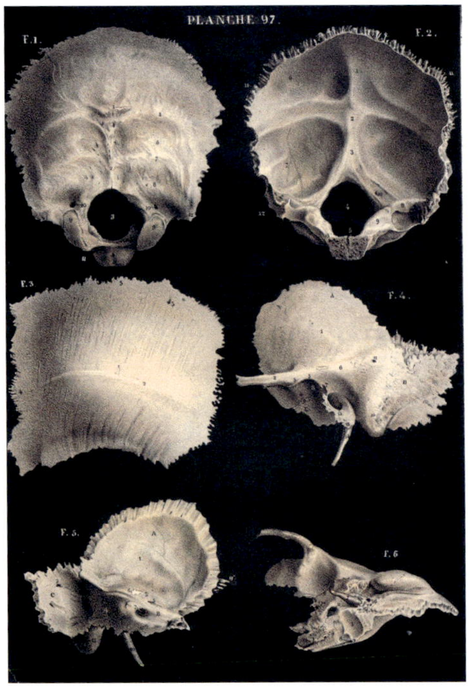

SELECTED EXHIBITIONS AND PROJECTS
2016–17

2016 (cont.)
'Hey You! – Who Me?',
YALE UNIVERSITY SCHOOL OF ART, New Haven (group)

'Human Interest: Portraits from the Whitney's Collection',
WHITNEY MUSEUM OF AMERICAN ART, New York (group)

'Black Pulp',
EDGEWOOD GALLERY, YALE UNIVERSITY SCHOOL OF ART, New Haven, toured to INTERNATIONAL PRINT CENTER, New York (group)

'The Grace Jones Project',
MUSEUM OF THE AFRICAN DIASPORA, San Francisco (group)

'Lucy's Iris: Contemporary African Women Artists',
MUSEO DE ARTE CONTEMPORÁNEO DE CASTILLA Y LEÓN (MUSAC), León, toured to ROCHECHOUART DEPARTMENTAL MUSEUM OF CONTEMPORARY ART AND CENTRO ATLÁNTICO DE ARTE MODERNO, Gran Canaria (group)

Receives the Cultural Leadership Award, American Federation of Arts, New York

2017
'Journeys into Peripheral Worlds',
DES MOINES ART CENTER, Des Moines, Ohio (solo)

'Ndoro Na Miti',
GLADSTONE GALLERY, New York (solo)

'Wangechi Mutu',
LEHMANN MAUPIN, Hong Kong (solo)

'Water Woman',
THE CONTEMPORARY AUSTIN (solo)

PERFORMA 17, New York (group)

4th CANADIAN BIENNIAL, Ottawa (group)

'We Are Here: I Am You,You are Here, We are Everywhere',
MUSEUM OF CONTEMPORARY ART, Chicago (group)

'Simple Passion, Complex Vision: The Darryl Atwell Collection',
HARVEY B. GANTT CENTER FOR AFRICAN-AMERICAN ARTS + CULTURE, Charlotte, North Carolina (group)

'Art Afrique: Le Nouvel Atelier',
FONDATION LOUIS VUITTON, Paris (group)

'Regarding the Figure',
THE STUDIO MUSEUM IN HARLEM, New York (group)

'All Things Being Equal',
ZEITZ MUSEUM OF CONTEMPORARY ART, Cape Town (group)

'Colonial Stories: Power and People',
GL HOLTEGAARD, Holte, Denmark (group)

'Journeys into Peripheral Worlds',
DES MOINES ARTS CENTER, Iowa (group)

'Il Cacciatore Bianco/The White Hunter',
FM CENTER FOR CONTEMPORARY ART, Milan (group)

Receives the National Artist Award, Anderson Ranch Arts Center, Aspen

SELECTED ARTICLES AND INTERVIEWS
2016–17

2016 (cont.)
Crichton-Miller, Emma, 'Goodman Gallery Marks 50 Years in Johannesburg', Financial Times, 11 November

Rosen, Miss, ''Africa Rising' Presents Cutting Edge Art, Fashion, Design', Crave, 29 November

A.M.B., 'Depicting the Diaspora: 'Africans in America' probes questions of identity and nomenclature', The Economist, 30 November

Royce-Greensill, Sarah, 'Liz Swig Launches Charmed: the bracelet that's more a work of art than a piece of Jewelry', The Telegraph, 7 December

Bernard, Joy, 'Art: South of the Sahara', Jerusalem Post, 18 December

2017
Wilson, Michael, 'Wangechi Mutu', Time Out New York, 15–28 February

Smith, Roberta, 'Wangechi Mutu', The New York Times, 9 March

Donoghue, Katy, 'Wangechi Mutu Gets Closer to The Landscape That Speaks To Her In 'Ndoro Na Miti'', Whitewall Magazine, March

Scobie, Ilka, 'Wangechi Mutu: Ndoro Na Miti', The Brooklyn Railway, March

Fateman, Johanna, 'Wangechi Mutu', Artforum, April

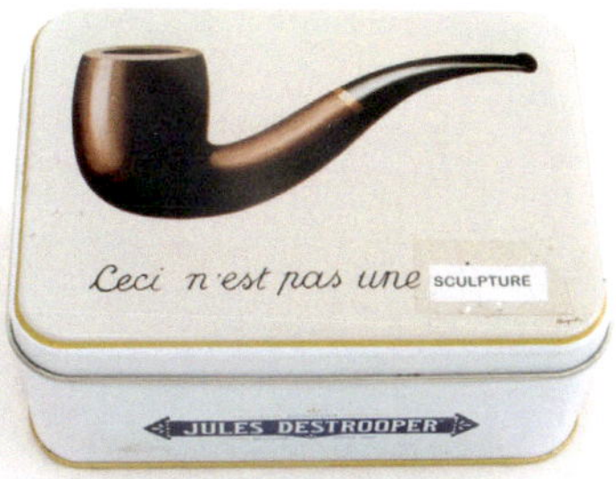

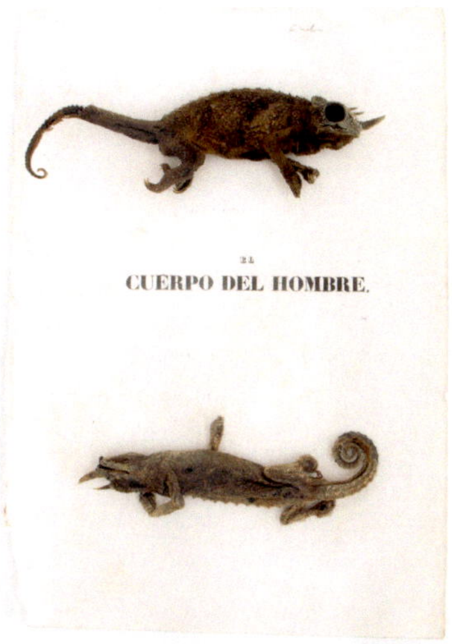

SELECTED EXHIBITIONS AND PROJECTS
2018–19

2018
'Wangechi Mutu: The End of Eating Everything',
BLANTON MUSEUM OF ART, Austin (solo)

'A Promise to Communicate',
INSTITUTE OF CONTEMPORARY ART, Boston (solo)

'Witness: Themes of Social Justice in Contemporary Printmaking and Photography from the Collections of Jordan D. Schnitzer and His Family Foundation',
HALLIE FORD MUSEUM OF ART WILLAMETTE UNIVERSITY, Salem, Oregon (group)

'People Get Ready: Building a Contemporary Collection',
NASHER MUSEUM OF ART, DUKE UNIVERSITY, Durham, North Carolina (group)

'The World on Paper: Deutsche Bank Collection',
PALAISPOPULAIRE, Berlin (group)

'Boss Lady',
GIRLS' CLUB WAREHOUSE, Fort Lauderdale, Florida (group)
'Tintoretto 500: The Madness of Painting',
CA' D'ORO, Venice (group)

'Multiply, Identify, Her',
INTERNATIONAL CENTER OF PHOTOGRAPHY, New York (group)

'Road to Justice',
MUSEO NAZIONALE DELLE ARTI DEL XXI SECOLO (MAXXI), Rome (group)

'Not a Single Story',
NIROX FOUNDATION, Krugersdorp, South Africa (group)

'Contemporary Magic: A Tarot Deck Art Project',
ART CAPSUL, New York (group)

'Making Africa: A Continent of Contemporary Design',
BLANTON MUSEUM OF ART, Austin (group)

'People Get Ready',
NASHER MUSEUM OF ART AT DUKE UNIVERSITY, Durham (group)

'Blind Faith: Between the Visceral and the Cognitive in Contemporary Art',
HAUS DER KUNST, Munich (group)

'Chaos and Awe',
FRIST CENTER OF VISUAL ARTS, Nashville, toured to CHRYSLER MUSEUM OF ART NORFOLK, Virginia (group)

'Unrecorded: Reimagining Artist Identities in Africa',
UNIVERSITY OF MICHIGAN MUSEUM OF ART, Ann Arbor (group)

'2017 Afro-Tech and the Future of Re-Invention',
HARTWARE MEDIENKUNSTVEREIN (HMKV), Dortmund (group)

'On Common Ground: Recent Acquisitions in Contemporary Art',
MUSEUM OF FINE ARTS, Houston (group)

Receives the African Art Award at the National Museum of African Art, Washington, DC

SELECTED ARTICLES AND INTERVIEWS
2018–19

2018
Wa Gacheru, Margaretta, 'Wangechi Mutu, Artist Who's Feted Abroad but Unknown in Kenya', Business Daily, 25 January

Valentine, Victoria L., 'Baltimore Museum of Art Swaps Works by Warhol, Kline, Noland, and Rauschenberg for Acquisitions by Whitten, Sherald, Mutu, and Yiadom-Boakye', Culture Type, June

Wilson-Goldie, Kaelen, '"Multiply, Identify, Her" International Center of Photography Museum (ICP)', Artforum, June

Brownell Mitic, Ginanne, 'In Nairobi, An Art Scene in Transition', The New York Times, 12 June

Spivack, Emily, "Why this artist is inspired by a chest of drawers', T: The New York Times Style Magazine, 20 June

Mutu, Wangechi, 'Ana Mendieta', Frieze Master's, no 7

2019
'The Met Facade Commission: Wangechi Mutu. The New Ones Will Free Us',
METROPOLITAN MUSEUM, New York (solo)

'Waking Dream',
RUBY CITY, San Antonio, Texas (group)

2019
Libbey, Peter, 'The Met Will Use its Facade and Great Hall to Showcase Contemporary Art', The New York Times, 21 March

Moffitt, Evan, 'The 2019 Whitney Biennial Is Unafraid to Be Beautiful', Frieze, no. 203, May

SELECTED EXHIBITIONS AND PROJECTS
2019–20

2019 (cont.)
WHITNEY BIENNIAL 2019, New York (group)

'Here We Are',
ART GALLERY OF NEW SOUTH WALES, Sydney (group)

'Afterlives of the Black Atlantic',
ALLEN MEMEORIAL ART MUSEUM, Oberlin, Ohio (group)

'The Academic Body',
AMERICAN ACADEMY IN ROME (group)

'I am... Contemporary Women Artists of Africa',
NATIONAL MUSEUM OF AFRICAN ART, Washington, DC (group)

'IncarNations. African Art As Philosophy',
BOZAR CENTRE FOR FINE ARTS, Brussels (group)

'Suffering from Realness',
MASSACHUSETTS MUSEUM OF CONTEMPORARY ART, North Adams (group)

'In the Wake',
ULRICH MUSEUM OF ART, WICHITA STATE UNIVERSITY, Kansas (group)

'Social Space',
JORDAN SCHNITZER MUSEUM OF ART, Pullman, Washington (group)

'Black Refractions: Highlights from The Studio Museum in Harlem',
MUSEUM OF THE AFRICAN DIASPORA, San Francisco,toured to GIBBES MUSEUM, Charleston; KALAMAZOO INSTITUTE OF ARTS, Michigan; SMITH COLLEGE MUSEUM OF ART, Northampton, Massachusetts; FRYE ART MUSEUM, Seattle; UTAH MUSEUM OF FINE ARTS, Salt Lake City (group)

'Word on the Street',
ARTPACE, San Antonio, Texas (group)

'Are we There Yet? Arts of the Black Atlantic',
ALLEN MEMORIAL ART MUSEUM, OBERLIN COLLEGE, Ohio (group)

'Serious Sparkle',
TANG TEACHING MUSEUM, SKIDMORE COLLEGE, Saratoga Springs, New York (group)

'Uptown to Harlem: African American Works from the Collection of Martin & Rebecca Eisenberg',
RIVERVIEW SCHOOL, East Sandwich, Massachusetts (group)

'Driving Forces: Contemporary Art from the Collection of Ann and Ron Pizzuti',
COLUMBUS MUSEUM OF ART, Ohio (group)

'Art for All',
JORDAN D. SCHNITZER FAMILY FOUNDATION, Portland (group)

2020
'Screenings 6: Wangechi Mutu',
UNIVERSITY OF SAN DIEGO (solo)

'Bodyscapes',
ISRAEL MUSEUM, Jerusalem (group)

'Duro Olowu: Seeing Chicago',
MUSEUM OF CONTEMPORARY ART, Chicago (group)

SELECTED ARTICLES AND INTERVIEWS
2019–20

2019 (cont.)
Loos, Ted, 'Why These 4 Whitney Biennial Artists Are Making Waves', Galerie Magazine, 10 May

Budick, Ariella, 'Whitney Biennial: an anthology of young America', Financial Times, 4 June

Catlin, Roger, 'Women's Voices Ring With a Resounding Roar in this New Show', Smithsonian Magazine, 17 July

MacSweeney, Eve, 'Art Sentinel: With new sculptures melding tradition and futurism, Wangechi Mutu brings a changing of the guard to the Metropolitan Museum of Art, W Magazine, 27 August

Morris, Kadish, 'In Pictures: Wangechi Mutu's Empowering Sculptures of African Women at The Met', Frieze, no. 205, September

Primat, Garance, 'La Lumière des Mondes, Domaine des Etangs', La Laiterie, September

Princenthal, Nancy, 'Wangechi Mutu: A New Face for the Met', The New York Times, 5 September

Cotter, Holland, 'At 19 Art Shows, From Los Angeles to Manhattan, All Eyes Are on Inclusion', The New York Times, 9 September

Sayej, Nadja, '"The works represent a new era": behind the Met's bold new sculptures', The Guardian, 16 September

Aldridge, Taylor Renee, '"We Ourselves Are Our Prize": Lasting Works in the Whitney Biennial Evoke Toni Morrison and Ancestry Through the Ages', ARTnews, 19 September

Collins, Ann C., 'Wangechi Mutu: The NewOnes, will free Us', The Brooklyn Rail, October

Trujillo, Maria, 'Liberating art history: Wangechi Mutu takes over the Metropolitan's empty niches', Art Critique, October

Murray, Cori, 'Wangechi Mutu Makes Her-story For The First Time In The Met's 117-Year History', Essence, November

Haigney, Sophie, 'Wangechi Mutu's Works to Grace the Met Facade Until June', The New York Times, 11 November

Quinn, Annalisa, 'Artist Wangechi Mutu: "I wanted them to sit upright and unafraid"', Financial Times, 4 December

2020
Durón, Maximiliano, '2020 Prospect New Orleans Triennial to Consider America's "Unprecedented" Political Moment', ARTnews, March

Libbey, Peter, 'Met Museum Acquires Two Sculptures by Wangechi Mutu', The New York Times, 28 July

Stapley-Brown, Victoria, 'Wangechi Mutu asks the Legion of Honor, 'Are you listening?', The Art Newspaper, October

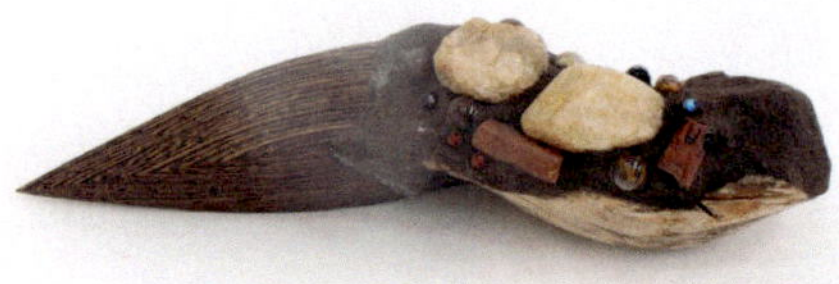

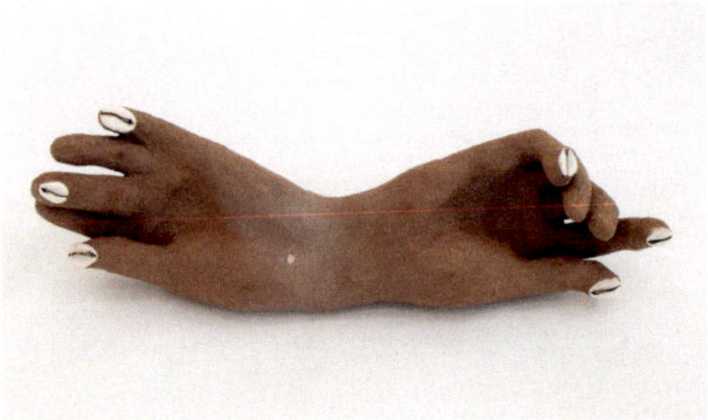

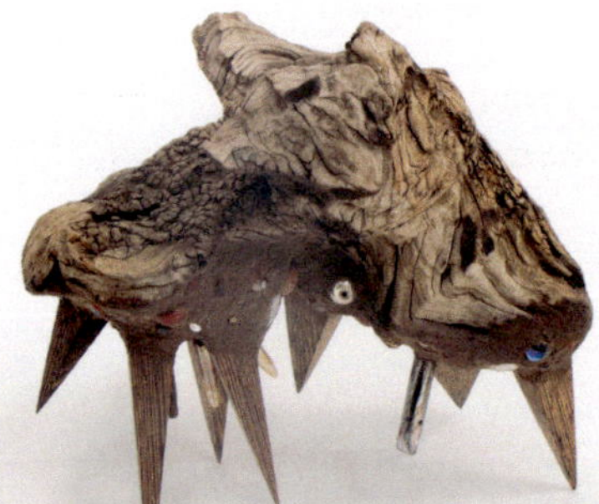

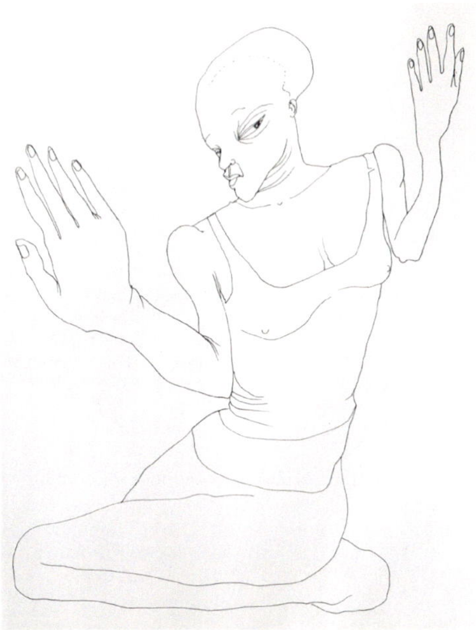

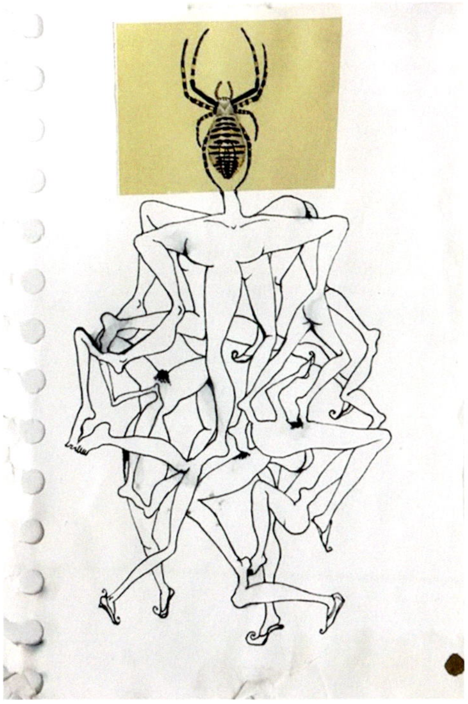

SELECTED EXHIBITIONS AND PROJECTS
2020–22

2020 (cont.)
'Abortion is Normal',
GALERIE EVA PRESENHUBER, New York (group)

'Indian Ocean Current: Six Artistic Narratives',
McMULLEN MUSEUM OF ART, Boston (group)

'Collective Constellation: Selections from The Eileen Harris Norton Collection',
ART + PRACTICE, Los Angeles (group)

'A Beautiful Struggle: Black Feminist Futurism',
URBAN INSTITUTE FOR CONTEMPORARY ART, Grand Rapids, Michigan (group)

'Riffs and Relations',
THE PHILLIPS COLLECTION, Washington, DC, (group)

'Neurones: Simulated Intelligences',
CENTRE POMPIDOU, Paris (group)

'Contemporary Female Identities in the Global South',
JOBURG CONTEMPORARY ART FOUNDATION, Johannesburg, South Africa (group)

'Ubuntu: Five Rooms from the Harry David Art Collection',
NATIONAL MUSEUM OF CONTEMPORARY ART, Athens (group)

'Word on the Street',
EMERSON COLLECTIVE, Washington, DC, (group)

'I'm Yours: Encounters with Art in Our Times',
INSTITUTE OF CONTEMPORARY ART, Boston (group)

'My Body, My Rules',
PÉREZ ART MUSEUM, Miami (group)

2021
'I Am Speaking, Are You Listening?',
LEGION OF HONOR MUSEUM, San Francisco (solo)

'Wangechi Mutu',
GLADSTONE GALLERY, New York (solo)

PROSPECT.5, New Orleans (group)

'Taking Space: Contemporary Women Artists and the Politics of Scale',
PENNSYLVANIA ACADEMY OF THE FINE ARTS, Philadelphia (group)

'Memoria: Récits d'Une Autre Histoire',
FONDS REGIONAL D'ART CONTEMPORAIN (FRAC) NOUVELLEAQUITAINE MÉCA, Bordeaux (group)

2022
STORM KING ART CENTER, New Windsor, New York (solo)

'Love as a Practice',
THE STUDIO MUSEUM IN HARLEM, New York (group)

'In the Black Fantastic',
HAYWARD GALLERY, London (group)

SELECTED ARTICLES AND INTERVIEWS
2020–22

2020 (cont.)
Weems, Carrie Mae, 'Wangechi Mutu and Carrie Mae Weems on the Profound Impulse to Make Art', Interview Magazine, December

2021
Mutu, Wangechi, 'Wangechi Mutu Hates Horror and Loves Silence', Frieze, no. 219, February

Loos, Ted, 'The Light-Filled "Dream Studio" of Kenyan-American Artist Wangechi Mutu', Wall Street Journal, 4 February

Gereben, Janos, 'Legion of Honor reopens with two original exhibitions', The San Francisco Examiner, 5 May

Zack, Jessica, 'Wangechi Mutu's Legion of Honor Exhibition creates a New Mythology', The San Francisco Chronicle, 6 May

Curiel, Jonathan, 'Wangechi Mutu Subverts Western Tropes', SF Weekly, 15 May

Loos, Ted, 'Museum Shows With Stories to Tell', The New York Times, 21 May

Chen, Jess, 'Art Seen: Wangechi Mutu', The Brooklyn Rail, July– August

2022
Ngozi Nwangwa, Shirley, 'Wangechi Mutu Brings Her Sculptures to Storm King', T: The New York Times Style Magazine, 2 June

BIBLIOGRAPHY

MONOGRAPHS, EXHIBITION BROCHURES AND ARTIST'S BOOKS

Mutu, Wangechi, and Christopher Miles, Wangechi Mutu, Susanne Vielmetter Los Angeles Projects, 2005

Mutu, Wangechi, and Peter Boswell, Wangechi Mutu: Amazing Grace, Miami Art Museum, 2005

Mutu, Wangechi, and Tara McDowell, New Work: Wangechi Mutu, San Francisco Museum of Modern Art 2005

Mutu, Wangechi, and Ekow Eshun, Wangechi Mutu: Yo.N.L, Victoria Miro, London, 2007

Mutu, Wangechi, Isolde Brielmaier, Malik Gaines and Michael Veal, Wangechi Mutu: A Shady Promise, Damiani, Bologna, 2008

Mutu, Wangechi, and Angela Steif, Wangechi Mutu: In Whose Image?, Kunstalle Wein, Vienna, 2008

Mutu, Wangechi, and David Moos, Wangechi Mutu: This You Call Civilization?, Art Gallery of Ontario, Toronto, 2010

Mutu, Wangechi, Friedhelm Hütte (ed.), Okwui Enwezor, Lauri Firstenberg, Courtney J. Martin and Klaus Ottman, Wangechi Mutu: My Dirty Little Heaven, Deutsche Guggenheim, Berlin, and Hatje Canz, Ostfildern, 2011

Mutu, Wangechi, and José Bélisle, Wangechi Mutu, ABC Books and Musée d'Art Contemporain de Montréal, 2012

Mutu, Wangechi, Trevor Schoonmaker, Kristine Stiles and Greg Tate, Wangechi Mutu: A Fantastic Journey, Duke University Press, Durham, North Carolina, 2013

Mutu, Wangechi, Adrienne Edwards and Binyavanga Wainaina, Wangechi Mutu: Nguva na Nyoka, Victoria Miro, London, 2014

Mutu, Wangechi, Rachel Kent, Mbugua wa Kimani, Dan Cameron and Adrienne Edwards Wangechi Mutu, Museum of Contemporary Art Australia, Sydney, 2013

Mutu, Wangechi, A Promise to Communicate, Ivorypress LiberArs, Madrid, 2019

Mutu, Wangechi, Isaac Julien and Claudia Schmuckli (ed.), Wangechi Mutu: I Am Speaking, Are You Listening?, DelMonico, New York, and Fine Arts Museums of San Francisco, 2021

Mutu, Wangechi, Adrienne Edwards, Courtney J. Martin, Kellie Jones and Chika Okeke-Agulu, Wangechi Mutu, Phaidon, London, 2022

SELECTED EXHIBITION CATALOGUES AND SURVEYS

Adams, Rachel, Wanderlust: Actions, Traces, Journeys 1967-2017, MIT Press, Cambridge, Massachusetts, 2017

Amrani, Sabrina, and Orlando Britto Jinorio, El Iris de Lucy: Artistas Africanas Contemporaneas, Centro Atlantico de de Arte Moderno, Madrid, 2017

Augaitis, Daina (ed.), and Stephanie Rebick, Visceral Bodies, Vancouver Art Gallery, 2010

Backstein, Joseph, Svetlana Boym, Catherine de Zegher, More Light: The Fifth Moscow Biennale of Contemporary Art, Institute of Contemporary Art, Moscow, 2013

Barwell Brownlee, Andrea, and Valerie Oliver Cassel. Cinema Remixed and Reloaded: Black Women and the Moving Image since 1970, Contemporary Arts Museum Houston and Spelman College Press, 2008

Bernhausen, Sara, and Britta Färber (eds), V15IONS: 15 Years Deutsche + Guggenheim, Deutsche Bank and Guggenheim Museum, Berlin, 2012

Barson, Tanya, and Peter Gorschluter, Afro Modern: Journeys through The Black Atlantic, Tate Liverpool, 2010

Betlach, Charles (ed.), Interrupting Entropy: Selections form the Betlach Collection, Santa Clara University Press, California, 2015

Biesenbach, Klaus, Greater New York, P.S.1. Contemporary Art Center, Long Island City and Museum of Modern Art, New York, 2005

Bilyeu, Elizabeth Anne, and & LeRonn Brooks, Witness: Themes of Social Justice in Contemporary Printmaking and Photography from the Collections of Jordan D. Schnitzer and His Family Foundation, Jordan D. Schnitzer and His Family Foundation, Portland, 2018

Bindman, David, Henry Louis Gates, Jr and Karen C. C. Dalton, The Image of the Black in Western Art: Volume V, Part II, Harvard University Press, Cambridge, Massachusetts, 2015

Bonami, Francesco, and Sarah Cosulich, Infinite Painting: Contemporary Painting and Global Realism, Villa Manin Centre for Contemporary Art, Codroipo, Italy, 2006

Bonham-Carter, Charlotte, David Hodge and Richard Cork, The Contemporary Art Book, Goodman Books, London, 2009

Bosland, Joost, Trade Routes Revisited, Michael Stevenson Gallery, Cape Town and Johannesburg, 2012

Brandstetter, Anna-Maria, and Marjorie Jongbloed (ed.), Violence/Trauma/Memory, Volkswagen Foundation, Hannover, Germany, 2006

Brielmaier, Isolde and Tu, Thuy Linh N., Rewind/Re-Cast/Review, Berrie Arts Center and Ramapo College Press, Mahwah, New Jersey, 2005

Burton, Johanna, Shannon Jackson, Dominic Willsdon and Lisa Phillips, Public Servants: Art and the Crisis of the Common Good, MIT Press, Cambridge, 2016.

Cachia, Amanda, Elizabeth McLuhan and Joan Borsa, Pandora's Box, Dunlop Art Gallery, Regina, Saskatchewan, 2008

Cameron, Dan, Matthew Drutt et al, 2004 Artpace Residencies and Exhibitions, Artpace, San Antonio, 2008

Cameron, Dan, Barbara Bleomink, Lolis Eric Elie and Claire Tancons, Prospect.1 New Orleans, Picturebox, New York, November, 2008

Chao, Marina, Multiply, Identify, Her, International Center for Photography, New York, 2018

Chave, Anna C., The Visible Vagina, Francis Naumann Fine Art and David Nolan Gallery, New York, 2010

Clark, Vicky A., and Sandhini Poddar, Figures of Thinking: Convergences in Contemporary Cultures, Pamela Auchincloss Arts Management and University of Richmond Museums, Virginia, 2005

Colburn, Bolton T., In the Land of Retinal Delights: The Juxtapoz Factor, Laguna Art Museum, Laguna Beach, California, and Gingko Press, Berkeley, 2008

Coleman, Teju, Known andStrange Things, Random House, New York, 2016

Colo, Papo, Holland Cotter, Mary Anne Staniszewski, Rachel Gugelberger and Jeanette Ingberman, Unfinished Memories: 30 Years of Exit Art, Steidl. Göttingen, Germany, 2017

Coomer, Martin, Protest, Victoria Miro, London, 2016

Coplan Hurowitz, Sharon, and Amanda Benchley, Open Studio, Phaidon, New York, 2021

Cornejo, Maria, Maria Cornejo: Zero 1997-2017+, Rizzoli, New York, 2018

Deitch, Jeffrey, Fractured Figure, Deste Foundation, Athens, and Distributed Art Publishers, New York, 2008

Della Monica, Lauren P., Bodies of Work: Contemporary Figurative Painting, Schiffer, Atglen, Pennsyilvania, 2016

Demand, Thomas (ed.), Ian McEwan, Ali Smith, Russell Ferguson, Christy Lange, Jonathan Griffin, Rainer Erlinger and Daniel McClea L'Image Volée, Fondazione Prada, Milan, 2016

Dexter, Emma, Jordan Kantor et al, Vitamin D: New Perspectives in Drawings, Phaidon, London, 2007

DiMeo Carlozzi, Annette, Kelly Baum, Anjali Gupta et al, American Art Since 1900, Blanton Museum of Art and University of Texas Press, 2006

Direktor, Ruth, Regarding Africa: Contemporary Art and Afro Futurism, Tel Aviv Museum of Art, 2017

Di Suvero, Mark, Thirty Years, Socrates Sculpture Park, New York, 2017

Ditner, Judy (ed.), Dress Codes: The Third ICP Triennial of Photography and Video, International Center of Photography, New York, and Steidl, Göttingen, Germany, 2009

Dunning, Stefani K., Black to Nature: Pastoral Return and African American Culture, Eurospan, London, 2021

Edwards, Adrienne, Blackness in Abstraction, Pace Gallery, New York, 2016

Enwezor, Okwui, and Colin Richards, Trade Routes: History and Geography, Johannesburg Biennale and Prince Claus Fund for Culture and Development, Amsterdam, 1997

Enwezor, Okwui (ed.), The Unhomely Phantom Scenes in Global Society, Seville Biennial, Spain, 2006

Enwezor, Okwui (ed.), Intense Proximité: Une Anthologie du Proche et du Lointain La Triennale 2012, Palais de Tokyo and Edition Artlys, Paris, 2011

Enwezor, Okwui (ed.), All The World's Futures, VEnice Biennale and Marsilio, Venice, 2015

Eshun, Ekow (ed.), In the Black Fantastic, Southbank Centre and Thames and Hudson, London, 2022

Eyene, Christine, Biennale Internationale De L'Art Contemporain Casablanca, Maroc Premium Foundation, Casablanca, 2016

Fall, N'Goné Fall, Ineke Van Hamersveld, Riet Van der Linden and Mirjam Westenrebelle, Art and Feminism 1960-2009, Museum of Modern Art, Arnhem, Netherlands, 2008

Farrell, Laurie Ann (ed.), Laurie Firstenberg et al, Looking Both Ways: Art of the Contemporary African Diaspora, Museum for African Art, Long Island City, New York, 2003

Franco, James, Isaac Julien and Glenn Scott Wright, Cinematic Visions Painting at the Edge of Reality, Victoria Miro, London, 2013

Genocchio, Benjamin, Art Studio America, Thames & Hudson, New York, 2013

Gioni, Massimiliano, Richard Flood and Laura Hoptman, Collage: The Un-Monumental Picture, New Museum of Contemporary Art and Merrell, New York, 2008.

Glesman, Amanda, The Campaign for Art: Gifts for the San Francisco Museum of Modern Art, San Francisco Museumof Art, 2016

Gopnik, Adam, and Michaelyn Mitchell (ed.), The Sleeve Should Be Illegal & Other Reflections on Art at the Frick, Delmonico, New York, 2021

Grovier, Kelly, 100 Works of Art That Will Define a Generation, Thames & Hudson, London, 2013.

Hall, Emily (ed.), Modern Women: Women Artists at the Museum of Modern Art, New York, the Museum of Modern Art, New York, 2010

Heartney, Eleanor, Helaine Posner, Nancy Princenthal, and Sue Scott, The Reckoning: Women Artists of The New Millennium, Prestel, London, 2013

Heuer, Christopher P. and Rebecca Zorac, Ecologies, Agents, Terrains, Yale University Press, New Haven, 2018

Higgs, Matthew, Nova Benway, Michelle Hyun, Nathan Lee, Manuela Moscoso, and Dylan Peet, At Home/Not At Home: Works from the Collection of Martin and Rebecca Eisenberg, Center for Curatorial Studies at Bard College, New York, 2010

Hill, Greg A., Candice Hopkins and Christine Lalonde, Sakahàn: International Indigenous Art, National Gallery of Canada, Ottawa, 2013

Hobbs, Robert, Franklin Sirmans and Michele Wallace, 30 Americans, Rubell Family Collection, Miami, and Distributed Art Publishers, New York, 2008

Hockley, Rujeko, and Jane Panetta, Whitney Biennial 2019, Whitney Museum of American Art, New York, 2019

Holm, Michael Juul, and Mette Marie Kallehauge, Africa: Architecture Culture Identity, Louisiana Museum of Modern Art, Humlebæk, Denmark, 2015

Holzwarth, Hans Werner (ed.), 100 Contemporary Artists, Taschen, Berlin, 2009

Holzwarth, Hans Werner (ed.), Astrid Mania et al, Art Now, Vol. 3, Taschen, Cologne, 2010

Hou, Hanru, The Spectacle of The Everyday: The 10th Lyon Biennale of Contemporary Art, Lyon, Les Presses du Réel, Dijon, France, 2009

Hou, Hanru, The Power of Doubt, La Fabrica, Madrid, 2011

Hudson, Suzanne, Painting Now, Thames & Hudson, New York, 2015

Keith, Naima J., Diana Nawi (eds), Jeffery U. Darensbourg, Amber Rose Johnson, Meg Onli, Thomas J. Lax and Kristina Kay Robinson, Prospect.5 New Orleans: Yesterday We Said Tomorrow, Rizzoli, New York, 2021

Kries, Mateo, and Amelie Klein, Making Africa: A Continent of Contemporary Design, Vitra Design Museum, Weil am Rhein, Germany, 2015

Kuramitsu, Kris and LeFelle-Collins, Lizetta, Linkages & Themes in the African Diaspora: Selections from the Eileen Harris Norton and Peter Norton Art Collections, Museum of the African Diaspora, San Francisco, 2005

Jackson, Zakiyyah Iman, Becoming Human: Matter and Meaning in an Antiblack World, New York University Press, 2020

Jones, Kellie, and Imamu Amiri Baraka, Life's Little Necessities: Installations by Women in the 1990s, Duke University Press, Durham, North CArolina, 1997

Kantor, Jordan, and Gary Garrels, Drawing from the Modern 3: 1975-2005, Museum of Modern Art, New York, 2006

Keith, Naima J., and Zoe Whitley, The Shadows Took Shape, The Studio Museum In Harlem, New York, 2013

Lee, Yongwoo (ed.), Kerry Brougher and Sukwon Chan, A Grain of Dust A Drop of Water, Gwangju Biennale, South Korea, 2004

Levi, Corwin, and Michelle Aldredge, Mirror Mirrored: A Contemporary Artists' Edition of 25 Grimms' Tales, Uzzlepye Press, Harrisville, Rhode Island, 2018

Lévy, Bernard-Henri, Les aventures de la vérité, Grasset, Paris, 2013

Lewis, Heidi, and Roland Mitchell, Beyond Mammy, Jezebel and Sapphire, The Jordan Schnitzer Family Foundation, Portland, 2017

Lowry Glenn, MoMA Highlights Since 1980s, The Museum of Modern Art, New York, 2008

Malbert, Roger, Simon Njami, David Elliott, Jean-Hubert Martin, Marie-Laure Bernadac, Abdelwahab Meddeb, John Picton and Lucy Duran, Africa Remix: Contemporary Art of a Continent, Kunstpalast Düsseldorf, Germany, and Hayward Gallery, London, 2004

Malbert, Roger, Drawing People: The Human Figure in Contemporary Art, Thames & Hudson, London, 2015

Malherbe, Anna, Sortilége, Fondation pour l'Art Contemporain, Claudine et Jean-Marc Salomon, Annecy, France, 2009

Mason, Daniel (ed.), and John Giorno, Bash: An Exhibition in Two Parts, Woodstock Byrdcliffe Guild, New York, 2014

Milbourne, Karen (ed.), Earth Matters: Land as Material and Metaphor in the Arts of Africa, National Museum of African Art, Washington, and Monacelli, New York, 2013

Mullins, Charlotte, Painting People: Figure Painting Today, Distributed Arts Publishers, New York, 2007

Nakamori, Yasufumi, Utopia/Dystopia: Construction in Photography and Collage, Yale University Press, New Haven, Connecticut, 2012

Noey, Christopher, The Artist Project, Phaidon, New York, 2018

Oguibe, Olu, and Okwui Enwezor, Reading the Contemporary: African Art from Theory to the Marketplace, Institute of International Visual Arts, London, 1999

Okeke-Agulu, Chika, and Joseph L. Underwood, African Artists, Phaidon, London, 2021

Olowu, Duro, Making & Unmaking, Ridinghouse and Camden Arts Centre, London, 2016

Ottmann, Klaus, Still Points of the Turning World, SITE Santa Fe International Biennial Exhibition, 2006

Pagano, Greer, Us is Them at the Pizzuti Collection, Columbus Museum of Art, Ohio, 2015

Pedrosa, Adriano, Amanda Carneiro and Andre Mesquita, Histórias Das Mulheres, Histórias Feministas, Volume 2, Museu de Arte de São Paulo, São Paulo, Brazil, 2021

Perez, Chris, and Noah Levine Color Wheel Oblivion, Marella Arte Contemporanea, Milan, 2004

Perryer, Sophie (ed.), Michael Stevenson, Joost Bosland and Taiye Tuakli-Wosomu, Distant Relatives/Relative Distance, Michael Stevenson Gallery, Cape Town, 2005

Phillips, Lisa (ed.), Johanna Burton, Lauren Cornell, Massimiliano Gioni, Joseph Grima, Julia Kaganskiy, Ned Rifkin, Lynne Tillman and Brian Wallis, New Museum: 40 Years New, New Museum of Contemporary Art and Phaidon, New York, 2017

Pilcher, Alex, A Queer little History of Art, Tate, London, 2017

Reilly, Maura, and Linda Nochlin, Global Feminisms, New Directions in Contemporary Art, Brooklyn Museum Merrell Publishers Limited,2008

Ryman, Kyla, What Do You See?, Home Grown Books, New York, 2016

Scala, W. Mark (ed.), Paint Made Flesh, Frist Center for Visual Arts and Vanderbilt University Press, Nashville, 2009

Scala, Mark W., Chaos and Awe: Painting for the 21st Century, MIT Press, Cambridge, Massachusetts, 2018

Schneider, Anna, Blind Faith: Between the Visceral and the Cognitive in Contemporary Art, Prestel, Munich, 2018

Schoonmaker, Trevor, Black President: The Art and Legacy of Fela Anikulapo-Kuti, The New Museum of Contemporary Art, New York, 2003

Shiobara, Masashi, Yumiko Kuwahara, Shogo Kakimoto, Kentaro Oshita et al, Global New Art: Taguchi Art Collection #1, Bijutsu Shurpan, Japan, 2010

Singleton, Douglas (ed.), Excerpt: Selections from the Jeanne Greenberg Rohayn Collection, The Frances Lehman Loeb Art Center, Vassar College, Poughkeepsie, New York, 2008.

Spector, Nancy, Simon Critchley, Angela Susan Thompson et al, The Luminous Interval: The D. Daskalopoulos Collection, Guggenheim Bilbao, Spain, 2011

Squires, Carol, A Different Kind of Order: The Fourth ICP Triennial of Photography and Video, International Center of Photography and, Delmonico-Prestel, New York, 2013

Storr, Robert, Interviews on Art, Heni Publishing, London, 2018

Sultan, Terry, David Pagel, Colin Gardner and Claudia Schmuckli, Damaged Romanticism: A Mirror of Modern Emotion, University of Houston Press, 2008

Thompson, Barbara (ed.), Black Womanhood: Images, Icons, and Ideologies of the African Body, University of Washington Press, Seattle, 2008

Thornton, Sarah, 33 Artists in 3 Acts, W. W. Norton & Company, New Yor, 2014

Villalongo, William and Mark Thomas Gibson, Black Pulp!, Yale University Press, New Haven, 2016

VV. AA., Africa Rising: Fashion, Design, and Lifestyle from Africa, Gestalten and Design Indaba, Berlin, 2016

VV. AA., Artemizia Foundation: Permanent Collection, Artemizia Foundation, Bisbee, Arizona: 2021

Weiss, Reydan, Everywhere and Nowhere: Works from the Reydan Weiss Collection, Villa Jauss, Oberstdorf, Germany, 2012

Wendt, Selene (ed.), Paco Barragán, Tommy Olsson, Michele Robecchi and Trevor Schoonmaker, Fresh Paint, Sternensen Museum, Oslo, and Charta Art Books, Milan, 2012

Wiedemann, Hillary and Robert Stephen Frankel, Awards in Painting, Sculpture, Printmaking, Photography, Video and Craft Media, The Louis Comfort Tiffany Foundation, Cold Spring Harbor, Long Island, New York, 2007

Wolin, Joseph R., Open This End: Contemporary Art from the Collection of Blake Byrne, Duke University Press, Durham, North Carolina, 2015

Zoubok, Pavel, The New Collage, Pavel Zoubok Gallery, New York, 2006

ILLUSTRATED WORKS

COMPARATIVE IMAGES

PUBLIC COLLECTIONS

ART GALLERY OF ONTARIO, Toronto

THE ALTOIDS COLLECTION, NEW MUSEUM OF CONTEMPORARY ART, New York

THE BALTIMORE MUSEUM OF ART

BLANTON MUSEUM, UNIVERSITY OF TEXAS, Austin

BROOKLYN MUSEUM, New York

CHRYSLER MUSEUM OF ART, Norfolk, Virginia

THE CONTEMPORARY AUSTIN

DES MOINES ART CENTER, Iowa

THE FINE ARTS MUSEUM OF SAN FRANCISCO

THE FRANCES YOUNG TANG TEACHING MUSEUM AND ART GALLERY, SKIDMORE GALLERY, Saratoga Springs

THE HAGUE, NETHERLANDS HOOD MUSEUM OF ART, DARTMOUTH COLLEGE, Hanover, New Hampshire

INSTITUTE OF CONTEMPORARY ART, Boston

JUDITH ROTHSCHILD FOUNDATION / THE MUSEUM OF MODERN ART, New York

THE METROPOLITAN MUSEUM OF ART, New York

MODERN ART MUSEUM OF FORT WORTH

THE MORGAN LIBRARY AND MUSEUM, New York

MUSÉE D'ART CONTEMPORAIN DE MONTRÉAL

MUSEUM OF CONTEMPORARY ART, Chicago

MUSEUM OF CONTEMPORARY ART, Los Angeles

MUSEUM OF FINE ARTS, Houston

MUSEUM OF MODERN ART, New York

THE NASHER MUSEUM AT DUKE UNIVERSITY, Durham, North Carolina

NASHER SCULPTURE CENTER, Dallas

THE NATIONAL MUSEUM OF AFRICAN ART SMITHSONIAN, Washington, DC

NEW ORLEANS MUSEUM OF ART

NORTON MUSEUM OF ART, West Palm Beach, Florida

NSU ART MUSEUM, NOVA SOUTHEASTERN UNIVERSITY, Fort Lauderdale

PENNSYLVANIA ACADEMY OF FINE ARTS, Philadelphia

PEREZ ART MUSEUM, Miami

PRINCETON UNIVERSITY ART MUSEUM, New Jersey

PIZZUTI COLLECTION, Columbus, Ohio

RUBY CITY, LINDA PACE FOUNDATION, San Antonio

SAINSBURY CENTRE FOR VISUAL ARTS, UNIVERSITY OF EAST ANGLIA, Norwich

SAN FRANCISCO MUSEUM OF MODERN ART

SCOTTISH NATIONAL GALLERY OF MODERN ART, Edinburgh

SMITH COLLEGE MUSEUM OF ART, Northampton, Massachusetts

SMITHSONIAN NATIONAL MUSEUM OF AFRICAN ART, Washington, DC

THE STUDIO MUSEUM IN HARLEM, New York

TATE, London

ULRICH MUSEUM OF ART, Wichita, Kansas

THE WALKER ART CENTER, CONTEMPORARY ART MUSEUM, Minneapolis

WHITNEY MUSEUM OF AMERICAN ART, New York

YALE UNIVERSITY ART GALLERY, New Haven, Connecticut

PHAIDON PRESS LTD.
2 COOPERAGE YARD
LONDON E15 2QR

PHAIDON PRESS INC.
65 BLEECKER STREET
NEW YORK, NY 10012

PHAIDON.COM

First published 2022

ISBN:
978-1-83866-164-9
Limited Edition:
978-1-83866-483-1
Signed Edition:
978-1-83866-482-4

A CIP catalogue record of this book is available from the British Library and the Library of Congress.

Commissioning Editor
Michele Robecchi

Production Controller
Nerissa Vales

Design
Melanie Mues, Mues Design, London

Layout
Cantina, London

Printed in China

PUBLISHER'S ACKNOWLEDGEMENTS

We would like to thank Astrid Meek, Jonathan Fraser, Sholeh Hajmiragha, Marissa Mackey, Emma Malmqvist and Taabu E. Munyoki at Wangechi Mutu Studio, Nairobi and New York; Victoria Miro, Erin Manns and Kathy Stephenson at Victoria Miro Gallery, London and Venice; Barbara Gladstone, Emily Bates and Simone Battisti at Gladstone Gallery, New York and Brussels; Bruna Aickelin, David Hammons, Melissa Larner, Anna Morton, João Mota, Esa Nickle, Adrian Piper, Betye Saar, Tracey Smith, Hans Stofregen, Carmen Thyssen-Bornemisza, Nari Ward, Fred Wilson.

We are also grateful to the following institutions: Fondation Alberto et Annette Giacometti, Paris; Museo Nacional Thyssen-Bornemisza, Madrid; Scottish National Gallery Of Modern Art/Gabrielle Keille, Edinburgh; Metropolitan Museum/Alfred Stieglitz Collection, New York; The Museum of Modern Art/Candace King Weir/The Modern Women's Fund/Committee on Painting and Sculpture Funds, New York; Hirshhorn Museum and Sculpture Garden/Smithsonian Institution, Washington, DC; Lehmann Maupin, New York; Musée d'Art Moderne Grand-Duc Jean, Luxembourg; New Museum of Contemporary Art, New York; The Contemporary Austin; Performa, New York; Roberts Projects, Los Angeles; Maryland Center for History and Culture, Baltimore; The Pinnell Collection, Dallas; The Estate of Jean-Michel Basquiat, New York; Adrian Piper Research Archive Foundation, Berlin; Artists Rights Society (ARS), New York; Design and Artists Copyright Society (DACS), London.

Photographers: Dawoud Bey, Guillaume Bonn, Paula Court, Randy Dodson, Cyntiah Edorh, Brian Fitzsimmons, LaToya Ruby Frazier, Maris Hutchinson/EPW Studio; Charles Mayer, J. Quazi King, David Regen, Adi Schniderman, Giulio Sciorio.

All works are in private collections unless otherwise stated.

ARTIST'S ACKNOWLEDGEMENTS

I am delighted to say that this book is now complete, and to acknowledge the people who put an immense effort into making it possible. I'm also thrilled to have the opportunity to share the project with everyone. This would have been impossible without the tireless work, dedication, understanding and care of the thinkers, collaborators, my studio team, galleries and friends.

I'm so grateful to Courtney J. Martin not only for her support, friendship and the time and work put into the interview, but also for introducing me to Michele Robecchi, whose dedication and patience have been invaluable throughout this process. Thank you to all the people at Phaidon who have put so many painstaking hours into this book!

Kellie Jones, you've been a long-standing supporter and such a beacon of inspiration, thank you for your strong contribution to this book.

Adrienne Edwards, I so appreciate the gift of our friendship, your sharp eye and mind.

Chika Okeke-Agulu, thank you for your thoughtfulness, depth and time.

Mario, Neema and Wathira, without you and my extended family, this work wouldn't be as important, meaningful and urgent.

I want to thank, in particular, Astrid Meek, my Studio Manager, without whom this would not have been possible.

Thanks to Jonathan, Taabu, Marissa, Emma, Charles and Maina, my Nairobi and New York teams who've all carried this along with me.

To Gladstone Gallery, Victoria Miro and Vielmetter Los Angeles, thank you so much for your consistency and unflinching support and work.

And then there are the friends and colleagues who have continuously lifted me and my work.

Forever grateful to Greg Tate, Okwui Enwezor, Binyavanga Wainaina, Mzee Richard Leakey and Jerome Stern, may you all rest in eternal peace.

Much appreciation goes out to you Trevor Schoonmaker, SantiGold, Suné Woods, Teju Cole, Arthur Jafa, Deborah Willis, David Adjaye, Kerry James Marshall, Kelly Baum, Max Hollein, Sheena Wagstaff, Thelma Golden, Sandra Jackson-Dumont, David Hammons, Claudia Schumkli, Isaac Julien, Ekow Eshun, Isolde Brielmeir, Maureen Mahon, Imani Uzuri, Damon Gorton, Paulina Pobocha, Ugochukwu-Smooth Nzewi, Karungari, Matthew Morgan and Jocelyn Cooper, Aisha Bell, Danilo and Saria, Jyoti Argade, Kambui Olujimi, Karen Del Aguila, Cy Nakpodia, Dawit, Alexandra Giniger, Dru and his team, Joaquin Jutt, Hiroko Ishikawa, Tuesday Smillie, Virginia Wagner, Hank Willis Thomas, Rujeko Hockley, Naima Keith, Diana Nawi, Julie Mehretu, Mbugua Kimani, Nora Lawrence, Robb Storr, Wokabi Mungai, Sam Messer, RoseLee Goldberg, Michael Armitage, Ashaka Givens, Oana Botez.

Thank you Cynthia Edorh for your photography and the unforgettable adventures. LaToya Ruby Frazier, thank you for the portraits and for your clear lens. I am grateful to Lacy, Swati and Ayo.

Maisie Broome and Jeffrey Spring from Modern Art Foundry, and Dylan Farnum for beginning all the work with me at Walla Walla Foundry. Thank you, Jonathan, Hannah and the terrific team at your Foundry.

CONTEMPORARY ARTISTS:

Contemporary Artists is a series of authoritative and extensively illustrated studies of today's most important artists. Each title offers a comprehensive survey of an individual artist's work and a range of art writing contributed by an international spectrum of authors, all leading figures in their fields, from art history and criticism to philosophy, cultural theory and fiction. Each study provides incisive analysis and multiple perspectives on contemporary art and its inspiration. These are essential source books for everyone concerned with art today.

MARINA ABRAMOVIĆ KLAUS BIESENBACH, KRISTINE STILES, CHRISSIE ILES / VITO ACCONCI FRAZER WARD, MARK C. TAYLOR, JENNIFER BLOOMER / AI WEIWEI HANS ULRICH OBRIST, KAREN SMITH, BERNARD FIBICHER / DOUG AITKEN DANIEL BIRNBAUM, AMANDA SHARP, JÖRG HEISER / PAWEŁ ALTHAMER ADAM SZYMCZYK, ROMAN KURZMEYER, SUZANNE COTTER / FRANCIS ALŸS CUAUHTÉMOC MEDINA, RUSSELL FERGUSON, JEAN FISHER, MICHAEL TAUSSIG / UTA BARTH PAMELA M. LEE, MATTHEW HIGGS, JEREMY GILBERT-ROLFE / LYNDA BENGLIS ANDREW BONACINA, BIBIANA OBLER, NORA LAWRENCE / CHRISTIAN BOLTANSKI DIDIER SEMIN, TAMAR GARB, DONALD KUSPIT / MONICA BONVICINI ALEXANDER ALBERRO, JANET KRAYNAK, JULIANE REBENTISCH / LOUISE BOURGEOIS PAULO HERKENHOFF (WITH THYRZA GOODEVE), ROBERT STORR, ALLAN SCHWARTZMAN / MARK BRADFORD ANITA HILL, SEBASTIAN SMEE, CONNIE BUTLER / CECILY BROWN COURTNEY J. MARTIN, JASON ROSENFELD, FRANCINE PROSE / CAI GUO-QIANG DANA FRIIS-HANSEN, OCTAVIO ZAYA, TAKASHI SERIZAWA / MAURIZIO CATTELAN NANCY SPECTOR, FRANCESCO BONAMI, BARBARA VANDERLINDEN, MASSIMILIANO GIONI / VIJA CELMINS ROBERT GOBER, LANE RELYEA, BRIONY FER / NIGEL COOKE DARIAN LEADER, TONY GODFREY, MARIE DARRIEUSSECQ / RICHARD DEACON PIER LUIGI TAZZI, JON THOMPSON, PETER SCHJELDAHL, PENELOPE CURTIS / TACITA DEAN JEAN-CHRISTOPHE ROYOUX, MARINA WARNER, GERMAINE GREER / MARK DION LISA GRAZIOSE CORRIN, MIWON KWON, NORMAN BRYSON / PETER DOIG ADRIAN SEARLE, KITTY SCOTT, CATHERINE GRENIER / STAN DOUGLAS SCOTT WATSON, DIANA THATER, CAROL J. CLOVER / MARLENE DUMAS DOMINIC VAN DEN BOOGERD, BARBARA BLOOM, MARIUCCIA CASADIO, ILARIA BONACOSSA / JIMMIE DURHAM LAURA MULVEY, DIRK SNAUWAERT, MARK ALICE DURANT, KATE NESIN / OLAFUR ELIASSON MADELEINE GRYNSZTEJN, DANIEL BIRNBAUM, MICHAEL SPEAKS / ELMGREEN & DRAGSET LINDA YABLONSKY, MARTIN HERBERT, CONNIE BUTLER / PETER FISCHLI AND DAVID WEISS ROBERT FLECK, BEATE SÖNTGEN, ARTHUR C. DANTO / TOM FRIEDMAN DENNIS COOPER, BRUCE HAINLEY, ADRIAN SEARLE / THEASTER GATES CAROL BECKER, LISA YUN LEE, ACHIM BORCHARDT-HUME / ISA GENZKEN ALEX FARQUHARSON, DIEDRICH DIEDERICHSEN, SABINE BREITWIESER / ANTONY GORMLEY ERNST GOMBRICH, JOHN HUTCHINSON, LELA B. NJATIN, W. J. T. MITCHELL / DAN GRAHAM BIRGIT PELZER, MARK FRANCIS, BEATRIZ COLOMINA / PAUL GRAHAM ANDREW WILSON, GILLIAN WEARING, CAROL SQUIERS / HANS HAACKE WALTER GRASSKAMP, MOLLY NESBIT, JON BIRD / MONA HATOUM GUY BRETT, MICHAEL ARCHER, CATHERINE DE ZEGHER, NANCY SPECTOR / SHARON HAYES JULIA BRYAN-WILSON, JEANNINE TANG, LANKA TATTERSALL / THOMAS HIRSCHHORN BENJAMIN H. D. BUCHLOH, ALISON M. GINGERAS, CARLOS BASUALDO / JIM HODGES JANE M SAKS, ROBERT HOBBS, JULIE AULT /JENNY HOLZER DAVID JOSELIT, JOAN SIMON, RENATA SALECL / RONI HORN LOUISE NERI, LYNNE COOKE, THIERRY DE DUVE / CHRIS JOHANSON CORRINA PEIPON, BOB NICKAS, JULIE DEAMER / ILYA KABAKOV BORIS GROYS, DAVID A. ROSS, IWONA BLAZWICK / ALEX KATZ ROBERT STORR, CARTER RATCLIFF, IWONA BLAZWICK, BARRY SCHWABSKY / ON KAWARA 'TRIBUTE', JONATHAN WATKINS, RENÉ DENIZOT / MIKE KELLEY ISABELLE GRAW, JOHN C. WELCHMAN, ANTHONY VIDLER / MARY KELLY MARGARET IVERSEN, DOUGLAS CRIMP, HOMI K. BHABHA / WILLIAM KENTRIDGE CAROLYN CHRISTOV-BAKARGIEV, DAN CAMERON, J. M. COETZEE / JANNIS KOUNELLIS 'TRIBUTE', PHILIP LARRATT-SMITH, RUDI FUCHS / YAYOI KUSAMA AKIRA TATEHATA, LAURA HOPTMAN, UDO KULTERMANN, CHATERINE TAFT / CHRISTIAN MARCLAY JENNIFER GONZALEZ, KIM GORDON, MATTHEW HIGGS / KERRY JAMES MARSHALL CHARLES GAINES, GREG TATE, LAURENCE RASSEL / PAUL McCARTHY KRISTINE STILES, RALPH RUGOFF, MASSIMILIANO GIONI, ROBERT STORR / CILDO MEIRELES PAULO HERKENHOFF, GERARDO MOSQUERA, DAN CAMERON / WANGECHI MUTU ADRIENNE EDWARDS, COURTNEY J. MARTIN, KELLIE JONES, CHIKA OKEKE-AGULU / LUCY ORTA ROBERTO PINTO, NICOLAS BOURRIAUD, MAIA DAMIANOVIC / JEAN-MICHEL OTHONIEL GAY GASSMANN, CATHERINE GRENIER, ROBERT STORR / TREVOR PAGLEN LAUREN CORNELL, JULIA BRYAN-WILSON, OMAR KHOLEIF / JORGE PARDO CHRISTINE VÉGH, LANE RELYEA, CHRIS KRAUS / NICOLAS PARTY STÉPHANE AQUIN, STEFAN BANZ, ALI SUBOTNICK, MELISSA HYDE / ADAM PENDLETON ALEC MAPES-FRANCES, ADRIENNE EDWARDS, ANDRÉA PICARD / RAYMOND PETTIBON DENNIS COOPER, ROBERT STORR, ULRICH LOOCK / RICHARD PRINCE ROSETTA BROOKS, JEFF RIAN, LUC SANTE / LILI REYNAUD-DEWAR ÉLISABETH LEBOVICI, DIEDRICH DIEDERICHSEN, MONIKA SZEWCZYK / PIPILOTTI RIST HANS ULRICH OBRIST, PEGGY PHELAN, ELIZABETH BRONFEN / UGO RONDINONE LAURA HOPTMAN, ERIK VERHAGEN, NICHOLAS BAUME, JASON SCHMIDT / DAAN ROOSEGAARDE NICO DASWANI, FUMIO NANJO, CAROL BECKER / STERLING RUBY KATE FOWLE, FRANKLIN SIRMANS, JESSICA MORGAN / ANRI SALA HANS ULRICH OBRIST, MARK GODFREY, LIAM GILLICK / DORIS SALCEDO NANCY PRINCENTHAL, CARLOS BASUALDO, ANDREAS HUYSSEN / WILHELM SASNAL ANDRZEJ PRZYWARA, DOMINIC EICHLER, JÖRG HEISER / THOMAS SCHÜTTE JULIAN HEYNEN, JAMES LINGWOOD, ANGELA VETTESE / STEPHEN SHORE MICHAEL FRIED, CHRISTY LANGE, JOEL STERNFELD / ROMAN SIGNER PAULA VAN DEN BOSCH, GERHARD MACK, JEREMY MILLAR / LORNA SIMPSON KELLIE JONES, THELMA GOLDEN, CHRISSIE ILES, NAOMI BECKWITH / NANCY SPERO JON BIRD, JO ANNA ISAAK, SYLVÈRE LOTRINGER / SIMON STARLING FRANCESCO MANACORDA, DIETER ROELSTRAETE, JANET HARBORD / FRANK STELLA ANDRIANNA CAMPBELL, KATE NESIN, LUCAS BLALOCK, TERRY RICHARDSON / JESSICA STOCKHOLDER BARRY SCHWABSKY, LYNNE TILLMAN, LYNNE COOKE, GERMANO CELANT / SARAH SZE OKWUI ENWEZOR, BENJAMIN H. D. BUCHLOH, LAURA HOPTMAN / WOLFGANG TILLMANS PETER HALLEY, JAN VERWOERT, MIDORI MATSUI, JOHANNA BURTON / LUC TUYMANS ULRICH LOOCK, JUAN VICENTE ALIAGA, NANCY SPECTOR, HANS RUDOLF REUST / BERNAR VENET FLORENCE DERIEUX, BARRY SCHWABSKY, CLAIRE LILLEY / ADRIÁN VILLAR-ROJAS HANS ULRICH OBRIST, CAROLYN CHRISTOV-BAKARGIEV, EUNGIE JOO / JEFF WALL THIERRY DE DUVE, ARIELLE PÉLENC, BORIS GROYS, JEAN-FRANÇOIS CHEVRIER, MARK LEWIS / GILLIAN WEARING RUSSELL FERGUSON, DONNA DE SALVO, JOHN SLYCE / LAWRENCE WEINER BENJAMIN H. D. BUCHLOH, ALEXANDER ALBERRO AND ALICE ZIMMERMAN, DAVID BATCHELOR / FRANZ WEST ROBERT FLECK, BICE CURIGER, NEAL BENEZRA / JONAS WOOD MARK GROTJAHN, HELEN MOLESWORTH, IAN ALTEVEER / YIN XIUZHEN HOU HANRU, WU HUNG, STEPHANIE ROSENTHAL / ZHANG HUAN ROSELEE GOLDBERG, YILMAZ DZIEWOR, ROBERT STORR